LAW ENFORCEMENT AND THE YOUTHFUL OFFENDER

LAW ENFORCEMENT AND THE YOUTHFUL OFFENDER

Third Edition

EDWARD ELDEFONSO
De Anza College
West Valley College
Santa Clara County Juvenile
  Probation Department

JOHN WILEY & SONS

NEW YORK
SANTA BARBARA
CHICHESTER
BRISBANE
TORONTO

OTHER BOOKS BY THE AUTHOR

Principles of Law Enforcement (with A. Coffey and R. C. Grace)

Human Relations: Law Enforcement in a Changing Community (with A. Coffey and W. Hartinger)

Police—Community Relations (with A. Coffey and W. Hartinger)

Youth Problems and Law Enforcement

Police and the Criminal Law (with A. Coffey and J. Sullivan)

Readings in Criminal Justice

Corrections: A Component of the Criminal Justice System (with A. Coffey and W. Hartinger)

An Introduction to the Criminal Justice System and Process (with A. Coffey and W. Hartinger)

Issues in Corrections: A Book of Readings

Process and Impact of Justice (with A. Coffey)

Process and Impact of the Juvenile Justice System (with A. Coffey)

Control, Treatment and Rehabilitation of Juvenile Offenders (with W. Hartinger)

Library of Congress Cataloging in Publication Data:

Eldefonso, Edward.
  Law enforcement and the youthful offender.

  Includes bibliographies and indexes.
    1. Juvenile delinquency—United States. 2. Juvenile
courts—United States. I. Title.
KF9779.E42   1978   364.36′0973   77-13331
ISBN 0-471-03234-4

Printed in the United States of America

10 9 8 7 6 5 4 3 2 1

Dedicated to
Cecelia Oliveras Eldefonso

and

Minnie ("Aunt Minnie") Lambert
whose
love, devotion, and compassion
will never be forgotten

PREFACE

In this, the third edition of *Law Enforcement and the Youthful Offender*, I have, as in previous editions, relied extensively on my twenty years as a practitioner in the juvenile justice system. Drawing on such pragmatic experience, as well as on fifteen years of classroom teaching in community colleges, where I offered courses specifically on juvenile procedures in programs on the administration of justice, I have endeavored to provide an introductory resource for police work with juveniles.

As an introductory text, this book starts with the premise that an elementary description of the field is necessary. In keeping with this philosophy, chapter one was revised extensively. Also, in recognition of recent developments in the field and in response to the constructive criticism of colleagues, this third edition reflects such contemporary issues as: *the status offender (and the impact of pornography); the female delinquent; the fragmented juvenile justice system; the increased use of alcoholic beverages by teen-agers; drug abuse; the upsurge of violent gangs; and the juvenile justice system—how it operates and where it is headed.*

The third edition still retains the philosophy of the first and second editions in that it describes the development of youthful misbehavior and the problem it presents to effective law enforcement. And because this philosophy is cast in the broadest possible definition of law enforcement, this volume also seeks to suggest and define appropriate avenues of solution.

This book is designed for the general student and for the student who is contemplating a career in law enforcement, specifically one in working with juvenile offenders. Because it covers the main aspects of police work with juveniles, it includes many subjects. All the recognized principles are treated fully, and all the tested concepts are examined. In keeping with its descriptive emphasis, however, conceptual and theoretical material is kept to a minimum.

Within the above framework, an effort has been made to capitalize upon the student's probable interest in police work. There is thus more material dealing with police work with the juvenile offender than is found in books on investigative techniques, juvenile court law, and special problems.

At the conclusion of each chapter, the student will find a brief summary to serve as a guide to the context of the chapter, a summary that can also help to refresh the memory on salient points after reading it. Also, at the end of each chapter the student will find a number of annotated references to encourage independent research in a particular area.

The third edition, I feel, provides the prospective police officer—or anyone interested in the field of juvenile crime—with ready access to a comprehensive, integrated, and authoritative assessment of all aspects of police work with juveniles.

The complexity of crime and delinquency virtually preclude, however, a definitive treatment. In fact, a single volume could scarcely *survey* the literature available on the problem. Yet, I have tried to clarify some of the specific and confusing aspects of the youthful offender that relate to the police and, to present at the same time, an overview of the entire problem of juvenile delinquency. By following such an approach, I hope to go beyond the mere presentation of subject matter toward the more rewarding goal of stimulating both an understanding of the problem and a pride in law enforcement careers.

E. Eldefonso

San Jose, California

ACKNOWLEDGMENTS

It is impossible to acknowledge all the assistance I received in preparing this third edition of LAW ENFORCEMENT AND THE YOUTHFUL OFFENDER. Much of it came from day-to-day contact through the years with teachers, probation officers, police officers, lawyers, criminologists, and many others. However, I must give special acknowledgement to several individuals. Grateful acknowledgement is due, Mildred Ann, my wife, whose amicable disposition made completion of the project less difficult; Naka Prastalo, for her contagious enthusiasm; B. Earl Lewis, Instructor, Department of Law Enforcement Education, DeAnza College; Walter Hartinger, Supervisor, Special Supervision Unit, Santa Clara County Juvenile Probation Department, who assisted in writing the section pertaining to "Juvenile Institutions: A Part of the Juvenile Court System"; and Robert Gerstenkern, for permitting me to draw extensively from his unpublished papers dealing with "The Family and Delinquency" and "Education and Crime."

I am also indebted to the following agencies for their cooperation in providing useful material: the International Association of Chiefs of Police; the National Council on Crime and Delinquency; the Federal Probation; the Children's Bureau, U.S. Department of Health, Education, and Welfare; the Campbell Police Department, Campbell, California; and the Federal Bureau of Investigation. For their individual contributions, I owe much to the following specialists and practitioners in the field of education and corrections: W. E. Thornton, former Chief Probation Officer, County of Sacramento, California; R. E. Rice and R. B. Christensen, County of Los Angeles Probation Department, Los Angeles, California; G. Geis, Professor, California State College, Los Angeles, California; and W. C. Kvaraceus, Boston University, Boston, Massachusetts. Each will recognize the points he has contributed.

E.E.

CONTENTS

x   Contents

Contents   xiii

LAW
ENFORCEMENT
AND THE
YOUTHFUL
OFFENDER

CHAPTER ONE an introduction to the problem

Juvenile delinquency is not a new invention; it is as old as time. Socrates is alleged to have observed: "The children now love luxury. They have bad manners, contempt for authority, they show disrespect for elders and love chatter in place of exercise. They no longer rise when their elders enter the room. They contradict their parents. Chatter before company. Gobble up dainties at the table, and tyrannize over their teachers."

History also suggests that the separation of juvenile and adult offenders dates back almost 2500 years, as early as the fifth century B.C. under Roman Law. The Twelve Tables of Roman Law, for example, made the theft of crops, when perpetrated at night, a capital crime. An offender under the age of puberty, however, was usually fined and, on some occasions, flogged. Thus, as far back as 451 B.C., juvenile crime existed. Although juvenile delinquency has a long history, youthful crime is now so alarming in extent and kind that we must modify our approach to juvenile offenders.

Just how serious is the problem?

In the last ten years, crime in the United States has increased four times faster than the nation's population! Serious crimes—larceny of fifty dollars or more, burglary, robbery, automobile theft, forcible rape, aggravated assault, and murder—have mounted steadily in the 1960s and reached their present peak in the first two years of the 1970s. The problem is much more chilling when one refers to statistics relating to juvenile crime. More crimes are now committed by children under fifteen—by our most precious asset, the youth of the United States—than by adults over twenty-five! Reports from the National Council on Crime and Delinquency and from the Federal Bureau of Investigation show a staggering 1600 percent upsurge in the number of juveniles arrested for serious crimes between 1952 and 1974. The following latest statistics spell out other alarming facts: More than half of all serious crimes—and one out of four are violent ones—are committed by youngsters. Of the enormous number of children—some 900,000—who will be released to the community by juvenile courts in 1976, three out of four will commit another crime. In 1976, according to the *Uniform Crime Reports,* published by the FBI, we witnessed the twenty-eighth consecutive year in which youthful criminality increased over the previous year. During that period, young offenders were represented in over 52 percent of total arrests. Delinquency remains primarily a boy's problem, but the disparity between the number of court cases on boys' and on girls' delinquency is narrowing. For many years, boys were referred to court for delinquency about four times as often as girls. Because of the accelerating increase in girls' cases as compared to those of boys, the ratio is now three to one. Nationally, girls' cases increased four percent as compared to a two percent increase of boys' cases. The overall increase in girls' cases in 1976 resulted primarily from an increase in urban and rural courts. Girls' delinquency cases disposed of by juvenile courts have been rising faster than those of boys every year since 1965. Between 1965 and 1976, girls' delinquency cases increased by more than 110 percent, whereas boys' cases increased by 52 percent. The latest data published by the FBI reveals that arrests of girls under eighteen years of age increased by 393 percent for "violent" crimes and by 333 percent for "property crimes"; for boys under eighteen years of age, the percentage increases were 236 percent and 82 percent, respectively. According to the authorities, specifically those of the Department of Health, Education, and Welfare, the rise in girls' delinquency has generally been attributed to their change in attitude toward society and to society's change in attitude toward them. Instead of the passive role assumed by girls in the past and society's protective role toward them, girls are becoming more aggressive and more independent in their day-to-day activities. Unfortunately, some of this behavior has resulted in much more running away from home and in drug use, to say nothing of such crimes as shoplifting, robbery, burglary and automobile theft,an offense not generally attributed to female juvenile offenders.

It is, however, the *status offenses* that show the highest volume of female juvenile offenders. Status offenses—*that is offenses not considered violations if committed by an adult* (e.g., being ungovernable, unmanageable, incorrigible, and sexually promiscuous; defying control by school officials; and engaging in other activities subjectively viewed by a community as "delinquent")—are phenomena difficult to appraise nationally. Yet it is particularly difficult to evaluate such data statistically by sex. Let us focus, then, on California and on its comparative statistics in an effort to gain some insight into the scope of our national problem.

Statistical data compiled by the California Bureau of Crime and Delinquency in 1970 tells the story: *Forty-four percent of all juvenile arrests in California were for law violations, but fifty-six percent were referred for status offenses.* It is depressing to note that the male-female ratio of law violators was eight-to-two—eight boys for every two girls. Within the *status offenses* group, however, the figures were 5.5 boys to 4.5 girls!

It is impossible to arrive at a national figure. Comparison with other jurisdictions is hampered by differences in vernacular, procedures, law, reporting, and so forth. But the problem of status offenders—males and females—is viewed as a number one priority by the Law Enforcement Assistant Administration (LEAA), which set aside in April 1975 $8.5 million to support public and private agencies in formulating innovative programs to keep juvenile status offenders out of detention and correctional facilities. Following the concern of the federal government about the growing number of status offenders, several states have modified their juvenile court law to exclude all such offenders from restriction in either detention or correctional rehabilitative facilities.

FEMALE JUVENILE "CRIME"

The special problems of the female juvenile "offender" have been neglected—or glossed over. The vast bulk of delinquency research, unquestionably, has concerned itself with youthful male offenders.

There are many reasons for this consistent neglect. The first and most primary one is that youthful female "offenders" comprise less than ten percent of the entire institutional population in the United States. There simply aren't so many "delinquent" institutionalized females as there are males.

Smaller proportions of "delinquent" females means that researchers interested in them will have fewer subjects to study, which complicates the statistical findings, and lowers the generalization of the data. During the last five years, however, we have seen an increase in research dealing with the youthful female "offender." Why? The answer is simple. We have, during the last five years, witnessed an increase in females inserted into the juvenile justice system. According to the U.S. Department of Health, Education, and Welfare, the arrest rates for female juvenile "offenders," are increasing faster than those for males, and more females are being processed through the juvenile justice subsystems.

Although the literature on female youthful offenders is comparatively limited, studies that have been done reflect the following:

> There is a great need to distinguish between types of girls (and boys) who run away. Among the several that are encountered, the principal traits of only three will be summarized here.
>
> 1. The rootless. *Pleasure-seeking, hedonistic, seeks immediate gratification. Cannot see consequences of her behavior. Guilt-free, narcissistic. Hence peer relations are impermanent and lack trust. Pseudointellectual, lacks self-discipline. She drops out of a series of schools and jobs. Likely to become sexually promiscuous and a drug user. As these*

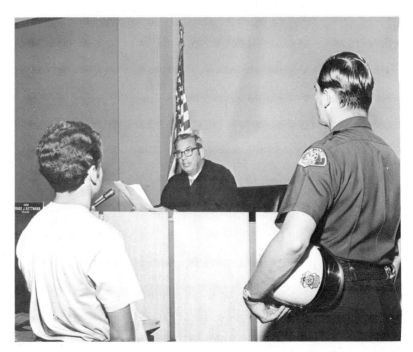

A police officer testifying at a juvenile court hearing
(Photo courtesy of Sgt. Jim Guido, Director, San Jose
Police Dept., San Jose, Calif.)

*increase, her mental and physical health suffer. A skilled manipulator,
especially of her family. They long treated her as special, exceptional, and
lavished praise upon her as a child. Gave her much freedom but never held
her to account. She grew up feeling on the one hand she was infallible and
on the other that her family did not love her because they never controlled
her. Her dependency needs were dismissed by her parents as incredible or
they were met by effusive material indulgence. Feelings of depression are
frequent and unresolved. Moves into middle and late adolescence emotionally a child and physically a woman. At this point the family becomes
frightened and for the first time sets limits on her. Girl rebels, runs away,
is soon taken into custody. Family rallies "to get her out of it." Girl dictates
the terms, family is often ready to concede. The process then repeats itself
as release from custody is followed by another of her whims, an effectual
blocking of this, protest, rebellion, flight, and again custody. Unless a
powerful regimen of conjoint family therapy is instituted, her prognosis, if
she survives disease and drugs, is unwed pregnancy. She loves her baby as
a toy but lacks the basic qualities to nurture it for sustained periods.
Eventually law enforcement steps in on complaint of neglect or abandon-*

ment. *The infant is often placed with its grandparents–who renew the pattern of relationship they developed with their daughter. Thus the daughter, through her child, has acquired a new tool to use in her attempt to control her family.*

2. The anxious. *Comes from a problem-loaded family. Has had to share adult responsibilities with her mother–household chores, rearing siblings, worry about finances, feeding, clothing. If father is present, she has had to worry about his excessive drinking, unemployment, and physical abuse of family members. Girl may feel ashamed of herself and her family. Knows she has problems and that parents do too. Wants help for herself and also for them. Often runs away for a few hours, overnight, or a few days. Spends this interval at a girl friend's home and enjoys talking to her friend's mother. Often asks for a probation officer so she can have someone to talk to and help her. Poor school performance, finds the work dull. Looks forward to marriage and children. Has no career goal or personal aspirations, says she would have no way of achieving them. Wants to talk with someone about boy-girl relations, sex, her own body, grooming, clothes, manners, but is reluctant to bring any of this up until firm trust is established. Fears and is confused by large bureaucratic impersonal agencies and services. Shows great feelings of powerlessness, anxiety, and depression. Runs away sporadically but is glad to return home, hopes this will lead to concrete help. May become pregnant out of wedlock. If so, she will need much careful support if she is not to repeat the cycle of her mother and grandmother.*

3. The terrified. *Most frequently, but not always, this is the girl who runs away because of the threat of incest with her father or stepfather, and an awareness of its hurricane consequences. The mother feels she has been prevented from realizing her potential because of her marriage and children. She withdraws from her husband increasingly over the years. The father works well at his job but is ineffective or disinterested in the family. He gradually finds he talks more easily to his daughter than his wife. In time, daddy's little girl becomes daddy's big girl. He begins to have sexual fantasies about her and acts these out with touches, kisses, opening the door when she is bathing, or walking about the house where she will see him nude. The mother becomes aware of this and subtly encourages it since it displaces her husband's sexual demands from herself to her daughter. The girl, on the other hand, resents her mother's lack of attention to her father as well as her father's increasingly insistent overtures to her. She tries to avoid being alone with him by pleading with her mother to stay home more often, inviting numerous peers to visit her, absenting herself as frequently as she can, or by running away. If the runaway is investigated and if she reveals her true motives, the mother reacts, first, by disbelief, but later by admitting she knew of it for a long while. Either as an incident to running away or to its subsequent investi-*

gation, the girl may attempt suicide. She has by this time probably developed a "bad me" concept, a severely and perhaps irreparably damaged self-image. She sees herself as the central agent of inevitable family collapse, that she caused it all, that somehow she could have prevented it but failed. Her sense of guilt is overwhelming. [1]

Other dynamics, as pointed out by Nancy B. Green and T. C. Esselstyn, help to produce the terrified girl.

She may be victimized by the mental illness of either or both parents. She may be repeatedly beaten by alcoholic parents. She may be the object of severe parental hatred or neglect. She may be compelled to act as a drug runner for her "pusher" father, brother or uncle. Most frequently, however, she is the product of a web of incest. In all these eventualities, the girl is literally in fear of her life, especially if she has to be returned home. She has also learned not to trust adults including those in the helping professions for if she does, the family unit may be shattered, someone may go to jail, her guilt will therefore be aggravated, and in the whole process she cannot conceive that anyone will accept her unconditionally. She is beyond control in the sense she feels she is beyond help. [2]

Studies[3] of female "delinquency" seem to indicate that struggles with adult authority are closely related to feminine aspirations and social expectations. On the other hand, male delinquents do not appear to be so dependent upon psychological states of mind as do female "delinquents." The male delinquent's behavior is generally aimed outward at social destruction whereas the female "delinquent" aims inward at her own destruction. Examples of outward destructive behavior are theft, malicious mischief, and so forth; examples of inward destructive behavior are promiscuity and drug abuse.

Outward destructive behavior is generally more easy to observe, and as a result the minor engaged in this type of behavior is apprehended sooner. Consequently, there is less likelihood that a strong habitual pattern will be formed. On the other hand, self-directed destructiveness tends to be secretive and often goes

[1] Nancy B. Green and T. C. Esselstyn, "The Beyond Control Girl," *Juvenile Justice*, The Journal of the National Council of Juvenile Court Judges, November 1972, vol. 23, no. 3, pp. 16-19.

[2] *Ibid.*, p. 18.

[3] Ruth Cavan, *Juvenile Delinquency: Development, Treatment, and Control*, 2nd ed., Lippincott, Philadelphia, 1972, p. 12. See also: Martin, L. H. and Snyder P. R., "Juvenile Court Jurisdiction Once Status Offenses Should Not Be Removed From the Juvenile Court," *Crime and Delinquency*, January 1976, vol. 22, no. 1, pp. 44–48; D. C. Gibbons, *Delinquent Behavior*, 2nd ed., Prentice-Hall, Inc., Englewood Cliffs, N.J., 1976, pp. 172–189, E. Eldefonso and W. Hartinger, *Control, Treatment, and Rehabilitation of Juvenile Offenders*. Glencoe Press, Beverly Hills, Calif., 1976, pp. 4, 29, and 89.

undiscovered until such habit patterns have been fairly well established. As a result, the girl who is a first-time referral to the juvenile justice system may be much more difficult to rehabilitate than might be expected from casual observation.

Delinquent behavior in girls seems to be closely related to their need for establishing a warm, affectionate relationship. Generally, their home environments can be characterized as lacking affectionate bonds. Behaviors such as truancy, promiscuity, and shoplifting all appear to be attempts to gain much-needed attention and to increase the possibility of establishing a close relationship. It is known that female delinquency is centered most often in the home. And, whereas boys are generally apprehended by the police, girls are most often reported to the police by their parents. Middle-class girls are expected to adopt their mothers as female role models, but when, for one reason or another, they are unable to do so, their rejection of female authority figures often is extended to teachers—which creates a dual problem of ungovernability at home and truancy at school. A background of disturbed family life is found more frequently in delinquent girls than in delinquent boys. Although the number of broken homes is constant for both boys and girls who are characterized by ungovernable behavior, it should be noted that a higher percentage of girls are *reported* for ungovernability. (Perhaps because our society maintains a different set of rules for boys and girls, behavior that may be labeled *"ungovernable"* when performed by a female may be labeled *"boys will be boys"* when exhibited by a male.) Seemingly, many parents of delinquent girls tend to be less responsive to their child's emotional needs during times of crisis. And much of the female delinquent's behavior does seem to suggest a psychological crisis. All too often, the solution to delinquent behavior among girls is seen as one of reducing the amount of trouble they cause. If the girl is going to school and obeying her parents, the problem is considered solved, whether or not the factor that precipitated the crisis is resolved, namely, that the girl may still be yearning for affection.

One of the more difficult aspects of this problem has been explored by Gisela Konopka, who indicates that girls seem to be more emotional than boys. Consequently, delinquent girls seem to feel more lonely than delinquent boys; they yearn for friends but at the same time seem to have few—they often regard their peers as childish.[4] The significance of this finding is that the delinquent girl, while seemingly in great need of a meaningful relationship, has rejected the traditional close attachment found among adolescent peers and, in so doing, has alienated the very source of the affection she desires.

Only infrequently is the female juvenile delinquent set on a life of crime; more often, her delinquent acts stand out as a cry for help. Female juveniles often outgrow their delinquent behavior, but not so frequently do they resolve the problems that gave rise to it. As adult women, who marry and bear children, they often perpetuate their problems in their offspring.

[4]G. Konopka, "Adolescent Delinquent Girls," *Children*, January-February, 1964, pp. 21–26.

FACTORS TO CONSIDER IN JUVENILE CRIME

So many elements must be considered with regard to the problem of delinquency that to give primacy to any one factor is extremely difficult. We know, however, that public opinion has been devastating. And it is difficult to dispute statistics from those who voice the opinion that the juvenile court's philosophy is too lenient. These individuals state that the juvenile court has become a "revolving-door" system of juvenile justice. To solidify their charge, they cite statistics which indicate that only ten percent of the million young violators who will appear in juvenile courts in 1976 will be detained in institutions. Public opinion has been taken up by the police and district attorneys' offices, who are calling for a much more punitive system. Perhaps, they are right; it is difficult to argue that the system is working—when data seems to indicate it is not. Perhaps, the juvenile courts *are* much more concerned about the need for "rehabilitating" the youthful offender than about protecting society.

Certainly, we cannot ignore the charge that most of the ideals and assumptions upon which juvenile courts are based may now be obsolete. As originally created, juvenile courts were instruments to study, diagnose, and prescribe treatment that would provide protection and rehabilitation. The juvenile court hearing was, therefore, in essence, considered much more important than any offense a youth may have committed.

Mason P. Thomas, Jr., in an address before the Juvenile Court Institute of the National Council on Crime and Delinquency, held in March 1971, brought the problem into focus when he stated:

> The Juvenile Court was born in an aura of social reform at the turn of the century. Its founders were closely associated with pioneers in the helping professions, including medicine, psychiatry, and social work. The Juvenile Court was designed to be as unlike the criminal courts as possible, so it avoided the usual formal trappings, the advisary process, traditional due process, or any emphasis on procedure. The Judge was to be the central figure in this socialized court with almost absolute discretion and power. Indeed, the Juvenile Court was designed to be more social than legal. While these aims were laudable, the Juvenile Court has been suffering from an identity crisis since its inception. Is it a Court or a social agency? The North Carolina Supreme Court refers to its powers as both judicial and administrative. The juvenile hearing was often so informal that the child and his family scarcely recognized the experience as a judicial proceeding. It was more like an informal conference. Further, juvenile courts have often assumed responsibility for services that were not available from existing child welfare agencies, such as Juvenile Probation, detention homes, foster homes, and others. The result has been even further confusion over

the identity of juvenile courts. They have seemed like child welfare agencies, yet the chief administrator has often been the juvenile Judge.

Thus, more often than we would want to believe, the juvenile is involved in another offense within ninety days after release by the court to the community on probation. And the cry of "revolving-door" justice emerges.

The Status Offender

The question of the "status offender," a topic the author will explore in detail later in this book, is a popular one, especially when we are searching for a readily available scapegoat. "Status offense" is a label concocted by the same individuals who managed to introduce the popular misconception of "victimless crimes."

Since adults are not punished for truancy, running away from home, violating curfew, and "promiscuous" behavior, is it unfair to punish children for such offenses? In other words, these offenses and others would not be regarded as offenses at all were not the perpetrator a child. Lately, considerable opposition has arisen to the idea of "status offenses." In August, 1976, the American Bar Association authored a new set of guidelines to revolutionize the juvenile court system. Included among them is a proposal to remove "status offenses" from the juvenile court's jurisdiction.

Perhaps the American Bar Association is correct. The basic premise of these guidelines is that what is proper for an adult should be proper for a juvenile. To support this premise, the equal rights clause of the Constitution is usually cited. There is, however, one significant problem—one salient fact—children aren't adults. Judgment tends to improve with maturity. A sense of responsibility or awareness of the consequences of one's action isn't something we are born with; rather it is something that evolves as we mature. Guy Wright, in an article on the subject entitled "New Fads in Juvenile Court Reform," in the *San Francisco Examiner* of February 17, 1976, took a pragmatic view of the problem:

> *Was there ever a child who thought the bedtime set by his parents was reasonable? Or who didn't need to be reminded to brush his teeth? How many of us would've got up every morning and gone to school if the grownups hadn't made us? But aren't we glad they did? Quite often children don't know what's best for them. They are easily exploited. That's why we have laws against child labor and statutory rape. Would the people campaigning to abolish "status offenses" also repeal those laws? To take it a step further, when a child makes a mistake, it's the parent who's expected to pay his doctor bill, replace the wrecked car or whatever. If the child defies all parental discipline, what are the parents supposed to do?*

In the same article, Mr. Wright "takes on" the myth of community resources:

According to the new enlightenment, "voluntary community services such as crisis intervention programs, peer counseling and crash pads" will take over. Any parent who ventured into the mumble-jumble world in search of help knows what a waste it is. Most youngsters who commit "status offenses" are actually begging for discipline. They want someone to set limits for them—limits that they are unwilling to accept from their parents or that their parents are unwilling or unable to impose. The Juvenile Court Judge who takes such a child into custody is really performing a rescue mission.

Mr. Wright points out that there is certainly room for improvement in the juvenile court system. But, he states court intervention is the only way to head off a disaster, and anyone who would prevent that intervention with gibberish about "status offense" is no friend of the troubled child.

But, then, there are many who disagree.

Many authorities feel that "status offenses" greatly resemble sumptuary laws against whoring, homosexuality, and drug-taking. Youngsters are taken to court and placed in temporary holding facilities for the mere crime of being young and having "tendencies" that society or their parents disapprove of. The youngsters are invariably told that they are being taken to court for "their own good." Statistical information in California alone reveals that an average of 100,000 status offenders are arrested annually. More than half of the boys and girls in California's juvenile halls have committed no crimes that an adult could be prosecuted for. They are, thus "crimes" that only children could commit. The National Council on Crime and Delinquency (NCCD) is in support of the American Bar Association. Milton Rector, NCCD's president, stated: "I'd say that within five years most States will adopt laws that exclude status offenders from the purview of the Juvenile Court. What this means is that the Court will be allowed to concentrate entirely on criminal offenders and communities will be developing more and better programs to deal with ungovernable and disturbed kids."

In 1966, President Johnson's Crime Commission recommended that the juvenile court system seriously consider ". . . complete elimination from the Court's jurisdiction of conduct illegal only for children. . . ." The Crime Commission argued that the very words that take away a child's liberty—"incorrigible," "unruly," "wayward," "stubborn"—are vague, and portmanteau labels bestowed by social workers, and by impatient parents and by judges acting in "the best interest of the child."

There is no denying, however, that the ramifications of status offenses —particularly runaways—have a destructive impact on juveniles and the community. The following is a vivid example:

"A twelve-year-old boy can earn up to $1,000 a day as a prostitute and a subject for pornographic pictures," stated Sgt. Lloyd Martin of the Los Angeles Police Department.

Sgt. Martin, who appeared before the House Subcommittee on Crime on Wednesday, May 26, 1977, also stated that "most receive less . . . a pimp will retain sixty percent of the earnings . . . the subjects we are concerned with are usually runaways; reasonably 'street wise,' emotionally troubled children who trade themselves for money or for what they interpret as affection."

The veteran officer produced a pamphlet entitled "Where the Young Ones Are" and said it was published four years ago in Hollywood. The pamphlet listed addresses of bowling alleys, beaches, arcades, parks and other places in fifty-nine cities where youngsters congregate.

The poorly contructed—cheap quality—pamphlet has, according to Martin, already sold 70,000 copies at five dollars per copy.

"Local and out-of-state runaways flock to widely-known locations knowing they can find shelter and money," stated Martin. Martin, at one point, advised the Committee to "close your eyes if you are offended;" then he proceeded to display magazines depicting boys and girls, mostly young teenagers, but some as young as six years old, posing in various sexual positions.

Robert F. Leonard, President of the National District Attorney's Association, expressed concern—along with Heather Grant Florence of the American Civil Liberties Union—about criminal sanctions being considered by the legislators. But he maintained that "federal legislation is desperately needed and that line-drawing, if it occurs (regarding language used in parts of the bill), should be to protect the defenseless minds and bodies of our children. . . ."

Leonard also pointed out that "an underground network of pornographers [child] extends nationally. Prosecutors in cities across the Nation have uncovered and compiled information pointing to a high degree of exchange and communication among those who prey on our children. . . ."

The explicit depiction of children engaged in sex acts is a big business venture involving organized crime and as many as 30,000 children in Los Angeles alone.

On Thursday, May 27, 1977, Daryl Gates, Deputy Chief of the Los Angeles Police Department, told the House Select Committee on Labor and Education that "intelligence has shown organized crime has rapidly moved into the area of child pornography" in California. He stated: "That State (California) has emerged as the world's film capital of 'kiddie porno. . . .' "

So, as we see, there are pros and cons about the "status offender." At any rate, this debate, which is confusing, is another factor that our society—and juvenile courts—must consider.

POLICE AND THE JUVENILE JUSTICE SYSTEM

Perhaps, the most important factor is police work that is good and not merely adequate. Good law enforcement depends, to a great extent, on the quality of men selected and on the effectiveness of the training they receive. Although the well-trained officer is a poor substitute for parental control, he is a vital component in effective delinquency control and prevention programs.

Almost any aspect of police work must involve juveniles. Statistics for 1976, reveal that the arrest of persons under eighteen years of age made up more than 52 percent of all arrests for criminal acts in cities and rural areas. Statistics indicate clearly the importance that must be attached to the problem itself and to the officer charged with the initial responsibility in the confrontation of that problem. In almost every situation involving a delinquent act, the police officer's role is a vital one, and he is *initially* involved. He sums up in his person and uniform, the true meaning of "Law Enforcement"; *he represents the law.* Therefore, his demeanor and actions impress a lasting image in the mind of the juvenile. This image relates directly to the child's understanding of law and law enforcement and, in many instances, to the subsequent behavior.

The police officer's role in delinquency control *does not*, as many suppose, automatically end with apprehension and detention. On the contrary, the Federal Bureau of Investigation's *Uniform Crime Reports* reveal that as many juvenile cases are handled within police agencies as are referred to juvenile courts. For example, in 1976, more than 48 percent of all juveniles taken into custody were handled on the police level with an admonishment and a subsequent release to parents or to community resources. The remainder were referred to juvenile courts, to criminal courts for trial as adults, or to other law enforcement agencies. This may be startling to many who, for the first time, are shocked into an awareness of the scope of police responsibilities with relation to juveniles. The need for good judgment, bulwarked by sound training, is apparent. The police officer inexplicably finds himself in a position where he must make a decision that will have its indelible effect on the young and impressionable person. The arresting officer must consider the child and the gravity of the offense. He must also ask and answer the following questions: Will the ends of justice and the best interests of the community and the juvenile be served merely by a verbal reprimand? Or shall the parents be advised of the offense and urged to exert closer supervision over the minor? Or is the offense one that requires referral to juvenile court or to a community agency? Thus, in many instances, the police officer sits as a surrogate judge or social worker. His findings determine the final disposition of almost half the cases involving juvenile offenders who are taken into custody. Therefore, law enforcement officers must learn to differentiate between the habitual, sophisticated juvenile offender and the impetuous, immature child who is acting a role. There is a difference. Certainly, the police—and the courts—must remove from circulation those who constitute a menace to the welfare of the community.

DELINQUENCY: AN OBSCURE TERM

Juvenile delinquency means different things to different people. To some, a juvenile delinquent is a boy or girl arrested for a law violation. To others, a single appearance in juvenile court identifies the delinquent. To many, the term covers a variety of antisocial behavior that offends *them*, whether or not a law is violated.

Juvenile delinquency is a blanket term that obscures rather than clarifies our understanding of human behavior. It describes a large variety of youths in trouble *or on the verge of trouble*. The delinquent may be anything from a normal, mischievous youngster to a youth who is involved in a law violation by accident. Or he may be a vicious assaultive person who is a habitual offender and is a recipient of some gratification from his conduct. As a blanket term, delinquency is like the concept of illness. A person may be ill and have polio or measles. The illness is different, the cause is different, and the treatment is different. The same is true of delinquency. Like illness, delinquency describes many problems that develop from varied causes and require different kinds of treatment.

The extent of juvenile delinquency in our country cannot be determined exactly, although the evidence indicates that delinquent behavior known to official agencies has increased in recent years, both absolutely and proportionately. The number of acts by which a juvenile can be identified as delinquent are almost limitless.[5] In addition to the major violations defined in the criminal codes, a juvenile is described, in some jurisdictions, as delinquent for habitually disobeying parents, for being truant, for being sexually promiscuous, for keeping late or unusual hours, for running away from home, and for other non-law-violating irregularities.

The term juvenile delinquency, then, is subject to wide variations in definition. A review of statutory definitions alone is enough to confirm this observation. First of all, such a survey indicates that a "juvenile delinquent" is identified by a statute in every state in the Union. In studying the juvenile court statutes in the United States, at least twenty-five acts or conditions that amount to "delinquency" were found. As previously indicated, these acts run the gamut from a simple refusal by a juvenile to obey his parents or guardian to the actual violation of a law. The Illinois statute, which is generally considered the prototype of juvenile court statutes because it was the first statewide juvenile court (July 1, 1899), originally covered only those juveniles who violated state statutes or municipal ordinances. It

[5]For a thorough discussion of delinquency laws in the United States, see: F. Sussman, *Law of Juvenile Delinquency*, 2nd Ed., Oceana Publications, New York, p. 21; R. Cavan, *Juvenile Delinquency: Development, Treatment, and Control*, 2nd Ed., Lippincott, Philadelphia, 1972, pp. 15–22; Sol Rubin, *Crime and Juvenile Delinquency*, Oceana Publications, New York, 1958, pp. 43–45; Sol Rubin, "The Lasr Character of Juvenile Delinquency," in Rose Giallombardo, eds., *Juvenile Delinquency*, 2nd Ed., John Wiley & Sons, New York, 1975, pp. 25–32; and D. C. Gibbons, *Delinquent Behavior*, 2nd Ed, Prentice-Hall, Englewood Cliffs, N.J., 1976, pp. 8–12.

was soon broadened, however, to include children jeopardized by their associates and those who were incorrigible, ungovernable, dissolute, and truant—in short, all children whose conduct did not conform to a model of wholesome, youthful activity. If delinquency were limited only to those youngsters who violate state statutes or municipal ordinances, the task of defining delinquent behavior would be simpler, but all jurisdictions, as previously indicated, except the federal, embrace prohibitions against various kinds of "child immorality"—acts or conditions that are not considered illegal when participated in by adults.

The many variations in juvenile court law are confusing. The age limitations of each particular state, however, adds to the problem. For example, in one state a child who commits a specific offense may be handled as a juvenile delinquent while in another jurisdiction one who commits the same offense may be handled as an adult criminal. This differential, therefore, makes an accurate definition or statistical count of juvenile delinquents almost impossible.

VARIATIONS IN DEFINING DELINQUENCY AMONG STATES

Although many of our states do not agree on how to describe a juvenile delinquent in precise terms, they have enacted statutory language that is sufficiently broad to cover virtually any form of juvenile antisocial conduct. For this reason, the characteristics of the delinquent juvenile tend to be largely the same throughout the United States. At the same time, it is important to point out the ambiguity and variation that exists in the definitions of delinquency as used in the United States.

In virtually all states, the behavior that can bring a child before the juvenile court may only be construed in terms of certain moral judgments of the community, which are derived from the older laws of chancery of the British common law courts. Thus, children may be judged for not only violations of state statutes or municipal ordinances but also for "noncriminal behavior" (i.e., incorrigibility, truancy, the habitual use of obscene language, absenting themselves from their homes, or associating themselves with vicious persons), which are fundamentally matters of community taste, standards, and discretion.

Besides the wide variety of behaviors that may be described as delinquency, there is the problem of age limits, which differ from one jurisdiction to another. The usual age limit, when specified, is seven years, but the upper limit varies. Most states set an arbitrary limit of eighteen, but some specify twenty-one, seventeen, or even sixteen. Several states also vary in the upper limit on the basis of the delinquent's sex. In some states that are limited in size and population, a special provision is found for children who would normally qualify as juvenile delinquents but who, because the juvenile court finds them unfit for its services, can be tried as adults when they are charged with committing serious crimes. In other words, there are legal exceptions to the delinquency status in a number of states. The provision in various states for concurrent jurisdiction of the criminal court and the juvenile court displays a similar anomaly in the purposes of delinquency statutes. On the one hand, they assert that a child is too immature to be held accountable for crime or to suffer punishment and, on the other, they make an exception of those crimes that are most retributively penalized in the law.

Adding further confusion to the ambiguity of the term juvenile delinquent is the problem of how to handle the abused neglected or dependent child. Technically, abused neglected or dependent children are distinguished from juvenile delinquents, but because of expediency, they are often included in the jurisdiction of the juvenile court. Thus, in most states, the juvenile court is empowered to determine these cases. This particular situation becomes more difficult when these children are detained in and sometimes committed to the same institutions where delinquents are incarcerated. Tappan writes that

> *Frequently, too, their [such neglected abused childrens'] conduct problems overlap with those of delinquents to such an extent that any realistic behavioral discrimination is impossible. Whether a child be held delinquent, neglected, or dependent may depend chiefly on a petitioner and his motive rather than either the child's conduct or his more basic problems of unadjustment. This suggests the large problem confronting children's courts as to the behavioral or situational elements that should be taken to constitute delinquency. . . . There are provisions in some states establishing, in the courts that handle delinquent and neglected children, jurisdiction over other related problems, e.g., the dependent child, adoption, custody, the physically handicapped child, the mentally defective or disordered child, illegitimacy, or marriage of girls under 16.*[6]

Juvenile delinquency is related to criminal behavior as such since patterns of antisocial youthful behavior are often carried over into adult activities. And much behavior that is termed delinquent when engaged in by juveniles involves the commission of acts that would also be considered criminal in most jurisdictions if committed by someone who is an adult.

The extent and nature of that ill-defined complex, juvenile delinquency, defies precise definition. What is delinquency? Who are the delinquents? How do they differ from nondelinquents?

> *Certainly there is no more central question in this study and probably none more difficult to answer. Yet it is important to see the nature of delinquency as clearly as possible and to understand the problems that have impeded efforts at definition. It is important, because on the interpretation of the term depend all those vital differences which set off the juvenile delinquent from the adult criminal at the one extreme and from the nonoffender at the other. In theory at least and, to a large degree, in fact, the*

[6]P. Tappan, *Juvenile Delinquency*, McGraw-Hill Book Co., New York, 1959, p. 13.

delinquent child is dealt with differently from the criminal: in the conduct involved; the court and its methods implored; the treatment philosophy, purposes, and methods applied; and in the individual's status, reputation, and civil rights in the community after adjudication.[7]

Discussions of the extent and treatment of delinquency are limited by conceptions of what delinquency is. As the following analysis will indicate, the question "What is delinquency?" may itself be highly misleading because it seems to suggest that a single answer is possible. In view of the variety of legal, administrative, clinical, and behavioral definitions available, the assumption that any directly factual, mutually consistent answers are possible may itself be one of the principle sources of confusion. Consequently, one of the first requirements of discussion is to reject the simple question "What is delinquency?" and to substitute the question "What is meant when the term delinquency is used?"

THE LEGAL DEFINITION

The legal definitions of juvenile misconduct in the United States have become so broad and diverse that in about one-third of the states there is not even a statutory definition of delinquency. This practice was recommended under the Standard Juvenile Court Act of the National Probation Association, which, following good casework principles, avoids the very concept of delinquency itself and simply establishes the jurisdiction of the children's court over those children who violate any state law or municipal ordinance. Legally speaking, then, a juvenile delinquent is a child (age defined by statute) who commits any act that would constitute a crime if done by an adult and who is adjudicated as such by an appropriate court. Children who are incorrigible, ungovernable, or habitually disobedient and beyond the lawful control of a parent or other lawful authority and require supervision and treatment are regulated to a separate category. But even laws that many may think of as being absolute or definitive are not so when it comes to juvenile delinquency.

As legal concept, delinquency is considerably broader and vaguer than the legal concept of crime—for two reasons: (1) it includes many behaviors that would not be considered illegal if committed by adults; and (2) a careful description of these behaviors is frequently much more ambiguous than would be constitutionally acceptable in criminal statutes, which generally requires precise specifications of activities labelled as illegal.

As previously stated, laws vary among different states. Just who is considered to be a child differs among states. So are the types of misbehavior included under the broad term of delinquency. Thus, it is quite possible for a child to be considered a delinquent in one state and not one in another. Yet even the most cursory review

[7]*Ibid.*, p. 32.

of this "typical" inventory of delinquent behavior leads one to conclude that it is reasonable

> *To believe that all, or at least a vast majority of, normal children some-*
> *times indulge in forms of behavior that might come within the purview of*
> *the juvenile court. Whether a given child will get into trouble depends*
> *largely on the interpretation that is attached to his conduct and the wil-*
> *lingness or ability of the parent to deal with it. Considering the broad scope*
> *of legal provisions on insubordination, "questionable behavior," "injuring*
> *or endangering the morals or health of himself or others," truancy, run-*
> *ning away, trespassing, and petty theft, it would be difficult to find any*
> *paragons of virtue who would be wholly exonerated of delinquency, save*
> *through parental understanding and leniency.* [8]

Many of the activities, then, specified as delinquent are no different from those activities engaged in, at one time or another, by all children. Since either all or the vast majority of children at one time or another engage in these activities, and since only a small proportion of these children are either socially labeled or officially processed as delinquents, something more than the mere engaging in these activities is required for the social identification of a child as a delinquent. This "something more" is formal, administrative action on the part of the law enforcement agents of society.

Before moving on to administrative definitions of delinquency, it is important to point out that because of the evergrowing and wide variation in definitions, the legal definitions of delinquency in the United States are almost nonexistent. As previously stated, many states—approximately one-third of the states—do not define delinquency in their statues. In these jurisdictions, delinquency is whatever the juvenile court adjudges it to be.

ADMINISTRATIVE DEFINITIONS OF DELINQUENCY[9]

Formal administrative action by law enforcement agents may take several forms, and estimates of the extent of delinquency will vary according to the index used. If police complaints are used, one figure will result; if commitments to an institution are used, another figure will result. In a study that investigated the estimates of delinquency made on the basis of different indexes of delinquency, it is noted that the formal law enforcement action often went beyond "recorded police complaints." These children were not taken to court, they were not formally adjudicated delinquent—and they were not institutionalized—though there is no reason

[8] *Ibid.*, p. 33.
[9] R. R. Korn, "The Counseling of Delinquents," Training Aid No. I (mimeograph), Santa Clara County Juvenile Probation Department, San Jose, Calif., 1969, p. 3.

to believe that their misbehavior was significantly less serious than the behavior of the adjudicated and institutionalized children. Therefore, it can be said that the only differentiation between nonadjudicated and noninstitutionalized delinquents from the others was not what they did but the manner in which their cases were handled by agents of the society. Needless to say, if police complaints are utilized as an index of delinquency (in contrast to court appearances or commitments to institutions), the rate of delinquency will show a drastic increase in any particular area. In other words, it is common knowledge that almost without exception, the police officer is the first to approach a child in trouble. It is also common knowledge that many youngsters are handled on an unofficial basis and not referred to a juvenile court. Thus, the police officer, in effect, sits as judge or serves as social worker in many instances. He may also determine the final disposition of almost half the cases involving juvenile offenders who are taken into custody. Therefore, a police officer is placed in a position of an "adjudicator." As an adjudicator, he may be an arbitrary despot in the application of his particular preferences. He may be enlightened, objective and nonmoralistic, or ignorant and prejudiced."[10] Thus, what happens to a delinquent youngster in any particular case depends a great deal on the attitudes and perceptions of the police officer as he decides to make or not to make an arrest.

DELINQUENTS AND NONDELINQUENTS: HOW DO THEY DIFFER?

Individuals not familiar with the problem of juvenile delinquency would readily agree that there is no similarity between a delinquent and a nondelinquent. However, studies by George Vold and Austin L. Porterfield (*Youth in Trouble*) ascertain that there is no significant difference between the delinquent and nondelinquent populations. Also, according to R. R. Korn:

> *There is no valid basis for assuming that the behavior of officially adjudicated delinquents differs significantly from the alleged behavior of vastly larger proportions of children, committing similar acts, who are not formally processed as delinquents. What strikingly differentiates the officially processed delinquents from those whose behavior is either not detected, or not officially acted upon, is a chain of social-like processes ranging from the (a) arrest, (b) formal adjudication as a delinquent, (3) official supervision and restriction within the open community, to (d) brief or prolonged incarceration in the enforced company of similarly processed children in correctional institutions.*

[10]Tappan, *Juvenile Delinquency*, p. 15.

Korn further states that:

> *The most visible and demonstrable difference derives not from the nature of the delinquent behavior itself, but rather from the nature and extent of the community reactions to this behavior—reactions ranging from tolerance to indifference, or indifference to prolonged correctional incarceration. We have, in effect, implied that it makes a difference whether or not juvenile misbehavior is tolerated and ignored ("Don't worry, he'll grow out of it"), informally dealt with in the family setting ("He'll get what's coming to him when Dad comes home"), or formally punished by the impersonal law enforcement agents of society ("We hereby commit you during the period of your minority to the New York Training School at Otisville").* [11]

The difficulty with defining delinquency is further compounded when agencies that deal with the problem begin to develop their own concepts of delinquent conduct. Agencies such as the police and the juvenile court have devised their own concepts of juvenile delinquents.

OTHER CONCEPTS

Police Concept

The police concept classifies the delinquent as the statistical delinquent and the personality-disordered delinquent. The statistical delinquent is a youngster who is involved in a delinquent act through impulsiveness or immaturity. As an example, he is involved in an automobile theft without, at that time, realizing the consequences of his actions. Such actions usually occur "on the spur of the moment" while the individual is involved with other youngsters. This youngster is not a recidivist and responds to agency services provided. However, he is a "statistic" because this impulsive delinquent act is reported by the arresting agency and, in some cases, in a subsequent referral to the juvenile court.

On the other hand, the personality-disordered delinquent is the youth who is often involved in a series of antisocial acts that necessitates, in most instances, a referral to the juvenile court and, in most cases, custodial care or some type of official help. The personality-disordered delinquent is the youngster who often "runs the gambit" of agency referrals. In other words, he may have received numerous warnings by law enforcement agencies prior to referral to the juvenile court. Furthermore, after being processed by the juvenile court, he may, on several occasions, be placed back in the custody of his parents on probation. However, when agency services fail, institutionalization is often the end result.

[11]Korn, "Counseling of Delinquents," p. 6.

School Concept

The school concept is a rather general one. It appears that schools, or the educational system, are concerned with delinquents who fall in several categories:

1. The academic delinquent—a minor who is not working to full capacity in school.

2. The behavioral delinquent—a boy or girl who is unable to respond to demands made by teachers or is continually involved in altercations with his peers.

3. The mentally or physically handicapped child—a child unable to compete with classmates because of severe emotional or physical handicaps that cause him to act in a hostile, unacceptable manner.

Generally, the schools are of the opinion that an unhappy child is a potential delinquent. The schools cite, as an example, the youngster who is unable to keep up with the manner of dress of his peers or who will not conform to school dress standards. This youngster may be teased and taunted by his peers. Eventually, he is provoked into striking back.

Juvenile Court Concept

The juvenile court concept deals with the juvenile who is actually referred to the juvenile probation department by various agencies, and a petition is filed in his behalf, alleging a law violation. The juvenile court, as previously discussed, processes numerous youngsters who show "predelinquent" behavior or are in dependency situations. Hence the juvenile court contends that only the youngster petitioned for a law violation should be classified as a delinquent.

According to the juvenile court concept, no juvenile is a delinquent unless he appears before the court on a petition alleging a law violation and the court sustains this petition. The juvenile court feels that it is unjust to declare that a juvenile is delinquent at the point of his apprehension, just as the adult court does not consider an adult a criminal at his point of apprehension. According to the juvenile court concept, the juvenile should be accorded the same presumption of innocence.

As was previously discussed, almost fifty percent of the juveniles apprehended after violating the law are released by police without official action and even if referred to the probation department, very few are referred to the court by the probation officer. Therefore, there is a legal difference between a youngster being apprehended as a juvenile law violator and one being declared a ward in a juvenile court proceeding. The juvenile court concept suggests that a minor does have due process and that his legal rights are protected. Until such time as a court of competent jurisdiction passes upon the evidence, sustains the petition, and declares the minor a ward, the child is no more delinquent, from a legal point of view, than is the adult who is not a criminal, at least not until properly charged with an offense against the law and found guilty as charged.

EMERGENCE OF JUVENILE DELINQUENCY AS A CONCEPT

In terms of historical prospective, three dominant movements have contributed to the emergence of the concept of the juvenile delinquent and the institution of the juvenile court as differentiated from crime and criminal proceedings.

The concept that *immaturity* exempts the individual from moral responsibility in choice of behavior is perhaps the earliest movement in this direction. The classical doctrine of *mens rea* (or a "guilty mind," one in which right is distinguished from wrong) was introduced in the first half of the eleventh century. The doctrine held that a child up to the age of seven was not capable of a *mens rea* and hence not accountable at law for his acts. Subsequently, through the interaction of state and church law, the relationship between criminal responsibility and moral guilt was firmly established. The *mens rea* concept suggested clearly both the justification for and the necessity of treating juvenile offenders differently than their adult counterparts. Furthermore, common law declared that the child from eight to fourteen years of age is presumed to be incapable of guilt, and thus irresponsible, because of immaturity—unless he can be shown to have sufficient intellectual capacity to perceive the difference between lawful and unlawful behavior.

The second movement is reflected in current juvenile court processes. The principle of *chancery of equity* was established by early English kings in reaction against the rigidity of the law and court as applied to minors and to those needing aid. Under the principle of *parens patriae* (the king as father of his country) and its more contemporary counterpart, *in loco parentis* (the state as standing in place of the parent), the child's rights have been ordered in civil law in such matters as neglect, dependency, and guardianship. From these principles comes the concept of the "ward of the state," which is applied to the juvenile handicapped by lack of effective parental supervision or control.

The third and most recent movement is derived notably from middle-class humanitarianism and from child psychology, both of which have striven to protect a child from the sweatshop, whipping post, and incarceration with adult offenders. At the same time, social and psychological research combined with modern penology to stress the causes of crime—how to diagnose treat and ultimately to eliminate them through individual study and therapy, especially in the cases of youthful offenders.[12]

These three developments led to the present day concept of juvenile delinquency as something quite different from adult crime. The earlier concept of the young offender to whom punishment is accorded to fit the crime has been replaced largely by the concept of the juvenile as a youngster needing guidance, much as

[12]*Ibid.*

any child in need of medical assistance in the form of diagnosis and treatment. The close affiliation of the early juvenile court with the child guidance movement, initiated in 1909 by Dr. William Healy of Cook County, Illinois, illustrates this point, although the focus was exclusively on the individual and his family rather than on environment.

Thus, the term *juvenile crime* represents a contradiction within a strictly legal framework since "crime," by definition, can be engaged in only by adults. *Legally, the term juvenile delinquency includes all the youngsters between ages set by state statutes whose behavior or series of behaviors involves infractions of rules and norms in such a manner as to bring them to the attention of authorities connected with official institutions.* The official institution may be in the form of the overall legal societal authority or a subinstitution such as an educational facility (school).

As indicated throughout this first chapter, two major kinds of violations are included in states and federal statutes. First, there are those violations of law that, if committed by an adult, would be called crimes. Second, there are those transgressions that are peculiar to the juvenile age group, such as truancy and incorrigibility, which have special significance only for members of this group. This category is often referred to as "Status Offenders." Hence, there are in our legal framework both the linear law that includes offenses ordinarily defined as "crimes" but that are now handled, because of the age factor, as "delinquencies" and the special infractions that are meaningful only when committed by persons of younger ages in the community. [13]

What does this mean? When an attorney speaks of tort, contract, or bailment, he has in mind something specific. When the police officer, probation officer, parole officer, or deputy sheriff discusses a burglary or a robbery or a rape, he speaks of crimes that have common law meaning. He knows the elements that make up the specific crime, and generally, he knows what actions come within the offense. But this is not so when someone speaks of juvenile delinquency. There are dissertations, periodicals, books, and many media that discuss juvenile delinquency. All profess alarm about it, but none tell exactly what it is that constitutes a delinquency. A noted authority on crime and delinquency, Professor Clyde B. Vedder, states that *"a very difficult problem in studying juvenile delinquency is deciding upon an exact definition of the term itself—no two authorities agree in this matter."* (Vedder's emphasis).

There seems to be a concerted effort on the part of the authorities to avoid labeling juveniles as delinquents. According to statistical information from the FBI and the Children's Bureau of the Department of Health, Education, and Welfare, law enforcement agencies handled almost fifty percent of juvenile police arrests informally. Scrutiny of statistical information from such agencies shows that more than 1,700,000 youths have had contact with various police agencies throughout

[13]W. C. Kvaraceus and W. E. Ulrich, *Delinquent Behavior: Principles and Practices,* National Association of the United States, Washington, D. C., 1969, p. 114.

the nation—but only approximately 500,000 actually appeared before juvenile courts throughout the states on petitionable offenses.

Thus, it is safe to say that more than half of the juveniles taken into custody by the various law enforcement agencies throughout the country are returned home without further action. It is also safe to say that half the juveniles who are referred to juvenile courts are released without a finding of delinquency.

THE NATURE OF DELINQUENCY

Many people view delinquency much in the same way that they view some physiological disease. They think of it as a specific pathology in the body of society. This is a misconception. Truancy, incorrigibility, delinquency are but symptomatic pictures of underlying conditions, the roots of which may be found in the family relationships, the school adjustment, the environmental background of the child, or in some psychological or physiological aspect of the individual's personality. In other words, delinquency is a symptom and not a disease. The medical profession recognizes a fever as a symptom, a symptom that may be present in many diseases. The doctor may prescribe something to allay temporarily the symptom, but if he is a good practitioner, he will spend most of his efforts in locating the focal point or points of infection and, by removing them, cure the disease and remove the symptom—fever. Delinquency is much like a fever. Many things or combinations of several things may cause it. Until a thorough diagnosis is made and until we treat fundamental causes as well as the symptoms, little progress can be expected. Moreover, delinquency is often the result of a combination of factors some of which may be found in the environment of the child and others within the child himself. The nature of delinquency, therefore, will differ both because of the environmental forces and because of the nature of the delinquent child. It is well to remember in this connection that one delinquent act does not necessarily mean that a child has a psychotic personality. In fact, many delinquents have quite well-adjusted personalities.

RELATION TO MENTAL ILLNESS

It is particularly important to clarify the relationship between delinquent behavior, as defined above, and psychological disturbance, character disorder, and actual mental illness. Psychological difficulties of youth and delinquent behavior are related and overlapping areas, but they are not the same thing. Psychological disturbance is a cause for only a portion, and it must be said an undetermined portion, of all delinquency. Some delinquency is "normal" in that it develops out of identifications that children make with their own neighborhood or special group within it. There are groups that are rebellious and defiant toward the norms and life patterns which the majority in the adult community accepts for itself and proposes as models for children and youth. The search for immediate rewards and the psychological satisfaction of acceptance by peers can lead youth to participate in what, in fact, may be delinquent behavior, although that behavior is quite understandable in terms of the individual's sense of personal worth. The problem remains of explaining the existence of the deviant and delinquency-oriented groups in our society, and this matter will be considered separately. It should, though, be clear that psychological pathology *is not a necessary condition* of delinquent behavior.

On the other hand, some kinds of psychological disturbance can predispose children and youth toward delinquent behavior. A child who has been subjected to hostility, rejection, or unfavorable adult attitudes toward him may learn to hate and mistrust the adult world. He may literally declare war on it. His method of attack may take the form of violating the norms that society officially protects; thus, he becomes a delinquent.

It should be noted, however, that in such children, the first act of delinquency may be preceded by much misbehavior that falls short of actual delinquency as defined here. This kind of personality development is well recognized and fairly well understood. Unfortunately, the same adults who view all adolsescent innovations as bad, dangerous, or productive of delinquency may be quite unaware of the real relationship to future delinquency exhibited in these rebellious and hostile behaviors of early and middle childhood. The future delinquent may give warning, but the danger signals are often overlooked. It is necessary, therefore, in talking about the various aspects of delinquency not only to avoid an improper extension of the term to all deviant or unconventional behavior of young folk but also to recognize that nondelinquent behavior may be predictive of future offenses. We will thus deal with delinquency as strictly defined as well as with other behaviors of children that are related.

The kind of personality development just discussed, in addition to other patterns, are considered clinically deviate and, to the extent that delinquent behavior stems from them, psychological disturbance and delinquency are casually related. It should be noted that not only parents but also other adults, among them teachers, neighbors, and policemen, have significant relationships with children. The child learns his attitudes toward society from interaction with his peers and from experience with adults. Parents have the greatest single influence, as will be seen in chapter 7, but they cannot be held solely responsible for the attitudes that children develop toward the adults or for the models of behavior that these adults represent.

Sociologists have long held the view that many forms of crime and delinquency may be well within the range of "normal" behavior. In other words, sociologists have advocated that certain types of criminal activity are, in actuality, no more than "normal" responses to situations in which the cultural emphasis upon material success has been absorbed without adequate opportunities to achieve such success in a conventional and legitimate manner.

Dr. [Richard] Jenkins concurs in this view and describes a major proportion of delinquency as the product of "the same motivation our culture sanctions as the force which keeps our competitive economy ticking. . . ."

Jenkins has called this type of delinquency "adaptive." Adaptive delinquents are distinguished from those whose clearly disturbed adjustment and poorly integrated behavior indicates an ideology based on compulsive response to frustration rather than on discriminative and adaptive goal-seeking. . . .

Implicit in this [discussion] of the possible relations between personal adjustment and personal activities are two assumptions: (1) The individual's total personal adjustment influences not merely what *he chooses to do and* why *(his motivation) but also* how *he succeeds in doing it (Thus, an individual can, for almost neurotic reasons, decide on a certain line of activity and have sufficient resources to carry it out effectively); (2) a line of activity, or a way of life (adopted because of any combination of psychological and situational determinants) involves the individual in* consequences *which are more or less rewarding or unrewarding in a social contact, the network of close relationships which are relatively supportive and approving or relatively non-supportive and disapproving. Sufficient reward and social support gives rise to* attitudes and values *in favor of the activity and powerfully reinforcing it. When these attitudes and values become firmly and harmoniously established in the self-concept: (i.e., become "egosyntonic"), the individual's continuing commitment to the activities becomes less and less dependent on his original motivation,* and hence, *less relevant to it and more and more dependent on the contacts of reward and social approval supporting those values and attitudes. At this point,* his purely psychological condition *tends less and less to influence* what *he does and tends primarily to affect* how *he does it. What we are thus, in effect, saying is that the complex of determinants which were originally etiologic to the behavior may not be the same which determine its continuity and persistence. . . .*

At some point a decision, a commitment is made: The bank clerk has decided to become a banker, the apprentice has decided to become a shoemaker, the juvenile delinquent has decided to become a professional thief. Sick or well, they will attempt to continue to function in these activities, and they will function, efficiently or inefficiently, until such time as they are either too disturbed to go on, have ceased to like or enjoy what they are doing, or have found something better. [14]

The above observation will gain greater importance when the causes of delinquency are discussed in chapter 5.

[14]Korn, "Counseling of Delinquents," p. 16.

SUMMARY

Chapter 1 presents an introductory overview of specific areas to be discussed in succeeding chapters. Basic queries such as who are the delinquents? Why are they what they are? What can be done about them? And the nature of delinquency are answered as well as the problem of defining the term delinquent. In addition, this chapter discusses delinquency not as unique to our contemporary society but as old as time. In order to substantiate this fact, several quotations are presented revealing that even during the time of Socrates, youthful problems were present.

Attempting to define a delinquent is extremely difficult. Juvenile delinquency is not a simple term. It is very elusive and means many different things to different individuals, and it means different things to different groups. When using this term "juvenile delinquency" properly, one realizes that almost everything a youngster does that does not meet with the approval of individuals or groups may be referred to as a delinquent act. For purposes of research, evaluation, or statistical records, such popular usage is not acceptable.

Chapter 1 also discusses the ambiguities and variations in definitions of delinquency in the United States. Many of the states do not agree on the description of a juvenile delinquent. Statutory language is extremely broad and covers virtually any form of antisocial conduct by juveniles. In virtually all states, moral judgments of the community are an important ingredient in defining a delinquent. Many children may be tried for not only violations of state statutes or municipal ordinances but also for "noncriminal behavior" such as incorrigibility, truancy, and the use of obscene language. These are crimes which, if committed by an adult, would result neither in arrest nor court appearance. These "crimes" are referred to as "status offenses." Age limitations here are a major problem because the states set various and arbitrary upper-age limits on behavior deemed to be delinquent.

In defining delinquency, there is always the problem of the neglected, dependent, or physically abused child. Although this youngster is technically separated from delinquency proceedings, he also appears in most states before the same court. Therefore, a stigma is attached to this youngster who is definitely not a delinquent but who, through no fault of his own, appears before the courts that serve delinquents.

An introductory overview is presented of the nature of delinquency. Delinquency is often the result of a combination of factors, some of which may be found in the environment of the child and others within the child himself. Taking this into consideration, the variables of delinquency thus reflect differences among environmental forces and differences in the natures of delinquent children. The relationship between delinquency, mental illness, and health is clarified in the section on the psychological difficulties of youth and delinquent behavior. In this part are discussed the important ramifications of the fact that psychological pathology is not a necessary condition of delinquent behavior.

The latter part of chapter 1 introduces the difference between delinquency and nondelinquency. It is easily seen that the difference is one based primarily upon the judgmental attitude of the community.

ANNOTATED REFERENCES

Coffey, A., *Juvenile Justice as a System: Law Enforcement to Rehabilitation,* Prentice-Hall, Englewood Cliffs, N. J., 1974, chaps. 1–3.

> Alan Coffey discusses the importance of viewing the phenomena of delinquency in its social and cultural contacts. Coffey's book serves as an excellent overview of the problem of delinquency and the law enforcement processes from arrest to rehabilitation.

Eldefonso, E. and Hartinger, W., *Control, Treatment and Rehabilitation of Juvenile Offenders,* Glencoe Press, Beverly Hills, Calif., 1976, chaps. 3 and 10.

> The authors offer, in nontechnical terms, a discussion that relates to information contained in chapter 1 of this text, Eldefonso and Hartinger discuss the problems of defining delinquency and the variety of definitions between states and certain age limitations.

Fredericksen, Hazel and Mulligan, R. A., *The Child and His Welfare,* 3rd ed. W. H. Freeman and Company, San Francisco, Calif., 1972, chap. 8.

> Chapter 8 deals with the concept of delinquency. The authors discuss the definition of delinquency, trends, factors relating to delinquency, and "society and juvenile delinquency." This source serves as an excellent reference for students who are involved in introductory courses in delinquency.

Gibbons, D. C., *Delinquent Behavior,* 2nd ed. Prentice-Hall, Englewood Cliffs, N. J., 1976, chap. 1.

> Gibbons explores the nature of juvenile delinquency and its impact on American society.

Konopka, Gisela, *Young Girls*: *A Portrait of Adolescence.* Prentice-Hall, Englewood Cliffs, N. J., 1976.

> A short book (176 pages) but informative. It delves into the problem of female delinquency; particularly in the area of the "status offender."

Phelps, Thomas R., *Juvenile Delinquency: A Contemporary View,* Goodyear Publishing Co., Pacific Palisades, Calif., 1976.

> As the title indicates, the author presents a detailed contemporary overview of the problem of juvenile delinquency in the United States. The book provides basic data information regarding the problems created by the delinquency laws as they finally control the status offenders. The author also covers the juvenile justice system and the processes which deal with the youth offender.

CHAPTER TWO the correlative factors of delinquency

Before turning to the various theories of delinquency causation that are discussed in the following chapter, it is important to point out the *correlative* factors of delinquency. Correlative factors relate not only to the physical contexts of delinquency (i.e., to slum areas, divorce, separation, rape, drug addiction, suicide, alcoholism, and psychosis), but to the social-psychological climates closely associated with delinquency.

The correlatives of delinquency are: *age, sex, poverty,* and *social class membership.* Because of their greater significance, two other correlatives, *primary group* (i.e., family) and *schools,* have been incorporated into chapter 7 and discussed there in detail.

AGE FACTOR

If the causal roots of delinquency are debatable, there can be no argument about the age factor. No matter what the category of time or delinquency statistics—and they are both highly variable and both open to serious question—one striking trend appears again and again:*there is an ever higher proportion of offenders* among those of young age.

Before examining the evidence for this trend, it will be helpful, once again, to review a few of the basic shortcomings inherent in today's crime statistics. Most importantly, since the statistics on the incidence of crime among various age groups are ordinarily in the form of arrests or convictions, they probably tend to exaggerate the crime rates of the young adults. Children are less likely than adults to be arrested for the same offenses, and older criminals commit crimes that are less likely to be detected than those committed by younger adults. Despite the dedicated efforts of the Federal Bureau of Investigation to gather uniform crime reports from every law enforcement agency in the nation, an enormous margin of error has been estimated. Furthermore, the reader need only refer to the statistical information presented in chapter 3 to be reminded that, although legal definitions of crimes are fairly exact, methods of enforcement, detection, prosecution, and judgment vary significantly throughout the United States.

But after some serious biases have been taken into account, the statistics do seem to justify the following set of conclusions: (1) the crime rate is highest during or shortly before adolescence; (2) the age of maximum criminality varies with the type of crime the age group of fifteen to nineteen years has the highest official rate for auto theft; the age group twenty to twenty-four has the highest rate for robbery, forgery and rape; and the age group thirty-five to thirty-nine has the highest rate for gambling and violation of narcotic drug laws); (3) the age of first delinquency and the type of crime typically committed at various ages varies from area to area in cities, the age of first criminality is lower in areas of high rather than low delinquency (boys aged ten to twelve commit robberies in some areas of large cities, while the boys of the same age commit only petty thefts in less delinquent areas); and (4) the age of maximum general criminality for most specific offenses is higher for females than for males.

In terms of prisoners received from court the overall felony rate in federal and state institutions has been gradually climbing for the fifteen to nineteen category over the past three decades with a slight leveling off for the last five years (1972–76).

But the ages at which delinquents are apprehended is largely a matter of *legal definition* and *customary practice*. In most states, the age of eighteen is defined as the dividing line between juvenile offenders and adult criminals. In some states, there is a statute providing for some latitude in handling a minor past the case defined by law. Usually, there are facilities to handle those younger past the legally defined age. In California, as an example, youths over eighteen (18–21) may be committed to the California Youth Authority. This trend is growing in many states and the importance of early rehabilitative procedures before the individual is remanded to adult penal custody is gaining wide support. Individualized treatment can best be accomplished, it is being recognized, when the individual is still young.

SEX FACTOR

Boys are apprehended for offenses approximately 3.5 times more frequently than are girls. The underlying reasons are not difficult to locate. They are certainly *not* due, as some may claim, to any "innate" sexual differences or predispositions to criminality! Rather, because of role-behavior differences and the status distinctions accorded to adolescence in the American culture, the society *expects* girls to act differently than boys, and surrounds their behavior with restrictions that act as barriers to delinquent activity. In *all* known cultures, children learn early to discriminate between potential roles and to develop "appropriate" behaviors expected of their sex. Girls in American culture tend to conform more closely to such standards (because the standards are flexible for them) than do boys. The expression "boys will be boys" shows acceptance of a of a certain degree of prankishness as a normal aspect of adolescent male behavior, whereas in other cultures the opposite is often the rule.

Studies conducted at the University of Minnesota by Elio Monachesi (utilizing sophisticated psychological tests) indicate that a higher percentage of female delinquents suffer emotional disturbance than nondelinquent girls, and both delinquent and nondelinquent boys. Such findings tend to support the hypothesis that *delinquency among boys is induced largely by opportunities presented by the environment, while among girls delinquency is due more often to emotional maladjustments and personal inadequacies.*

POVERTY

Few of the variables associated with crime and delinquency have been more misunderstood than that of poverty. Contrary to early investigations, recent studies indicate almost "null" relationship between poverty and delinquency. This is in part due to the obvious fact that delinquency rates are higher during today's era of relative prosperity than they were during the depth of the Great Depression of the 1930s.

During the early part of the century, it was readily apparent that poverty and delinquency were positively and closely associated. This does *not* mean, however, that conditions of poverty no longer breed crime and delinquency. It means simply that while economic conditions have improved, rates of delinquency are still high and are becoming more dispersed among the general population. In short, the improvements in our economic life during the past several decades—bringing in their wake steadier and more widespread employment, social security, high wage standards, aid to dependent children, and increased social benefits—have not produced the decline in delinquency that might reasonably have been expected. Instead, other factors are becoming increasingly instrumental in producing delinquent disorders.

Adverse economic conditions, nevertheless, do appear to be a potent stimuli to delinquency. Wealth and economic status function *relatively* as limiting conditions in producing delinquency. The highest incidence of delinquency is always induced among the marginal, economic groups, and as these groups contract in size, the relative incidence appears to shrink accordingly.

Why, then, the high correlation between poverty and crime? The answer is not difficult to come by; it is the same answer, further, which we shall call upon to explain the apparent relationship between delinquency and broken families. It is this: low economic status is not a direct cause of delinquency. It is rather one of many variables that more or less automatically "go together," (including broken families, suicide, certain types of psychosis, and alcoholism). Relative poverty is one of *many* characteristics that plague the slum zones of transition. It is therefore only naturally correlated with high crime and delinquency rates. But correlations and cause-and-effect relationships are *not* necessarily synonymous. We can safely assert, then, that although poverty and low economic standards are concomitant with delinquency, they are not indispensible characteristics. To be "poor but honest" is, in fact, the rule rather than the exception.

SOCIAL-CLASS MEMBERSHIP: MIDDLE-CLASS AND LOWER-CLASS DELINQUENCY

Despite the professed democratic ideal of a "classless" society,[1] a realistic appraisal of the contemporary social-economic map dictates an irrefutable fact: Americans *are* stratified into a hierarchical system of power, prestige, and value-oriented groupings. Whether or not the typical American will admit to the reality of social classes, the fact remains that they do exist. Awareness of social stratification groupings is unnecessary so long as people's life styles, values, ideals, motivations, and social intercourse are limited to sets of cliques of like-minded, similarly oriented people.

American middle-class and lower-class subcultures differ from one another at highly significant points. But the most crucial differences, in terms of delinquency, relate to the vastly different child-rearing techniques and social values instilled in children by the two classes. No matter where the American class structure has been studied—in the rural South or Midwest, in virtually all our great metropolitan centers, in small towns and villages, ranging from New England through California—social scientists have arrived at similar conclusions.

At the risk of generalizing, it can be asserted that where the middle class typically stresses parent/child relationships geared to love and dependence through late adolescence, the lower classes tend to give their children physical and psychological freedom well before the adolescent years. The middle class is far more stringent in its child-rearing pattern, weaning and toilet training its youngsters far earlier, stressing an early assumption of responsibility, instilling ideals of progress and diligence, emphasizing social and gregarious skills, discouraging physical or oral aggressiveness, restricting sexual impulses, and highly evaluating "nice manners." The typical lower-class parent, in contrast, is more permissive and laissez-faire in rearing his child, devalues formal education, pushes the child into the street at an early age, and does not discourage aggressive physical and sexual impulses.

Middle-class norms are in effect a tempered version of the Protestant ethic which has played so important a part in the shaping of American character and

---

[1]For a more comprehensive analysis of social-class membership as it relates to delinquency, see H. M. Hodges Jr., *Social Stratification*. Schenkman Publishing Co., Cambridge, Mass., 1971.

American society. Briefly, this ethic prescribes an obligation to strive—by dint of rational, ascetic, self-disciplined, and independent activity—to achieve in world affairs. A not irrefutable but common correlary is the presumption that 'success" is itself a sign of excess of these moral qualities. Perhaps the chief middle-class virtue is ambition; its absence is a defect and a sign of maladjustment. And ambition means a high level of aspiration—aspiration for goals, difficult of achievement. It means also an orientation to long-range goals and long-deferred rewards. It means an early determination to "get ahead." It is incumbent upon the "good" middle-class parent to encourage in his child those habits and goals that will help him to be "better off" than himself, and his first duty is to make his child want to "be somebody." The middle-class ethic is also an ethic of individual responsibilities; it applauds resourcefulness and self-reliance, a reluctance to turn to others for help.

The ability to conform to these norms does not depend upon a simple effort of will. Conformity comes easily when a child has internalized (subconsciously adopted as his own) these norms because he was grown up in a world where, for example, precept and reward have always emphasized them and where training has equipped him with the necessary skills and habits.

It is worthy of note at this juncture that in referring to cultural differences between middle-class and working or lower-class society, the author does not mean to imply that there are two sharply demarcated and culturally homogeneous classes. In most communities, the categories merge. Some of the most traumatic effects of "middle-class culture" are to be found, in fact, in the upper, mobile, lower-class families. Thus, in speaking of lower-class culture, we are speaking of cultural characteristics that do not characterize all lower-class families—but that do tend, in a statistical sense, to distinguish the cultural milieu of the two class subcultures.

Planning and foresight are less typical of lower-class families; provision for the future is more likely to be concerned with maintaining an accustomed level of living than with raising it. Jobs or occupations are evaluated in terms of their present yield in income, other immediate satisfactions, and security; they are not seen, as in the middle-class, as a stage in an upward career.

In general, the lower-class person appears to be more dependent upon and "at home" in primary groups and avoids secondary, segmenteal and formal relationships more than the middle-class person. He appears to be more spontaneous, emotionally irrepressible, to give freer and less disguised expression to his aggression, and to find it more difficult to play roles with which he does not basically identify. He is less likely to possess, to value, or to cultivate the polish, the sophistication, the affluence, the "good" appearance, and the other-directed "personality" so useful in selling one's self and manipulating others in the middle-class world.

Middle-class socialization, in comparison with lower-class socialization, is conscious, rational, deliberate and demanding. Relatively little is left to chance and "just growing." Middle-class parents are likely to be concerned and anxious about their children's achievement and age-graded norms, and this anxiety is often communicated to the child. The middle-class child is constantly aware of what his parents want him to *be* and to *become*. And he is probably more properly motivated to conform to parental expectations; for his home is likely to generate a "need" for dependence upon parental love. This love is not only a supreme value to the child, it is in Margaret Mead's terms, "conditional love." It is something to be merited, to be earned by effort and achievement. To the degree that this love is precarious and contingent, there is generated what is often referred to by behavioral scientists' as "adaptive" or "socialized" anxiety, which is to be allayed only by avoidance of prescribed behavior and by constant striving.

Lower-class socialization, on the other hand, tends to be relatively easygoing; the child's activities are more likely to be governed by his *own* present inclinations, his parent's convenience, and his momentary unpremeditated impulses. He is more often thrown upon his own or the company of an autonomous group of peers. He is freer to explore in many areas forbidden to the middle-class child, and to encounter a variety of trouble, scrapes, and personally meaningful problems.

Furthermore, the sanctions that the lower-class parents administer are probably less effective than those of middle-class parents. It is doubtful that the effects of physical punishment, which is more common in the lower-class home, are so lasting or so deterring as the effects of the threat of the loss of love. And because of the structure of his home, the lower-class child is less likely to develop the overwhelming emotional dependency on the love of one or two adults, which is so typical of the middle-class child. At the same time, it appears likely—although this aspect of differential socialization has not been well explored—that *the lower-class child is more dependent upon his relationships with his peer groups* for the satisfaction of many emotional and practical needs.

Physical prowess and aggression also have a different significance in lower-class socialization. In both classes physical competence and readiness to stand and fight when attacked are important expectations for the male role. But there are important differences of emphases. For the lower-class boy, fighting is more frequently recognized as a normal, natural, and legitimate way of settling disputes; he often sees his parents and other adults fighting on what would seem inadequate provocation. For the middle class, physical prowess as a criterion of status tends to be channeled into organized, competitive sports, governed by strict rules of "fair play."

It is far from surprising, then, that delinquency finds far more fertile ground in the lower-class sectors of the typical city—and particularly in those that are situated in slum areas. Bearing in mind what we have already observed about the adolescent rejection of parental values and need for peer-group identifications, we can readily see the intense grip that the gang—delinquent or "legitimate"—holds on the lower-class adolescent's loyalties. In such a cultural milieu, any well-socialized "normal" child will take part in gang activities. If his gang's activities are delinquent in character, *he will become a delinquent.* If it is the normal, well-adjusted and, as several studies have indicated, the *physically superior and more energetic boy* who is most frequently delinquent in the lower-class subculture, then what of the typical middle-class delinquents?

The *middle-class delinquent* is, apparently, one of two types. Atypically, he too runs with an adolescent gang with delinquent propensities. Such gangs are rare in middle-class ranks, but they are often composed of youngsters whose families (1) ignore, for several possible reasons, the middle-class child-centered norms practiced by their neighbors: (2) have work or social obligations that preclude the close personal relationships and cautious supervision typical of other middle-class families; or (3) have obliterated normal family ties as a result of divorce or separation.

More frequently—almost typically, in fact—the middle-class delinquent is a diametric counterpart of the lower-class delinquent. Where the lower-class delinquent is smoothly socialized and well-liked by his peers, the former middle-class delinquent is often seriously maladjusted and at odds with his fellow adolescents. What little research has been done in this area (for the theory is relatively new and middle-class delinquents are *statistically* rare) vividly portrays that such children, either too *leniently* or too *strictly* reared as youths, are emotionally crippled by either varying degrees of neurosis or psychopathic (*not* psychotic) personality makeups. They are the deviants, the socially shunned, the isolates, the "odd balls" who are rejected, or sense that they are rejected, by their age-grade mates. They typically resort to one of two basic adjustment mechanisms: (1) they withdraw into a private, introvertive dream world; or (2) they turn to bizarre, attention-getting devices. More rarely, they may seem to be smoothly adjusted, serious-minded youngsters ("who'd ever dream he'd shoot his teacher—he was such a nice, well-behaved boy!'), but they actually bear hidden grudges toward peers or adult authority figures. There are occasional instances, too, of middle-class children who have turned to delinquent acts as the apparent consequence of failing in school, being taunted by other children because of some oddity or defect, having failed in normal prestige-granting activities (such as sports, club membership, or social cliques), or feeling unloved and unwanted by their parents. But whatever the causal factor, "psychological" delinquents such as these have one thing in common: *they are essentially lone wolves, and they commit their delinquent acts alone.* It bears repeating, however, that such cases are relatively rare, although they receive more attention because they make ideal "news copy." It is conservatively estimated that 80 percent of delinquent acts are committed by *gang-oriented* lower-class adolescents. This is not to discount the occasional gang-centered delinquencies in the lower reaches of the middle-class—man estimated five percent of total delinquent acts.

Aside from "slums" (as though the physical aspects of the slum zones—rather than the social factors concomitant with life in the slum—somehow "cause" crime), no correlative factors of delinquency have been more frequently and fervently blamed than those mentioned in this chapter. In a sense, such inaccurate reasoning is justified. For not only is the issue to find correlative factors such as age, sex, poverty, and social class membership as relatively clear-cut scapegoats—but also sociology and psychology have repeatedly asserted that these factors are the prime matrix in shaping both cultural behavior and personality growth. (The family as the primary factor in shaping personality and cultural growth will be discussed in chapter 7.)

To deny that the correlative factors discussed in this chapter *cause* delinquency is not, however, to deny that such factors typically go in hand in hand with delinquency. But, as was previously pointed out, a *correlation* is one thing, a *cause and effect* relationship another. Trees bud in spring, so does love. Few would seriously contend, though, that budding trees *cause* love affairs

SUMMARY

This chapter points out the correlative factors of delinquency. *Age, sex, poverty,* and *social class membership* afford us an in-depth study of the correlative factors closely associated with delinquency.

Although statistics pertaining to age as a correlative factor in delinquent activities may be debatable, this chapter points out that there is one factor that is not debatable: the striking trend, which crops up again and again, of *an ever higher proportion of offenders in the young category.*

In discussing age and delinquency, this chapter views the basic shortcomings inherent in today's crime statistics. Even after serious biases have been taken into account, statistics do seem to justify the conclusion set forth in chapter four: (1) the crime rate is *highest* during or shortly before adolescence; (2) the age of *maximum* criminality varies with the type of crime (the age group fifteen to nineteen has the highest official rate for auto theft; the age group twenty to twenty-four has the highest rate for robbery, forgery and rape; and the age group thirty-five to thirty-nine has the highest rate for gambling and violation of narcotic drug laws); (3) the *age of first delinquency* and the type of crime typically committed at various ages varies from area to area—in cities, the age of first criminality is lower in areas of high rather than low delinquency; and (4) the age of *maximum general criminality* for most specific offenses is higher for females than for males.

With regard to *sex,* boys are apprehended for offenses approximately 3.5 times more frequently than girls. The underlying reasons, as pointed out in the chapter, are not difficult to locate.

Contrary to early investigations, recent studies indicate almost no relationship between *poverty* and delinquency. Poverty may have been an important factor in the earlier part of the century, but it certainly is not significant in today's era of relative prosperity. This does *not* mean, however, that conditions of poverty no longer breed delinquency. This chapter discusses the failure of the improved economic conditions over the several decades to produce the decline in delinquency that might easily have been expected.

Social class membership does have a definite relationship to the amount and type of crime. This chapter discusses the crucial differences, in terms of social class membership, in the area of child-rearing techniques and social values instilled in children by the parents. These differences in child rearing and social values are discussed in relation to their impact on delinquent activities.

ANNOTATED REFERENCES

Reese, C. D. "Police Academy and its Effects on Racial Prejudice," *Journal of Police Science and Administration*, No. 1, Sept. 1973.

> This journal discusses the gamut of social problems, placing a great deal of emphasis on deviant behavior pertaining to the correlative factors of delinquency.

Gans, Herbert J., *The Urban Villages*, Free Press, Glencoe, Ill., 1970

> Chapter three gives a vivid detail of different definitions of virtues and faults from the viewpoint of different classes—an area that is discussed in this chapter.

Gibbons, Don C., *Delinquent Behavior*, 2nd ed., Prentice-Hall, Inc., Englewood Cliffs, N.J., 1976.

> Middle class delinquency is discussed in Chapter six. Also discussed (Chapter seven) is female delinquency.

England, R. W., "A Theory of Middle Class Delinquency," *Journal of Criminal Law, Criminology, and Police Science*, 1960 Vol. 50, No. 6, pp. 535–540.

> Covers the title subject.

Kolbrin, Solomon, "The Conflict of Values in Delinquency Areas," *American Sociological Review*, October, 1951.

> Although dated, the author's remarks still hold true regarding conflict as it relates to delinquency and class values.

Miller, Walter B., "Lower Class Culture as a Generating Milieu of Gang Delinquency," *The Journal of Social Issues*, vol. 14, 1958.

> Miller, in his classic study, discusses the lower class and its impact on youngsters who are *potential* delinquents as well as on those who are already involved in delinquent activities. The culture, according to Miller, has a significant impact on the amount and type of crime committed.

Vas, Edmund W., *Middle Class Juvenile Delinquency*, Harper & Row, New York, 1974.

> The author discusses lower-class and middle-class delinquents and differ-

ences in their values and their behavior patterns. Vas points out that these classes differ chiefly in that significantly more lower-class delinquents feel themselves to be "loyal and daring." This is an excellent resource for enriching the information pertaining to lower-class and middle-class delinquents discussed in this chapter.

CHAPTER THREE delinquency: myths, misunder- standings, and theories

Most problems, most questions can be studied from more than one point of view. It is a misconception to assume that there is only one way of considering delinquency. Certainly one must consider not only the delinquency but the delinquent as well. There is no one, nor even a known, correct attitude to take toward the problem. Students of the problem must recognize all possible attitudes and points of view. A juvenile may steal because he is hungry; he may steal because it is more exciting than doing something better; he may steal to please some adult, even a parent; he may steal because he is a kleptomaniac; or he may steal something for no discoverable reason.[1]

Delinquent behavior is complex and, as pointed out in chapters 1 and 2, has many different meanings in different social contexts. To the judge and policeman, stealing, for example, is contrary to criminal law and the child who steals is a delinquent; to the psychologist, who is interested in the theory of learning, the child has learned to steal—a lesson that society as a whole wishes he had not learned; to the psychiatrist, stealing may be viewed as a way of resolving some emotional conflict or tensions that have arisen from the child's inability to cope with life's situations; to the citizen who owned the stolen property, the child is a threat to the safety of property and should be punished; to the parent, the child's stealing may be viewed as the work of the devil, as a mental disorder, as an act of

[1]E. Eldefonso and W. Hartinger, *Control, Treatment and Rehabilitation of Juvenile Offenders,* Glencoe Press. Beverly Hills, Calif., 1976, Chapter 4., pp. 74–94.

rebellion, as an attempt to ruin the family reputation, as a bad habit, or even as an act of carelessness about getting caught that the child should avoid the next time he steals. To the child's playmates, stealing may be an act in an exciting and dangerous drama, and the young thief may be judged by whether he lives up to their code, shares with them, or refuses to tell on those who have stolen with him. And, of course, it is most important to know what stealing means to the child himself.[2]

From the educator's point of view, delinquency is learned, and in looking for conditions that give rise to delinquency he finds many that are common to other kinds of poor learning development—broken homes, poverty, emotional conflicts in family life, retarded mental development, or poor neighborhood background. It is necessary, therefore, to study these conditions, to discover how some children learn delinquency in these conditions, and how other children in the same home, school, and neighborhood, often with the same intelligence and basis for emotional conflict, learn socially acceptable behavior. It is also necessary to learn how children can unlearn delinquent behavior, and most of all we must know how more desirable social behavior can be learned.[3]

Many believe that delinquency has definite causes. Some blame poverty, others slum conditions, and still others find the cause for delinquent acts within the warped personalities of the delinquents. One reads that the home or the parents are to blame, that the school and teachers are at fault, or that the churches have in some way failed to meet the needs of modern youth. The lack of recreational facilities, the increased amount of leisure time, the laws making it impossible for children under sixteen or seventeen years of age to go to work, have been cited as causes. Progressive education with its increased freedom for pupils in modern schools, even modern religion with less emphasis upon hellfire and damnation, have been blamed for increases in juvenile delinquency. Modern urban society, with its increased facilities of communication, with better and faster means of transportation, with greater concentration of population, quite different from the rural life of a generation or two ago, has also been attributed as the cause of the present problem of juvenile delinquency. Delinquent parents, broken homes, bad politicians, insufficient police protection, the presence of adult vice and crime are often mentioned. The movies, the comic books, television and radio programs, filthy literature, suggestive art, are other causes frequently given. These causes given for delinquency are almost as numerous as those who write or talk about the subject.[4]

No doubt some of these beliefs are more or less correct. The careful student, however, must try to determine whether or not any one or all of the causes given may or may not be other symptoms, just like delinquency, of more fundamental

[2]*Ibid.* p. 75
[3]*Ibid.* p. 77
[4]E. H. Stullken. "Misconceptions About Delinquency", *Journal of Commerce Law, Criminals and Police Science*, Vol. 46. No 6, Mar. and Apr. 1966. pp. 833–842.

reasons why some juveniles become delinquents while others do not. If he wants to understand the problem, the educator, the student of the law, the psychologist, the psychiatrist, the social worker, must strive to dig down deeper than many of the superficial reasons that are often given for producing delinquents.

Just as there are those who believe they know the cause of delinquency so there are those who think they know how to cure it. Some believe that more, better, or stricter laws will solve the problem. They often forget that laws are only as effective as the public concern in their enforcement and that adding more legal prohibitions will not deter juveniles from becoming delinquent. Many today say that parents should be held responsible for acts of their children and that we should fine or imprison the parents whenever a juvenile commits some delinquent act. No doubt parents should be awakened and educated to their responsibilities, but it is questionable whether mere punishment will accomplish the end in view.[5]

> *Others believe that if proper recreational facilities are provided in greater degree, if more athletic activities are sponsored by schools, churches, or other agencies of the community, and if more playgrounds are available to all boys and girls, then delinquency will be reduced. Some in Illinois believe that an Illinois Recreation Commission, created by legislative action and supported by the state will prevent delinquency. The enactment of such legislation will probably be good for many children but it is doubtful whether the argument that it will prevent delinquency has much validity.*
>
> *Many also believe that the schools can provide a panacea for juvenile delinquency. The school today, is concerned with helping students to guide their conduct by reason, to use intelligence in reaching decisions rather than blind obedience, habit, or prejudice, and to acquire a knowledge of self and an understanding of the consequences of behavior. The school today aims to develop young people physically, spiritually, and morally as well as intellectually so that they can take a competent and effective part in daily life, contribute to the welfare of others and make their own lives happy and good. The schools recognize and integrate all those aspects of life—moral, ethical, economic, civil, social—in which people need to exercise intelligence and understanding. Schools, therefore, are concerned with all the problems of life, the delinquency problem included; but their concern is primarily one of dealing with all children in such a way that delinquent behavior will not likely result on the part of individual children.*
>
> *Others advocate punishment as a cure for delinquency. One hears and reads much about a return to the historic "woodshed scene"; but the fact that most juvenile delinquents have already been the recipients of a great deal of physical and often unintelligent punishment, casts doubt upon punishment as a cure for delinquency. The delinquency problem is*

[5]*Ibid.*

less likely than any other crime problem to respond to the purely negative measures of punishment.[6]

Just as there is no single cause for delinquency, so it is doubtful that there is any single, simple solution to the problem. It is a misconception of the problem to believe there is a simple solution or that one can be found. Only as local communities become aroused, only when all agencies will cooperate and coordinate their efforts, and only when the citizens of a given community will work together for the welfare of all children can they hope to attack the problem successfully.

MYTHS AND MISUNDERSTANDINGS

Throughout the ages, it has been quite popular for each generation to believe that they have discovered the true cures or causes for juvenile delinquency. Contacts with various groups of people—experts and laymen alike—indicate that very strong opinions are held on this subject. And each group holds to its own concept with unusual tenacity.

As with many social problems, nearly everyone forms a snap judgment, becomes a self-appointed expert, and is anxious to "do something about juvenile delinquency." Individuals and groups often forget that "doing something about delinquency" means that the public and the community at large must be willing to do something about itself.

Fortunately, community action is seldom guided by the popular misconceptions about juvenile delinquency. Nevertheless, these misconceptions and myths are sufficiently widespread, to warrant critical examination.

It is thus necessary to explore some of the ideas that are misleading or incorrect but that, like legends, still persist in the folklore surrounding delinquency. Although there may be an element of truth in some of the misconceptions regarding delinquency, such misconceptions are open to serious challenge as *absolute* or *categorical* statements concerning the nature and sources of delinquency. To place credence in half-truths that have been falsified through overgeneralization and indiscriminate application is to erect a psychological "Berlin Wall." Subscription to such fallacies prevents clear and innovative thinking when programs are designed for the prevention and treatment of the youthful offender.

The problem of popular misunderstandings is vividly captured by Joseph S. Roucek and Roland L. Warren, who state,

> *An adequate, scientific approach to problems of delinquency and crime is hindered by the popular misunderstandings remaining in the folklore and common sense approach to the problem. In the following paragraphs, the term "criminal" will be used to include "delinquent" merely for purposes of brevity.*

[6]*Ibid.*

The first misunderstanding is that criminals are a separate type of people. *Popular thinking tends to lump together all criminals as being people who are different from other human beings and who, among themselves, are pretty much the same. Actually, the range of individual differences among criminals is as wide as that for the general population, and their behavior can be interpreted and understood according to the same principles which govern the behavior of law-abiding persons. Nevertheless, the misunderstanding persists, and it militates against the institution of programs which would deal with the criminals by recognizing the individual circumstances surrounding each case and seek their rehabilitation through an application of scientific principles of human behavior.*

Another misunderstanding is the viewpoint that criminals have no morals. *This involves the fallacious notion that criminals are not motivated by normal human desires and that they are lone wolves who do not seek or need the approval and affection of other people. Actually, most crime is a group phenomenon, involving cooperative association of several parties. In addition, criminals are found to subscribe to many of the* mores *to which law-abiding people give their loyalty, and in addition have strong group mores, such as that of loyalty to one's own group and the duty not to squeal, or inform legal authorities about one's fellow criminal.*

Another important misconception is that crime has a single cause. *Criminologists, through careful research over many decades, have found that crime is usually associated with a combination of factors, rather than any single one like feeblemindedness, broken homes, etc.*

A fourth important misconception is that crime is prevented by strict penalties. *Many people advocate severe punishment as a deterrent to crime. However, no such relationship has been found to exist between the frequency of crime and the intensity of punishment. It is said that during the reign of Henry VIII pickpockets did their most extensive business among the crowds gathered to watch the public hanging of criminals, many of whom were being hanged for stealing.*[7]

Fallacies such as those cited by Roucek and Warren lead the expert into impractical, mirage-like plans and create hopes that can not possibly be successful, no matter how much time, effort, and money is put into them. There are other misconceptions that should be discredited, such as the idea of a simple cause.

SIMPLE CAUSE

Perhaps the most common misconception is that juvenile delinquency is caused by *one thing.* Some people will argue until they are blue in the face that delinquency is

[7]J. S. Roucek and R. L. Warren, *Sociology, An Introduction,* 3rd ed. Littlefield, Adams and Co., Ames, Iowa, 1970, pp. 330–327.

a result of a single factor, such as inadequate housing, lack of discipline, or a progressive educational system.

The serious student should not be misled into accepting any simple causal explanation of the problem of delinquency. This common tendency to overemphasize a single factor is quite prevalent in society; it is usually utilized by frustrated individuals and groups as a convenient scapegoat. Such groups or individuals believe that if a simple explanation can be found, then there is a simple solution to the problem. The sooner such convenient scapegoats are laid to rest, however, and people realize that there is no simple panacea, no ready-made solution, the sooner they will be able to face the problem realistically.

The myth of the simple cause treats delinquency as an isolated act cut off from the rest of society. Delinquency, however, cannot be self-contained or isolated from its social setting. It must be viewed from the perspective of multiple causes and the complex relationship of many factors. So thoroughly is the problem of delinquency a part of other aspects of community life that it can be seen as a "cave-in of asphalt pavement"; consequently to understand delinquency is in actuality to study the underlying structure of society. Only within the broader perspective can the complexities of the problem be properly set and the solution sought.

BROKEN HOMES

Causative theories concerning the broken home and delinquency are popular, timeless. Although the concept of "broken homes," like the concept of the "working mother," has some utility, more precise definitions of broken homes are required and the precise effects these have in different milieus need to be determined. There is, for example, the problem of the *psychologically broken home*, where even though both parents are living together, the parents are continually at odds and are unable to communicate with each other. Therefore, there is continual turmoil within the family constellation and one questions whether this is healthy emotionally. There is also a question of a lower-class culture pattern, in which separation is the standard or acceptable style, and thus, a broken home has a different connotation in this frame of reference than it does in others.[8]

There are many other factors here that need to be investigated, and perhaps the most important question is the impact of the *physically* broken home on the first four or five years of a child's life, as against the impact of breaks that may occur later in life.

In a massive study of nine thousand juvenile delinquency cases handled by the Philadelphia Court in 1964, Thomas P. Monahaan ascertained that broken homes were twice as prevalent among delinquents as among the general population of the city. However, the inference that the broken home is the cause of delinquency has been questioned on several grounds. *First* of all, it was found that

[8]James Dobson, *Dole to Discipline*, Wheaton Illinois, Tyndale House Publishing, 1970, pp 7–10.

the percentage of serious offenders from broken homes is less than the number from intact homes. *Secondly,* it has been pointed out that such a study (an examination of court cases only) has a built-in flaw: when apprehended for an offense, the child with an intact family is more apt to be sent home, whereas the youngster from the "broken home" is apt to be sent to court and, very often, to an institution.

LOWER-CLASS CHILDREN AND DELINQUENCY

The myth that delinquency is confined to the lower class, is one that seems plausible from statistics, for the statistics do bear out that a preponderance of lower-class youngsters are juvenile offenders. But the reader should know that these statistics, based on Federal Bureau of the Investigation Uniform Crime Reports and Children's Bureau of Department of Health, Education, and Welfare, only record those violators of law who, are *legally* apprehended or who appear in court.

In chapter 3, it was pointed out that more than two-thirds of the youngsters apprehended never appear before the juvenile court. Further, over 15 percent of the youngsters who actually appear before the juvenile court have their petitions dismissed. These large numbers of youngsters who are caught for an offense or never appear before the juvenile court, and who are fortunate enough to have their petitions dismissed, are more likely the middle-class youths whose parents "know the right people" and use the correct channels to apply pressure at the proper points. Youngsters from "good" white-collar families have parents who possess the ability to conceal or eliminate the evidence of their offspring's indiscretions. Unfortunately, parents of lower-class children simply do not have the contact or "know the ropes" to avoid legal apprehension or a subsequent appearance before the juvenile court.

> *Most official delinquents come from the ranks of the poor, a fact which has led to the easy conclusion that poverty, poor housing and related conditions cause delinquency. This conclusion is based on the fallacious reasoning that if two things vary together, one is the cause of the other. There is no doubt that most official delinquents are poor, and that they live in rundown dwellings, but neither is there any doubt that a few official delinquents are rich, and that still others come from moderately wealthy families.* [9]

Furthermore, as Martin and Fitzpatrick point out, when a youth is not referred to court (i.e., an unofficial case), cases do not show a significant difference. In other words, delinquency knows no boundaries and is scattered throughout the general population, "although the form it takes and the frequency with which it occurs may vary by economic and social rank. [10]

[9]J. M. Martin and J. P. Fitzpatrick, *Delinquent Behavior, A Redefinition of the Problem,* Random House, New York, 1965, p. 77.
[10]*Ibid.*

Taking this factor into consideration, one can correctly assume that social reformers in the early 1900s placed too much emphasis or credence on the relationships between delinquency and poverty. It is, therefore, ridiculous to take the position that clearing the slums or simply raising the standards of living of the poor will eliminate delinquency or criminal behavior. Clearing slums as well as raising the living standards alone will be ineffective and cannot control a social problem that is deep rooted and whose origin is traced to multiple factors.

THE RECREATIONAL MYTH

Perhaps the greatest, most general, and most misleading fallacy of all is the belief that all we need to do to eliminate or drastically alleviate delinquency is to supply playgrounds and conduct recreational programs. This particular belief represents a highly organized school of thought, which believes that "give the boy a place to play and he will not get into trouble" and "a community with an excessive number of playgrounds is a community with little delinquency." But research indicates there is no direct or discernible relationship between the *usual recreational program* and delinquency rates.

Recreation, as organized and conducted at present, cannot drastically reduce youthful crime because the children who need the program are usually not present at the playground. Regardless of how adequate the program or the leadership is, if these children who need it the most are not present, recreational facilities or programs cannot be a significant influence in their lives. Furthermore, because recreation is skill-centered, it is not unusual to find that the vulnerable children cannot compete successfully, and any effort to induce them to compete only lowers their ego and increases their frustration. The majority of recreational leaders, moreover, are trained in skills and activities and are unable to understand delinquency and its related problems. Such lack of training or understanding makes it difficult for these leaders to do a promotional job with the potential delinquent. Partnership, cooperation, and adherence to rules are stressed in all recreational programs, and leaders expect the children to abide by them. This in itself causes a great many problems for the highly vulnerable youth, who resents any kind of supervision and when pressured can create an explosive situation. Delinquents and potential delinquents find it difficult to respond to authoritative figures, and certainly most directors and program leaders do not, will not, and cannot tolerate this type of behavioral problem in their groups.

CURFEW LAWS AND DELINQUENCY

Although many communities utilize curfew laws, it is naive to believe that curfew laws will help materially to prevent juvenile delinquency. The children who need the curfew most obey it least. It is most difficult to enforce and when enforced, it is not enforced consistently, but only when pressure is placed on law enforcement agencies. The curfew ordinances throughout the country have not actually stood the test of constitutionality. Many people working in the field are of the opinion that curfews are mere legislative "gimmicks" that do not ensure any long-term success in keeping children out of trouble.

Curfew laws have existed for years with scant evidence of any effectiveness and the Children's Bureau has stated: "The most effective curfew is one applied by parents. It can be flexible to meet different circumstances, and children are more likely to obey it."

DELINQUENCY AS AN URBAN PHENOMENON

Every major American city has its traditional neighborhoods of high delinquency, and, therefore, it is a common assumption that delinquency is a product of urbanization.

This attractive notion has more basis in fantasy than in fact. Much juvenile delinquency is hidden in rural areas because, as we have seen, the same media of communication do not exist to publicize it. The Federal Bureau of Investigation and Children's Bureau statistics reveal that the suburbs have shown a tremendous increase in delinquency activities in 1969. In fact, the increase of youthful crime in the suburbs during the last several years has far outstripped the rate of youthful crime in the urban areas.

Moreover, forces other than official ones often step in to control youthful crime in the rural areas or suburbs. Families and friends in these areas do what police and courts accomplish in the large urban areas. Nevertheless, many people seriously suggest that residence in rural areas or suburbs is the answer.

Although urban communities have a higher rate of juvenile delinquency when compared with the suburbs, recent statistics (refer to chapter 3) from the Federal Bureau of Investigation and the Children's Bureau reveal that delinquent activity is increasing at an alarming rate in the outer fringes of the city.

THEORETICAL APPROACHES TO CRIMINAL BEHAVIOR

Why does crime occur and why does it increase at a rapid rate? The assumption often is made that a clear knowledge and understanding of the causes leading to criminal behavior can lead to a clear understanding of how to control and prevent crime.

This type of reasoning is based on the frequent experience of solving a problem successfully after its causes are determined. The problems of infectious diseases, flood control, and highway construction have been solved in this manner—by understanding and forming a clear picture of the causes. It should be noted, however, that in such instances the causes are relatively simple and few. This is certainly not true of human behavior.

Knowledge of causes does not always result in the ability to control a problem when the causes are both extremely complex and numerous. For example, much is known about the cardio-vascular and metabolic fields, yet there is not a corresponding knowledge of how to control or prevent these illnesses. In some such instances, the causes themselves are very complex and not subject to control. Causation of crime has more in common with this latter circumstance than it does with the more simple and hopeful relationship described for many infectious diseases and the threats of natural environmental forces.

It should be noted that, although control of problems may be aided by the knowledge of causes, it does not always depend completely on full understanding of causation. Medicine has many instances of the development of successful treatments, and even of preventive methods, before the causes of some illnesses were known. Similarly, efforts to control or prevent criminal behavior need not and must not, in fact, await a comprehensive statement of causes.

A number of factors associated with crime have been identified in a fairly complete way. Many factors are part of broad social and economic problems that are, themselves, as difficult to control as is criminal activity. These statements are not made to indicate any attitude of defeatism, but only to indicate the complexity of the problems of criminality and the limitations of the advantages that can be expected from a delineation of the factors that relate to criminal behavior.

It is not illogical for a person engaged in prevention and treatments to be concerned with factors related to criminal behavior; indeed, he is better prepared to treat, prevent, or rehabilitate if he knows what causes such antisocial behavior. Yet it is astounding what a wide variety of answers will come, even from the experts, from the simple question,"What factors contribute to criminal behavior?"

For teaching purposes the answers to this question are classified in three general categories of factors relating to crime: *sociological, psychological,* and *physiological.* Extensive treatment of these categories will be made in the following pages by presenting various theoretical approaches to crime and delinquency.

SOCIOLOGICAL FACTORS

From time to time, various factors have been found, or are alleged, to be related to criminal behavior. Unless a specific theory is discussed, it is preferable to speak about related factors rather than about causal factors, since causal factors imply a simple set of relations that exist. Criminal behavior, like other forms of behavior, is responsive to social and economic conditions, and other dominant features of society. Deviant behavior has occurred ever since laws and moral codes began. City life; population mobility; divergence in values, in life styles, and in opportunities for social and economic advancement; family instability; the lure of quick wealth; and social success through activities on the fringe of conventional society—all these characteristics of modern society are not in themselves necessarily the causes of crime, but they are contributory factors. Such characteristics provide the context within which patterns of antisocial behavior arise and are transmitted. They make more difficult the operation of informal social control, which has always been more important than formal legal controls in maintaining the moral order of society.

A part of the increased rate of criminality is related to an increased tendency to use the police and the courts to settle minor disputes that formerly would have been considered private matters. For effective control of crime, then, we must seek ways of compensating for those counteractions that either encourage or foster deviant behavior.

As we have seen, many studies of crime and delinquency suggest that the rates of deviant behavior are highest in the deteriorated areas of our larger cities. These are the areas in which the most recently arrived low-income immigrants settle. Also living in such areas are those who have drifted there because of failure to compete successfully for the most desirable living space (because of lack of skills, disease, or other disability) and persons who have located in those districts because of a desire for freedom from conventional restraints. These neighborhoods are characterized not only by physical deterioration, but also by great heterogeneity of background and moral standards, lack of neighborhood solidarity, lack of opportunities for youth to participate meaningfully in the kinds of activities that are available to children in more favored neighborhoods, and by the presence of "successful" members of the underworld, who are regarded as heroes by the youths. These circumstances of life often are associated with unstable families and a high incidence of illegitimacy and desertion, leading both to marginal employment, with inadequate supervision for the needs of children, and to the absence of father figures with whom children can identify and look to for supervision, guidance, and affection.

Antisocial behavior has been found to be particularly high among the minority groups or second-generation immigrants (children of foreigners who have settled in the United States) owing to conflicts of American customs with the culture of their parents. Such children often are disorganized personally, and this personal disorganization frequently contributes to delinquent behavior patterns.

A high proportion of criminals and delinquents come from homes that have been broken by deaths, desertion, or divorce. The importance of the family in the development of personalities is well known. Homes characterized by marital conflict or by absences of an important member, understandably contribute more than their share to crime and delinquency. Yet not all children from broken homes become criminals, thus other factors must be at work.

In underprivileged environments crime and delinquency may not express economic need so much as an individual maladjustment—an open, behavioral reaction to the basic conflicts that confront the child, adolescent, and adult. Neither the basic conflict of values nor crime, of course, is confined by any means to urban slums. Each finds its most favorable expression in such an atmosphere, but each may also be found in society at large.

Theoretical Approaches to Criminal Behavior   **49**

Another aspect of the contemporary environment, that is significantly involved in the problem of delinquency, arises from the very high premium put on certain forms of success and the preoccupation of many parents with their own social and occupational standing. When this is coupled with the freedom that adolescents can achieve from parental restriction, the family as a source of sound values and as a mechanism of social control is weakened further. There is evidence that middle-class youths emulate for "kicks" many of the behavioral patterns that have their origins in relatively deprived areas. These expressions of rebellion from parents are likely to appear when parental standards are inconsistent or too stringently applied to the adolescent and not wholly manifested in parental behavior.

There have been major fluctuations in the amounts of criminality that appear to be associated with major social and economic changes. At least in recent years, crime has increased in times of economic prosperity, which are marked by hedonistic values in many circles—such as the 1920s, the 1950s, and the 1960s—and has fallen in times of depression. We do not yet know about the factors that mediate between these broad changes and criminal behavior. Detailed studies along these lines and other areas mentioned earlier should be most enlightening.

PSYCHOLOGICAL FACTORS

Psychological factors relate primarily to an individual psychological pathology, some forms of which are related to a predisposition to criminal behavior. Psychological factors that underlie antisocial behavior involve inner tensions and emotions, unresolved conflicts, and unsatisfied needs of the individual. It should be noted that many of the factors described as productive of criminal and delinquent behavior also contribute to psychological pathology. Personality disturbances can occur in any section of society, whereas sociological factors such as deteriorated neighborhoods are confined to identifiable areas. Occurrence of criminal behavior by an individual residing in an area not considered conducive to antisocial behavior frequently reflects personality disorders rather than the existence of a widespread criminal or delinquent culture. Furthermore, the conditions of family life in underprivileged areas operate to increase the probability of psychological disorders among children. The end results, therefore, are that individuals with personality disorders tend to be numerous where there is a deviant culture that stimulates negative behavior. In less criminally oriented areas, however, psychological disturbances on the part of a few individuals may still be expressed through criminal or delinquent behavior. The persons may even be able to recruit other individuals who do not otherwise exhibit criminal behavior. Such relationships further illustrate the extreme complexities of the psychological factors related to crime and delinquency.

Many psychiatrically oriented psychologists consider the criminal and the delinquent to be products of personality maladjustments. The socialization process is regarded as producing either healthy or unhealthy personalities, and criminal behavior is considered a correlative of the latter.

Psychiatrists have, on the whole, amended an earlier belief that the criminal or delinquent is essentially a psychotic person. Other schools of criminology, however, have not yet entirely ruled out psychosis as a factor related to crime and delinquency. They have concentrated their focus largely on one psychosis, namely, schizophrenia, which which appears to be directly related to criminology: they also have devoted a great deal of attention to the relationship between the "psychopathic personality" and crime. If schizophrenia is the most frequent psychosis found among prisoners or delinquents in institutional facilities, it is also the most frequent in society. The rates of schizophrenic symptoms are higher, however, in the deteriorated sectors where criminal and delinquent behavior is at its maximum.

Psychologically oriented students of delinquency, on the other hand, tend to emphasize the personality attributes that distinguish delinquent from nondelinquent behavior. Research studies indicate, for instance, that the average delinquent boy is more psychopathically manic than the average nondelinquent boy. Psychologists think the source of personality deviation among delinquents is lack of parental acceptance and affection for a child. This psychologiaal theory argues that feelings of insecurity, inadequacy, withdrawal, frustration, and rebellion develop in the child.

PHYSIOLOGICAL FACTORS

If crime resulted from a sole physical factor, and that factor were a wart on the end of the nose, then it would be a simple matter to collect all criminals and delinquents with warts on the ends of their noses and remove the warts by surgery, thereby eliminating crime. As we well know, however, the physical factors in criminal behavior are more subtle and complex. In fact, there may be many who would question any physiological basis for antisocial behavior. Most investigators feel that health and disease play a rather minor role, but let us briefly examine what we call physiological factors and attempt to ascertain their importance in understanding criminal and delinquent behavior.

Factors such as body build, intelligence, sex, race, general appearance, and the presence or absence of congenital defects are some of the physiological factors that may or may not have a direct relationship to criminality. In the past the validity of such factors was given impetus by numerous studies, especially genetic studies of family groups such as the "Jukes" by W. Dugdale and the "Kallikaks," by Henry Goddard, which showed that long lines of members of the same families committed crimes of all sorts and were dangerous social misfits. Out of these studies came the idea that defective heredity played a major role in criminal behavior. This particular belief continued until 1930 when further studies revealed that the most mentally retarded do not become criminals or delinquents and those who do become involved in deviant behavior are gullible and easily led. Furthermore, although feeblemindedness has long been associated with criminal and delinquent behavior, the validity of such studies is weakened by the fact that the extent of feeblemindedness in the noncriminal and nondelinquent population is not precisely known, and that a larger proportion of the more intelligent criminals elude the law.

Although it is true that physiological factors may play a minor role in the overall picture of crime, some factors require closer scrutiny. What is the significance of the high percentage of abnormal electroencephalograms among those involved in criminal acts? How much do we really know of the birth of the criminal and/or delinquent and that all-important first fifteen minutes of life? The picture is confused and until answers are found to these questions, and many others, there can be little hope that the student of criminality will be enlightened in the near future.

THEORETICAL APPROACHES TO CRIME AND DELINQUENCY

In many penal institutions, doctors, lawyers, editors, engineers, and public officials swing into line with fellow convicts when the bell rings for meals or lock-up time. But still crime marches on. Murder, robbery, assault, kidnapping, and the like continue to flourish in all parts of the world.

Mistakenly, the uninformed public believes that it has the solution to the paramount problem of crime and delinquency. "Stop gambling" was one of the earliest suggestions, and laws accordingly were passed prohibiting gambling in almost every state. "Close houses of prostitution" and "Get rid of dope peddlers" were additional remedies offered by well-intentioned, but ill-informed persons.

Equally convincing was the contention years ago, and even today, that if every child were given a fair chance to obtain an education, his criminal tendencies would be restrained and crime could be greatly diminished. Thus, playgrounds have been established in most of the towns and cities of America, but still crime and delinquency spread at an alarming rate.

For every situation arising in connection with crime and delinquency, which captures the attention of the public for the moment, ignorant persons mistakenly believe that they have the one and only answer to the perplexing problem.[11]

Many criminologists have stopped trying to find a single theory that will explain crime and delinquency. They find particular factors that often repeat themselves—for example, factors of gang membership, lack of status in constructive groups, tensions in homes, and perhaps, a sense of failure in competition.

Harry Elmer Barnes and Negley K. Teeters, however, make the following flat statements:

[11]A. Vollmer, *The Criminal*, Foundation Press, Brooklyn; 1959, p. 18.

No physical abnormality, no degree or type of insanity, no extent of mental retardation, no extremity of poor health, no degree of physical deprivation, no extreme of poverty, no filth of slum life, no lack of recreation, no stimulation of press, movie, radio or television, no hysteria or crime wave, no family discord or broken home, will surely and without exception produce crime. A crime is committed only when a peculiar combination of personal and social factors comes into juxtaposition with an utterly unique physical structure of a human being, to create a specified crime situation. And, viewed in a merely external fashion, the same apparent constellation of factors might not produce a crime the next time they merge simply because the precise sameness can never absolutely reoccur. [12]

In general, attempts to formulate more satisfactory theories of human behavior constitute the principal content of the whole group of "human behavior" sciences, namely, biology, physiology, medicine, psychiatry, psychology, social psychology, and sociology.[13] But these various theories can be viewed only in relation to some intellectual or cultural frame of reference because the specialist tends to theorize only in his field.[14]

The rest of this chapter examines the principal explanations of crime and delinquency expounded by the various disciplines. No attempt has been made to be all-inclusive. All that has been attempted is the examination of one or two illustrations of each type of explanation offered by various disciplines. The theories are presented in a sentence-structured outline in order to give a more concise statement covering the main points of each theory.

1. The Anthropological Approach

This approach attempts to discover whether the criminal is significantly different in his physical structure from the noncriminal. It examines the physical traits of behavior.

A. Cesare Lombroso (a Italian army physician)

In his writing, Lombroso affirmed the atavistic origin of the "born" criminal and suggested a close relationship between crime, epilepsy, insanity, and degeneracy, as a whole. In other words, he viewed the criminal as a type of man more primitive and savage than his civilized counterpart.

1. He studied a series of 383 skulls of criminals and recorded the percentage frequency of a considerable number of forehead and other cranial features.

---

[12]H. E. Barnes and N. K. Teeters, *New Horizons in Criminology*, 3rd ed; Prentice-Hall, Englewood Cliffs, N.J., 1969, p. 116.

[13]S. Schifel, *Theories in Criminology*, Random House. 1969. Chap. 2.

[14]*Ibid.*

2. Comparison of these skulls with savage and prehistoric skulls led him to emphasize the "born" criminal as a physical type characteristic of primitive man and even animals.[15]

B. Ernest Hooton

He contends that criminals are organically inferior and that crime results from the impact of environment on the low-grade human organism. It follows from his theory that the elimination of crime can be effected only by elimination of the physically, mentally, and morally unfit, or by their complete segregation in a socially aseptic environment.[16] Hooton makes the following conclusions:

1. Criminals are inferior to noncriminals in nearly all their bodily measurements.

2. Physical inferiority is significant principally because it is associated with mental inferiority.

3. The basic cause of the inferiority is due to heredity and to situation or circumstance.

4. Dark eyes and blue eyes are deficient in criminals and bluegray and mixed are in excess.[17]

5. Tattooing is more common among criminals than noncriminals.

6. Long and sloping foreheads, long, thin necks, and sloping shoulders are also in excess among criminals in comparison with civilians.

C. William H. Sheldon

He developed the technique of applying body type to individual delinquents.

1. There are three basic body types:

a. Endormorphic—having a predominance of visceral and fatty tissue.

b. Mesomorphic—having a predominance of muscle, bone, and connective tissue.

c. Ectomorphic—having a predominance of skin and nervous tissue.

2. According to Sheldon, each body type is characterized by specifice traits of temperament and personality.

a. The endormorph is fat and characterized as a slow-moving individual who is warm and affectionate.

---

[15]G. C. Killinger and Paul F. Cromwell Jr., *Penology*, West Publishing Co., St. Paul, Minn. 1973. p. 40.
[16]Schafel, *Theories*, Chap. 2.
[17]*Ibid.*

    (i) Very gregarious, enjoys comfort, soft clothes, soft food, and soft, slow music.

    (ii) When irritated or confronted with a problem the endormorph "seeks advice " from a well-stocked refrigerator.

b. The mesomorph is the muscular boy who is characterized by loud speech and laughter and excessive, vigorous discharge of physical energy.

    (i) He thrives on competition and communicates more favorably with people in physical competition.

    (ii) Solutions to his problems are found through physical activity regardless of whether such activity is negative or positive behavior.

    (iii) In examining delinquent boys in the Boston area, Sheldon found that they tended to cluster in the mesomorph section of his typological triangle; that is, they were more physically aggressive, muscular, and physically stronger than average.

c. The ectomorph is the tall and lean type who appears to be a "bundle of nerves," is continually displaying short, quick, jerky movements, and has strained speech.

    (i) Food is viewed as a necessary nuisance and little pleasure is found in meals. He is a shy individual who prefers silence and refrains from becoming involved in close relationships or competitive endeavors.

    (ii) Problems are solved by withdrawing and reflecting about them.

2. The Psychological Approach

This approach analyzes motivation and diagnoses personality deviations. It holds that inner tensions and emotions, unresolved conflicts, and unsatisfied needs of the individual underlie antisocial behavior. Psychology tends to stress the individual rather than the group. Psychological research has chiefly contributed facts concerning deprivations in human needs, desires, and individual deviations in personality.

A. Sheldon and Eleanor Glueck

They concerned themselves with the personalities of delinquents and how they differed from those of nondelinquents. The Gluecks made the following assertions:

1. Delinquents are more extroverted, vivacious, impulsive, and less self-controlled than the nondelinquents. They are less fearful of failure or defeat than the nondelinquents.

2. Delinquents are less concerned about meeting conventional expectations and are more ambivalent toward or far less submissive to authority. They are, as a group, more socially assertive.

3. To a greater extent than the control group, the delinquents expressed feelings of not being recognized or appreciated.[18]

B. W. I. Thomas
He contends that the individual needs an adequate and wholesome outlet for the expression of his psychic drives and wishes.

1. The individual requires satisfying implementation of his social drives or "wishes."

2. Frustration of these basic, psychological demands or the impossibility of securing socialized satisfaction may channel them into law-violating activity.

3. Lack of affection and security easily leads to sexual delinquency, theft, and incorrigible behavior in children.[19]

3. The Psychiatric Approach
This approach originally specialized in the diagnosis of mental illness. Increasingly, however, psychiatrists have extended their activity into the analysis of all degrees of personality deviation and even of normal behavior.

A. One of the major assumptions of psychiatry is that the origin of behavior difficulties is to be found in emotional tensions originating early in life in conflicts in the family. Moreover, behavior patterns established then are thought of by the psychiatrist as relatively fixed and permanent.

B. Franz Alexander
He defines antisocial behavior as "meaningful substitute behavior" growing out of an individual's conflicts and deep, unconscious inner urges.[20]

1. The only difference between the criminal or delinquent and the normal individual is that the normal man partially controls his criminal drives and finds outlets for them in socially harmless activities.

2. This power of controlling and domesticating the primitive, unsocial tendencies is acquired by the individual as a result of education. In other words, criminality, generally speaking, is not a congenital defect, but a defect in upbringing.[21]

---

[18]S. Glueck and E. Glueck, *Unraveling Juvenile Delinquency,* 3rd ed. Commonwealth Fund, New York, 1969, p. 115.
[19]H. E. Barnes, *The Story of Punishment,* 2nd ed., Patterson Smith, Montclair, N.J. 1972.
[20]L. B. Vold, *Theoretical Criminology,* 3rd ed. Oxford University Press, New York, 1969, p. 28.
[21]*Ibid.,* p. 125.

4. The Psychoanalytical Approach

    A. This approach traces behavior deviations to the repression of basic drives. Such repression is occasioned by the mores or demands of civilized life and produces a conflict between the superego or conscience and the basic drives such as sex and hunger.

    B. There is also a conflict between desire for success and limited life opportunities. The source of these mental conflicts is unknown to the victim. He seeks release from conflicts either by some mental substitute such as day-dreaming and other flights from reality, or by overcompensatory behavior, which may be delinquent or criminal. Thus, delinquent and criminal behavior is seen as an unconscious effort to solve an emotional problem.

    C. Sigmund Freud.

        1. The central core of his ideas involves the notion of basic mental conflicts because of certain incompatible elements of the personality.

            a. The unacceptable elements are repressed into the unconscious mind and kept there by the "censor"—a term used to describe the mechanism that creates unity and harmony in the conscious personality by repressing the undesirable elements into the subconscious.

            b. The repressed ideas, impulses, or complexes continue to exist, even though put out of the conscious mind; and a considerable portion of ordinary mental activity consists of the "roundabout" ways in which the repressed elements of personality seek to evade or outwit the censor and achieve some sort of indirect expression.

            c. The three basic elements of the personality that must be brought into balance are the *id,* the *ego,* and the *superego.*

        2. Delinquent and criminal behavior, under this general theoretical orientation, is to be understood, simply and directly, as a substitute response—some form of symbolic release of repressed complexes. The conflict in the unconscious mind gives rise to feeling of guilt and anxiety with a consequent desire for punishment to remove the guilt feelings and restore a proper balance of good against evil. The delinquent or criminal therefore, acts in order to be apprehended and punished.[22]

5. The Ecological Approach
This approach shows the influence of the spatial distribution of men and institutions on behavior patterns.

---

[22]S. Brokel and R. Rock. *The Mentally Disabled and the Law,* University of Chicago Press. Chicago, 1971, p. 343.

A. Clifford Shaw

    1. He indicated on spot maps the home addresses of no less than 55,998 delinquents divided into eight groups, including juveniles, youthful felons, adults, and delinquents of both sexes. Data from as early as 1900 and as late as 1927 were included in his first study.

        a. Delinquency was very unevenly distributed in the city of Chicago. For example, in 1926 some areas showed no complaints of juvenile delinquents by police or probation officers, whereas in one area 26.6 percent of boys of juvenile court age had been involved in some act that resulted in complaints to the police in that single year.

        b. Delinquency rates varied inversely with the distance from the city's center (the Loop), except where outlying industrial areas increased the rates locally.

        c. Areas where delinquency was concentrated were found to be characterized by proximity to industry and commerce, physical deterioration, and decreasing population in a period when the city as a whole was growing rapidly.

    2. The major explanation for the concentration of delinquency was found to be in the deterioration of the neighborhood as an agency of social control.

        a. As the city grew and became industrialized, former residential areas were invaded by industry or commercial establishments.

        b. Population became mobile. People lost interest in the appearance and moral reputation of the neighborhood because their residence was shorter. Consequently, neighborliness declined.

        b. Immigrant groups brought conflicting patterns, and conflicts between the first and second generation multiplied. The neighborhood ceased to be a primary group defining behavior and regulating it in the interest of a common standard. It became indifferent. Hence, patterns differed widely, and criminal groups could exist side by side with noncriminal. Finally, a stage was reached in some areas where certain types of delinquency and crime were not considered to be inappropriate.[23]

B. Frederick Thrasher
His book *The Gang* involves a study of 1,313 gangs in Chicago and indicates their concentration in a twilight zone of factories and railroads radiating from the central Loop district.

---

[23]C. R. Shaw and H. D. McKay, *Juvenile Delinquency in Urban Areas,* University of Chicago Press, Chicago, 1942, p. 55. For an update on this subject, see D. B. Kennedy and A. Kerber, *Resocialization: An American Experiment.* Behavioral Publications, Inc. New York, 1973.

1. According to Thrasher, "gangland represents a geographically and socially interstitial area" between the Loop and the residential districts and in other midpositions. The concept of traditional or interstitial area was important, for it suggested that crime originates on the edges of civilization and respectability and in communities imperfectly adjusted to normal conditions.

2. Thrasher's work called attention to the appeal of the gang for adventurous recreation, its importance as a social group, its cultivation of an intense spirit of loyalty, and to other qualities it possesses that have social values.[24]

6. The Social, Sociological and Cultural Approach

   A. The *social* approach includes consideration of educational, religious, recreational, occupational, and other factors.

   B. The *sociological* approach concerns the effects of group life, social attitudes, and group patterns of behavior as well as the influence of social status, of the role the individual plays and his conception of it, and of various other types of social institutions and relationships.

   C. The *cultural* approach considers the influence of various institutions and social values that characterize groups and social disorganization. Culture generally is considered to be the sum total of the achievements of the group; sociologists and anthropologists use the cultural approach.

      1. Edwin H. Sutherland

         a. A person becomes a criminal because of an excess of definitions favorable to violation of law. When any person becomes criminal, he does so because of contacts with criminal patterns and also because of isolation from anticriminal patterns. Any person inevitably assimilates the surrounding culture unless other patterns are in conflict.[25]

            (i) The hypothesis suggested here as a substitute for the conventional theories is that white-collar criminality, just as other systematic criminality, is learned; that it is learned in direct or indirect association with those who already practice the behavior; and that those who learn this criminal behavior are segregated from frequent and intimate contacts with law-abiding behavior.

            (ii) Whether a person becomes a criminal or not is determined largely by the comparative frequency and intimacy of his contacts with the two types of behavior.

               • This may be called the process of *differential association*. It is an

[24]Barnes and Teeters, *New Horizons in Criminology*, p. 155.
[25]*Ibid.*, p. 159.

experimental explanation both of white-collar criminality and lower-class criminality.

- Those who become white-collar criminals generally start their careers in good neighborhoods and good homes, graduate from colleges with some idealism, and, with little selection on their part, get into particular business situations in which criminality is practically a folkway and are inducted into a system of behavior just as into any folkway.

- The lower-class criminals generally start their careers in deteriorated neighborhoods. Families find criminals at hand from whom they acquire the attitudes toward, and techniques of, crime, through association with delinquents and, in particular, through segregation from law-abiding people.

- The essentials are the same for the two classes of criminals. This is not entirely a process of assimilation, for inventions are frequently made, perhaps more frequently in white-collar crime than in blue-collar crime. The inventive geniuses for blue-collar criminals are generally professional criminals, whereas inventive geniuses for many kinds of white-collar crime are generally lawyers.

b. A second general process by which a person becomes a criminal is through social disorganization in the community. Differential association culminates in crime because the community is not organized solidly against that behavior. The law presses in one direction while other forces press in the opposite direction.

(i) In business, the "rules of the game" conflict with legal rules. A businessman who wants to obey the law is driven by his competitors to adopt their methods. This is well illustrated by the persistence of commercial bribery in spite of the strenuous efforts of business organizations to eliminate it. Groups and individuals are individuated; they are more concerned with their specialized group or individual interests than with the larger welfare. Consequently, it is not possible for the community to present a solid front in opposition to crime.

(ii) The Better Business Bureaus and crime commissions, composed of business and professional men, attack burglary, robbery, and cheap swindles, but often overlook the crimes of their own members. The forces that infringe on the lower class are similarly in conflict. Social disorganization affects the two classes in similar ways.

c. The factor or process that is suggested here as the explanation of both upper-class and lower-class crime is that criminal behavior is learned in direct and indirect association with persons who had practiced the same behavior previously and in relative isolation from those who opposed such behavior.

(i) In both socioeconomic classes, a person begins his career free from criminality, learns something about the legal code that prohibits certain kinds of behavior, and learns in various groups that other kinds of behavior that conflict with the general code may be practiced.

(ii) Through contact with these variant cultures he learns techniques, rationalizations, and the specific drives and motives necessary for the successful accomplishment of crimes.

- If he is reared in the lower socioeconomic class, he learns the techniques, rationalizations, and drives to be used in petty larceny, burglary, and robbery: if he is reared in the upper socioeconomic class and is engaged in an occupation characteristic of that class, he learns techniques, rationalizations, and drives to be used in frauds and false pretenses.
  zThe process of acquiring criminal behavior is identical in the two situations, although the contents of the patterns which are transmitted in communities differ.[26]

2. Albert K. Cohen

- **a.** In his analysis of the culture of the gang, he sees much delinquency flowing from a subculture that persists primarily in urban areas, generation after generation.

- **b.** He maintains that most middle-class and working-class children grow up in "significantly different social worlds," and, owing to difficulty experienced by working-class boys in measuring up to the conventional materialistic standards and socially acceptable behavior norms, they tend to engage in "negativistic" delinquency.[27]

SUMMARY

This chapter explores some of the ideas regarding delinquency that are misleading or incorrect, but that still persist in the folklore surrounding delinquency. Al-

[26]W. C. Reckless, *The Crime Problem*, 3rd ed., Appleton-Century-Crofts, New York, 1969, pp. 244–25.
[27]For a contemporary treatment of Cohen's theory, see R. E. Clark, *Reference Group Theory and Delinquency*, Behavioral Publications, New York, 1972.

though there may be an element of truth in some of the misconceptions regarding delinquency, such misconceptions are open to serious challenge as absolute or categorical statements concerning the nature and sources of delinquency. The chapter goes on to attack and challenge the half-truths that have been falsified through overgeneralization and indiscriminate application. The main concern, here, is that such fallacies prevent clear thinking when innovative programs are designed for the prevention and treatment of the youthful offender. The popular misunderstandings that are analyzed and discussed in this chapter are (1) criminals are a *separate type* of people,(2) criminals have *no morals*, (3) crime has a *single cause*, (4) crime is prevented by *strict penalties*, (5) *broken homes cause* delinquency, (6) delinquency is *confined* to lower classes, (7) the use of *recreational facilities eliminates* delinquency, (8) *curfew laws help to prevent* delinquent activities, and (9) that delinquency is an *urban phenomena*.

The latter part of this chapter discusses theoretical approaches to criminal behavior and as such, for teaching purposes, theories are classified in three brief general groups of categories or factors leading to crime: *sociological, psychological, and physiological.*

Sociological factors such as urbanization, family instability, population, and morality as well as economic advancement, are not in themselves necessarily the causes of crime, but they are contributory factors. Such characteristics, provide the context within which patterns of antisocial behavior arise and are transmitted. This chapter also points out that the rates of deviant behavior are highest in the deteriorated areas of our largest cities. These are the areas in which the most recently arrived immigrants have settled. Also living in such areas are those who have drifted there because of failure to compete successfully for more desirable living space (because of lack of skills, disease, or other disability) and persons who have located in those districts because of the desire for freedom from conventional restraints. These circumstances of life are often associated with unstable family ties and a high incidence of illegitimacy and desertion, leading to marginal employment, to inadequate provision for the needs of children, and to the absence of a father figure with whom the child can identify and look to for supervision, guidance, and affection. Naturally, the effect of the social problems contribute more than their share to crime and delinquency.

Psychological factors are discussed in this chapter and relate primarily to an individual psychological pathology, some forms of which are related to a predisposition to criminal behavior. Psychological factors that underlie their social behavior involve the inner tensions and emotions, the unresolved conflicts and unsatisfied needs of the individual. Personality disturbances can occur in any section of society, whereas sociological factors such as deteriorated neighborhoods are confined to identifiable areas. This chapter also points out that the conditions of family life in underprivileged areas operate to increase the probability of psychological disorder among children. Furthermore, the end results are that individuals with personality disorders tend to be numerous in criminal and delinquent areas where there is a deviant culture that stimulates negative behavior.

The final section of this chapter discusses the importance of such *physiological factors* as body build, intelligence, sex, race, general appearance, and the presence or absence of congenital defects. These are some of the physiological factors that may or may not be related directly to crime and delinquency. The validity of such factors are discussed, particularly the genetic studies of family groups such as the "Jukes" by Dugdale and the "Kallikaks" by Henry Goddard, which showed that long lines of members of the same families committed crimes of all sorts and were dangerous social misfits. The picture regarding physiological factors is confused and until answers are found to many questions, there can be little hope that the student of criminology will be enlightened in the near future.

The rest of the chapter examines the principal explanations of crime and delinquency expounded by the various social science disciplines. The various theories are presented in a sentence-structured outline in order to provide a more precise statement covering the substance of each topic.

ANNOTATED REFERENCES

Coffey, A. C., *Juvenile Justice as a System: Law Enforcement to Rehabilitation.* Prentice-Hall, Englewood Cliffs, N.J., 1974.

> A descriptive book with a cursory—but informative—discussion on the theoretical causes of delinquency.

Clark, R. E., *Reference Group Theory and Delinquency*, Behavioral Publication, New York, 1972.

> A thorough treatment of E. Sutherlands "Differential Association Theory." Part two of this book discusses how reference groups influence behavior—an excellent extension of Cohen's theory on gangs.

Gibbons, D. C., *Delinquent Behavior*, Prentice-Hall 2nd ed., Englewood Cliffs, N.J., 1975.

> Chapter Four covers Delinquency Causation. Gibbons also takes into consideration the future of delinquency theory.

Taft, Donald R., *Criminology*, 3rd ed., Macmillan, New York, 1966.

> For an excellent discussion of the anthropological approach and an introduction to criminology, Taft's volume is a classic.

Vollmer, August, *The Criminal*, Foundation Press, Brooklyn, N.Y. 1969.

> First published in 1949, Vollmer's book provides a lucid analysis of the causes

of crime and contains information useful for the law enforcement practitioner as well as the academician.

Yablonski, Lewis, *The Violent Gang*, Macmillan, New York, 1962.

Yablonski describes a violent gang by means of sociopsychological theory. Furthermore, he discusses the sociopsychological influences, and pathological personalities, thus exploring this area in more detail than was possible in this chapter.

CHAPTER FOUR juvenile justice in operation

In California alone, if present population and crime and delinquency trends continue, we can look for an increase of about seventy-five percent or more all along the line by 1980. In round figures alone, that would mean an operating cost of about $685 million a year and a minimum capital outlay of about $600 million for additional state and local facilities.

The criminal and juvenile justice process, then, will have to work at peak efficiency in order to handle such a load. Since the subject of this book is the juvenile offender, it seems appropriate, at this time, that the juvenile justice system and its processes be examined.

THE SYSTEM AND HOW IT WORKS

Before concentrating on the juvenile judicial process, namely, the function that initiates and carries out the adjudication of juvenile delinquency, the status offender, and the neglected—physically abused child, let us focus our attention briefly on the primary agency from which the juvenile judicial process draws its clientele. This agency, the police, is the backbone of the judicial system that deals with children, usually under the age of eighteen. Much has been said, already, of the importance of police work with juveniles—much more will be said later on. At this time, let us examine how a minor is apprehended and injected into the process—a decision that usually lacks clearly defined guidelines.

DISCRETIONARY PRACTICES

Some law enforcement units that deal with juveniles operate on a very well-defined basis regarding the criteria for diversion from the juvenile courts, and in the use of discretion. Others are seemingly without departmental guides, directions or policies. In such units, staff assigned are likely to handle juvenile cases on a purely personal basis. If the officer is prevention-oriented, the use of discretion is possible. If there is no firm departmental policy regarding the handling of cases, the officer may be more likely than not to refer to the juvenile court. Juveniles who are handled by the staffs of units not structured for them run the risk of being referred to the juvenile courts more frequently than youths handled by the staffs of agencies that operate with clear-cut policies and guidelines.

Although discretion should be practiced on an equal basis for all youth, without regard to race, color, creed, sex, economic status, influence, or personal appearance, this is, unfortunately, not the case. A youth's attitude, studies have shown,[1] is an important factor in the officer's decision whether to refer to the juvenile court. Law enforcement personnel tend to hold for court and/or to detain securely certain youth on the basis of their "attitudes." Piliavin and Briar,[2] have shown that attitude factors such as surliness, lack of respect, talking back to the officer, the use of curse words, and so on are important in determining the disposition the law-enforcing officer makes. Other factors frequently considered are mode of dress, residence in the poorer sections of the city, hair styles, and so forth. The result of such a process is that a sophisticated youth, by showing his "best side," or apparent remorse for his involvement, can deceive an officer into making a favorable disposition in his case, either outright release or citation to court, even though the facts of the case themselves may warrant a referral to juvenile court, or at least secure custody pending a court hearing. The youth with a negative attitude, on the other hand, is likely to wind up in juvenile court, even though a more appropriate disposition may be referral to an alternative service in the community.

The available arrest information asks more questions than it answers regarding the processing of the juvenile. We know, for example, the gross number of juveniles arrested as well as their sex, their age, and even their racial or ethnic breakdowns. While it would appear that the seriousness of the offense plays a key role in determining referrals to probation, we know also that factors such as attitude are just as important.

At the present time, too many youngsters are referred for official adjudication. In 1975, for example, in California referrals to probation police agencies were 51 percent of total arrests, and they accounted for 82 percent of all new referrals to the probation department. Of all cases in which police made referrals, approximately 90 percent were referred to probation.

This wide range of probation services raises two important issues: The first concerns the paucity of noncorrectional community resources such as children's protective services. Most protective services bureaus are currently very small operations within public welfare departments. The second issue concerns the police policy regarding the preponderance of these referrals to probation.

---

[1]Olson, Jay and Shepard, George H., *Intake Screening Guides: Improving Justice for Juveniles*, U. S. Department of Health, Education, and Welfare, U. S. Government Printing Office, Washington, D. C., February 1975, p. 5.
[2]*Ibid.*

THE PROCESS: SUBSYSTEMS OF THE JUVENILE COURT.

The function of the juvenile judicial process is, as previously indicated, to initiate and carry out the adjudication of a youthful "offender."

But since not all cases are adjudicated in court, how is a youngster screened out of the system?

The screening out of minors inserted into the system is carried out by a subsystem of the juvenile court—a system commonly referred to as detention and intake investigation. Probation departments are variously organized, but most departments follow basically the same procedure. A large department may have an intake section, a detention section, and an investigation section. The intake section must establish a close working relationship with the detention facilities. The intake section screens cases and takes *initial* action on those minors referred to the probation department. Usually, when a minor is in custody (detention), the intake deputy probation officer must make an immediate investigation into the circumstances of the case. Therefore, it is not unusual for the screening officer to hold repeated interviews, interrogations, or both with the minor who is being detained.

The initial investigation of an alleged offense concerns itself with court reports and recommendations for those cases petitioned and appearing before the court. In most cases, statues determine procedural requirements of the police and juvenile court. For example, statutes in the State of California set forth the manner in which a minor is handled by the police and probation officer. Section 626 of the California Welfare and Institutions Code describes the procedure to be used by the police officer after arrest. If a minor under eighteen is arrested, the procedure for disposition is as follows:

---

1. He may release the minor.

2. He may cite the minor to appear before the county probation officer. The procedure for citing is as follows:

   A. Prepare in duplicate a written notice to appear before the probation officer.

   B. The notice should contain a concise statement on the violation and the reason why the minor was taken into custody (facts making up a violation of law).

   C. A copy of this notice is to be given to the minor or parents; each may be required to sign a promise to appear; and the minor must then be immediately released.

   D. As soon as practicable, one copy of this notice to appear, including the facts of the offense, shall be filed with the probation officer.

3. The arresting officer must take the minor without unnecessary delay before the probation officer of the county and deliver custody of such minor to the probation officer. In determining which of the three dispositions he will make, the arresting officer shall select the one *that leasts* restricts the minor's freedom of movement, providing such is compatible with the best interests of the minor and community.

As previously indicated, most juveniles who appear in juvenile court are sent there by the police. Extensive screening and informal adjustments by police, both on the street and in the police stations reduce, to a degree, the number of apprehended juveniles referred to the court. Extensive screening, too, is carried out by the probation department at the entry level. It is incumbent upon the screening-intake unit to make a preliminary inquiry to determine whether the interests of the child or the police require court action. The inquiry may vary from cursory investigation to a full-fledged social study involving contact with numerous persons and agencies in the community. It may include a hearing at which the child, his parents, and the attorney representing the child are present. As previously stated, in many juvenile courts, especially in the large metropolitan areas, the preliminary screening function known as *intake* is performed by a special division of the probation department. Depending upon the deputy probation officer's judgment as to the basis for the court's jurisdiction, the adequacy of evidence, and the desirability of court action, the intake officer may *dismiss* the case, authorize the filing of a *petition*, or, in many courts, dispose of the case by *"informal adjustment"* (i.e., a period of six months on probation *without* court action).

Judge Wallace Waalkes, in an article in *Crime and Delinquency*,[3] described juvenile court intake as a unique and valuable tool:

> *Intake is a permissive tool of potentially great value to the juvenile court. It is unique because it permits the court to screen its own intake not just on jurisdictional grounds, but, within some limits, upon social grounds as well. It can cull out cases which should not be dignified with further court process. It can save the court from subsequent time-consuming procedures to dismiss a case. It provides an immediate test of jurisdiction at the first presentation of a case. It ferrets out the contested matters in the beginning and gives the opportunity for laying down guidelines for appointment of counsel and stopping all social investigation and reporting until the contested issues of fact have been adjudicated. It provides machinery for referral of cases to other agencies when appropriate and beneficial to the child. It gives the court an early opportunity to discover the attitudes of the*

[3]Waalkes, Wallace, "Juvenile Court Intake—A Unique and Valuable Tool," *Crime and Delinquency*, vol. 10, no. 2, April 1964, p. 123.

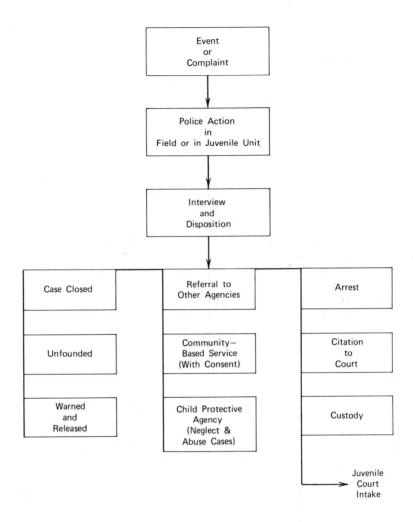

child, the parents, the police, and any other referral sources. It is a real help in controlling the court's caseload, because it operates in the sensitive area of direct confrontation with the police, the school and other community agencies, intake can make or break the community's good communication with an understanding of the juvenile court's role.

FACTORS IN DECISION-MAKING[4]

The first decision made at the point of intake is whether the complaint is one over

[4]Adapted from Olson and Shepard, *Intake Screening Guides: Improving Justice for Juveniles*, pp. 22–23.

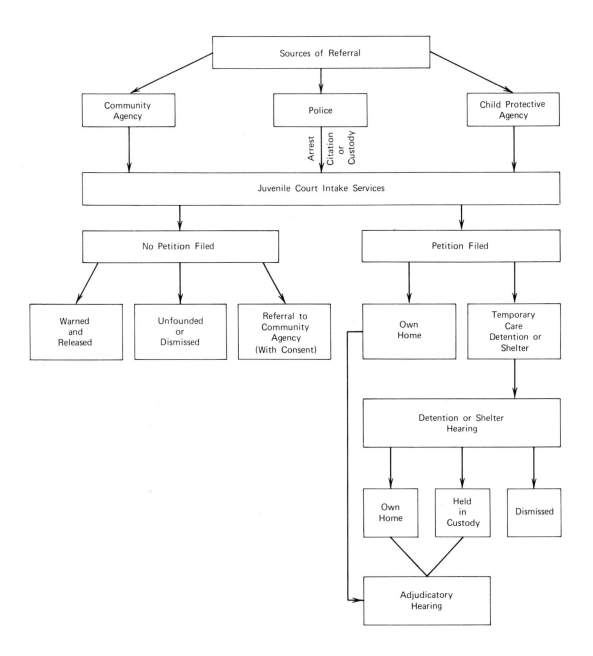

which the juvenile court has jurisdiction. This requires knowledge of the jurisdiction of the court and generally presents no complex legal problems.

In order for the court to have jurisdiction, certain specific conditions must be present. The youth must be *within* the age jurisdiction of the court; must be allegedly *involved* in an act or a situation described by the state juvenile court act; and there must exist *prima facia* evidence of such involvement. Should any question arise concerning the sufficiency of the evidence, the matter should be referred to the prosecutor for a final decision.

In cases involving an act that would be a crime if committed by an adult, the nature of the act becomes very important, but it is not always the controlling factor. The public certainly has the right to be protected, and crimes such as murder, rape, robbery, aggravated assault, and arson are serious enough to justify the filing of a petition and the scheduling of a court hearing, assuming sufficient legal evidence.

A *second* factor to be considered is previous history. Access to police and court records should be readily available to determine if the youth or family are known to either agency. If the case is active with the court, the youth's probation officer should be consulted. However, this does not shift any of the intake decisions from the intake worker to the probation officer.

Other important factors are the age and time of day the offense occurred.

Among the very young, the offense may be an impulsive act without great significance or could be a danger signal and a "cry for help." Only a skillful intake worker will be able to make such determinations. Of equal significance is the time of day an offense occurred. For example, a child under fourteen who commits a delinquent act late at night, or during early morning hours, should trigger a concern. The time the act takes place is often a clue to the type of supervision afforded by the parents or guardian.

Still other questions to be considered are:

What is the nature of the child-parent relationships?

What is the attitude of the youth and parent toward the situation?

Is there a recognition by the youth of the seriousness of the situation?

Was the youth alone or in the company of others who are accomplices?

The objective of helping youth to live within the limits set by law is not realized by routinely funneling more youth into the system. Unless it is determined after careful screening that a youngster is a serious threat to person or property or is a repetitive offender, official action cannot be justified.

The juvenile court should be primarily concerned with offenses that, if committed by adults, would be crimes:

> The juvenile Court should serve as a last resort, used only when questions of restraint and coercion arise. In this perspective, the business of the juvenile court should usually be limited to offenders whose conduct would be a violation of the criminal law if committed by an adult. The juvenile court should not be saddled with the role of a child welfare agency or with the rehabilitation of children who run away, smoke, refuse to attend school

or are otherwise "incorrigible." For those problems, other suitable agencies must be found in existing or new social service agencies. [5]

If the intake worker recommends the filing of a petition and places the youth in detention, the first of three judicial hearings, the *detention hearing,* is immediately set into motion.

THE DETENTION HEARING

The detention hearing must be scheduled within a prescribed period of time; the *Standard Juvenile Court Act* [6] stipulates that such a hearing be scheduled within twenty-four hours after a petition has been filed. Presiding over such a hearing is a juvenile court referee:[7]

> *The judge, or senior judge if there is more than one, may appoint suitable persons trained in the law, to act as referees, who shall hold office during the pleasure of the judge. The judge may direct that any case, or all cases of a class or within a district to be designated by him, shall be heard in the first instance by a referee in a manner provided for the hearing of cases by the court, but any part may, upon request, have a hearing before the judge in the first instance. At the conclusion of a hearing, the referee shall transmit promptly to the judge all papers relating to the case, together with his findings and recommendations in writing . . .*
>
> *Written notice of the referee's findings and recommendations shall be given to the parent, guardian, or custodian of any child whose case has been heard by a referee, and to any other parties in interest. A hearing by the judge shall be allowed if any of them files with the court a request for a review, provided that the request is filed within three days after the referee's written notice. If a hearing de novo is not requested by any party or ordered by the court, the hearing shall be upon the same evidence heard by the referee, provided that new evidence may be admitted in the discretion of the judge. If a hearing before the judge is not requested or the right to review is waved, the findings and recommendations of the referee, when confirmed by an Order of the judge, shall become the decree of the court . . .*

[5]*Model Acts for Family Courts and State—Local Children's Program,* Department of Health, Education, and Welfare, U. S. Government Printing Office, Washington, D.C., 1975, sec. 2, (19). Taken from Olson and Shepard, *Intake Screening Guides: Improving Justice for Juveniles,* p. 23.

[6]*Standard Juvenile Court Act,* 6th ed., National Council on Crime and Delinquency, New York, 1969, art. 1, sub.1.

[7]*Ibid.*

States vary in the use of the referee; some states—in fact, some counties—utilize judges at a detention hearing.

A detention hearing is, basically, to decide whether the minor shall be detained in detention (i.e., in the juvenile hall) pending the hearing of the petition on file. State statues specify the reasons for detaining a minor. As an example, in California, the referee (or judge) cannot detain a minor unless there is a finding of one of the three following criteria: (1)*Continued detention of the minor is a matter of reasonable necessity for the protection of the minor or the person or property of another.* (2)*The minor is likely to flee the jurisdiction of the court.* (3)*The minor has violated an order of the juvenile court.*

The use of detention should be confined only to a youth alleged to be a serious threat to the community and considered dangerous. If a youth presents a threat to his own personal safety, e.g., suicidal threats, but is not otherwise dangerous, temporary care should be provided in a hospital or mental health facility appropriately equipped for such patients.[8]

Detention of youth in jails and juvenile detention facilities throughout the nation has, according to the Department of Health, Education, and Welfare, been scandalous.

Professor Rosemary C. Sarri calls attention to the problem:

> *Despite frequent and tragic stories of suicide, rape, and abuse of youth, the placement of juveniles in jails has not abetted in recent years. The overuse of jails for adults and juveniles has been denounced by justice system personnel and lay critics, but this criticism has not produced any significant change in the vast majority of States.*
>
> *. . . Detention in physically restricting facilities built for the exclusive use of juveniles has been characterized generally as positive when contrasted to juveniles in adults jails. Although many juvenile facilities may be more helpful or humane than their jail counterparts, they still are jail-like facilities and are often even located adjacent to jail. Confinement in such a facility may be equally harmful, particularly in cases where the person has not committed a criminal violation.*[9]

That brings us to the juvenile court hearing; of which there are two such sessions—*jurisdictional* and *dispositional*.

JUVENILE COURT HEARING

As might be expected, juvenile courts vary in philosophy, procedure, and facilities

[8]Eldefonso, Edward and Coffey, Alan R., *Process and Impact of the Juvenile Justice System*, Glencoe Press, Beverly Hills, Calif. 1976, p. 144.

[9]Sarri, Rosemary C., "The Rehabilitation Failure," *Trial: Juveniles and Justice*, The National Legal Magazine, Cambridge, Mass., September-October 1971, vol. 7, no. 5, p. 18. (Emphasis added)

from state to state. In a strict sense, it is incorrect to speak of a juvenile court, or a juvenile court system, as though juvenile courts throughout the country were uniform in their structure, philosophy, and activity. In fact, one may find variations among the courts from county to county within the same state. Although wide variations of philosophy, procedure, and functions exist among juvenile courts, there are, however, certain important traits that all have in common. The proceedings are divided into three stages: the first, already discussed, is called the *prejudicial stage*, which is commonly referred to as the "detention hearing;" the *jurisdictional hearing* is the second stage, during which the facts are established by presentation of evidence and testimony; and the last stage is a *dispositional hearing*. After jurisdiction is established, the court must decide what action would be most likely to help the juvenile avoid further difficulties. From the time he is taken into custody, the stages must comply with a definite time schedule. Once again, using the California Juvenile Court Statute as an example, the *petition* must be filed within forty-eight hours after the minor is taken into custody; a *detention hearing* must be held within twenty-four hours after a petition has been filed; and a jurisdictional hearing must be set within fifteen days after the minor has been detained.

Juvenile courts are tribunals that deal in special ways with young people's cases, and they exist in all jurisdictions. The cases they deal with include law violations, status offenders, and neglected children. The young people they deal with are those below a designated age, usually set between sixteen and eighteen, and their authority extends until the youth reaches his majority. Juvenile courts differ from adult and criminal courts in a number of basic respects: First, the primary purpose of a criminal trial is to determine publicly if there is sufficient evidence to *convict* the person accused of a specific crime; to expose him as guilty or prove him innocent. The secondary purpose is to determine the appropriate *disposition* of his case. If proven innocent, he is, of course, set free. If proven guilty, the judge must usually follow the statutory recommendations for fine or imprisonment—the traditional, punishment-oriented route. In minor crimes, the judge may place the defendant on probation, or assign him to one of the numerous treatment and education programs that involve some supervision and restriction of freedoms but enable him at the same time to work toward rehabilitation in the community.

In a juvenile court, the primary purpose of the hearing—as laid down by the philosophy of juvenile justice—should be to *protect* the offender from publicity that may be unfair, from the traumas and pressures that can accompany a full-fledged advisary criminal proceeding, and from the harsh consequences that may follow an adult criminal conviction. In short, the judge's first concern should be the *welfare* of the minor. Unlike the criminal court judge, he is not supposed to consider the punishment option in his disposition of the case; rather, his recommendations should provide for guidance and rehabilitation.

Procedurally, there is a definite difference between the juvenile and adult courts. In criminal courts, the trial is usually a *public* one, and a *jury* is used unless it is waived in accordance with law. In juvenile courts, the hearing is *private*, and only nine states provide for a jury trial if the defendant wishes; but even in these states, juries are only *rarely* used in juvenile court. Sentencing procedures, also, are different in criminal and juvenile courts. In criminal courts, if a defendant is convicted, he is sentenced for punishment *as prescribed by law.* The judge does not have broad discretionary powers in exercising his own discretion in sentencing the convicted person. The emphasis is on the crime rather than the needs of the person who committed it. In juvenile court, if a youth is adjudged a delinquent, the court has *broad discretionary powers* to provide for his care and rehabilitation. Theoretically, the court is supposed to emphasize the youth's individual needs and cooperate with the probation department in working out the treatment or educational plan that has a good chance of changing his delinquent behavior pattern.

A statement by the United States Supreme Court (State v. Owens, 416P. 2d259, 269 [1966]) emphasize the philosophical concept of the juvenile justice system:

> *The validity of the whole juvenile system is dependent upon its adherence to its protective, rather than its penal, aspects. Dispensing with formal constitutional safeguards can be justified only so long as the proceedings are not, in any sense, criminal. We hope confinement in a penal institution will convert the precedents from juvenile to criminal and require the observance of constitutional safeguards. . . . If, after a juvenile procedent, the juvenile can be committed to a place of penal servitude, the entire plan of* parens patriae *becomes a hypocritical mockery.*

JUVENILE CORRECTIONS

The juvenile court is simply one important component of the entire process of the administration of juvenile justice. When a youthful offender is handled by the juvenile court and the petition is adjudicated, the process does not terminate; it continues. Decisions must be made as to what services can be provided to meet the minor's needs. So, the correctional process takes over. The function of juvenile corrections is the care, custody, and supervison of minors who have been declared wards of the juvenile court.

There is a great deal of furor over the failure of corrections to rehabilitate. Disenchantment with rehabilitation programs have been directed both at the adult and at the juvenile justice systems. Professor Rosemary C. Sarri, University of Michigan School of Social Work, focuses on the extent of the problem:

> *From the findings already available it is apparent that career patterns are a consequence of the interaction of organizational and individual characteristics. For example, in one state 90% of all those adjudicated may be assigned to probation, whereas in another state nearly half of the adjudicated offenders will be institutionalized . . .*

Many, in all levels of government and in the lay community, interested in change have seized the opportunity to foster innovative treatment and rehabilitative technologies. At the same time, some persons responsible for these programs are pessimistic about meeting society's rising expectations in the face of the serious and harmful conditions prevailing in many states and localities. For example: Twice as many children are detained in jails as in specialized detention facilities for children. Large numbers of youths continue to be committed to institutions for behavior that would not be law violations for adults. This is particularly true for girls, 75% of whom in some states are institutionalized for behavior that is not criminal for adults or for juvenile males. Mentally ill and mentally retarded youths in many states are committed to the same institution with delinquent youths for lack of adequate facilities . . .

Although a vast amount of research has been directed at other areas such as the causes and cures for juvenile delinquency, relatively little research has been conducted specifically for application to correctional rehabilitation facilities . . . [10]

The use of such facilities is, unfortunately, an alternative that the juvenile court must consider.

Unfortunately, in many cases the home environment is so poor that it is not in the best interest of the child for him to remain there. In these instances, the child is removed from his home and placed in the care of the Probation Officer to be boarded out or placed with some suitable foster family. . . . Many boys and girls whom it is felt that neither probation supervision nor foster home placement is indicated, [may] profit from the routine and discipline offered by an institution. [11]

RESIDENTIAL FACILITIES

There are five primary types of residential facilities customarily utilized by juvenile courts: *Reception-diagnostic centers;* county facilities such as *ranches and/or camps; traditional training schools;* community relocation facilities such as *group homes;* and, although not exclusively used by correctional clientele, *foster homes.* [12]

The traditional training school is generally utilized for the more aggressive minors; county ranches and/or camps and group homes are for the less

---

[10]*Ibid.*
[11]*Ibid.*
[12]Eldefonso and Coffey, *Process and Impact of Juvenile Justice, Op. cit.,* pp. 144–145.

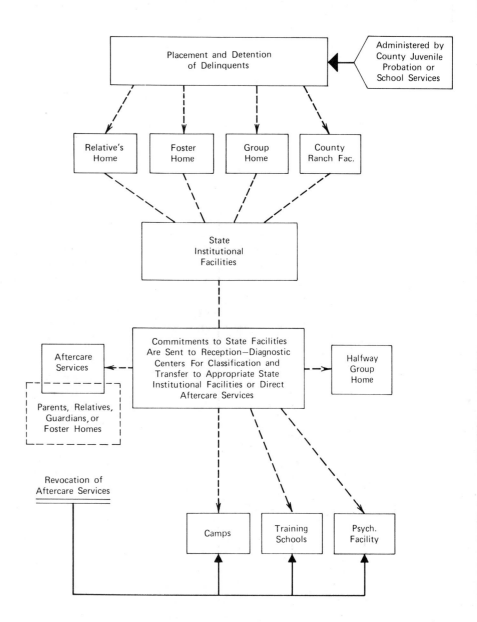

aggressive minors; and foster homes are not exclusively utilized by correctional agencies. There are many different types of foster homes: foster homes for a dependent/neglected child; mental hygiene homes for the emotionally disturbed minor; foster homes for the child with family problems; homes for boys or girls just released from institutional facilities; and foster homes for the child released for adoption. The reception-diagnostic facility is a specialized facility that is found only in populous states that have a *number of juvenile-correctional institutions programs to choose from. The primary purpose of reception-diagnostic facilities is to select the proper program for each minor who is committed. In a large system, the facility has access to a wide range of correctional programs. In areas that have no reception-diagnostic facilities, each institution must perform this type of service for itself.*

Historically, these different institutions were created as a result of varying pressures on the juvenile correctional system. Training schools for juveniles originated from private agencies.

Juvenile correctional institutions can be operated by state or local governments. Generally, all state governments operate juvenile correctional facilities, but in large states, local branches of government often operate these institutions. Within the different states and local jurisdictions, these juvenile correctional institutions are administered by any number of agencies, such as correctional agencies, welfare departments, probation departments, and so on. With the exception of foster homes, which are family (husband, wife, and children) administered, the chief administrator of each institution is the superintendent or director.

The program is concerned with (1) reception-orientation; (2) custody; (3) treatment; (4) education; and (5) recreation. By and large, these programs are run by the counselor-supervisor or by the house-parent and the teachers within the institution. Because these people are in daily contact with the committed minors, their attitudes and general competence are closely examined: a program in a juvenile correctional facility is only as good as the personnel who administer it . . .

Generally, it is felt that correctional facilities serving delinquent minors offer a system that combines controls, protection, and totality of treatment that is experienced in the community setting. However, the minor committed to the juvenile correctional facility generally are unaware of these values and consequently view their commitment as punishment for wrongdoing. A juvenile offender typically arrives at the institution fearful, suspicious, and distrustful of its intentions. Although he does not see the institution as a source of help in adjusting to society, he may quickly recognize the need to conform, at least within the institution, so that he can return home as quickly as possible. The predominating factor the minor's point of view is that he is there not by his own choice. This does not necessarily prevent his acceptance of the situation or impede his cooperation in the retraining process, but his first and primary objective is to get out of the facility. . . .

AFTERCARE

The correctional process that deals with the juvenile *after* institutionalization has taken place is referred to as *aftercare* services. Such services are identified as parole.

The distinction between parole and probation is not difficult to comprehend: Juvenile probation permits the minor to remain in the community under the supervision and guidance of a probation officer. It is a legal status created by the juvenile court and it usually involves a *judicial finding* (sustainment of a petition); certain conditions imposed on his continued freedom; and determining the flexibility of such conditions. Aftercare services take place *after* a juvenile is released from an institution. Often referred to as parole, these services and condition for the minor's continual freedom within the community are similar to probation services. In actuality, it is the clientele that makes the difference—usually, the minor released from institutionalization is a sophisticated, hardcore delinquent, and recidivism is not an unusual occurrence. The minor on probation, conversely, is much more rehabilitatable.

Over 95 percent of all persons committed to institutions are eventually released. For community protection, as well as the benefit of the individuals themselves, both control and treatment measures following release from an institution are necessary. Aftercare (parole) supervision takes on added importance to the community in view of the fact that clientele released from institutions consists of a high ratio of more difficult offenders because of the expansion of probation services and other local offender-management techniques. As previously indicated, the institutional population takes on more prone-to-failure cases. As these individuals return to the community, the parole agent's caseload reflects the higher ratio of the more difficult and harder-to-maintain type of offender.

The role of the probation and parole agent is extensively studied in another chapter.

THE FRAGMENTED JUVENILE JUSTICE SYSTEM

As one can see, the juvenile justice system has many segments. Police, courts, correctional institutions, and aftercare services. The interrelationship between various segments of the system is, apparently, the most significant problem in the juvenile justice system.

Juvenile justice can function systematically only to the degree that each segment of the system takes into account all of the segments. In other words, the system is no more systematic than the relationship between police and court, court and probation, probation and correctional institutions, correctional institutions and aftercare services. In the absence of functional relationships between segments, the juvenile justice system is vulnerable to fragmentation and ineffectiveness. Consider, for example, the relationship depicted below.

Fragmentation and ineffectiveness can be measured simply in terms of delinquency rates that are not reduced and by youthful law violators that continue to offend. To assume the fragmentation produces ineffectiveness, then we must conclude that American society is not coping *effectively* with juvenile crime when its juvenile justice system is fragmented.

It is worth noting, however, that the precise manner in which the juvenile

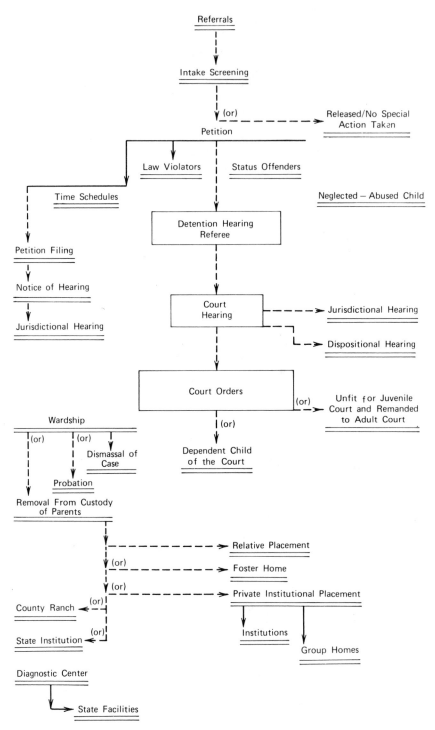

justice system produces fragmentation can vary from one part of the United States to another. Ineffective juvenile justice through fragmentation may have many causes. For example, when the police operate without regard to the juvenile court, the system is clearly fragmented. Another example elsewhere in this system is a juvenile court showing indifference to probation officers, institutional facilities, or the police.

The point is that when one segment of the system functions in isolation from the rest, the resulting fragmentation reduces the effectiveness of the whole. Effectiveness in this case is the measure of the success of society's approach to juvenile crime in general.

THE ELEMENTS OF THE JUVENILE JUSTICE SYSTEM

The elements of the juvenile justice system—law enforcement, courts, and corrections—are related to each other to the degree that each is effected by the other's policies and practices. Difficulty of coordination between the aforementioned agencies is primarily attributable to the manner in which the juvenile justice system in the United States developed. As the President's Commission on Crime and Delinquency concluded, the overall system of juvenile justice in the United States is neither a unitarian nor even a consistent system. It is not designed as a unitary system. It's philosophical basis is that a juvenile is to be accorded the care and treatment he would ordinarily receive at home—and if, and only if, it is in the best interest of the community, should the minor be removed from the care and custody of his parents. In accordance with that philosophy, institutions and procedures have been created. Some of these have been quite carefully constructed; others have been improvised. Some have been aspired by principals; others have been a matter of expediency. Consequently, our juvenile justice system deliberately sacrifices much of its proficiency, and probably its effectiveness, in order to preserve our autonomy and to attempt to protect the best interests of the minor.

The systems approach must deal with causes and effects, which in turn have to deal with interaction. All human interactions are effects of some kind, and every interaction whether large or small, has some effect. Even the supposed absence of interaction has effect on those who notice the absence. It is through this fundamental observation of our system that the vital role of the juvenile offender emerges.

Interaction of a youthful burglar with the victim is the effect of the burglar, but it is also the cause of another interaction with police, and with the court, probation, correctional institutions, and aftercare services. Interaction of police with the court is similarly a variety of both causes and effects, as are the interactions of juvenile corrections with courts and police.

The limitless effects are also the causes of other effects. Consider any possible reaction to police making an arrest. The arrest is an interaction that itself is an effect, but a reaction to this effect is a cause of another effect. And the endless cycle goes. The system is simply a chain of these causes and effects. The system may or may not cause favorable effects; indeed, many effects tend to cause unfavorable effects (or results).

The need for each segment in the juvenile justice system to relate to other segments have already been noted. When fragmentation prevents this relationship, it should not be surprising that the system produces extremely unfavorable effects (or results) despite the fact that effects are still causes. A system that produces *unfavorable* effects may continue to work but with little or no *effective* impact on the problem for which it was intended. A consistent effective impact is the measure of success on any system.

The existing fragmentation of federal and state agencies and programs and the lack of coordination among them is probably the single greatest obstacle to the development of an effective juvenile justice system. One can only agree with the observation that in its operation the juvenile justice system functions so that the total is less than the sum of its parts. Most state systems are made up of several interrelated parts, usually separately administered at different levels of government. Consequently, no one body oversees the entire system, and the allocation of funds for programs and personnel are generally uncoordinated.

What does this self-contradictory system mean for the juvenile offender? Is it designed to breed respect for law and order, or is it designed to engender a kind of cynicism that only permits him to find his way through the maze—to make his peace with probation and with the courts and to adjust to the police?

Some sense of balance must remain out of the old system. The various segments of the juvenile justice system (as well as the criminal justice system) must be joined to make something other than a conglomerate, heterogeneous mess of competing and conflicting agencies. In some measure, it is necessary to coordinate them and approximate a system of juvenile (and criminal) justice that each is supportive of the other.

The advantages of having a central information source are obvious. Too often the individual delinquent has suffered because his state has received and processed fragmented information, or lacked—or even completely misunderstood--—the resources and knowledge available only to a few. Increased knowledge and awareness of each other's activities would bring a high level of cooperation and coordination between often isolated and fragmented agencies and programs. In addition, new techniques successfully innovated in many courts and communities would be more readily brought to the attention of those in other areas of the country, where they could be adopted when suitable. And most important, more complete systematized information would aid in the search for more adequate explanation of the causes of juvenile crime as will as in the development of solutions. We certainly need to learn a great deal more than we now know if we are to formulate successful policies and devise effective measures to combat these problems.

SUMMARY

In this chapter, the juvenile justice system of the United States has been presented as American society's method of coping with juvenile delinquency.

It was noted that a great deal of discretion is available to those segments (police, courts, probation, correctional institutions, and aftercare services) of the juvenile justice system that deals with the youthful offender. Unfortunately, discretion may not be used properly. Often there is a lack of departmental guides, direction, or policy. In these cases, the juvenile offender is handled on purely a personal basis and, therefore, bias enters the picture. Also, discussed in chapter 4 were the factors inherent in decision making. It was noted that in order for the court to make decisions—decisions having a significant impact on the minor—they must have jurisdiction of the case. In other words, the youth must be within the age jurisdiction of the court; must be allegedly involved in an act or a situation described by the state juvenile court acts, and there must exist prima facia evidence of such involvement.

In discussing the juvenile justice system, the subsystems of the juvenile courts were examined: detention hearing, jurisdictional hearing, and dispositional hearing—all important segments of the juvenile court—were dissected. The latter part of chapter 4 covered juvenile corrections and fragmentation. It was pointed out that the juvenile court was simply one important component of the entire process of the administration of juvenile justice. When the minor is adjudged a ward of the court, the correctional arm—an apparatus that is constructed specifically for the rehabilitation of the juvenile offender—enters the arena. The correctional subsystem takes into consideration the services provided by probation, correctional institutions and aftercare measures. All such services must interrelate; all such services must be coordinated—but as indicated in chapter 4, most often they are not. The problem of fragmentation of not only the "secondary" arm of the juvenile court—corrections—but also fragmentation throughout the system was discussed. Fragmentation, is thus characterized by an overlapping of jurisdictions, a diversity of philosophies, and a hodgepodge of organizational structures that have little contact with one another. Fragmentation is probably the single greatest obstacle of the development of an effective juvenile justice system.

ANNOTATED REFERENCES

Cohen, Lawrence E., "Juvenile Dispositions: Social and Illegal Factors Related to the Process of Denver Delinquency Cases," National Criminal Justice Information and Statistics, Washington, D.C., 1975.

> This short 75-page pamphlet is the third in a series that addresses issues concerning the processing of juvenile offenders. It uses data collected on juvenile court dispositions in Denver during 1972. The study is comprehensive; it is possible to assist the importance of variables of two general types—legal and status—in the disposition of juveniles.

Davis, S. M., Rights of Juveniles—The Juvenile Justice System, Clark Boardman Company, New York, N.Y., 1974.

In this document, the author explores the issues of the juvenile court—defining delinquency and court jurisdiction over status offenders. The author also gives attention to the subsystems of the juvenile court—sub-systems which have been explored in this chapter.

Dineen, John, "Juvenile Court Organization and Status Offenses—A Statutory Profile," National Center for Juvenile Justice, Pittsburgh, Penn., 1974.

This short pamphlet (54 pages) provides factual information on the state of the juvenile court law. Comments are made on child level and organization of courts with juvenile jurisdiction. A table provides information on the organization of courts by state for all 50 states and the District of Columbia.

Eldefonso, Edward and Coffey, Alan R., *Process and Impact of the Juvenile Justice System*, Glencoe Press, Beverly Hills, Calif., 1976.

To illustrate the impact of juvenile justice on youthful offenders processed through the system, four composite case histories represented a synthesis of hundreds of juvenile justice cases were devised. The perceptions of two young men, one female status offender, and two dependent children of the court incorporate many of the most common responses to the system. And their backgrounds suggest many of the reasons for these responses. Descriptions of each stage of the juvenile justice process—the juvenile justice system as it exists now, the role of the police, the teenager and the impact of the juvenile court, and the nature and impact of corrections—are coupled with the stories of these composite characters. What emerges is a formally rounded picture of the workings and the effects of juvenile justice on the individual. Because the book emphasizes the impact of juvenile justice while describing the process itself, it constitutees an effective supplement to juvenile justice literature in police and corrections courses alike.

Sarri, Rosemary C., "The Rehabilitation Failure," *Trial: Juveniles and Justice,* September-October 1971, vol. 7, no. 5, pp.18–20.

Trial, a national legal magazine published by American Trail Lawyers Association addresses the problem of the rehabilitation of the juvenile offender. As Professor Sarri points out, the rehabilitation of the juvenile offender has been a failure. Professor Sarri takes into account the lack of research directed at correctional rehabilitation agencies. The author discusses thr five-year national assessment study that has been launched by the Institute of Continuing Legal Education at the University of Michigan, by the Institute of Law Enforcement, and by the Criminal Justice of the Law Enforcement Assistance Administration. Professor Sarri feels that the study will unearth important information, which has been lacking, thus far, in research on juvenile delinquency.

CHAPTER FIVE prevention is the answer

Delinquency prevention is perhaps one of the most misunderstood concepts in the field of social science because of an inability to agree on what actually constitutes prevention. As previously noted, delinquency is a phenomena as old as history and as complex as nuclear physics. Its causes are multiple, and the emphasis shifts with the changes in society. Nor are all delinquents cast from the same mold—they are individual human beings with all their differences.

Because there are so many possible causes of delinquency, a wide variety of factors tend to be held responsible—separately or in combinations. The individual himself, his family, his neighbors, his school, his church, his place of residence, his government—an endless list which is, thus, the reason for ambiguities in theories. The result: everyone is responsible for delinquency and, of course, when everyone is responsible for something, no one really is.

Since the original Juvenile Court Act of 1899, there has been a great deal of discussion and instruction of delinquency prevention programs. Such discussions and actual implementation of delinquency prevention programs have, in most cases, brought forth disappointing results. A vivid example is given by William C. Beeleman and Thomas W. Steinburn who completed a study titled "The Value and Validity of Delinquency Prevention Experiments":

> Five major delinquency prevention experiments conducted in the open community among voluntary juvenile subjects reveal uniformly disappointing results: the provision of the preventive service seems no more effective in reducing delinquency than no service at all. The controlled procedures governing these experiments make these negative findings particularly convincing and thus constitute a challenge to services offered in the name of "delinquency prevention."
>
> However, these experiments need not constitute the final judgment of the effectiveness of prevention services as they had two major deficiencies. The first is a shortcoming in the execution of service; the available data suggests that the experimental subjects were so lightly exposed to the

services given that positive change could not be expected. The second shortcoming is in the design and evaluation of the experiments; instruments were not devised for the collection of baseline data that would clarify the fundamental dimensions of the services given. Thus data pertaining to the attention given experimental subjects by service agents are so sparse that is extremely difficult and sometimes impossible to accurately assess the amount and kind of attention the experimental subjects received. To avoid the duplication of ineffective efforts, we will need to know with more precision what has failed to work thus far. [1]

Traditionally, all efforts in prevention have been aimed toward containing and repressing incipient delinquents through law enforcement agencies. In recent years, there have been strong efforts to imporove rehabilitative processes for already identified delinquents so that the amount of recidivism might be reduced. But there has been *little concerted effort* toward development of a prevention program.

FOCUSING ON PREVENTION[2]

The way to solve the delinquency problem is to prevent boys and girls from becoming delinquents in the first place. Society is not solving that problem because the emphasis is not placed on that all-important job: prevention. Moreover, it appears that society is blocked by a psychological wall of fallacies which keep everyone busy with impractical plans that are doomed to fail right from the start. The correctional program in the United States seems to be content with treating individual delinquents after they have already committed delinquent acts, while such programs overlook almost entirely the factors that contribute to delinquency.

Society must find a way to correct the faulty home and environment *before* the child becomes a police case. It is both unfair and impractical to rely upon a few private agencies to do this large-scale, complex public job.

In the last analysis, according to the *Task Force Report: Juvenile Delinquency and Youth Crime,* the most promising and also the most important method of dealing with crime is by preventing it by ameliorating the conditions of life that drive people to commit crimes and that undermine the restraining rules and institutions erected by society against antisocial conduct. This report by the President's Commission on Law Enforcement and the Administration of Justice professed doubts that even a vastly improved criminal justice system can substantially reduce crime

[1]W. C. Beeleman and T. W. Steinburn, "The Value and Validity of Delinquency Prevention Experiments," *National Council on Crime and Delinquency,* vol. 15, no. 4, October 1969, p. 471.
[2]Adapted from *Task Force Report: Juvenile Delinquency and Youth Crime,* The President's Commission on Law Enforcement and the Administration of Justice, U.S. Government Printing Office, Washington, D.C., 1967, pp. 41-42.

if society fails to make each of its citizens feel a personal stake in the good life that society can provide and the law and order that are prerequisites to such a life. That sense of stake in society can come only through a real opportunity for full participation in society's life and growth. Providing opportunity is the basic goal of prevention programs.

The *Task Force Report* also states that it is with young people that prevention efforts are most needed and for whom these efforts hold the greatest promise. It is more critical that young people be kept from crime; for they are the nation's future, and their conduct will affect society for a long time to come. The youth are not yet set in their ways; they are still developing, still subject to the influence of the socializing institutions that structure—however skeletally—their environment: family, school, gang, recreation program, and job market. But that influence, to do the most good, must come before the youth has become involved in the formal criminal justice system.

> *Once a juvenile is apprehended by the Police and referred to the Juvenile Court, the community has already failed; subsequent rehabilitation services, no matter how skilled, have far more less potential for success than if they had been applied before the youth's overt defiance of the law.*[3]

Bill Ellison, former Delinquency Prevention Officer of Santa Clara County (Santa Clara County Juvenile Probation Department) now on California Governor Brown's staff, succinctly answers the question "Delinquency Prevention: What is the Problem?"

> *It must be understood that crime and delinquency are not isolated phenomena that can be attacked directly but are by-products of the social, cultural, and economic conditions under which people live.*
>
> *The prime effort against the problems of crime and delinquency should be concentrated on improvement of services to people in the areas of health, education, welfare, employment, housing, recreation, and human relations. Research in metropolitan areas reveals that a positive relationship does exist between the incidence of crime and delinquency and economic deprivation. This does not mean that only poor kids get into trouble, but the unstable, disorganized environments in which they live make them more vulnerable to crime and delinquency. This pattern is very clear in Santa Clara County.*
>
> *Most people hope to develop a cure-all program that will solve the problem permanently. But preventing delinquency is much like keeping in good physical condition; you must work at it constantly. It involves com-*

---

[3]*Report of the President's Commission on Crime in the District of Columbia,* U.S. Government Printing Office, Washington, D.C., 1966, p. 733.

munity organization—the process of making services consistent with the needs of the people.

Delinquency prevention by our staff is interpreted to be a measure taken before a criminal or delinquent act has actually occurred for the purpose of forestalling such an act. Control is a measure taken after a criminal or delinquent act has been committed. Both prevention and control should be viewed as sub-categories of society's negative attitude on action against crime and delinquency.

This seems to indicate that much of our effort should be focused on the removal or improvement of conditions that lend themselves to crime. Economic deprivation is a prime target.

Delinquency prevention can best be described in three general ways:

1. Delinquency prevention is the sum total of *all activities* that contribute to the adjustment of children and to healthy personalities in children. *(Primary)*

2. Delinquency prevention is the attempt to *deal with particular environmental conditions* that are believed to contribute to delinquency. *(Secondary)*

3. Delinquency prevention consists of *specific preventative services* (health, recreation, employment, counseling or child guidance, probation, parole, etc.) provided to individual children or groups of children. ((*Tertiary)*[4]

Basically, Ellison is referring to a broad approach to the problem of preventing delinquency which has five major categories:

1. *Control* measures by law enforcement agencies.

2. *Individualized* casework on incipient delinquents.

3. *Educational* campaigns to encourage every parent to "keep his own house in order."

4. *Promotional* efforts by civic-minded groups to develop the needed recreational, vocational, educational, psychiatric, psychological, and medical services to meet these special needs of many children.

5. *Reduction of recidivism* by delinquents through the improvement of supervision techniques and practices.

In essence, the broad approach to the prevention of juvenile delinquency is

[4]B. Ellison, "Delinquency Prevention: What is the Problem?" Santa Clara Country Juvenile Probation Department Training Bulletin, San Jose, Calif., 1970.

assisting the *highly maladjusted family in reaching some stability result in a referral to the probation department.* School authorities, probation officers, police, family casework agencies, and neighbors, are often aware of these situations, but frequently they do nothing about them because there appears to be no way of entering the picture until some drastic official action must be taken. Procedures must be developed to focus on this type of preventative work on the community level!

Another problem area in the treatment of delinquent children is an area discussed in chapter seven pertaining to *delinquency and the school.* There is no question that the complex relationship between the school and the child varies greatly from one school to another. The process of education is dramatically different in the slum and in the middle-class suburb. The child and the problems he brings to school are different; the support for education that receives at home and in his neighborhood is different; the school systems themselves are very different. The slum school faces the greatest obstacles with the least resources, the least qualified personnel, the least adequate capability for effective education.[5]

The school, unlike the family, is a public instrument for training young people. It is, therefore, more directly accessible to change through the development of new resources and policies. And since it is the principal public institution for the development of a basic commitment by young people to the goals and values of our society, it is imperative that it be provided with the resources to compete with illegitimate attractions for young people. Anything less would be a serious failure to discharge our nation's responsibility to its youth.[6]

Perhaps the most serious failing in prevention programs is our inability to reach the *slum dwellers.* Delinquency in the slums, which represents a disproportionately high percentage of all delinquency and includes a disproportionately high number of dangerous acts, is associated with certain phenomena: (1) the weakening of the family as an agent of social control; (2) the prolonging childhood; (3) the increasing impersonality of technological, corporate, and bureaucratic society; and (4) the radical changing of moral standards with regard to such matters as sex and drug use. All of these phenomena are not lacking in the slums and statistics and observation clearly demonstrate that they are associated with undesirable conditions of life. Among the many compelling reasons for changing the circumstances of inner-city existence, one of the most compelling is that it will prevent crime.[7]

SLUMS AND SLUM DWELLERS[8]

The slums of virtually every American city, harbor an alarming amount of not only physical deprivation and spiritual despair, but also doubt and cynicism about the

[5]*Task Force Report,* p. 49.
[6]*Ibid.*
[7]*Ibid.,* p. 42.
[8]*Ibid.*

relevance of the "outside" world's institutions. Furthermore, slum dwellers question the sincerity of efforts to close the gap. Far from ignoring or rejecting the goals and values espoused by more fortunate segments of society, the slum dweller wants the same material and intangible things for himself and his children as those who are more privileged. Indeed, the very similarity of his wishes sharpens the poignancy and frustration of the discrepancies in existing opportunities for fulfillment. The slum dweller may not respect a law that he believes draws differences between his rights and other's, or a police force that applies laws so as to draw such differences, but he does recognize the law's duty to deal with lawbreakers, and he respects the policeman who does so with skill and impartiality. Living in a neighborhood likely to have one of the city's highest rates of crime, he worries about crime and wants police protection as much as people living in the same city's safer regions.

The slum dweller may not have much formal education himself, or many books in his house, and he may hesitate to visit teachers or attend school functions, but studies show that he too, like his college-graduate counterpart, is vitally interested in his children's education. And while some inner-city residents, like some people everywhere may not be eager to change their unemployed status, it is also true that many more of them toil day after day at the dullest and most backbreaking of society's tasks, travelling long distances for menial jobs without hope of advancement. Very likely he or his parents left home in the deep South or Appalachia, or Mexico, or Puerto Rico, looking for a better life, only to be absorbed into the more binding dependency and isolation of the inner city. Claude Brown in his *Manchild in the Promised Land* pointed a vivid picture of children who live under these conditions:

> *The children of these disillusioned colored pioneers inherited the total lot of their parents–the disappointments, the anger. Added to their misery, they had little hope of deliverance. Where does one run to when he is already in the Promised Land?*[9]

PROFILE OF THE DELINQUENT RESIDENT OF THE SLUMS[10]

A sketch drawn from the limited information available shows that the delinquent is frequently a child of the slums, from a neighborhood that is low on the socioeconomic scale of the community—where conditions are harsh in many ways for those who live there. He is fifteen or sixteen years old (recently, there has been a noticeable drop in age; in fact, in New York City, the age of "involvement" has dropped to 13 to 14), one of numerous children—perhaps representing several

[9]C. Brown, *Manchild in the Promised Land,* The Macmillan Company, New York, 1965, p. 10.
[10]Task Force Report, *Op. cit.,* p. 43.

different fathers—who live with their mother in a home that the sociologists call "female-centered." It may be a broken home; it may never have had a resident father; it may have a nominal male head who is often drunk or in jail or in and out of the house (welfare regulations, which prohibit any payment where there is a "man in the house," may militate against his continuous presence). He may never have known a grown man well enough to emulate him or identify with him. From the adults and older children in charge of him he receives leniency, sternness, affection, and perhaps indifference, in erratic and unpredictable succession. All his life he has had considerable independence, and his mother has had little control over his comings and goings, little way of knowing what he is up to until a policeman brings him home or a summons from court comes in the mail.

The delinquent may well have dropped out of school. He is probably unemployed, and has little to offer an employer. The offenses he and his friends commit are much more frequently thefts than crimes of personal violence, and they rarely commit them alone. Indeed, they rarely do anything alone, preferring to congregate and operate in a group, staking out their own "turf"—a special street corner or candy store or poolroom. They may adopt their own flamboyant titles and distinctive hair styles or ways of dressing, of walking, or of talking to signal their membership in the group and show that they are "tough" and not to be meddled with. Their clear belligerence toward authority does indeed earn them the fearful deference of both adult and child, as well as the watchful suspicion of the neighborhood policeman. Although the common conception is that the gang member is a teenager, in fact, the lower-class juvenile begins a gang career much earlier than his teen years, and he is usually in search not of "conspirators in crime," but of companionship. It is all too easy for them to drift into minor, then major, violations of law.

This is not to suggest that his mother, or his father (if he has one) or an uncle or older brother, have not tried to guide him. But their influence is diluted and undermined by the endless task of making ends meet in the face of debilitating poverty, by constant presence of drugs, drinking, gambling, petty thievery, prostitution, by the visible contrast of relative affluence on the other side of town.

DELINQUENCY PREVENTION

Assuming that it is feasible to prevent delinquency, a family-based prevention strategy would have to deal simultaneously with a number of related social problems. In other words, strategies aimed at intervention must converge with other programs directed at related problems. Thus, the aim of prevention strategy should be to produce a new set of influences and conditions more likely to control the frequency with which delinquent events occur. All communities have some type of existing system for both generating and controlling delinquency. What prevention policies and strategies seek to do is to supplement the existing systems with another that would produce more desirable effects.

The problem arises when delinquency prevention is subjected to secondary objectives and agencies and institutions, responsible for exerting some control within the community, relinquish their responsibility in this area. The agencies and institutions listed below are in an excellent position to develop and/or to support delinquency prevention programs. Unfortunately, however, their role in the community may be regulated to tasks of more *immediate* concern.

1. The police catch criminals.

2. The schools educate the young.

3. The church ministers to spiritual well-being.

4. The family has many roles, but the delinquent's family is itself so frequently disordered that it tends to encourage rather than prevent delinquency.

5 The state provides some leadership, technical assistance, and financial aid, but too often the state is too far removed to be of much help, and the state is fully cognizant of this fact.

The development and implementation of a national strategy for youth development and delinquency prevention have not met the challenge of youthful crime. William C. Beeleman and Thomas W. Steinburn made a study which revealed that delinquency prevention experiments conducted in the open community among voluntary juvenile subjects revealed uniformly disappointing results.

LIMITATIONS OF PREVENTION

The Annual Report of the Youth Development and Delinquency Prevention Administration *(Delinquency Prevention Report,* April 1971) calls for a "fresh look" at the delinquency prevention effort.

In examining the national delinquency prevention effort, this report substantiates the study of Beeleman and Steinburn. The report presents these major findings:

1. There is *little coherent national plan* or established priority structure among major antidelinquency programs.

2. The overall effectiveness of federal efforts to combat the problem is *less than the sum* of its parts.

3. There is a *lack of effective national leadership* in dealing with youth and delinquents.

4. Current anti-delinquency efforts *do not make the maximum use* of existing resources.

5. *State planning has been sporadic and ineffective,* due in large part to the lack of theoretical knowledge base and a shortage of technical assistance.

6. *No model systems* for the prevention of delinquency or the rehabilitation of the delinquent youth have been developed.

The report relates how the emerging national strategy for youth development and delinquency prevention can help to overcome these shortcomings. According to William C. Kvaraceus, noted author and Chairman of the Department of Education, Clarke University, current efforts to prevent and control delinquency

> *are preoccupied with trying to obtain improved legislation, a more adequate base of financial support, and a stronger law enforcement and police protection, reflecting the myth that the panacea for reducing crime and delinquency rates is better laws, more money, and better trained police--three* necessary but insufficient *means for solving the problem.* [11]

THE NEED FOR PREVENTIVE EFFORTS

In spite of the limitations and the disappointing results of prevention efforts, our society cannot avoid or abrogate its responsibility in attempting to prevent and control delinquent activities. Practitioners in the field of corrections and law enforcement will readily agree that focusing only upon controlling crime and correcting offenders will not eliminate the problem of youthful crime. This is a proven fact—one need only refer to correctional institution information pertaining to the recidivism rate of youngsters who have been institutionalized. There are many arguments for a maximum effort to prevent delinquency among young people:

1. *The evidence suggests that, in terms of cost effectiveness alone, corrective measures are highly expensive.* The average costs of maintaining a youngster in a public training school is $3,020 per year. In private institutions for delinquents, costs are considerably higher. In California, it is estimated that an average combined juvenile and adult criminal career costs (per year) the governmental system $10,000. By 1975, this state is expected to spend almost $900 million per year on its police functions, adjudication functions, probation, incarceration, and parole functions directly related to crime and delinquency. This does not include the costs of crime itself measured in "value of property" lost or destroyed, or intangible emotional and psychological losses.

[11]W. C. Kvaraceus, "Delinquency Prevention: Legislation, Financing, and Law Enforcement Are Not Enough," *National Council on Crime and Delinquency*, Vol. 15, No. 4, Oct. 1969, p. 463.

2. *Further, much of the money spent for such correctional programs seems ineffective.* Recidivism among young people who have been institutionalized is exceedingly high; considerable numbers of young people placed on probation commit further offenses. And few programs have been evaluated to determine whether it was the corrective service that was responsible in the case of the nonrepeater or whether the youngster might not have avoided further delinquency, even without the corrective or rehabilitative service. In the face of such meager success, it seems appropriate to prevent young people from those initial encounters with police and courts that frequently mark the beginning of delinquent and criminal careers rather than their end.

3. *In addition to the actual costs of apprehending, adjudicating, and rehabilitating juveniles, there are other costs to the nation in terms of wasted human resources when lives become enmeshed in delinquent careers.* The earning power and contribution to the economy of persons who enter or are processed through juvenile and criminal justice and corrections is considerably reduced.

4. *It is clear that the delinquent or criminal label, even if the individual does not continue in the delinquent paths, imposes upon him a stigma that is difficult to erase, and blocks him from access to the full resources of society.* Consequently, every effort should be made to prevent marking young people with this indelible stamp.

5. *The case for the early implementation of improved preventive programs,* whether they are treatment-oriented or part of the general upgrading of basic education, seriousness, opportunities, and living conditions [refer to "Slums and Slum Dwellers"] is bolstered by our psychological insights into the importance of the earlier years as a period when personalities and behavioural patterns are more likely to be affected than in the later years when they are more firmly fixed.

6. *A disproportionate amount of illegal activity occurs in later adolescence and early adulthood.* The Uniform Crime Report for 1976 noted that nearly 59 percent of all persons arrested by police in that year were between 16 and 21. The youth population of the nation is growing proportionally and will continue to increase. It seems clear that we can predict larger amounts of delinquency and crime, unless something is done to impede its rise.

7. *Prevention programs are frequently similar to those required to correct other social imbalances.* Successful prevention programs, many of which will not be specifically against crime, will have multiple payoffs,

providing visible benefits in other areas as well. Not only will they reduce the costs of correctional and rehabilitative programs but also they will equip individuals for more effective social and economic performances.[12]

Since authorities in the field agree that there is no single cause of delinquency, any effective prevention program must be many-sided.

A PREVENTION PROGRAM

Programs for the effective prevention and control of juvenile delinquency and youth crime continue to elude decision-makers at the national, state, and local levels. Despite rapidly expanding efforts during recent years, illegal behavior by young people has grown more excessive since the post Viet Nam conflict. During the past decade especially, the problem has been further compounded by the emergence of new patterns of juvenile crime (e.g., drugs, alcohol, status offenses such as runaway, incorrigibility, and sexual promiscuity) on the part of many young people. Moreover, among some youths today, both rich and poor alike, misbehavior has been replaced by collective withdrawal and sometimes calculated violence in far too many instances. Along these lines, we have seen an increase in gang activities. Thus, today as yesterday, the vast majority of young violators continue to be involved in petty thefts, truancy, and, in some instances, vandalism; but there have now been added to these familiar forms of delinquency, such violations as drug abuse and planned violence against established institutions.

Clearly a fresh look at the problem of delinquency is warranted. There needs to be reassessment of the present public policies for dealing with youthful offenders and development of new understanding of the causes of delinquency, as well as what can and should be done about it at the federal, state, and local levels. Unfortunately, much of what is known is not being used at present to direct intervention strategies; much of what needs to be learned is not even being addressed in a systematic and comprehensive manner.

PRIMARY PHASES OF THE JOB

Responsibility for the prevention of delinquency should remain with local communities. The federal and state governments can and must provide leadership for a prevention program, but the ultimate responsibility for taking corrective action must remain at the local level. A good prevention program requires the cooperative effort of many citizens and organizations.

There are two primary phases to the job: the delinquent—the youth who is

---

[12]*Task Force Report,* pp. 354–55.

apprehended for some type of antisocial activity—and the youth exposed to delinquency. Although neither one can be ignored, it is the youngster who has *not* been actively involved in delinquent activities that promises the "greatest return."

It is apparent that the people we refer to as delinquents come largely from certain backgrounds, and just as various sources of weakness in the social fabric may operate as causes of delinquency, the context in which delinquent behavior occurs are similarly varied. Such contexts, or social settings, may be identified as *the inner-city slum areas, the suburbs, the rural communities,* and *the college and high school campuses.* In each of these social settings, the elements that obstruct youth development and operate to weaken the young person's tie to the social order, as well as the types of events and situations that precipitate episodes of delinquent or destructive activity, combine in many different ways. Each of the contexts of delinquency has unique features; no single type of program of intervention is likely to be able to deal effectively with all situations. Neither the patterns of delinquency nor their significance for the individual or the community are identical in each of these social settings. Within each of these social settings, moreover, it is possible to specify the types of institutional activities that have the most direct and immediate impact on the emerging commitment of many youths to violate the legal norms of society. These activities may be thought of as occurring in and around distinctive "arenas of action" wherein adolescents forge their identities with respect to their support or rejection of lawful activities. [13]

Inner-City Slum Areas: Schools [14]

With the development of great metropolitan complexes, many youngsters predisposed to delinquent activities (e.g., the poverty-stricken, the minorities, the undereducated, the deprived, the children of broken and unstable homes) tend to become concentrated in particular neighborhoods—chiefly in the hearts of cities.

Such a concentration of marginal families tends to perpetuate itself and strengthen those factors that are associated with delinquency.

Typically, housing is squalid, overcrowded, lacking in privacy, depressing. There is little opportunity to study school lessons, but there is plenty of chance to observe alcoholism, mental illness, violence, promiscuity, prostitution, illegitimacy, disease, narcotics addiction, criminality, and racism.

In inner-city slum areas, for example, a primary arena of action is the school, notably the secondary school, where the educational processes of ranking and rating frequently tend to segregate nonachievers into low-status groups. A wealth of available evidence clearly indicates that such status groups have persistently

[13]Adapted from *Delinquency Prevention Report,* "National Strategy for Youth Development and Delinquency Prevention," U.S. Dept. of Health, Education and Welfare, U.S. Government Printing Office, Washington D.C., March 1971, p. 1.
[14]*Ibid.*

served as centers for the development of oppositional and often explicitly delinquent subcultures. Furthermore, the schools reflect the residential pattern so that there is no leavening effect of pupils of other social and economic backgrounds. School attendance and achievement are below normal. The dropout rate is much higher, but employment opportunities are lower.

THE SLUM AREAS: YOUTHFUL ALIENATION[15]

For a variety of reasons, group and cultural support is given to youthful alienation, withdrawal, and *delinquency* in the slum areas. Here links are forged between younger youths who are in the market for delinquent solutions and the older, more established, and sophisticated offenders. Here the more conventional socializing agencies of family or church frequently fail to perform adequately their functions, and the culture of the street takes hold.[16]

Because of the group and cultural support given to youthful alienation there is a question as to the positive or negative effects of encounters between the young and law enforcement, judicial, and correctional agencies. The central problems involve the *deterrent* effects of using the official machinery of the juvenile justice system in response to particular types of offenses, as opposed to using more informal, less stagmatizing procedures for dealing with infractions. Questions relate to the purposes, program content, and efficiency of the official control agencies, specifically the police, courts, and corrections:.

The slum neighborhood breeds a sense of alienation, bitterness, and hopelessness that combines to create and solidify negative views of the social system and of law enforcement in particular. Effective prevention requires that we substitute hope for hopelessness, motivation for apathy, and opportunity for lack of it.

THE SUBURBS, RURAL COMMUNITIES. COLLEGE AND HIGH SCHOOL CAMPUSES[17]

For the *suburbs,* the *rural communities,* and the *college and high school campuses,* the developmental problems of youth seem to require specification of crucial areas of action peculiar to each setting. Most likely each of these social settings represents a distinctive problem which, in turn, requires a *different local approach and strategy.* Yet, it also seems likely that the three underlying principles described earlier—(1) access to acceptable social roles, (2) escape from the entrapment of labeling, and (3) avoidance of the reciprocal processes of rejection, alienation, and estrangement-

[15]*Ibid.*
[16]*Ibid.*
[17]*Ibid.*

—are applicable in certain ways in all social settings. However, the current state of knowledge, as well as the "state-of-the-art," do not permit altogether competent prescription. Clearly what is called for is a carefully differentiated approach to what may become recognized with experience as basic differences in the four social settings identified.

Such a differentiated approach requires not only a capacity to distinguish between the significant features of different social settings, but also the capacity to distinguish between more conventional or more traditional forms of delinquency and more recent cultural, political, and social developments that have added novel features to what we have characterized as youth and delinquency problems for some time. Of these recent developments, two may be tentatively identified: growing ideological hostility among youths to what is globally referred to as "the Establishment," and the politicizing of some forms of serious illegal activities in response to the racial prejudice in American society.

PRIMARY AND SECONDARY PREVENTION

There are a great variety of prevention programs in communities throughout the United States. Some communities are presently engaged in activities designed to forestall delinquency by early treatment or other measures of "primary" prevention. Most of the communities, according to a study completed in 1964 by the United States Department of Health, Education, and Welfare, concentrated on "secondary" prevention measures directed toward those already adjudged delinquent or toward youngsters manifesting behavior that might lead to serious delinquency.

An illustration of "primary" prevention is contained in the report of activities submitted by the Welfare Council of Metropolitan Chicago. The council, in the early 1960s, came to the conclusion that juvenile delinquency was one of Chicago's major social welfare problems and that it was increasing year by year. A project called Community Mobilization for Youth was undertaken, and the prevention and treatment of juvenile delinquency became a major concern of the council. A number of "task forces" sponsored by the council and by the Mayor's Committee on Youth Welfare were set up. They produced working papers on delinquency prevention and treatment programs, "ranging from the preventive roles of child guidance and case-work, schools, health services, and churches and recreation, to the treatment function of courts and correctional programs."[18]

Another major activity directed toward "primary" prevention was reported by the Welfare Federation of Cleveland. A description of this work is contained in the

[18]M.B. Novick, Consultant, Division of Research, "Community Programs and Projects for the Prevention of Juvenile Delinquency," *Juvenile Delinquency, Facts and Facits*, no. 14, U.S. Department of Health, Education, and Welfare, U.S. Government Printing Office, Washington, D.C., 1964, p. 3.

council's pamphlet, "Toward Better Adjusted Children." The undertaking is based on "the thesis that schools and community agencies must work together to serve troubled children and their families." This cooperative program came into being when one of the three boards of education asked to join the council's Committee on Juvenile Delinquency. Projects of this sort were reported to the U. S. Department of Health, Education, and Welfare by several communities, their main aim being to detect "maladjusted school children" in their early years.[19]

Another type of "primary" prevention activity is that which concentrates on extending or improving existing leisure-time programs or on developing new programs of this sort for children and youth. Some of the communities reporting this type of interest said these leisure-time activities were designed specifically for the reduction or prevention of delinquency. In at least one city, a study of the leisure-time activities of neighborhood centers resulted in the employment of "roving group leaders" in areas of hard delinquency. In many communities, such efforts by the community councils have resulted in the establishment of new athletic and recreational programs for preadolescent boys, without specific reference to delinquency.

One community activity in the area of "secondary" prevention centers around the serious shortage of foster homes suitable for the care of adolescents who are delinquent-prone or adjudged delinquent. The United States Department of Health, Education, and Welfare reports that many communities have been active in studying detention facilities for youthful offenders awaiting court disposition.

Many communities reported surveys or studies that touched on juvenile delinquency but were not necessarily focused on delinquent supervision. These studies ranged from the collection and analysis of data about juveniles apprehended by law enforcement agencies to studies of facilities for service to all children. Among the latter were studies of children's services in the community, foster-home care, and leisure-time activities for youths.[20]

In one community, a study is underway to identify "hard-core" families and to propose methods for providing them with rehabilitative services.[21]

Some community councils have for many years maintained statistics on juvenile delinquency in their communities, while others are just beginning to keep such information and analyze it periodically. A few community councils reported statistical activities as a recent development in the field of juvenile delinquency.[22]

One community council reported making intensive studies, area by area, of the "behavior of youths" with particular emphasis on leisure-time activities and the need for agencies to provide such services.

In another community, a project is getting underway in cooperation with the university to make an intensive study of a sample of juvenile court cases in which

[19]*Ibid.*
[20]*Ibid.*, p. 4.
[21]*Ibid.*
[22]*Ibid.*

the family or youth has appeared before the court five times or more in a recent period.

INCREASING PUBLIC UNDERSTANDING[23]

Communities involved in constructing a prevention program—regardless of whether the program is directed toward "primary" or "secondary" prevention—must be concerned with community understanding.

In any preventive program, increasing public understanding of the problem is vital. Many methods should be utilized: town meetings; radio and TV programs; community newspapers; and community and "research" projects relating to juvenile court practices, qualifications of judges and probation officers dealing with youthful offenders, and identification of the problems of youths. The utilization of influential citizens of the community increases their understanding of the problems of delinquency prevention and insures their support of recommendations growing out of these studies. Workshops or institutes on juvenile delinquency for the staffs of social agencies and schools, for juvenile law enforcement officers, probation officers, and court personnel is another tool which can increase the public awareness of the delinquency problem in their community.

The appointment of committees of professional persons and qualified laymen to review programs adopted by other cities for the control, treatment, and prevention of juvenile delinquency, is another effective method for increasing public understanding. The United States Department of Health, Education, and Welfare ascertained public understanding of delinquency can be attained through a wide range of activities:

1. Studying local situations and available services to help delinquents.

2. Alerting the public to local conditions and national trends through radio, TV, and newspapers.

3. Holding "town-meetings" on the subject aimed at informing the public and eliciting support for proposals to change local situations and to improve services.

4. Augmenting existing treatment or rehabilitative programs for delinquents.

5. Extending and improving leisure-time programs for youth, such as detached worker services to street clubs and youth gangs. This is usually accomplished by providing added subsidies to established agencies, such as settlement houses and neighborhood centers, so that special workers can be employed to work with street clubs.

[23]*Ibid.*

Funds for this extension usually come from community chests or foundation grants.

6. Supporting educational programs and workshops for workers who deal with delinquent youths. Often this type of activity involves cooperative work with local universities and other professional training centers.

7. Encouraging and supporting special employment-placement programs for youths who have left school.

8. Collecting and disseminating information from welfare councils in other communities to aid local member agencies and communities in developing their plans to reorganize services or add new ones.

9. Taking a lead in establishing intensive coordination of existing services in designated sections of their cities where incidence of delinquency is high.

COMMUNITY PROJECTS AND PROGRAMS

In order to prepare an appropriate prevention strategy, the initial task of the local community planning group would be to secure information to answer a series of questions about the delinquency problem in the community and the responses now being made to it. It would be necessary to secure answers to such questions as the following:[24]

1. What are the types of delinquency that occur most frequently or cause most harm?

2. What types of delinquency concern the community most, and what is the basis for this concern?

3. What is the community now doing about these offenses?

4. What do experienced persons say is the effect of the current measures now being used?

5. What data exists to support this evaluation or other trends with regard to the delinquency problem?

6. Taking a situational view of these different delinquency problems, what are the aspects of the problem that are now being disregarded?

7. Considering the various components of the situational model of delinquency events, which of these components seem to be most crucial for the different types of delinquency problems? Which ap-

[24]Novick, "Community Programs," pp. 6, 7, and 464.

pear to be most out of control? Which appear most accessible to strategic intervention?[25]

By evaluating the problem of youthful crime within the community, delinquency prevention programs can be guided by an awareness of the priorities within that particular community. Familiarity and awareness of community problems will lead to a more intelligent use of the resources available.

To find out what assistance local communities needed in preventing juvenile delinquency, the United States Department of Health, Education, and Welfare designed a questionnaire that was sent to community welfare planning councils requesting answers in as detailed a form as possible. The questions were specifically directed toward delinquency prevention; the main purpose of the inquiry was to discover (1) the variety, and if possible, the frequency of programs already in existence to prevent delinquency (rather than to treat adjudicated delinquents); and (2) the extent of their impact on the delinquency problem.

Projects or programs were reported in all but one of the cities with populations over five hundred thousand. Eleven cities in the population bracket one hundred thousand to five hundred thousand also had projects, as did seven cities with populations of less than one hundred thousand, according to the questionnaires returned. Several projects were reported for some large cities, while for others there were only one or two. According to the information on delinquency prevention projects already in the files of Children's Bureau, a considerable number of projects, now in existence, were not reported. Why the response was so poor is not known. It may indicate that in some cities the welfare councils are not in close touch with developments of this kind. Another possible reason is that the questionnaire was sent at the time when many councils were involved in community fund drives.[26]

Yet in spite of the deficient coverage, the projects reported on are probably typical of most delinquency prevention projects in the United States.

TYPES OF PROGRAMS OR PROJECTS[27]

While the delinquency prevention programs and projects described by the respondents differed in detail, they fall into the following broad categories:

---

1. *Detached worker services:* This service sends out social group workers or recreation leaders to locate groups of adolescent boys or girls who do not or will not use

[25]L. E. Ohlin, "A Situational Approach to Delinquency Prevention," *U.S. Department of Health, Education, and Welfare, Social and Rehabilitation Service,* U.S. Government Printing Office, Washington, D.C., 1970, pp. 11–20.
[26]*Ibid,* p. 7.
[27]*Ibid.*

existing leisure-time programs and who, because of idleness, frustrations, or boredom, appear to be heading toward delinquency or are already known to the police as delinquents. Usually these workers are not actually separated from established social agencies, but they operate and work with youth outside the agency wall and on a very different work schedule than that of the staff in the traditional recreation and leisure-time agency. These programs attempt to redirect the aggressive or delinquent behavior of members of hostile youth groups and street clubs by providing them with an adult leader or guide who is a friend, skilled in helping them to find legitimate outlets for their feelings of frustration, and desirous of guiding them into new behavior patterns that may lead to improved social adjustment.

2. *Area projects:* This term is used to describe the kind of work that Clifford Shaw started in Chicago forty years or so ago. These projects are based on the idea that delinquency is due partly to the poor quality of the social and physical environment in low-income areas of large cities and, even more, to the fact that slum neighborhoods have lost the sense of mutual responsibility for children's behavior. The area projects attempt to improve this situation with the help of adults living in such neighborhoods. Attempts are made to arouse residents to a greater sense of responsibility for the welfare of children, and channels are opened through which adults can work to make significant contributions to child welfare. This method is often described as "locating and training indigenous leadership."

3. *Intensive coordination of services:* Another approach to delinquency prevention is based on the idea that within small fairly circumscribed neighborhoods that are "high delinquency areas," coordination of existing programs will result in getting these services to individuals, families, and groups early enough to prevent incipient delinquency or its recurrence. Thus the best skills of every agency and organization are brought to bear on the problems of the given community. With this team approach, referrals from one agency to another are quicker and less complicated, and the efforts of each worker are integrated with those of other workers.

4. *Intensive group work services:* This sort of service is provided for "hard-to-serve" groups of children and youths and sometimes, for their parents. Major differences between these services and those traditionally provided are:

   A. Group members are selected because their behavior problems are noted by group leaders in the conventional programs and by school personnel, police, probation workers, and the like, including the "detached workers"

   B. Professionally trained group workers who are especially skilled in therapy lead the groups.

   C. Usual care is employed in programming for these groups and emphasis is placed on the social behavior problems of the member rather than on

Community Projects and Programs   **103**

wholesale use of leisure-time.

D. Emphasis is given to helping group members to help each other.

5. *Intensive casework services:* These are usually an extension of ongoing programs in public or voluntary agencies. Special units are set up to provide easily accessible, highly integrated counseling to individuals. Group caseworkers on this sort of service are assigned only a small number of clients, so that they may give more intensive service than is usual, and have time free for emergencies.

6. *Parent education programs:* These seek as clientele the parents of delinquent youths or of those children who seem to be heading toward delinquency. The program is often carried on in cooperation with a juvenile court. Special parent groups are set up in local agencies, such as neighborhood houses where they discuss a wide range of subjects relating to child rearing, family life, and community problems that contribute to delinquency. The support that the parents get from each other and from knowing that others are struggling with similar problems seems to be one of the most important aspects of these programs.

7. *Youth employment programs:* These are planned to bridge the gap between school and work, particularly for young people who leave school before regulation. In them, out-of-school youths are given training in good work habits and disciplined behavior on the job and are then guided into jobs. Employers cooperating in the work recognize that they are contributing to a delinquency prevention program and thus are inclined to overlook some of the deficiencies of these selected youths as workers.

8. *Recreational programs:* These are extensions of the usual organized recreational activities of the community. Such extensions have been made in some communities in the hope that they will assist in preventing delinquency by involving young people in wholesome activities during their free time. Although the effectiveness of such programs is questionable for youths already oriented to delinquency, such activities do tend to meet the interests of youth generally. Thus, they contribute to the total social climate of a community and may indirectly serve as a delinquency prevention measure.

Responsibility for the prevention of delinquency should remain with local communities; however, the state should provide leadership. The state of California, fortunately, does recognize its responsibilities in this area. The 1965 State Legislature passed, and Governor Edmund Brown signed, a bill allowing the state to enter into contract with private and governmental agencies for the development of delinquency prevention projects. This bill was sponsored by the relatively new California Delinquency Prevention Commission after a survey of the state disclosed that prevention efforts were fragmentary, poorly defined, and in many cases, overlapping. The bill provided for the establishment of the County Delinquency Prevention Commission to coordinate preventive efforts in the county and to permit an integrated and organized approach.

The state of California and the city of San Diego have been engaged in a cooperative effort for many years to prevent unexploited juveniles from crossing the international border at San Ysidro. For many years, juveniles from all over California have been flocking to the town of Tijuana, Mexico, and the border check station had made a significant contribution toward shutting off this traffic.

The California Delinquency Prevention Commission, in concert with the Department of Employment, has worked to develop "jobs for youths" campaigns in various parts of the state. It was largely through their efforts that the first Youth Conservation Camp in the country was set up in 1970 near San Bernardino to provide job opportunities and job motivation for young school dropouts. This camp has now been turned over to the federal government for use with the Youth Job Corps.

The commission sponsored a statewide conference on delinquency prevention that permitted youth groups throughout California to share ideas on how to set up different types of prevention projects. Out of this conference was developed a publication, "21 Ways to Prevent Delinquency"—a compilation of twenty-one different projects currently in existence in various California communities.

Since 1960, California has extended former Governor Edmund Brown's fourteen point program for delinquency prevention. Essentially, this is a broad-gauged attack on delinquency, calling for a united effort by eleven different departments of state government. This is based on the concept that delinquency can be solved best when there is full participation at the local level. The state, therefore, provides leadership, technical consultation, and service as a catalyst in getting communities to develop their own programs. The state sets standards, prepares pamphlets, and newsletters, and develops conferences and promotional and educational campaigns. The following are some recommendations taken from the California Delinquency Prevention Commission's suggestions for developing a more comprehensive blueprint for action.

SPECIAL SERVICES IN SCHOOLS

The major contribution by the schools toward the control and prevention of delinquency is that of helping children and youths to grow into competent and responsible adults. Most people want to meet the expectations set for them by their families, their schools, and their communities, and most people do so with reasonable success. The person who achieves whatever is expected of him is not likely to become a delinquent. However, a certain proportion find difficulty in making the transition from childhood to adulthood. These are the potential delinquents. Therefore, the schools must be prepared to take certain actions to help such people avoid trouble. These actions should include:

1. *Identifying potential problem pupils* at the earliest possible ages.

2. *Providing sufficient flexibility* in the school program to permit adjustments for these pupils.

3. *Providing intensive work* with individual pupils who present special social and emotional problems.

4. *Accepting* the responsibility for cooperation with other community agencies and organizations in providing and using needed services.

JOBS FOR YOUTH

Job opportunities for young people, particularly the school dropout and the delinquency-prone, need to be made available in increasing numbers. Many young people get into difficulty because their failure in school is reflected by their later failures to secure satisfactory employment. Existing and additional youth employment committees should be encouraged, involving representation from labor, management, the schools, and state departments of employment.

These committees should continue to concern themselves with developing summertime and part-time employment for children still in school, and full-time jobs for those young people who end their schooling with graduation from high school. Consideration should be given to some kind of employment internship program that would involve selecting terminal students in high school and junior college to begin work one year prior to graduating, while taking appropriate skill courses for school credit.

MENTAL HEALTH SERVICES

Because good mental health is a by-product of other favorable factors, individuals look to the area of everyday social activity to build defenses against mental breakdown. This includes the home, school, church, jobs, and recreation, public health and safety, and economic security.

The provision for basic health and welfare services effectively administered serves as a deterrent to disturbed behavior. Additional and better coordinated services providing early identification, diagnosis, and treatment are essential to a comprehensive program of prevention.

Modern psychiatric approaches demand that children and their families receive early treatment with as little dislocation as possible from their home, school, or community so that there is a minimal disruption of the patient's community ties and relationships.

To achieve the degree and quality of services required for mental health, responsibility must be shared among federal, state, and local, public and private agencies. The potential of such citizen participation should be encouraged to the fullest by vigorously furthering this partnership.

ASSISTANCE PROGRAMS

Strengthening a child's own home is the most effective way of preventing juvenile delinquency. An examination of delinquent histories shows that disorganization in the family is frequently the forerunner of overt delinquent acts.

The contributions that can be made by the social welfare services to the prevention of delinquency lie mainly in the area of mitigating the *negative effects of deprivation* faced by underprivileged families whose earnings are neither stable nor adequate enough to afford a decent standard of living. This refers to those who ordinarily lack sufficient opportunities to afford decent housing and the basic needs of health, recreation, and education. It also refers to those who lack the protection afforded by coverage under programs for survivors, disability, and unemployment insurance.

To some extent the general assistance programs of the various counties throughout the United States function for this purpose, but are too varied and too limited to do more than support people at a standard that cannot possibly provide stable and wholesome living conditions.

The Aid to Federally Dependent Children Program also has as its basic purpose the strengthening of family life. Moreover, it includes many of the most deprived, and hence high delinquency risk, children. In numbers it affects more children in home interviews than any other social welfare program. These children are in families where major family breakdown has already occurred, e.g., incarceration, death, disability, desertion.

It is important to provide social services in addition to financial aid to these families to prevent further disintegration and to rehabilitate them if possible.

ROLE OF VOLUNTARY SOCIAL WELFARE AGENCIES

Voluntary social welfare agencies have an important contribution to make in the prevention and treatment of delinquency, both individually and in cooperation with public agencies. They have professional family service programs, child-care institutions, foster-care services, day-care centers, and group work activities that reach many thousands of families and children yearly. But they must develop the means to reach many more families and children in trouble and provide treatment for them. They must continue to encourage the boards of directors of volunteer groups, representing as they do a broad cross-section of our communities, to be concerned with the welfare of *all* citizens, to engage in experimental programs, demonstration projects, and basic research in the behavioral sciences.

In recent years, more and more social agencies have been caught in a squeeze of spiraling costs and shrinking income from the volunteer dollars, and frequently they have been forced into emergency retrenchment. Thus, an extra burden has been thrust upon tax-supported agencies. Consequently, the low cost and greater diversification of private agency programs are lost to the public agencies. Therefore, special incentives should be provided the voluntary agencies to give additional family and child-welfare services to predelinquent and delinquent children and their families both in their own homes and while the youngsters are away from home in foster care.

PROBATION SERVICES

Probation departments must be encouraged to develop more preventive services. Very few counties have developed procedures for the discovery and treatment of delinquency-prone children. Little has been done by probation agencies to utilize volunteer groups and citizen action committees engaged in preventive work.

Increased emphasis needs to be placed on the treatment of delinquents in their local communities where family relationships can be strengthened. The state institutions should be reserved for the delinquent children and youths and those who are so emotionally and mentally disturbed that they cannot be treated properly in local facilities.

YOUTH SERVICE BUREAUS

Delinquency prevention is an intangible, difficult for the nonprofessional to buy. The public has felt an obligation to help delinquents, but the only thing that they could see for their money was brick and mortar. Hence, institutionalization has become the major method of treatment, while delinquency prevention receives low priority in appropriations. As an example of the limited appropriations for delinquency prevention, one need only review the current spending habits of the state considered the most progressive in the handling of youthful problems—California. California is currently spending more than $170 million annually in processing and treating juvenile offenders. It has been estimated that the total costs of crime and delinquency in California run to well over $300 million. Little is spent for *prevention* of delinquency. Less than 5 percent of the California Youth Authority budget is now being spent on prevention and only twenty-eight of the fifty-eight County Probation Departments (some of which are part-time probation officers actually carrying caseloads as well as doing preventive work) have any organized programs in delinquency prevention.

The President's Commission on Law Enforcement and Administration of Justice has also concluded that "once a juvenile is apprehended by police and referred to the Juvenile Court the community has already failed; subsequent rehabilitative services, no matter how skilled, have far less potential for success than if they had been applied before the youth's overt defiance of the law."

With the growing awareness of the lack of any major delinquency prevention program throughout the United States, efforts are now being made to begin a concerted, planned prevention approach. In most communities, the youngsters who come to the attention of the juvenile court tends to be limited to specific geographic sections, since delinquent behavior is not uniformly distributed across the geographic face of the community. These geographical concentrations appear to encompass the location and distribution of minority groups, the white poor and other powerless groups whose children make up most of those handled by the juvenile justice system.

Furthermore, experience indicates that those youngsters who are dealt with on an official level in juvenile court, as well as most of the cases dealt with by law enforcement agencies and correctional facilities, were usually involved in offenses which, if committed by an adult, would not be considered a crime (e.g., incorrigible and disobedient behavior, curfew violation, truancy) and relatively minor law violations which are essentially threatening or menacing to the welfare and common interests of the local community.

It is, therefore, mandatory that any preventive type program, in order to be effective, must be incorporated through the community development approach. Such programs, basically, divert those cases, which because of no other available services, usually end up as referrals to the juvenile probation department. *The real answer to delinquency prevention* lies in the ability and willingness of the community to accept responsibility for their youth and to become involved in removing delinquency-producing factors, in influencing agencies and organizations to expand services to fill gaps, and in providing direct services to youths based upon normal, warm, love-centered relationships.[28] It is the belief of the practitioners in the field of juvenile justice that the best method to accomplish this goal is the *youth service bureau*. The youth service bureau, with its particular structure, functions, and intent, has the potential of being the vehicle for this community involvement. John M. Martin, noted author, lecturer, and teacher, emphasized the need of such bureaus:

> *Perhaps the best-known mechanism being offered at present along these lines is what are now called Youth Service Bureaus. As recommended by the President's Commission on Law Enforcement and Administration of Justice, there would be local, community-based servicing agencies situated outside of the Juvenile Justice System. The police, Juvenile Courts, parents, schools and others, would refer adolescents, delinquent and nondelinquent, who are in need of special attention to such bureaus. Properly staffed and managed, such bureaus could be used to divert cases out of the juvenile justice system, thus avoiding many of the negative consequencies*

[28]J. M. Martin, "Toward a Political Definition of Juvenile Delinquency" U.S. Department of Health, Education, and Welfare, U.S. Government Printing Office, 1970, p. 11.

which faced individuals which in fact remained under the care of the system.[29]

With regard to the location of the youth service bureau, Martin emphatically states that the youth service bureau should be a "local community-based" and controlled service. Under no circumstances, should the service bureaus be under the auspices of state, county, or municipal agencies. Such bureaus should be autonomous, following the President's Commission dictum that such bureaus *are not* to be run by the juvenile justice system itself.

A strong case can be made for situating youth service bureaus in the private sector rather than in the public sector. In the private sector they would be operated to the maximum extent possible by the representatives of the groups whose children are being cared for by the juvenile justice system. Such an arrangement would serve to meet the goal that cases should be diverted out of the system whenever possible. It could also begin to address the imbalance of power between the juvenile justice system and those who receive its care. Supported by tax dollars, and administered by private organizations responsive to the needs of indigenous populations, such bureaus would accomplish goals that would not even be approached by bureaus run by some division of government.[30]

The rather limited amount of literature on youth service bureaus points to certain basic functions of the youth service resource bureau:

1. *Make separate referrals* (on a voluntary basis) from agencies, schools, etc., of youth who are beginning to exhibit problems that could lead to eventual judicial processing, refer these youth to existing agencies or programs for a particular service, and ensure that the service is provided.

2. *Strengthen existing resources* through purchasing services and assisting the agencies with special problems.

3. *Develop new programs* to fill gaps that may be evident in community services.

Normal *court intake* services are supposed to provide short-term counseling and appropriate referral of youths to service agencies. Thus one may say that the youth service bureau is only duplicating an existing service, a problem that continually plagues social service systems. However, in many states, actual court intake services are extremely limited and consequently, rather ineffective in almost every instance. Only a very few juvenile courts have a separate community-financed intake service. In the majority of counties throughout the United States, services on the intake level of the juvenile probation department are limited. The budget limitations placed on most juvenile probation departments—which are also

[29]*Ibid.*
[30]Ibid., p. 12.

responsible for adoptions, foster care, services to unwed mothers and others-—results in limited staff, which ultimately affects the quality and quantity of intake services. Therefore, the very existence of youth service bureaus throughout the county and in specific areas of high delinquency will strengthen rather than duplicate the intake process. In addition, the primary trust of the bureau is to *prevent delinquency* at a stage earlier than that which demands court intake processes.

Perhaps the strongest point in the youth service bureau concept is the function of resource development to communities through community response and support. However, additional factors are the practical limitations of staff and the lack of enough professionally trained social workers, juvenile probation officers, correctional and law enforcement personnel, to deal with the problems of people. The final conclusion is that the only effective and possible means of meeting the full range of problems is through citizen involvement in direct services to youth. This is coupled with a new brand of citizen committees. The youth service bureau's structure provides an excellent avenue for the *involvement of lay citizens as a major resource* within a community. They serve youth directly, help build systems to prevent juvenile delinquency, and strengthen the legislative constitnency.

It should be noted that many states are encouraging the establishment of youth service bureaus *on a trial basis* and not as a panacea for the problem of delinquency in every county and community in the state. The federal government is directly involved in financing the operations of youth service bureaus in numerous counties throughout the United States. An ongoing comprehensive, outside evaluation of the effectiveness of the Youth Service Bureau approach is a part of every problem and if the evaluation results that the problem is not viable, federal monies are withheld.

THE POLICE ROLE IN DELINQUENCY PREVENTION

Law enforcement has a positive role to play in delinquency prevention. Trained juvenile officers alert to happenings in the adolescent's world can frequently avert trouble before it develops.

This brings us to the question: *Is the police role in prevention a proper one?* Some criticism has been noted as to the propriety of the police engaging in what might be termed "the treatment" filed of combating delinquency. Certainly the police are qualified, for the most part, to enter this field, although admittedly there are many elements of treatment in this approach. In fact, the official contact between a child and a police officer is, in a sense, a phase of treatment. The officer's attitude and conduct toward the child may have a decided effect on the child's outlook and feeling toward those in authority.

A reply to this criticism may be found in the answers to two simple questions: "Is crime prevention a police responsibility?" and "Is delinquency prevention crime prevention?"

It is obvious that *crime prevention is a police responsibility,* and it logically follows that if most of the adult criminals were juvenile delinquents, preventing delinquency is crime prevention. To intelligently apply these fairly new concepts in law enforcement by trained personnel for the purpose of delinquency prevention is, without question, a proper function of a police department as part of its responsibility to a community.[31]

Proper surveillance of hazardous areas can prevent unwitting youngsters from becoming accomplices in criminal activies. Close cooperation of community agencies with law enforcement officers would help spotlight community needs in the field of delinquency prevention. This would often permit effective action to be taken before trouble begins.

A preventive activity that clearly falls within an acceptable function of the police is to act to control or suppress conditions in a community that might lead to delinquency or crime. These conditions are generally part of certain types of group activities, such as:

1. The pool halls, drive-in restaurants, bowling alleys, or roller rinks in or around which children are allowed to loiter to unreasonably late hours and where the very young may be allowed to become involved in the use of narcotics, beer, or hard liquor.

2. "Rock sessions," which should be closely supervised and where it is not unusual to find many youngsters involved in activities that could very well lead to serious law enforcement problems.

3. Establishments or houses that harbor and/or attract children who are runaways and that contribute to the delinquency of minors.

During normal patrols of a city, police officers become aware of such danger areas. It is obviously a reasonable performance of their duty to be aware of those factors that can encourage youngsters to become involved in antisocial activities. On occasion, business establishments, although operating within the letter of the law, may still have undesirable atmospheres insofar as the welfare of children is concerned. It is advantageous then, in all cases, for the police officer to become well acquainted with the proprietors of such businesses to elicit their help in protecting and contributing to the welfare of young people. Such an approach may, in the long run, produce better results than the constant use of threat of "action."

However, there may be cases where sympathetic appeals, warnings, and threats are to no avail. In such instances, the police may have to take court action or repeal permits to do business from licensing agencies. A civil court injunction is often an effective solution, and, of course, the prospect of losing his license will ordinarily make a proprietor more cooperative. Those establishments that cater to

---

[31] J.E. Winters, "The Role of Police in the Prevention and Control of Delinquency," *Federal Probation*, vol. 21, no. 2, June 1957, p. 5.

young people and provide entertainment in the form of "rock music" and dancing have posed an extremely serious problem for law enforcement personnel.

In the areas where undesirable conditions exist through no fault of a particular establishment or person, the police should call the matter to the attention of some community-planning body. In many cities, cooperation between the police and the youth service agencies has resulted in various projects to combat situations. For example, information provided by the police on delinquency areas and gang activities has led to the establishment of new recreational facilities and to the use of "detached workers" by social agencies in an effort to solve the problem.

The police are, of course, tremendously interested in efforts to create a better environment for juveniles to lead them away from delinquency; yet, there is often some question as to the extent to which they should participate in such efforts. For example, it is questionable whether a police officer should attempt to work with a gang in the same manner that detached workers from social agencies do. However, in some other areas of his work there are indications that police officers can be very effective without prejudice to their responsibilities as law enforcement agents. This is particularly true in the case of recreational activities (Police Athletic League). Illustrations depicting such activities by the San Jose Police Department's Police Athletic League vividly portray the importance of such programs.

Certain organizations, particularly agencies exclusively concerned with leisure-time activities and recreation, have questioned the appropriateness of recreational programs conducted under police auspices. In response to such critics, proponents of police recreational programs have pointed out that:

1. *Insufficient recreational facilities* force the police into these programs to meet crucial needs.

2. Actual experience in some communities has shown that *the police can be very effective in work with so-called predelinquents,* that is, children in underprivileged areas who are not interested in programs of conventional recreational activities. Only the police seem to speak the language of these youngsters and seem to understand their motivations and aspirations.

3. Such programs are invaluable in *impressing children* with the concept of the police officer as a friend.

Strong as such arguments may be, many people still hold that they do not justify police participation in such programs. They ask whether the police would countenance recreational agencies engaging in police functions on the grounds that the police department's performance is inadequate. These critics of the police also contend that the development of the child's concept of police officers should come about through the child's observation of officers engaged in their proper duties, and through standard educational techniques. This desirable goal, it is pointed out, can be obtained without permitting the police to perform functions that are asserted not to be properly theirs.

The Police Role in Delinquency Prevention   113

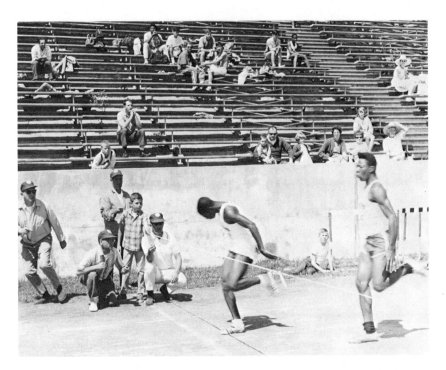

Photos courtesy of Sgt. Jim Guido, Director, San Jose
Police Athletic League, San Jose, Calif.

114   Prevention Is the Answer

In recent years, a number of organizations have considered this question and have taken a somewhat middle-of-the-road point of view. They have emphasized the importance of calling the attention of the community to recreational needs. They have seen police engaged in these programs only as a last resort. They have called for police recreational programs that employ *trained* recreational personnel and meet the standards of national recreational organizations.

Considering these arguments, it is clear that there are four points that should be reviewed prior to having police undertake recreational programs:

1. The police have the responsibility to *keep the community informed* of recreational needs, particularly in underprivileged areas.

2. All communities should provide recreation *based on community needs* and develop facilities through broad community programs involving leisure-time activities.

3. Police participation in providing recreational service should be *determined through joint group community planning.*

4. Recreation supervisors should be *trained in the field* of recreation and recreation programs should *meet recognized standards.*

Traffic safety is another dimension in which the police play a significant role. In nearly every community, police handle juveniles who violate traffic rules and regulations in the same manner that they handle adults. Quite often the enforcement of traffic laws is the responsibility of a special traffic division, but no distinction is made between juveniles and adults; a citation is simply issued for the violator to appear before the appropriate judicial agency.

However, in connection with this traffic question, the police do regard juveniles differently from adults in one respect. They know the juvenile driver will eventually become an adult driver, and they would like that juvenile to become, and remain, a safe driver. For this reason, police departments in many communities have undertaken certain traffic safety programs for young automobile drivers. Bicycle safety education and junior safety patrol programs have been set up. These three programs cover most of the police activity in traffic safety.[32] Those departments that have traffic divisions usually entrust these programs to that unit as it is best qualified for such work. Some of the activities found in these traffic division programs are

---

1. *Traffic Safety for Young Automobile Drivers.* Such a program includes:

   A. Planning and assisting with driver education and training in the schools.

   B. Using public education media available to impress upon juveniles, as well as adults, the need for safe driving.

   C. Sponsoring or operating traffic schools for junior operators.

2. *Bicycle Safety Education.* This follows the same general pattern as the program for automobile drivers but is directed toward a younger age group with the principle approach through the school.

3. *Junior Safety Patrol.* This is carried out with cooperation of the schools and the parent-teacher associations. This program gives the police an opportunity to develop an extensive safety education program in the schools, as well as to promote good relations with juveniles.

As in the case of other preventive activities, there is generally complete approval of traffic safety programs, but there may be objections to certain types of programs being conducted by the police. It is apparent that the need for such

[32]*Police Services for Juveniles,* U.S. Children's Bureau, Department of Health, Education, and Welfare, U.S. Government Printing Office, Washington, D.C., 1964, pp. 52–54.

A police student cadet program is a very integral part of any lawenforcement agency. Photos courtesy of Sgt. Jim Guido, Director, San Jose Police Athletic League, San Jose, Calif.

117

programs be defined and the agency best qualified and most appropriate for the task should be entrusted with it. In any case, police interest and their cooperation in these programs cannot be excluded.

POLICE IMAGE AS IT AFFECTS YOUTHFUL BEHAVIOR

There are no limitations as to the amount and type of delinquency preventive programs which law enforcement officers can become involved in. Programs may run the gamut of activities ranging from gun safety instruction for juveniles, to Boy Scout explorer posts, to school lectures on driving safety and the danger of narcotic addiction, to public speaking at civic functions, to school scholarship drives, to citizen awards programs, to stamp-out-crime crusades, to area service centers, to in-service human relations training, and to YMCA building programs.[33]

What has not been discussed thus far is the use of community-relations units (law enforcement agencies in larger cities are activating community-relations units to gain the support of citizenry in their areas of jurisdiction) in an endeavor to improve police relations with youths. The use of police-community relations must be utilized if law enforcement expects to be effective in successfully performing its task. This factor is brought into focus by George H. Shepard who defines "police-community relations" and summarizes their use in the field of delinquency prevention:

> The term "police-community relations" has been described as a field of social action within which Police activities have direct relevance to the general effort toward community betterment. This relationship can become not only the very foundation by which the Police in a free, democratic society can maintain peace and harmony in their jurisdictions, but it can serve as the means by which the best kind of public "cooperation" in fighting crime and disorder can emanate as an output of the Police effort to gain public support.
>
> This was illustrated in the City of Philadelphia, Pennsylvania, after its disastrous riot in July 1964. With the aid of Community-Relations Bureau personnel, several ring-leaders of the riot were identified by residents of the affected area and, subsequently were arrested and brought to trial. . . . Police must come to realize that in "prevention" lies the key to decreased criminal activity and that one of the best ways to prevent crime is by active citizen report. . . .
>
> Young people everywhere have become receptive to, and often activated by, the exciting challenges offered by leaders of revoluntary movements. Perhaps Police should take a long, hard look at the success of some

[33]L. Brown, "Dynamic Police Relations at Work," *Police Chief*, vol. 35, No. 4, April 1968, pp. 44–50.

extremist groups with segments of our youths to see if there are some valuable lessons to be learned from them.[34]

George H. Shepard's article in *Police Chief*, deals with the use of the juvenile specialist in community relations and, as such, the report emphasizes the innovative approaches the juvenile officer has initiated, as well as some of the effects of his community-oriented activity. Shepard is of the opinion that the juvenile specialist's "knowledge of community agencies, youth, and their parents, together with his experience in dealing with schools, courts, and the public and private sectors involved in community betterment, has placed him in the forefront of Police-Community affairs.[35]

Recalling the significance of the saying "as the twig is bent so grows the tree," it does not seem surprising that many human-relation programs in fact do focus on the subject of youth. For indeed "bending the twig" in the direction of respectful police goals yields results that cannot be measured throughout the ensuing non-criminal adult life. But more than human-relation programs are required for such ideal crime prevention; often needed is a sensitivity to the profound impact on children who come into contact with police authority. The need for a positive police image when dealing with the citizenry is extremely crucial—especially when dealing with juveniles:

> *It is in early adolescence that a youth begins to fit the world to his own individual personality as he replaces the value systems that he has copied from the adults around him with a value system of his own. This is a period of great physical and emotional upheaval, of rapid changes in both body and mind. It is a period of discovering, of exploration, of experiences that will have a lasting effect upon the complex psychological system of the adult. Educators have long been aware of the importance of the early adolescent years and have designed special schools (junior high schools) and programs for this crucial age. It is generally recognized that the attitudes tend to crystalize at this time of life, and that the most successful attempts to modify attitudes take place during this period of time. (The tremendous success of the Boy Scout in dealing with youngsters of early adolescent ages is a case very much to the point in any discussion of this age level.)*
>
> *It is important, therefore, that a Police Department interested in building favorable attitudes towards law and law enforcement take a special interest in the early adolescent within the department's sphere of influence. These young people from the ages of 12 through 16 comprise a very special group toward which special programs and procedures should be directed.*

[34]G. H. Shepard, "The Juvenile Specialist in Community Relations," *Police Chief, j2vol. 35, no. 4, Jan. 1970, p. 1.*
[35]*Ibid.*

It is equally important to take note of the fact that certain militant and revolutionary groups within American society are gradually becoming aware of the special nature of the early adolescent within our midst. There is certain realization that these young minds are shaping the value systems that will eventually point the direction of American life in the forseeable future.

A race to capture those young minds has begun. It would seem self-evident that the forces of law and order must join in that race, so that the value systems of our next generation of adults include sets of attitudes that are favorable toward law and law enforcement in a free and democratic society.[36]

The problem, of course, is twofold: first, there must be the special police sensitivity just implied, but there must also be sufficient firmness to justify the child's respect. The question of firmness will be discussed further in chapter 11, "Police Services for Juveniles." With regard to special police sensitivity, law enforcement agencies throughout the United States have begun to recognize the need for special police participation in community programs designed to "improve the police image." Special programs dealing with youths have been developed by law enforcement agencies throughout the United States. There are programs such as those reflected in a publication by the late Nelson A. Watson entitled "The Fringes of Police Community Relations" (Police Administrator's Conference, Indiana University Medical Center, June 29, 1966). Another example is reflected in the following "handout:"

The purpose of these talks is to develop a more positive relationship between the young people of the community and the Police, and to foster a greater degree of social consciousness on the part of these young people. Rather than dealing simply in what the law is and how it affects young people, which tends very often to be somewhat sterile, we dwell more on motivating good behavior in general. We attempt to define a role for the vast majority of young people who do not get into trouble but at the same time assert little influence if any on those that do. This represents the first phase of the presentation.

The second phase of the presentation is devoted to a colored slide program showing Juvenile Hall, the ranches and a Youth Authority Institution. What we are striving to do is to take the glamour away from young people who go to these facilities. Very often they come back to school and become leaders because the rest of the young people think that this is some sort of achievement after listening to the stories fabricated by these individuals. Also, we find that most of the questions by students previ-

[36]R. Portune, *Changing Adolescent Attitudes toward Police*, W. Andersen Co., Cincinnati, 1971, pp. 12–13.

ously were directed to the nature of these facilities and the slides provide the closest thing to a guided tour.

The third phase of the program is devoted to answering any questions that the students may have. This interaction hopefully develops a positive nature to the contact between students and someone who represents the Police Department. It is with this in mind that we desire to keep presentations at the classroom level to develop the highest degree of communication and interaction.

This handout is presented to teachers prior to addresses at schools by officers assigned to the Community-Relations Unit of the San Jose, California, Police Department. Although the handout deals primarily with improving the police image with youths, it seems reasonable to assume that this activity may gain the respect of the community at large. Even citizens completely satisfied with *conventional* police services will be likely to respond favorably to the program.

Still more relevant to programs geared to improving police image, specifically among groups ordinarily resentful of police, is the message of the following letter:

Mr. Nate Shaffer
Council of Community Services
431 Sixth Street
Richmond, CA

Subject: Relation of Police Community, Relations Aids to Police-Youth Discussion Group Program

Dear Sir:

There has been exhibited throughout the Nation a dislike, distrust and, in some cases, hatred of Police by large segments of our Negro citizens. The City of Richmond, with one fourth of the population Negro, falls into the National pattern. I shall not attempt to go into the "whys" of this situation at this time. I would rather accept this situation as a fact and seek solutions.

It is my strong conviction that in today's society, we must attempt to reach the youth with a concentrated effort to establish more meaningful lines of communication between them and the Police. In particular, with Negro youth. We must try to bring about a better understanding, a deeper appreciation for one another, and our problems.

We have in the City of Richmond taken steps to reach the Negro youths through a series of Police-Youth Discussion Groups. Our method of setting up such groups is quite simple. Take a small geographical area of the city, seek out the youths who have exhibited anti-social behavior, get them to a meeting with selected Police Officers. At such meetings the youths are

The Police Role in Delinquency Prevention   **121**

encouraged to speak their minds, regardless of how hard it is on the Police. On the other hand the Police are to answer all questions, avoiding none. They explain their responsibility, the law and the policy with which the Police must govern themselves. I hasten to add that such a meeting is not attempted on the basis that all ills or misunderstanding will be cleared away at a single meeting or a dozen meetings. However, we have, through Discussion Groups, brought about far better understanding between these two forces. This is demonstrated by a lessening of crimes committed by those youths who have participated and by many, having been school dropouts, having returned to school.

Much of the success of the Police-Youth Discussion Groups can be attributed to the work and dedication of the five Police-Community Relations Aids. It is they who go out into the community and invite the youths to the group meeting. They pick them up at their homes (or wherever they can be located), bring them to the meetings and take them home at the close. Further, the personal contact with the youths in their homes, oftentimes bridges the gaps of communications, counsels both the youth and their parents.

At the present time, the Richmond Police have conducted two 12-week Police-Youth Discussion Groups within the Negro community. Both groups are continuing as structured clubs. Just during the past two weeks, three new Discussion Groups have been formed. We cannot, at this time, even offer a guess as to the number of groups that might form within the next six months. Regardless of the number now or in the future, we can see the Police Community-Relations Aid has a very important part in a program that shall have a present and lasting value to those in the various Groups, their families and the community.

Very truly yours,

*[s]C. E. Brown
Chief of Police*

Again, although youth seems to be the primary subject, the entire community stands to gain by this human-relations activity.

Community-relations programs dealing with youths attempt to prevent the incidents which "give police a black eye." This suggests that the officers' efficiency should be reduced. Indeed, to achieve the ultimate respect of a good police image demands vigorous and conscientious performance of all duties; but also demands sensitivity to anything that could give the police a bad name. The necessity of working with juveniles in this particular area is quite evident and community programs dealing with delinquency prevention must take into consideration the apparent reasons for disrespect of law enforcement by youthful offenders. It seems reasonable that a youthful offender brutally mishandled by one policeman may have difficulty in conceding how helpful most policemen really are. This possibility alone should afford a more convincing argument for eliminating force wherever possible. Behavioral scientists believe that a kind of "selective perception" sets in which causes an unjustly abused individual to look for and "see" only those incidents that prove the police are brutal. Years and years of looking for and seeing incidents, combined with reassurances from others doing the same thing, of course, create such an individual's undesirable image of police—thus creating a greater void between police and youth in their communities.

There is no reason why attitudes cannot be changed. Data from a study by Robert L. Derbyshire[37] conducted with third-grade youngsters in the Los Angeles area shows that social class and ethnic background influenced children's perception of the police. Following is the sample upon which the data were gathered: thirty Negro youngsters from an area of low social and economic stability; thirty Mexican-American youngsters from a neighborhood having average to below-average social and economic stability, and thirty Anglo-American youngsters from an area of high social and economic stability.

The research consisted of asking the children to draw pictures of policemen at work. The results were analyzed and assigned basically into two categories. These categories were scored: (1) aggressive police behavior, such as fighting, chasing fugitives, and shooting, or police assistance having negative overtones such as searching a building, unloading a paddy wagon, driving in a car with prisoners, or giving a traffic ticket; or (2) neutral behavior, such as directing traffic, riding in a car, or walking, as well as assisting with positive overtones such as talking with children or giving directions.

Negro and Mexican-American youngsters differed significantly from the upper-middle-class Caucasian/Anglo youngsters in that the minority-group children were *much more likely* to picture police as aggressive or with negative behavior connotations. On the other hand, Anglo-American upper-middle-class children tended *not* to see the policemen's task as aggressive, negative or hostile, but rather as being neutral, nonaggressive, and assisting.

There is every reason to believe that these children actively respected the attitudes of their parents and/or other significant persons in their environment.

After the children had been tested, the Los Angeles Police Department in conjunction with the Los Angeles Public Schools exposed them to their "Policeman Bill Program." In essence, this program is one in which a police officer presents a twenty-minute discussion to first, second, and third-grade children. In it he de-

[37]R. L. Derbyshire, "Childrens Perceptions of the Police: A Comparative Study of Attitude Change," *The Journal of Criminal Law, Criminology and Police Science,* vol. 59, no. 2, June 1968, pp. 183–90. See also: A. Coffey, E. Eldefonso, and W. Hartinger, *Human Relations: Law Enforcement in a Changing Community,* Prentice-Hall, Inc., New Jersey, 1976, pp. 200–217. (Attitudes of young children toward police as well as the means of effecting positive change are thoroughly discussed.)

scribes the function of the police. After this discussion, the youngsters are taken outside the school building and allowed to sit in the police car, blow the siren, etc.

When the thirty Negro children were retested two days after being exposed to the Policeman Bill Program, their pictures revealed a somewhat different content. They showed significantly *less hostility* toward the police after their short contact.

This research seems to confirm the learning theorist's assumption that attitudes are learned from one culture and/or subculture. The most significant finding for the practicing policeman, however, is that with little effort, *attitudes learned from one's culture and/or subculture can be changed.*

Changes in attitudes are brought about in various ways. Some involve the change in an *individual situation.* An example of this is a young man's having a new attitude toward police upon his being sworn in as a policeman. Change in *group membership,* too, may cause a shift in attitude. An example of this is the youngster's ceasing to be a gang member and consequently improving his attitude toward police. Other changes in attitude are brought about through the impact of *education.* Broadly speaking, each policeman can do something about effecting attitude changes through education.

SUMMARY

Since the original Juvenile Court Act of 1899, there has been a great deal of discussion and construction of delinquency prevention programs. However, such prevention programs have, in most cases, brought forth disappointing results. Some examples are presented in this chapter showing the negative results of delinquency prevention programs.

The way to solve the delinquency problem is to prevent boys and girls from becoming delinquents in the *first place.* However, society is not solving that problem because the emphasis is not placed on the all important phrase; prevention. In the last analysis, according to the *Task Force Report: Juvenile Delinquency and Youth Crime,* the most promising and also the most important method of dealing with crime is by preventing it, while ameliorating the conditions of life that drive people to commit crimes and that undermine the restricting rules and institutions directed by society against antisocial conduct. The *Task Force Report* goes on to state that it is with young people that prevention efforts are most needed and hold the *greatest promise.*

The chapter further explores some of the prevention programs installed by juvenile probation departments throughout the United States. Within this particular context Bill Ellison, Delinquency Prevention Officer of Santa Clara County Juvenile Probation Department, set forth his own ideas as to what prevention is and how it can be best initiated. Ellison succinctly described prevention as: (1) *the sum total of all activities* that contribute to the adjustment of children and to healthy personalities in children; (2) the attempt to deal with *particular environmental conditions* that are believed to contribute to delinquency; (3) *specific preventive services* (health, recreation, employment, counseling or child guidance, probation, parole, etc.) provided to indiviudal children or groups of children. Basically, Ellison advocates a broad approach to the problem of preventing delinquency. This chapter discusses the five major categories to the broad approach of delinquency prevention.

The emphasis in the broad approach to prevention of juvenile delinquency should be on removal of gaps in our society: the biggest gap, perhaps is our failure to get into the highly maladjusted home before serious problems start to develop.

The latter part of this chapter discusses the need for preventive measures and argues that maximum effort is needed in terms of cost effectiveness, questionable programs, wasted human resources, and segmentation of the youngster. Preventive efforts are a responsibility of the local communities; the federal and state governments can and must provide leadership for a prevention program, but the ultimate responsibility for taking corrective action *must remain at the local level.* A good prevention program requires the cooperative effort of many citizens and organizations.

The two primary phases of a prevention program are the *delinquent*—the youngster who is apprehended for some type of antisocial activity—and the *youth exposed to delinquency.*

The contents of the prevention program should include *primary and secondary prevention;* for example, "primary" prevention activity is that which concentrates on extending and improving existing leisure-time programs or on developing new programs of this sort for children and youth.

Furthermore, it is necessary to *increase public understanding,* through developing programs specifically designed to prevent delinquency (i.e., on programs of special services and schools, jobs for youths, mental health services, assistance programs, voluntary social welfare agencies, and probation services). Finally, youth service bureaus are important agencies in coordinating delinquency prevention programs.

ANNOTATED REFERENCES

Empey, LaMar T., *A Model for the Evaluation of Programs in Juvenile Justice.* Published by National Institute for Juvenile Justice and Delinquency Prevention, Office of Juvenile Justice and Delinquency Prevention, Law Enforcement Assistance Administration, U.S. Department of Justice, Wash. D.C. 1977.

> A short pamphlet discussing the need for an exclusive model to be attached to every problem. The author emphasizes that "collaborations between program and research people is essential if we are to avoid errors of the past. . . ." (i.e., many problems have proven to be ineffective)

Federal Juvenile Delinquency Programs, vol's 1 and 2. Office of Juvenile Justice and

Delinquency Prevention, Law Enforcement Assistance Administration, U.S. Department of Justice, Washington, D.C. 1977.

An analysis and evaluation of delinquency programs throughout the United States.

O'Brien, K.E. and Marcus, Marvin, *Juvenile Diversion: A Selected Bibliography*, National Criminal Justice, Reference Section, Wash, D.C. 1977.

An excellent resource for up-to-date references dealing with diversion programs.

Ohlin, Lloyd E., "A Situational Approach to Delinquency Prevention," *U.S. Department of Health, Education, and Welfare, Social and Rehabilitation Service, Youth Development and Delinquency Prevention Administration*, U.S. Government Printing Office, Washington, D.C., 1970.

In this brief but cogent publication, Ohlin, Professor of Criminology at the Harvard Law School, comments on the broad subject of delinquency prevention strategies. He offers no theory of delinquency causation or examples of delinquency prevention programs—nor is that his intention. However, he does advocate implementing long-term strategies involving a "systematic approach" to both research on causes of delinquency and planning community-based prevention programs.

Shepard, George H., "The Juvenile Specialist in Community Relations," *Police Chief*, International Association of Chiefs of Police, Washington, D.C., January, 1970.

Shepard presents an excellent view of the use of the juvenile specialist in crime prevention activities. He believes that the juvenile specialist is in an excellent position to offer his experience and expertise in preventive programs.

American Correctional Association, *Juvenile Diversion:* A Prospective, College Park, Maryland, 1972.

This is an incisive analysis of diversion programs sponsored by court and local police departments.

Caven, Ruth and Ferdinand, T., *Juvenile Delinquency*, 3rd ed., J. B. Lippincott, Philadelphia, 1975, pp. 423–440.

CHAPTER SIX the family and schools: impact on juvenile delinquency

Before one can consider the question "How does the institution of the family contribute to deviant behavior?" one must first define the social functions of the family as they relate to the child. The family gives to the child, through procreation and socialization, the *status* that affects its relationships with the social system. As well as introducing the child to his culture, the family also acts as a *buffer* between the child and his environment, while at the same time giving him his capacity to cope with the world. The family also *gratifies* the child's need to be loved and wanted by offering him emotional as well as material security.[1] Until the child has attained social and financial independence, his family, unless disrupted, is considered the single most important factor in exercising social control over him.[2] Peer groups and other social institutions may be significant, but a child learns from his parents a complex of norms centering around values and regulating modes of behavior. Therefore, the early socialization process is usually considered one of the key factors in determining the individual's proneness to deviancy.[3]

Most studies reveal that delinquency diminishes with age; the majority of

[1]E. H. Johnson, *Crime, Correction, and Society,* 2nd ed. Dorsey Press, Homewood, Ill., 1970, p. 187.
[2]G. Konolka, *Young Girls: A Portrait of Adolescence,* Prentice-Hall, Englewood Cliffs, N.J. 1976, Chap. 2.
[3]P. H. Hahn, *Community Based Corrections and the Criminal Justice System,* Davis Publishing Co. Inc., 1975, p. 120.

juvenile deviants do not go on to become adult criminals.[4] Matza describes delinquency as a status whose "incumbents intermittently act out a role."[5] All delinquents are capable of conventional activity; no child is totally deviant. The delinquent is an actor who is usually neither compelled to perform misdeeds, nor does he freely choose them. He conforms to some traditions, is unreceptive to others, is a drifter in limbo between convention and crime.[6] No moral conversion or reevaluation of behavior occurs to motivate the majority who conform as they reach adulthood. Instead, other pressures, such as marriage, combine with the nonpurposeful nature of most deviant behavior to pull the delinquent into socially conforming patterns.

THE FAMILY AS A CAUSAL FACTOR IN DELINQUENCY

There are several ways of analyzing the family as a causal factor in delinquency. The *psychologist* views the family variables as they contribute to personality development, while the *sociologist* is concerned with the family's relationship to the total society as the family transmits its class-differentiated patterns to the child. The *psychologist* views the delinquent as a disturbed personality. The *anthropologist* and *sociologist*, in focusing on social class and delinquent gangs, generally ignores the family because the socialization process doesn't usually support delinquent patterns within the family. Few families *teach* criminal behavior to their children. Parents superimpose their values on their children, even delinquent ones.[7] However, in passing along to the child the narrow range of norms accessible to its own particular social group, the family often transmits, through its unspoken evaluations of groups and goals, a conflicting orientation toward the world.[8]

In 1955, Cohen's *Delinquent Boys* marked the turning point in delinquency research by combining the sociological and psychodynamic factors into a single causal process.[9] In undertaking a systematic approach to the understanding of the family's relationship to delinquency, it is necessary to consider many mutually compatible causal factors. The study of delinquency is based on one of two assumptions: that deviant behavior is produced by the variables under study, or that deviant behavior occurs through the ineffectiveness or absence of social controls.

[4]D. Matza, *Delinquency and Drift,* John Wiley and Sons, Inc., New York, 1964, p. 54. See also S. Glueck and E. Glueck, *Unraveling Juvenile Delinquency,* 2nd ed., Commonwealth Fund, New York, 1970; J.M. Martin and J. P. Fitzpatrick, *Delinquent Behavior: A Redefinition of the Problem,* Random House, New York, 1965.
[5]Matza, *Delinquency and Drift,* p. 26.
[6]*Ibid.,* p. 28.
[7]*Ibid.,* p. 47.
[8]Robert K. Merton, *Social Theory and Social Structure,* 2nd ed., Free Press, New York, 1972, p. 242.
[9]Preface to *Journal of Social Issues,* vol, 14, 1958, p.3.

In other words—what makes people commit delinquent acts or what prevents them from committing delinquent acts?[10]

The *personality maladjustment* theory shares the first assumption with Cohen's delinquent subculture and Sutherland's differential association theories; the social disorganization, culture-conflict, and means-and-formulations theories share the second assumption (i.e., lack of social controls.).

FAMILY RELATIONSHIPS AND FAMILY STRUCTURE: ROLE IN DEVIANT BEHAVIOR

Another way of analyzing the family's role in deviant behavior is to separate the institution of the family into two entities, *family relationships*—how members feel about and act toward one another—and *family structure*—the ascriptive variables that place the child into the total society. The quality of family relationships may be a more important variable in the cause of deviant behavior than is family structure.

Most sociological studies deal with the outward structures of the family, its size, its social class, its location, or its cohesiveness. Yet the structural variables, influential as they may be to the child's development, fail to answer the question of why all children in a high delinquency area are not delinquent, or why one child among several in a family avoids delinquent behavior. Delinquency may be a group phenomenom, but deviant behavior is still determined by individual choice, whether tentative or purposeful. First, let us examine the role that the family plays in the causation of delinquency.

What infuence does social class have on an adolescent's behavior? In their study of self-reported delinquency, Nye, Short, and Olson found no relationship between behavior and class.

Sutherland asks if lower-class urban parents unwittingly sanction or encourage delinquency by raising their children with slaps and crude language, and "subculture of violence" which the children in turn transfer to the outside world.[11] Walter Miller, in his classic study, describes lower-class behavior not as being in rejective conflict with middle-class norms but as positively motivated by its own long-established and distinctive traditions of activity. The one-sex peer group street gang is an adolescent variant of the female-based household, which is the predominant lower-class child rearing unit.[12] A unique lower-class value system supports delinquent behavior.[13]

Miller's concept of lower-class values contrasts with Cohen's. Cohen claims that lower-class delinquents share middle-class values and want a better life.[14]

[10]Hahn, *Community Based Corrections*, p. 127.
[11]E. Sutherland, *Principles of Criminology*, 8th ed., J. B. Lippincott Co., Philadelphia, 1966.
[12]W. B. Miller, "Lower-Class Culture as a Generating Milieu of Gang Delinquency," *Journal of Social Issues*. vol. 14, 1958, p. 6.
[13]*Ibid.*, p. 19.
[14]A. Cohen, *Delinquent Boys*, Free Press, Glencoe, Ill., 1955.

Rodman coordinates the contrasting views by claiming that delinquents use "value stretch" to approve both lower and middle-class values, while at the same time they have a lower degree of committment to any value in the range.[15]

How are values related to delinquency proneness? Does the impact of social anomie on the one institution most directly related to the behavior patterns of the individual cast any light on the problem? Applying Durkheim's concept of normlessness to the family, Jaffe uses "family anomie syndrome" to explain the malfunction of individual control in a disorganized family.[16] In a study comparing Negro institutionalized and nondelinquency-prone children, he found a positive correlation between confusion or lack of family consensus regarding values, feelings of powerlessness in the children of these families, and problems of parental identification, with value confusion as the key variable.[17] Children in anomalous families have a problem working out an identification with their parents' values in the face of real-live situations, and delinquent behavior may be an effort to restore some sense of personal power.[18]

Few parents teach their children deviant behavior, yet home conditions seem to play a large role in the child's acquiring of deviant values. Sutherland, who claimed that deviant behavior was learned, discusses five processes by which home conditions are related to delinquency:

1. The child may assimilate by observation within the home an attitude regarding respect or disrespect for the law, as well as the attitudes and behavior patterns of deviancy.

2. Parents determine the geographic location and social class of the home within the community.

3. The parents also make value judgments determining the prestige of other's behavior.

4. A child can withdraw or be driven from an unhappy home, and the resulting isolation increases delinquent associations.

5. The home may be neutral and fail to teach the child inhibitions against delinquency.[19]

The degree of *family tension* plays a more important role in creating criminal tendencies than either the economic or social position of the family. In seemingly cooperative and concerned families, hostility and resentment can be unconsciously

[15]H. Rodman Hyman, "The Lower-Class Value Stretch," *Social Forces,* vol. 42, 1963, pp. 205–15.

[16]E. Jaffe, "Delinquents Proneness and Family Anomie," *Journal of Criminal Law, Criminology, and Police Science,* vol. 54, 1963, pp. 146–54.

[17]*Ibid.,* p. 147.

[18]*Ibid.,* p. 152.

[19]Sutherland, *Principles of Criminology,* p. 225.

transferred to the child.[20] According to Abrahamson, delinquency rates were higher in unbroken and unhappy homes than in broken homes.[21]

The *broken home*, once thought to be the prime villain of delinquency, is considered a key variable by Monahan, who notes the higher rates of broken homes among female than male delinquents.[22] In observing the differential effect of broken homes on girls, Toby noted that adolescent males are weakly controlled in both well-integrated and disorganized families, while girls in well-integrated families get firm supervision, which the disorganized family is unable to provide. Therefore a girl from a broken home is more influenced by criminogenic factors.[23] Even though more children from broken homes, as compared to unbroken homes, become delinquent, the critical concern to some is not the break, per se, but the fact that death, divorce, or desertion connote tension and unsatisfactory emotional relationships. A cohesive family insulates a child against the antisocial influences of peer group and neighborhood. A well-integrated home lessens the attractions of the delinquent gang.[24]

What about that other scapegoat, the *working mother?* Perhaps the key factor for the generally higher rates in this category is that the child of a working mother may be unsupervised for long periods of time. Being thrown on his own resources, he comes in contact with deviant behavior patterns outside the home. The chance for a neglected slum child encountering delinquency is high.[25]

The opportunities available within the family to attain the goals valued by both the family and society is the last and perhaps most important role of family structure. Cohen describes deviant behavior as a response to the strain resulting from ambivalence relative to "institutionalized expectations."[26] Delinquents seek to achieve valued ends and conditions through the cultural means most readily available to them.[26] They may be seeking the success goals of the middle class, or performing the ritualized patterns of lower-class gang warfare. If the success goals are blocked by low social-class standing, illegitimate means are found.[28] Like all parents, slum parents have dreams for their kids—they want them to be "good," to be "successful." Our society demands, even screams "Success"—the American Dream—you can make it to the top of the heap if you just try hard enough. Parents

[20]D. Abrahamson, "Family Tension, Basic Cause of Criminal Behavior," *Journal of Criminal Law and Criminology*, vol. 40, 1949–1950, pp. 330–43.

[21]*Ibid.*

[22]T. Monahan, "Family Status and Delinquency," *The Sociology of Crime and Delinquency*, ed., M. Wolfgang, John Wiley and Sons, Inc., New York, 1962, p. 326.

[23]J. Toby, "The Differential Impact of Family Disorganization, "*The Sociology of Crime and Delinquency,* ed., M. Wolfgang, John Wiley and Sons, Inc., 1970, p. 334.

[24]McCord and McCord, *Origins of Crime,* p. 86.

[25]Sutherland, *Principles of Criminology,* p. 223.

[26]A. Cohen, "The Study of Social Disorganization and Deviant Behavior," *Sociology Today,* 4th ed., Robert Merton, Harper & Row, New York, 1970, p. 467.

[27]Miller, "Lower-Class Culture," p. 17.

[28]R. Cloward and L. Ohlin, *Delinquency and Opportunity,* Free Press, Glencoe, Ill., 1970.

least able to provide access to opportunity for success often project their own ambitions onto their aspirations for their children.[29]

FACTORS REINFORCING CONFORMITY

Are all children in disorganized homes delinquent? The answer, of course, is no, only a small percentage are. Therefore, *family structure* cannot be the determining factor in deviant behavior. What factors in the socialization process reinforce conformity? How have the antideviant norms been successfully internalized by the child, thus enabling him to withstand the deviant pressures of tension and noncohesiveness, lower-class values, and lack of opportunity in the face of rising expectations in an affluent society? If the quality of family relationships plays a key role in preventing delinquency, as even ecologically oriented sociologists such as Shaw and McKay admit,[30] what are the factors of family dynamics that reinforce the adolescent's conformity? *Discipline and affection-rejection* seem to be the critical interactional variables. Each child in a family has a different relationship with his parents; each is both treated, and responds to, the same parent differently.

The longitudinal study of the McCords reveals the effect that parental attitudes have on criminal behavior.[31] Because their 253 male subjects were restudied after they had reached adulthood, and thus their backgrounds were not dependent on memory but on extensive records, there is perhaps an accuracy to their findings that retrospective studies lack. The McCords found that maternal affection was of primary importance in the genesis of crime—if the mother was loving, the son was insulated regardless of the father's attitude. If the mother was rejecting, the son was likely to become criminal, especially if the father was also rejecting.[32] Two rejecting parents produced the highest criminal rate, two loving parents produced the lowest. A passive father produced a conforming son, perhaps because if such a boy identified with his father's withdrawn attitudes, he would be ill-prepared for the extroverted demands of gang membership. A rejecting father, more often than a cruel one, created a criminal son. A neglecting or a passive mother, each a contrast to the active role expected of American mothers, produced a deviant son. A loving mother, no matter how neurotic, usually produced a conforming son. Of all the influences in criminality, the McCords found *maternal affection and role model* to be the most fundamental.[33]

If a child's affectional ties with his parents are disrupted during the socialization process, he will have little opportunity or desire to identify with them and to

---

[29]Merton, *Social Theory*, p. 212.
[30]C. Shaw, and H. McKay, "Are Broken Homes a Causative Factor in Juvenile Delinquency?" *Social Forces*, vol. 10, 1932.
[31]McCord and McCord, *Origins of Crime*, p. 86.
[32]*Ibid.*, p. 115.
[33]*Ibid.*, p. 103.

internalize control of aggressive feelings.[34] The main index of a boy's identification with his parents is how much he consciously regards them as models. Aggressive boys are more likely to have their impulses held in check by external threats than by selfcontrol.[35]

A child's conscience develops from his identification with his parents. Anxiety and conformity to his parents' wishes result from withdrawal of love or physical punishment. The McCords discuss two important variables relating discipline to crime—the withdrawal of love backed by consistent demands tend to decrease crime, while punitiveness combined with *inconsistent demands* increase crime. Erratic discipline varying between laxity and punitiveness have the most harmful effects. Consistency of parental behavior is more important than the methods used; in fact, fourteen severely punished but consistently treated boys showed the lowest rate of delinquency.[36] On the other hand, Ulrich asks if pain be the cause of human aggression.[37] More research on the syndrome of the "battered child" may answer his question.

To sum up the relationship of discipline and love to crime, consistent discipline counteracts the influence of a boy raised by a criminal father.[38] The McCords found that conscious values even in a deviant subculture support the noncriminal values of society; and a consistently disciplined son follows the expressed values rather than the actual behavior of a criminal father, even when the behavior contradicts conscious values.[39] This finding opposes those who, like Merton, maintain that children follow their parents values only if the parents actions reinforce those values.

The family controls the child while he grows, but in the last analysis the child must learn to control himself. Reiss defines personal control as the "ability of the individual to refrain from meeting needs in ways which conflict with the norms of the community."[40] The primary group, or family, is the institution that develops personal controls during the socialization process. This process is self-enforcing and pervasive but never completed or no other controls would be needed. This failure comes from a social lack of agreement on mores, as well as from the fact that few children totally accept parents' teachings.[42] As a child changes his role to that of an adolescent, his rejection of parental mores interrupts the internalization

[34]M. Phillipson, *Understanding Crime and Delinquency:* A Sociology Introduction. Aldine Pub. Co., Chicago, 1974, Chap 2.

[35]*Ibid.,* p. 64.

[36]McCord and McCord, *Origins of Crime,* p. 78.

[37]R. Ulrich, "Pain as a Cause of Aggression", *American Zoologist,* vol. 6, p. 659.

[38]W. McCord and J. McCord, "Effects of Parental Role Model on Criminality," *Journal of Social Issues,* vol. 14, 1958, p. 71.

[39]*Ibid.,* p. 75.

[40]A. Reiss, "Delinquency as a Failure of Personal and Social Controls," *American Sociological Review,* vol. 16, 1951, p. 196.

[41]*Juvenile Division Through Family Counseling,* by National Institute of Law Enforcement and Chamber Justice, Law Enforcement Assistance Administration, Wash, D.C., 1976, p. 120.

The Family as a Causal Factor in Delinquency

process, and creates friction in the family.[42] Indirect controls are associated with the adolescent's affectional identification with the conforming parent, and parental effectiveness decreases as negative feelings toward the parent increases. If conscious and affectional control fail, the family resorts to direct supervision of the adolescent.

The development of a positive self-concept is equally important in enabling an adolescent to withstand deviant pressures.[43] A study of sixth-grade boys judged by their teachers as unlikely to engage in delinquency revealed that they saw themselves as obedient and worthwhile children, confident of their ability to stay out of trouble. Although closely supervised by their parents, they didn't feel unduly restricted. How did these boys acquire their self-esteem? Was it from the social definition of their role by the significant people in their life? Was it a by-product of effective socialization? Was the satisfaction of being a "good" boy sufficient compensation?[44] No one has yet answered this question, but there is little doubt that both self-esteem and self-control play an important part in helping the individual to avoid deviant behavior. And, for whatever reason, the child as a social creature reflects in some measure the attitudes and expectations of those who have nurtured him.

THE SCHOOLS AND THEIR IMPACT ON DELINQUENCY

Many critics advocate a sweeping change of juvenile court laws. This change would, among other things, treat the juvenile delinquent more like an adult in that he would be given full constitutional rights when charged with crime, such as entitlement to bail, trial by jury, and the protection afforded by the requirement that the proof against him be "beyond a reasonable doubt."

It would also restore punitive powers to the juvenile court and end the so-called informal handling of juveniles, with its emphasis on counseling by the juvenile divisions of police and probation departments.

The controversy over the proper function of the juvenile court must be set against the background of some fundamental forces at work in our democracy today which include: (1) the guarantee of *more protection* to individuals who are in apparent conflict with society as evidenced by recent decisions by the now conservative (Nixon's appointments) United States Supreme Court; (2) the guarantee to *minority group citizens* that they can participate more fully in the opportunities afforded by American citizenship, because attempts to realize that guarantee on a local level have often brought large numbers of our citizens into open defiance of local authority; (3) the growing *impersonalization* of our urban society and the con-

---

[42]*Ibid.*, p. 120.
[43]W. Reckless, S. Dinitz, and E. Murray, "Self Concept as an Insulator against Delinquency," *American Sociological Review*, vol. 21, 1956, p. 744.
[44]*Ibid.*, p. 746.

sequent de-emphasis of personal social responsibility; and, (4) the need to continu-ally *improve the quality of police personnel* to meet the challenge of more sophisticated equipment and more complex situations.

These are only a few of the dynamic trends in our democratic society today. Their significance is that they are forcing upon us profound changes in police administration, law enforcement, and the techniques of criminal prosecution. These changes cannot help but affect our attitudes on juvenile delinquency. In-deed, much of the dialogue about the efficacy of juvenile courts has its roots in the changes of modern society.

It is within this broad framework of the role of the juvenile court and other agencies within our developing society that we should consider an approach to the disciplinary and juvenile delinquency problems in our schools. These problems of the schools cannot be isolated from the disciplinary and juvenile delinquency prob-lems of the community. If one considers a juvenile delinquent from the aspect of what governmental and private agencies affect his life, that the schools become merely one of a number of agencies that influence the child. The juvenile division of the police department, the juvenile court and its "good right arm," the juvenile division of the probation department, the local welfare department, and perhaps private casework agencies and churches, are among those groups that might share "jurisdiction" over the juvenile delinquent.

In formulating an approach to the disciplinary and juvenile delinquency prob-lems in the schools, it is important to define the role of the schools as one of the several agencies influencing the child. It is necessary to ascertain what kind of impact the schools could have on the juvenile delinquent. The schools are, "as is clearly recognized," in a strategic position to provide leadership in meeting the problem of deviant behavior[45]. . . .

Violence In Schools

On February 25, 1977, Senator Birch Bayh (Democrat, Indiana), Chairman of the Senate Sub-committee on Juvenile Delinquency, released a report on critical prob-lems in American education. The report estimated that six million dollars is spent each year as a result of vandalism in the schools—more money than was spent for textbooks in 1972 and enough to hire fifty thousand more teachers! The report further stated that seventy thousand serious physical assaults on teachers occurs annually and the number of assaults on students are in the hundred thousands.

Speaking before the National Education Association on violence in schools, Senator Bayh stated: "While certainly not every school in the country is faced with serious crime problems, it is clear that for a growing number of students and teachers, the primary task is no longer education but self-preservation. . . ."

The sub-committee report, a summation of three years of hearings based on a nationwide survey of 757 school systems, enrolling about one-half of the public

[45]*California Youth Authority Quarterly,* Winter, 1977, Comment by Governor Jerry Brown.

elementary and secondary school students in the nation, revealed that the number of assaults increased fifty-eight percent in 1970 to 1974. Also, sex offenses were up sixty-two percent, drug related crimes rose eighty-one percent, and robbery was up one hundred seventy percent—all school related!

Bayh's sub-committee ascertained that the problem of school violence was not confined to urban areas. Problems of school violence occur in small towns and affluent communities, as well as in large cities. "It is also time to stop pointing accusatory fingers at our educational system as being solely responsible for these problems," Senator Bayh said. "Our schools are only one facet of a society that has had juvenile arrests increase by 245 percent over the last decade. . . . The recommendations of Bayh's sub-committee were:

1. Alternative schools to provide academic and educational attention for frustrated and resentful students.

2. Optional education programs to help cut truancy rates. "Our studies showed that a significant number of incidents of violence and vandalism can be traced to young school-aged intruders who are out of school, out of hope and too often out for revenge against a system they feel has failed them," Bayh said.

3. Alternatives to suspension from school for lesser rule violations such as truancy or smoking. Bayh mentioned such alternatives as cool-off rooms, behavior contracts and additional counseling strategies.

4. Prevention of overcrowding in the classroom. Bayh's final comment was: "Classrooms which are overcrowded result in poor relationships between students and teachers, a poor education for students and poor discipline for everyone. Such alienation, frustration and resentment at school are classic ingredients for violence and vandalism."

Basic Responsibility: Schools

The basic responsibility of the schools now is to educate the children of the community. The schools generally see their function as preparing a child to be a responsible, productive citizen. A private school has the luxury of deciding what kind of children it will accept in its classrooms; the public school does not. The public school, because of state compulsory attendance laws, must accept every child for whom the state has made provision. In many states, the public schools must accept certain physically and mentally handicapped children. Any child who comes within the terms of the compulsory school attendance laws has a right to attend the public school, and the public school has a duty to admit him to classes.

Does this duty of the schools mean, however, that the schools must admit or keep in school children whose conduct is inconsistent with the learning atmosphere so necessary in the classroom? The answer obviously is no. But the schools have the burden to show that the conduct of every child kept out of the classroom to which he normally would be assigned is in fact inimical to the purpose of education.

Showing that a child's conduct in school is inimical to the purpose of education depends on resolution of the question "What is the impact of disciplinary and juvenile delinquency problems on the schools?"

A child whose conduct makes him a disciplinary problem hurts himself. If he cannot be corrected, his own chances for a meaningful education are seriously impaired. He can hardly benefit from an intellectual experience when his intellect is not focused on the main purposes for his presence in school.

More regretfully, however, his conduct also intereferes with the rights of others in a most serious way. By creating disturbances in the classroom, or other places, which tend to injure the good order and discipline of the school, he distracts others from the main purposes of education. Moreover, public monies are diverted from educational programs and facilities to such juvenile delinquent-induced expenditures as repair of damage caused by vandalism and disproportionate attention from counselors and teachers.

Most state constitutions have given the schools jurisdiction over children for purposes of education. It is important to observe, however, that total jurisdiction over children was not given to educators. The schools have children only to educate them. It would seem that if a child's conduct is such that education will suffer if he remains in the classroom, the schools best sanction is the removal of that child from school. But, to what extent should such a child be removed? Should he be expelled? Suspended? Transferred to a different school? Given home tutor services? In other words, what is the extent of the school's duty to educate a child who has shown that he cannot get along in the normal kind of classroom environment?

There would seem to be no question that the schools owe their primary solicitude to the group. That is, as long as the classroom theory of teaching is with us, schools will have to protect the classroom environment and do everything they can to insure that the classroom group can function effectively. The schools will remove irritants to the efficient working of the classroom.

It is this recognition by school people that the rights of the majority group are paramount that sometimes causes problems with other agencies that are called into a situation because of the nature of a child's misconduct. These agencies, such as the juvenile court and its probation department, focus primarily on an individual child who has become delinquent, and they address themselves to the problem of rehabilitating that child. In other words, the schools emphasis is on the group; the other agencies' emphasis is on the individual child.

The school can share actively this concern for rehabilitation only to the extent that it has programs to deal with the problem. If the child has participated in all of the rehabilitative programs that the schools can offer an errant pupil, and he still cannot be tolerated, the schools will remove him from the school environment.

This removal from school, whether through suspension or expulsion, makes the effort to rehabilitate the child considerably more difficult. It is definitely a source of irritation between other agencies and the schools.

The ultimate sanction of the schools for misconduct is removing the offending pupil from the classroom environment by suspension or expulsion. There are various forms of punishment that teachers and principals impose on misbehaving pupils short of this ultimate sanction. Most students have probably experienced such minor punishment for misconduct, which concerns the schools only.

The real question is whether expulsion for misconduct, which is more the concern of society than of the schools, solves any problems. It appears to be an answer for the schools because it removes a child whom the schools are not equipped to handle. But, from the standpoint of society, or the child himself, suspension or expulsion from the school resolves nothing. While such suspension or expulsion might be a public exorcism, dramatically announcing that responsibility for the child has been shifted from the schools to the rest of society, the problem of the expelled child meeting life in our society on some kind of socially acceptable terms is certainly not solved. Society demands that somebody or some agency take responsibility for the school "kickout," and many citizens think that schools are best equipped for this task. The line of demarcation between a school "dropout" and a "kickout" is often disregarded because the basic problem of a child on the streets is the same.

THE EDUCATIONAL SYSTEM AND CRIME

Most persons who have studied the problem of delinquency agree that commitment to illegitimate rather then legitimate patterns of behavior results from a multitude of conditions and forces: defective families, overcrowded housing, adult criminal influences, access to automobiles, poverty and lack of economic opportunity, decline of influence of the church, and many others. Most persons also agree that anything approaching complete elimination of delinquency rests on major social changes at each of these points.[46]

At the same time, available evidence suggests strongly that delinquent commitments result in part from adverse or negative school experiences of some youths, and, further, that there are fundamental defects within the educational system, especially as it touches lower-income youths, that actively contribute to these negative experiences, thereby increasing rather than decreasing the chances that some youths will chose the illegitimate alternative. Despite the fact that the schools are meant to be the major agency for promoting progress along legitimate

[46]*Task Force Report: Juvenile Delinquency and Youth Crime*, U.S. Government Printing Office, Washington, D.C., P. 222.

avenues to adulthood, prevailing conditions in education deter such progress for some youth and make the delinquent alternative more attractive.[47]

Negley Teeters of Temple University said,

> *I'm so sick of hearing that the broken home is the cause of delinquency, or the motion picture, or our speed-up life. The fact is we've got to live with our culture. And if you ask me, the crux of our delinquency is not the parents; it's the schools. Our schools are filled with misfits, kids who don't belong. Our education is geared for all our kids and that's the heart of our problem. We need some kind of program for the kids who don't fit into our school picture, who are not interested in middle-class norms or in becoming a lawyer some day.*[48]

William Kvaraceus of Boston University said, "Our schools face the imminent danger of becoming the most expensive irrelevancy of the twentieth century."[49]

The only alternative offered to traditional education is the vocational high school. These schools exist in many large cities, but on the whole they are for boys and girls with fairly good academic qualifications, but there are some exceptions. A few—very few—of the big cities have trade programs which take youngsters of lower-than-average ability and attempt to instruct them in paperhanging or upholstery or needlework. But such programs touch the merest fraction of school enrollments. In the country at large, there is little place in our system for the boy or girl with few or no academic qualifications.

According to the American dream, everybody must want to be—and be able to be—a first-class citizen; anything less is Un-American. Consequently, a largely uniform school system has been geared to this ideal. It is book-centered and college-oriented, which is fine for those going on to higher education, but it leaves no alternatives for the child with a slightly lower than average I.Q.[50]

The results of this rigid approach are crushing. *Almost one million youngsters a year drop out of high school.* Many just sweat it out, doing little or nothing, until the legal age of leaving (sixteen in some states, seventeen in others). Some are embittered, frustrated and, worse, functionally illiterate. In the name of democracy, and with high humanitarian purpose, we have shortchanged a large segment of our juvenile population; we have not given them the kind of education that would have been right for them.

Realizing that something was wrong and yet unable to lower the legal age at which children might leave school, the education authorities have tried to fill the gap with substitutes—counselors, phychologists, playgrounds, "practical"

---

[47]*Ibid.*, p. 173.
[48]H. E. Burnes and Negley Teeters, *New Horizons in Criminology,* 5th ed. Prentice-Hall Inc., Englewood Cliffs, N.J., 1971, p. 172.
[49]*Ibid.*, p. 173.
[50]*Ibid.*, p. 174.

courses, and extracurricular activities. Some of these have been helpful, but they have not reached the heart of the problem. For example, counselors are worthwhile, but there are only eleven thousand counselors for nine million high school students.[51] One can see how little individual help can be given, especially when there are no adequate educational alternatives for the counselors to recommend anyway.

Kvaraceus estimates that only about 35 percent of our youth have the ability to profit from a traditional college preparatory curriculum, and that the academically untalented youngsters, the "reluctant learner" as some educators like to call him, is unprovided for. This point of view was confirmed by a recent National Education Association study of the teachers themselves. After listing "overlarge classes" as their number one problem, the teachers designated the "reluctant learner" as problem number two. Forty-five percent of the teachers urged that some provision be made outside the regular classroom for nonlearners, and almost half the principals endorsed this suggestion.[52]

Curriculum is irrelevant to latter life. The curriculum for the teen-ager would be more realistic if it used the neighborhood as a classroom, instead of textbooks, for the subject known as social studies. Actually, the neighborhood provides a better learning situation for many things that are beyond the definition of social studies.[53]

Stullken's comments about the application and realization of the overall philosophy of education are extremely important. He said that treatment of every child according to his own needs would go a long way to reduce not only juvenile delinquency, but adult crime as well. For example, research has indicated that schools without facilities to help individual children contribute the largest percentage of referrals to juvenile court. *School truancy* is the first symptom of the unadjusted school child. The majority of these school truants in our juvenile courts are found to be slow learners. With the rigid curriculum and without special help, such children are unsuccessful in meeting the requirements of the normal curriculum; they become frustrated, hostile, and, quite naturally, begin to express themselves through delinquent behavior. A child who is rejected in his school group, and who experiences school failure, easily develops patterns of delinquency. A rejection of school learning means rejection of authority and community standards.[54] One really doesn't need to stretch his imagination to see that this type of situation does, in fact, foster crime, both juvenile and adult. Rigid schools and rigid curriculums increase rather than lower juvenile delinquency.

It hardly need be said that this is a period of extremely rapid change in noneducational areas of American life. Technological and economic shifts have

[51]*Ibid.*, p. 175.
[52]*Ibid.*, p. 176.
[53]A. H. Rice, "Commission Blames Schools for High Juvenile Delinquency Rate," *Nations Schools*, vol. 80, December, 1967, p. 6.
[54]S. Glueck and E. Glueck, *The Problem of Delinquency*, Houghton Mifflin Company, Boston, 1959, p. 162.

resulted in a changed occupational structure and new manpower demands. Moreover, past decades have seen major shifts in the American population. More and more families have moved off the farm, many of them resettling in metropolitian areas. Expansion has not been uniform within those areas, however, as urban fringes have experienced rapid growth, while central cities have remained stable in size or have actually declined. Nor has the distribution of economic and racial groups within large cities remained stable. Rather, central cities have increasingly come to be made up of lower income and nonwhite families, at the same time that suburbs have remained or become predominantly white and middle-class. Accompanying these economic, social, and population changes has been a reawakening of the demand for equal educational and economic opportunity.[55]

These changes, as well as others, have combined to place new demands on the educational system and have called for major adaptations by the public schools. It is our contention that, although there is a stir in the air, the schools and the public that supports them, have largely failed to respond, with the result that there are serious gaps between the educational system and other parts of the society.[56]

One specific way the schools have unconsciously augmented feelings of alienation among lower-income and nonwhite pupils, especially in large cities is by introducing children to the world of reading and books through *readers that hold up as an exclusive model a cultural pattern of the white middle-class suburban family.* The child knows in his heart that the school gives the highest prestige value to books, and yet everything that is familiar to him is excluded from the ways of life presented in the books that the schools provide.[57]

In short, current textbooks and other curriculum materials are largely *irrelevant to the experiences, language, style, skills, and orientation of lower-class children,* especially in the urban slums. The language, the pictures, the content of lessons—all are from a world many steps removed from the disadvantaged child. As Klineberg has remarked, reading materials are generally oriented to the middle-class suburbs where "life in general is fun, filled almost exclusively with friendly smiling people including gentle and understanding parents, doting grandparents, generous and cooperative neighbors, even warm-hearted strangers."[58]

A program of community action will do much; a revision of school procedures will do more. Courses of study must be revised radically; classes must be reduced in size; much greater freedom of curriculum adjustment must be taken by supervisors and teachers; diagnostic and remedial teaching must be stressed; active, creative, and constructive units of work must find fuller application. "No child must be a failure" must become our slogan, or at least our ideal in the schools. We must discover, in each child's case, that area in which he and she can be successful and build upon it. Socialized programs and individual techniques of instruction

[55]*Task Force Report,* p. 226.
[56]*Ibid.,* p. 226.
[57]J. Niemeyer, "Some Guidelines to Desirable Elementary School Reorganization," *Task Force Report,* p. 237.
[58]O. Klineberg, "Life is Fun in a Smiling, Fair-Skinned World," *Task Report,* p. 237.

The Schools and Their Impact on Delinquency   141

must be extended. We must eliminate any regimentation of children that still obtains in our schools, any uniformity of objectives and of standards of judging children, any attempt to hammer all out in the same mold and to measure all by the same preconceived standards. Character-building programs must be extended, but must not be formalized through artifical devices or be reduced to the glib vocalizations of words relating to good sentiments and ideas. Nor should they be reduced to formal, set lessons. The program should be concrete and practical and should be integrated with the entire life of the child in school and out of school.[59]

SUMMARY

Chapter 7 discusses the impact of the institution of the family and schools on deviant behavior. The family gives to the child, through propagation and socialization, the status or nonstatus that affects his relationships with the social system. The family also acts as a *buffer* between the child and his environment, while at the same time giving him his capacity to cope with the world. Finally, the family *gratifies* the child's need to be loved and wanted by offering him emotional as well as material security.

There are various ways of analyzing a family as a causal factor in delinquency. Several views are presented by psychologists and sociologists. The psychologist views the family variables as they contribute to the personality development, while the sociologist is concerned with the family's relationship to the total society as it transmits its class-differentiated patterns to the child.

The turning point in delinquency research was the study presented in 1955 by Cohen and his subsequent book entitled *Delinquent Boys*. Cohen combined the sociological and psychological factors into a single causal process. In undertaking a systematic approach to the understanding of the family's relationship to delinquency, Cohen pointed out the necessity to consider many mutually compatible causal factors.

The influence of social class on adolescent behavior was studied by Nye, Short, and Olson who found that there is no relationship between behavior and class. However, Sutherland, a noted author and sociologist, disagrees and states that lower-class urban parents unwittingly sanction or encourage delinquency by raising their children with slaps and crude language, a "sub-culture of violence" that children in turn transfer to the outside world.

The impact of family on juvenile delinquency is presented by Sutherland, who claims that deviant behavior is learned. He discusses the process by which conditions are related to delinquency: (1) the child may assimilate by observation within the home an attitude regarding respect or disrespect for the law, as well as the attitudes and behavior patterns of deviancy; (2) parents determine the geographical location and social class of the home within the community; (3) parents also make

[59]Glueck and Glueck, *Problem of Delinquency*, p. 110.

value judgments concerning the prestige of the behavior of others; (4) a child can withdraw or be driven from an unhappy home, and the resulting isolation increases delinquent associations; and (5) the home may be neutral and fail to teach the child inhibitions against delinquency.

The degree of family tension, broken homes, working mothers, and the opportunities available within the family to attain goals valuable to both the family and society also have a relationship to juvenile delinquency.

The schools impact on delinquency is an extremely controversial topic. It is clearly recognized that the schools are in a strategic position to provide leadership in meeting the problems of deviant behavior. The position of the schools is extremely important because they have contact with virtually every child in the community at an early point in his development. The responsibilities of the school and the manner in which it handles such responsibilities are extremely important.

Most who have studied the problems of schools, and their impact on juvenile delinquency, agree that delinquency results in part from the adverse or negative experiences of some youth. Furthermore, there are fundamental defects within the educational system, especially as it touches lower-income youths, that actively contribute to these negative experiences and thereby increase rather than decrease the chances that some youths will choose illegitimate alternatives. The prevailing conditions in education stimulate progress for some youngsters, yet make the delinquent alternative more attractive for others. For example, research has indicated that schools without facilities to help individual children contribute the largest percentage of referrals to the juvenile courts. *School truancy* is the first symptom of the unadjusted school child; the majority of school truants in juvenile courts are found to be slow-learners. With a rigid curriculum and without personalized help, some children are not successful in meeting the requirements of the normal curriculum and become frustrated and hostile. Quite naturally they begin to express themselves in delinquent behavior. A child, therefore, who is rejected in his school group and who experiences school failure, easily develops patterns of delinquency. A rejection of school learning means a rejection of authority and community standards.

ANNOTATED REFERENCES

Glueck, Sheldon and Glueck, Eleanor, *Unraveling Juvenile Delinquency,* 2nd ed., Commonwealth Fund, New York, 1976.

> The Gluecks call attention to the fact that two-thirds of the fathers of delinquents, as compared with only one-third of the fathers of nondelinquents, have a history of criminality. The Gluecks also investigate the case of mothers who have a history of criminality. This study took a number of years and involved over five hundred delinquent and nondelinquent children.

Shulman, Harry M. *Juvenile Delinquency in American Society*, Harper & Row, New York, 1961.

> This book (though dated, still holds true) examines the percentage of juveniles involved in delinquent activities who come from broken homes. Shulman also examines the peer groups with which such juveniles identify. These peer groups are vital in guiding and directing behavior of the juvenile.

Konopka, G., *Young Girls: A Portrait of Adolescence*, Prentice-Hall, Inc., Englewood Cliffs, N.J., 1976.

> A study of 920 girls: opinions on schools, adults, sexuality, sociopolitical concerns, friends, and clubs. Offers new insight about teenage girls.

Goush, A. and Geilli, M.A., "The Unruly Child and The Law: Toward a Focus on The Family," *Juvenile Justice*, v. 23, No. 3; pp. 9–12. Nov. 1972.

> This article examines the juvenile court system with suggestions for a new approach on handling children, . . . and providing counseling for the child's family.

Cavan, Ruth S., 3rd ed. *Readings in Juvenile Delinquency*, J. B. Lippincott, Co., Philadelphia, 1975.

> An Anthology that supplements information covered in Chapter 6.

Murray, C., *Learning Disabilities and Juvenile Delinquency–Current Theory and Knowledge*. National Institute of Juvenile Justice and Delinquency Prevention, Washington, D.C. 1976.

> Concise study of "Learning Disabilities" as a noncitizen in the causing of getting-out behavior.

CHAPTER SEVEN the history, philosophy, and function of the juvenile court

It is difficult to imagine that the first juvenile court statute is now over seventy years old. The first juvenile court statute made inevitable the collaborative relationship of law and social work with a definite intention of helping those youngsters whose antisocial behavior were symptoms of deeper internal problems. This close association between law and social work was spelled out in the formulation of the juvenile court concept as pronounced in 1899 by the Chicago Bar Association, which sponsored the act creating the juvenile court system. The association summed up the purposes of the new law:

> The fundamental idea of the juvenile court law is that the state must step in and exercise guardianship over a child found under such adverse social or individual conditions as to develop crime . . . It proposes a plan whereby he may be treated, not as a criminal, or legally charged with crime, but as a ward of the state, to receive practically the care, trust, and discipline that are accorded the neglected and dependent child, and which, as the Act states; shall approximate as nearly as may be that which should be given by its parents.[1]

[1]R. Pound, "The Juvenile Court and the Law," *National Probation Parole Association Yearbook,* 1944, vol.1 no. 13.

As indicated by this statement, the juvenile offender is viewed as a youngster in need of the court's protection, not punishment. The court, therefore, is defined as the nonpunitive parent.

Like all public institutions and services in our rapidly changing democratic society, the juvenile court, as a system, as an agency of government, and as a social service, is undergoing change to meet the diverse needs of the variety of courts, communities, and individuals that it exists to serve. The juvenile court has become the primary judicial agency for dealing with juvenile criminology, the single most pressing and threatening aspect of the crime problem in the United States. In order to realize the impact of youthful crime on the juvenile court system of today, one need refer only to the statistical information presented in previous chapters. It is apparent that responsibility for meeting the problems of crime rests more heavily on this judicial institution.

PHILOSOPHY

The juvenile court system was founded by society on the basic assumption—and a radical assumption if the tenets of the centuries that preceded it are considered—that there was one factor, the factor of age, of youth alone, which overcame the previously assumed notion of complete and total responsibility of the "normal" child for all his acts. This assumption of partial responsibility was predicated on the understanding that the child's immaturity and the conditions inherent in his immature state made it impossible for him to act as a responsible adult. As soon as this assumption was established, there followed the need for some instrument or instruments that could determine the nature and the extent of the maturity or immaturity present in the child. Logically, this led to the demand that each child be looked upon as an individual and that all his assets and liabilities be evaluated before the extent of his maturity—and, hence, responsibility—was determined. Thus, the principle of *mens rea* (criminal intent) was brought into focus and related to the juvenile court concept. The principle of *mens rea* was adapted from Roman Law, which mitigated or removed criminal responsibility of children depending on their age:

> *Under this doctrine a child of seven is held to be incapable of having the criminal intent which is a necessary ingredient of the crime; between seven and fourteen, he is deemed presumptively incapable and after fouteen he is deemed presumptively capable. Even within this doctrine, shocking sentences were meted out as late as the 19th century which contributed to a development of humanitarian movement for greater protection of the child. Blackstone refers to the hanging of an eight-year-old boy, a ten-year-old boy, and burning of a girl of thirteen in England; and similar brutalities were all too common in this country. However, the concept of curtailed criminal responsiblility for children, resting upon the child's presumed*

incapacity to form the necessary criminal intent remained a living force in the law.[2]

An additional legal antecedent was the doctrine of *parens patriae* (the state as the guardian of its ward the child) by which the state intervenes in the family and can alter or terminate parental rights. This doctrine developed out of appeals for justice in behalf of neglected and dependent children of the king's chancellor in feudal England. Since the common law courts, restricted to awards of damages as remedies, provided no adequate solutions in the courts of law for such emerging problems of human relations, the king's chancellor evolved a system of hearings in hardship cases. These hearings became known as chancellery hearings; later, with more precedents, as courts or equity in contrast to the courts of law. The doctrine of *parens patriae* therefore is technically a doctrine of equity, and it is often for this reason that juvenile courts have been held to be noncriminal, similar to civil courts of equity, with jurisdiction extended through the delinquent as well as the dependent and neglected child. This is more than a technical distinction since one's constitutional rights in criminal proceedings differ markedly from those in equitable proceedings.

The juvenile court emerged from the conflux of many different practices and thoughts, many of which were centuries old, others of which were relatively recent responses to our rapidly changing society and social conditions.

Originally, the concept of the juvenile court was derived from the English courts, which had differential treatment for children. The best-known source of the ideal of the juvenile court is summed up in the Latin phrase, *parens patriae*. The English concept of the king in the role of parent was the basis of the *parens patriae* theory accepted in the United States as the foundation of the juvenile court.

The essential philosophy, then, of the juvenile court, and of other specialized courts handling juvenile cases, has been referred to as "individualized justice." This in essence means that the court "recognizes the individuality of a child and adapts its orders accordingly"; that it is a "legal tribunal where law and science, especially the science of medicine, and those sciences that deal with human behavior, such as biology, sociology, and psychology, work side by side"; and that its purpose is remedial and, to a degree, preventive, rather than punitive.[3]

DEVELOPMENT OF THE JUVENILE COURT IN THE UNITED STATES

When the English legal system was transplanted to the United States, the chancery court's activities were extended to include protection of minors in danger of per-

[2]H. W. Sloane, "The Juvenile Court: An Uneasy Partnership of Law and Social Work,"*Journal of Family Law*, vol. 5, no. 2, Fall 1965, pp. 171–72. See also *The Law and Tactics in Juvenile Cases*, 2nd ed., The National Juvenile Law Center, St. Louis Mo., 1974.
[3]Pound, "The Juvenile Court and the Law," *op. cit.*, p. 14.

sonal as well as property injury, and it is because of this inheritance of the chancery court's protective powers that the juvenile court in the United States has most commonly been justified against constitutional attack.

The chancery court however, dealt only with the neglected and dependent children, not with children accused of criminal law violations. Thus the historical basis of the present-day juvenile court's delinquency jurisdiction has been a matter of some dispute. Such jurisdiction, however, seems to have had its logical justification in the recognition of the failure of the older courts to prevent crime and in the ongoing experimentation in judicial methods and procedures. Another rationale for the present-day juvenile court's delinquency jurisdiction lies in the social sciences. The social sciences were regarded as capable of identifying methods of appropriate treatment for potentially criminal youths. An emphasis upon sociological jurisprudence became a major force in the juvenile court. Social resources were seen as an integral part of the judicial process.

The social conditions prevailing in the nineteenth century played an important role in intensifying the movement for reform of the treatment of children. Industrialization and immigration drove people into cities by the thousands causing overcrowding, disruption of family life, increasing vice and crime, and other destructive factors characteristic of rapid urbanization. Because of these factors, delinquency—and those activities associated with delinquency such as incorrigible behavior, truancy, formation of gangs, curfew violations, malicious mischief—rose rapidly, and society became duly concerned with its youth. There was a rising concern, throughout the nineteenth century, about the official treatment of children; there was a growth of what has been called the spirit of social justice. The ascendant social sciences, along with their optimistic claims to diagnosis and treatment of the problems underlying deviant behavior, seemed to provide the ideal tool for treating wayward children humanely and alleviating their antisocial conduct.

The specialized juvenile court owes its origin to the humanitarian impulse and initiative of many lawyers, social workers, ministers, and others who had become increasingly troubled by the treatment of children under the criminal law and whose efforts to correct this condition resulted in the establishment of the world's first juvenile court in 1899, in Cook County, Illinois.

The juvenile court grew out of a long series of efforts to mitigate the harshness of the common law toward children. Reform efforts sought to modify the application of criminal court procedures and penalties to children, and to avoid mixing children with adult offenders in jails and prisons. Separation of children from adults was carried into the court process in limited form as early as 1861 in Chicago; and in 1869, a Massachusetts law provided for the presence of an agent or officer of the State Board of Charity in all criminal proceedings against children under sixteen to "protect their interests." In 1877, another Masssachusetts law provided for "Sessions for Juvenile Offenders" where separate records and dockets were kept. In 1877, a New York law supported by the Society for the Prevention of Cruelty to Children in the city of New York, prohibited mixing of juveniles with adults in prisons or places of confinement. Furthermore, the Boards of Children's Guardians Law of Indiana, passed in 1891, and amended in 1893, authorized the Board of Children's Guardians to file a petition in the circuit court if it had probable cause to believe that a child under fifteen years of age was dependent, neglected, truant, incorrigible, or delinquent. If the court judged the petition to be true, the child could be committed to the custody and control of the Board of Children's Guardians until he became of age.[4]

This was an interesting and progressive rule toward the improvement of juvenile justice. Very clearly, it expresses a belief that certain young children are in need of protection of the state, rather than punishment for their offenses, at least before a certain age of responsibility.

The Juvenile Court was established essentially as a response to social problems—society's concern over the callous, indifferent treatment of children accused of criminal activity. The first court especially for children was authorized by the Illinois legislature in 1899; within twenty-five years, every state but two had authorized juvenile courts.[5]

The rapid spread of the juvenile court was in effect a response of society to widespread conditions which created special difficulties for children. Mass immigration and rapid urbanization which followed industralization produced slums where families were crowded into unsavory housing. On the streets children were exposed to vice and crime. The strong paternalism that had marked American and European family life gave way to disruption and loss of control over children. The juvenile court came to be seen as an effort to produce social justice by offsetting some of these conditions.

> *The Juvenile Court, then, was born in an aura of reform, and a spirit with amazing speed. The conception of the delinquent as a "wayward child" further specifically came to light in April 1899, when Illinois legislature passed the Juvenile Court Act, creating the first statewide court especially for children. It did not create a new court; it did not include most of the features which have since come to distinguish the Juvenile Court. The original Act and the amendments to it that shortly followed brought together under one jurisdiction cases of dependency, neglect, and delinquency—the less comprehending incorrigibles and children threatened by immoral associations as well as criminal law breakers. Hearings were to be informal and nonpublic, records confidential, children detained apart from adults, a probation staff appointed. In short, children were not to be treated as criminals nor dealt with by the process used for criminals.*

[4]C. E. Reasons, "Guilt: Procedural Change and Substantive Effect," *Crime and Delinquency*, vol. 16, no. 2, 1970, p. 164.

[5]D.C. Gibbons, *Delinquent Behavior*, 2nd ed., Prentice-Hall, Inc., Englewood, N. J. 1976. Chapter 1.

A new vocabulary symbolized the aura: Petition instead of complaint, summons instead of warrant, initial hearing instead of arraignment, finding of involvement instead of conviction, disposition instead of sentence. The physical surroundings were important too: they should seem less imposing than a court room, with the judge at a desk or table instead of behind the bench, fatherly and sympathetic while still authoritative and sovereign. The goals were to investigate, diagnose, and prescribe treatment, not to adjudicate guilt or fix blame. The individual's background was more important than the facts of the given incident, specific conduct relevant more as a symptomatic of a need for the court to bring its help and powers to bear and then as a prerequisite to emphasize jurisdiction. Lawyers were unnecessary—adversary tactics were out of place, for the mutual aim of all was not to contest or object but to determine the treatment plan best for the child. The plan was to be devised by the increasingly popular psychologists and psychiatrists; delinquency was thought of almost as a disease, to be diagnosed by specialists and the patient timely but firmly diagnosed. [6]

Although the Illinois law set up a statewide system with juvenile courts; actually only Cook County initially had both the population and facilities to operate a court. The law applied to children under the age of sixteen, and restricted the definition of a delinquent child to a person under the age who violated any law of the state, or city, or village ordinance. At least one judge from the circuit court was to be designated to hear juvenile cases in a special court room, labeled the Juvenile Court Room. The act also eliminated arrests of children by warrant, the use of indictment, and any other forms of criminal procedure. It provided separate records and informal procedures.

JOHN AUGUSTUS: THE FIRST PROBATION OFFICER

Not so long ago, you could become a lawyer by "reading law" in an attorney's office, or you could teach in a country school with no more than a grade-school education. You could even start out as a preacher if you "heard the call" and answered it. Probation and parole had a similar early history dating back to the mid-nineteenth century. They were, to a large extent, dedicated services without pay.

The first of these devoted probation volunteers was John Augustus, a Boston shoemaker, who in 1841, on an impulse of mercy, bailed out a common drunkard and, with the judge's permission, took the man home with him and, indeed,

---

[6]*Task Force Report: Juvenile Delinquency and Crime,* The President's Commission on Law Enforcement and Administration of Justice, U.S. Government Printing Office, Washington D. C., 1967, p. 3.

reformed him. The court was so impressed with this reformation that more and more cases—juveniles and adults under suspended sentence—were turned over to Augustus. His home was filled to overflowing with those whom he sheltered until they could find places in the outside world. He finally had to give up his shoe business and become a full time probation officer.

Judge Peter Thatcher worked quite closely with John Augustus in the Boston Municipal Court during his term of office, and if John Augustus can be referrred to as "The Father of American Probation," Judge Peter Thatcher is frequently referred to as "The First Juvenile Court Judge."

The pioneer work of John Augustus spread gradually at first, largely among adults, and then at the turn of the century a giant step was taken with the establishment of the first juvenile court in Chicago. Laws providing for separate courts and informal handling of children spread rapidly. A demand arose for probation officers to supervise children and work with their parents. Thus, over 130 years ago, came the beginnings of volunteer service in probation and the making of the first probation and parole officers.

SPECIAL ACTS SIGNIFICANT TO THE DEVELOPMENT OF THE JUVENILE COURT

As social and medical knowledge advanced, the emphasis shifted from concern with the symptoms of the study of causes. Lying, stealing, truancy, retractory behavior, and sex offenses—the principle manifestations of delinquency—were placed in "test tubes" and studied.

Thus, the clinical approach to juvenile delinquency was initiated by Dr. William Healy, in a laboratory established for the Chicago Juvenile Court in 1909. Dr. Healy suggested that a combination of factors was associated with delinquency and that the combination varied with individual cases. Subsequently, child guidance clinics were organized in all the large cities of the United States. They served as diagnostic and consultative centers for both individuals and courts. This philosophy has spread and influenced the development of clinics associated with hospitals and universities, adult education centers, and various welfare agencies. To this day, the clinical approach is still expanding.

The passage of the Social Security Act in 1935, stimulated the rapid development of diagnostic and consultative centers throughout the states. Of particular significance in relation to juvenile delinquency were the grants authorized under this act to assist public welfare agencies in establishing, extending, and strengthening public welfare services for children, including those who were in danger of becoming delinquent.

Gradually, under the provisions of this act and other legislation, a variety of resources for services and care for children have developed. The Social Security Act gave impetus to social insurance programs, public assistance, child welfare, public health services, maternal and child health services, and other services of this nature—all of which are basic in providing conditions conducive to the well-being of children and youths. The Public Health Service Act in 1948 was amended to authorize grants to the states for extending and improving community health services. Federal grants for demonstration projects in mental services were authorized after the Health Service Act was further amended to provide funds from the government.

JUVENILE INSTITUTIONS AS PART OF THE JUVENILE COURT SYSTEM: A HISTORICAL PERSPECTIVE

During the beginning of the juvenile court movement in the first quarter of the nineteenth century, society began to see the juvenile offender as a child needing treatment different from that received by an adult criminal. The movement to provide separate institutions for child offenders grew out of three somewhat interrelated, historically interesting factors.[7]

1. The practice of *indenturing uncared for children:* Indenturing was the practice of contracting to work for several years in return for transportation fare to the American colonies.

   The first record of indenturing was noted by the public authority in Massachusetts. Benjamin Eaton, a child, was indentured in 1639 by the governor to a Bridget Fuller, a widow for fourteen years. The Articles of Indenture specified that Benjamin was to go to school for two years and to perform such services as Mrs. Fuller desired. Furthermore, he was not to be bound over to anyone else without the consent of the governor.

   As an accepted child-care practice, it was natural that indenturing became an early part of the program of institutions for juvenile offenders. The daily *Journal* of the Superintendent of the New York House of Refuge (considered by correctional historians to be the first institution for delinquents), dated May 10, 1828, reveals that eight youngsters were released to be indentured to persons in Ohio. The indenturing practice, it appears, was the forerunner to the present-day foster home system.

2. *The apprentice system:* Initially the early release (indenturing out) from institutions was specifically accomplished so that the youngsters could act as apprentices to individuals (referred to as a master tradesman) involved in a specific trade. Because of the increased

[7]This section on "institutions for child offenders" was taken, with permission from an unpublished paper authored by a colleague and co-author on other books. *Walter Haringer, Supervisor, Santa Clara County Juvenile Probation Department Aftercare Unit, San Jose, Calif.*

Photo courtesy of the California Youth Authority, Sacramento, Calif. Preston School of Industry, about 1900.

emphasis during the late 1800s on industry, some concern was given to having apprentice programs within the institutions. Also, the former houses of refuge, or reform schools, as they were called, changed their names to industrial schools. In California, the Preston School of Industry remains from that era.

3. *The use of the alms houses or orphanages:* Orphanages were not originally built for delinquents, but children often had to steal to survive there. The first orphanage in the United States was established in 1729 in New Orleans and was known as the Ursuline Orphanage. In 1790, the Charleston Orphan Home in Charleston, South Carolina, was founded.

   In 1800, the Magdalen Society was formed in Philadelphia with the intention of institutilizing young girls who "in an unguarded moment have been robbed of their innocence and sunk into wretchedness and guilt." This is perhaps the first group in the country to deal with the problem of prostitution.

The first house of refuge, opened in New York City in 1825, was a barracks on Madison Square leased from the government by the Society for Reformation of Juvenile Delinquents with a budget of $18,000. The most famous of the original founders of the society were John Griscom, a Quaker schoolteacher who had been

Ventura School for Girls, about 1930.

impressed with the work of several correctional practitioners in Switzerland, and the Reverend John Stanford. This first house of refuge institutionalized both females and males.

The second house of refuge opened in Boston in 1826, was officially known as The House of Reformation. The third House of refuge opened in 1828 and subsequently moved to new quarters in 1850. At the turn of the century, the boys and girls were separated into two institutions; at present the boys' institution is known as the Glen Mills School for Boys, while the girls institutions are known as Sleighton Farms.

Despite the glowing language written about these three early schools, they were little better than prisons. Neither in architecture nor in personality did they differ much from conventional prisons. While it is true that the first superintendents were educators and men of some vision, little was accomplished. The Boston and New York schools developed a crude type of self-government with a system of rewards and penalties that was unique and revolutionary for that day and age.

Prior to the establishment of houses of refuge, many children were thrown into county jails, especially in the large cities. They were subjected to the crudest forms of treatment; usually they were not segregated by sex nor by the crimes they committed. Adults who had been sent to jail or prison for every conceivable crime or vice were housed together. There was no juvenile delinquency problem because juvenile delinquents were treated in the same manner as adults. The poor and orphaned children were sent to jail for the pettiest offense. England and, consequently, the United States which adopted English law, were two of the last jurisdictions to accept the idea of diminished responsibility for juveniles. A youth of thirteen caught stealing a spoon in England in 1801 was handed before the magistrate, convicted, and promptly hanged. There was "no specific problem of juvenile delinquency"; children who broke the law suffered the punishment of their elders.

The cottage type of juvenile institution came into being in 1854 when a girls' reformatory was opened in Lancaster, Massachusetts. Four years later, a boys' school was opened at Lancaster, Ohio. Both institutions featured the cottage of family plan. The idea of the small family unit is generally regarded as coming from the well-known school at Mettray, France, which was opened in 1839 by Frédéric Auguste Demetz.

The first cottages in Lancaster, Ohio, were log cabins of which each housed forty boys. The custodians were known as "Elder Brothers." In these cottage-type institutions an attempt was made to group boys according to their dispositions and characters and in separate cottages under special supervision. These groups were the first crude forms of a classification system that was initially worked out in the Borstall System in England and has been carried to quite a refinement in reception centers and clinics throughout the United States.

The original program was an arduous school schedule followed by hard work on the farm; consequently, the staff was able to send their young charges to bed completely tired. There was a crude form of self-government; but the regime was military in nature. Early institutions were often organized so that each cottage was called a company, and some of the "better adjusted inmates" became noncommissioned officers, while the superintendent was often referred to as "Major" or "Colonel." This practice led to the "Duke" system where the noncommissioned officers were often the bitter boys who commanded respect and got the other boys to go along with the program in lieu of being physically abused. These noncommissioned officers were rewarded with special privileges.

Historically, the guiding principle underlying the juvenile court from its founding in Cook County, Illinois, in 1899, was to inquire whether or not the juvenile manifested a condition—the condition of being delinquent—not whether he had committed an offense. If it was established that he manifested the conditions of delinquency, it was assumed that these conditions were due to reasons beyond his control. The remedy, then, was not to punish him, but to remove the condition or to neutralize its effects. This called for careful study, various forms of therapy, and guidance, rather than the imposition of penalties. Historically, too, proceedings in the juvenile court were civil, not criminal. There was a hearing, not a trial. The formal trappings of the juvenile court were replaced by informality. The rules of evidence were modified since the issue was not one of fact, but went to the problem of how to select treatment in the juvenile's behalf.

MODIFICATIONS IN THE JUVENILE COURT SYSTEM SINCE 1899

Since 1899, there have been extensive modifications in these earlier views as to how the juvenile court should function. The legalistic modifications are discussed fully in the following chapter, "Legal Aspects of the Juvenile Court," but it is appropriate at this time to review some of the factors that relate to the history of the juvenile court.

While jurisdictions vary, it is safe to say that today, in most parts of the United States there is more formality in court procedures and a greater concern with elements of proof than there used to be. While the rules of evidence in a juvenile court hearing are much more relaxed than a hearing in the adult court, they have not been waived. While the concept of delinquency is somewhat difficult to define, most juvenile courts have required more precision in defining this term and in dealing with its forms than was true decades ago. The earlier courts required an investigation into the background of the juvenile before making disposition of him, and this practice has been continued and improved upon, and some functions have been added to the court. It is not uncommon for courts in these days, through their probation departments, to operate institutional facilties. Courts vary in their jurisdictional exercise over traffic cases involving juveniles, over issues of dependency and neglect, over adults who contribute to delinquency or dependency of a minor, over truancy, and over parallel matters concerning the health and welfare of the young.

Nevertheless, the basic concern of the juvenile court with the growth and development of juveniles and youths, and with the hazards to which they have been exposed, still remains today but public criticism regarding the welfare of the minors as compared to that of the community may be weakening a seventy-year philosophy.

As indicated in Chapter One. The jury is still out regarding a more "restrictive and severe approach to juvenile offenders."

FUNCTIONS OF THE COURT

Since their inception, juvenile courts have often found themselves without community resources with which to make their judgments effective. For example, in a community without proper facilities, a child who required foster-home care might be left in a damaging home situation, be "committed" to an institution, or placed in a substandard facility. None of these solutions would have met the child's needs. Because of such lack of necessary resources within the community, many courts find themselves forced to develop child-care facilities within their own administrative structures, much against their will and principles. The courts, believing that the administration of some of these child-care facilities was an appropriate role for the court to play, developed such facilities with a great deal less reluctance. Still others have simply accepted the lack of proper facilities without taking any action.

There are different ways of looking at this development. At one extreme are those authorities who believe that the court should itself administer most of the child-care and treatment facilities, such as have been developed by voluntary and, more recently, public agencies. In their view, the court would thus become the primary public child-care agency in the community. At the opposite extreme are those who would limit the court's function more drastically by transferring its powers of disposition to an administrative panel or tribunal as has been done in some European countries.[8]

In the United States, there would be serious question as to the constitutionality of such an administrative tribunal. Such a tribunal would be making decisions that would deprive parents of the custody of their child or would deprive a child of his freedom.[9] An administrative tribunal made up of experts in the social sciences, as the proponents of such a tribunal usually conceive it to be, is not necessarily trained to protect the rights of people coming before it. Moreover, an administrative tribunal would be no more likely than a judge to come to decisions that are sound for the child. Like the judge, the tribunal must rely for its decision on the study made by the probation staff, with the help of medical, psychiatric, and community resources. The members of the panel cannot themselves make social studies; nor should they, if they are to act in a judicial capacity.

On the other hand, it does not seem desirable to center all child-care services in a court. The kind of detailed planning, for instance, involved in the day-to-day care of residential treatment of children should not be a matter of judicial decision, nor should a court review its own acts as it well might be called upon to do in such a situation. An agency providing specialized child-care services should be part of the executive branch of government or a voluntary agency, and should be under the direction of an executive trained in social work. It should not be a part of the judicial branch of government and should not be under the direction of a person whose primary qualification for the job is legal training. Also, the court ought not to be burdened with the details of administration or policy that such an agency requires. A question of duplication is also of importance. Many social agencies that render excellent service to children entrusted to their care by court are privately supported. Others, although publically supported, may need also to provide care for children who have not come to them through the courts. A parent who needs and wants care for a child who does not require a change in legal status, should not be compelled to go through a court. To create two public services, one in the court and one outside giving the same type of care, would seem unnecessary.

Neither extreme point of view would, therefore, seem to meet the situation. A

[8]P. Lerman. *Community Treatment and Social Order—A Critical Analysis of Juvenile Correctional Policy*, The Univeristy of Chicago Press, Chicago, 1975 p. 10.

[9]F. R. Prassel, *Introduction to American Clinical Justice*, Harper and Row, New York, 1975.

point of view that places some services in the court and others in an agency in the executive branch of government or a volunteer agency seems to be more practical and to be in line with the American tradition regarding the separation of powers. What services should be administratively subject to each must depend on the essential nature of their contribution to the total process. To say that the court should undertake the judicial function and that the agency should handle the administrative function, although basically sound, is an oversimplification of the problem and should not be taken too literally. Actually, there is no agreement as to what is "administrative" and what is "judicial," nor can the two processes always be separated in relation to court process. Instead, it may have to be said that the court should control the services that are necessary or closely related to its judicial function. Services that do not fall into this category should be administered by an agency in the executive branch of government or by a voluntary agency. Even then, it will be found that some services are so closely related to both functions that the choice may have to depend on pragmatic or incidental factors.

For example, in the case of neglect or delinquency, he process by which the state assumes partial authority over the upbringing of a child and implements this authority can be divided into eight steps:[10]

1. *Investigation of Complaint and Filing of Petition.* Investigation as used here is the action required to secure the facts necessary to determine whether an act of delinquency has actually been committed or a condition of neglect actually exists. The individual or agency that received the complaint, made the investigating, and sought authorization from the court to file a petition is responsible for providing the evidence to support the allegations made in the petition. It seems clear that investigation, as defined here, and the filing of the petition are not appropriate functions of the court. A court through, the use of its own staff, should not be placed in the position of investigator and petitioner as well as act as the tribunal deciding the validity of the allegations in the petition. Generally, therefore, investigating complaints and filing of petitions require services proper to the police or to such other administrative agency providing protective services for children as may exist and as are vested by law with these functions. In certain situations, however, it may be desirable for the court, through its own personnel, to take such action, for example, in the case of a child on probation who is alleged to have committed a delinquent act.

2. *Determination of the Need for and Nature of Court Action.* When a situation is brought to court for action, the court should have the power to determine whether action is needed and, if so, the nature of such

[10]*Essentials of Adoption Law and Procedure,* Children's Bureau, Department of Health, Education, and Welfare, Washington, D.C., 1969, pp. 16–18.

action. Generally, the court's intake service is primarily responsible for making a preliminary screening to determine whether the protection of the child and the community require further action. Since this is the responsibility of the court, it is appropriate that the intake service be placed within the administrative structure of the court.

3. *Establishing the Fact That the Child is Within the Jurisdiction of the Court.* This action, calling as it does for legal determination as to the authority of the court to act in the case, is clearly a judicial function.

4. *Establishing the Facts As Alleged in the Petition.* This action is similar to that of number 3 above, and is clearly a judicial function.

5. *Making the Social Study.* The social study is made for the specific purpose of helping the court determine what treatment disposition to make. The court's determination will, of course, be based on all relevant facts presented to it, whether presented as a result of the social study or as outside of such a study, through other testimony. The cardinal principle should be that the court should have before it all the facts necessary to make an intelligent decision. The judge has responsibility for making decisions and the community holds him accountable. In most cases, however, he relies to a considerable extent on the social study made by other persons in arriving at his decision. He needs, therefore, to have confidence in such persons and to be able to hold them accountable for the adequacy of the social study and general performance of their duties. In neglect or delinquency cases, the social study is so closely related to the judicial process that it should normally, but not necessarily, be done by personnel administratively attached to the court. When this service is provided by a worker in another agency, such as a child-welfare worker in the public welfare department, or in a voluntary agency, the worker should be administratively responsible to the court for service performed for the court.

6. *Determining What Action Is Needed and What Rights, If Any, of the Parent or Child Should be Limited.* This action, involving possible limitations on the rights of the child or his parents or a change in the legal status of the child, is clearly judicial.

7. *Providing Needed Care and Treatment.* The operation of facilities for the care and treatment of children away from their homes is a function appropriate to administrative agencies. In the case of detention (secure detention), a second principle is involved. Detention involves protection of the community, as well as of the child. Detention also involves limiting the rights of the parent and child. For this

reason, the court must have control over intake and release. Following this second principle, good detention has been developed under the administration of courts, particularly in the urban communities. However, it should be possible to combine the two principles by placing administration of detention facilities under an administrative agency and ensuring that the court has control over intake and release and has a part in the developing administrative policy.

The administration of shelter care facilities for children awaiting court hearing is more closely related to the general child-care functions of administrative agencies and should be provided by them.

Providing treatment in his own home to the child who has come before the court may involve two different situations, it may involve the legal status of *probation*. This status, similar to the making of the social study, is so closely related to the judicial process in delinquency cases that it should be performed by personnel administratively under the direction of the court, or responsible to the court. Such action is especially warranted since it enables the same person who makes the study to continue to work with the child and parents during the probation period.

Treatment of a child in his own home in *neglect situations* may also involve *protective supervision*. This involves casework service to the family, which is generally more closely related to that given by family or children's agencies. Because this service involves responsibilities to and by the court it requires that the service be given by the court where no agency is willing to undertake this responsibility.

8. *Releasing a Child from the Control of the State.* This action involves removing the limitation placed on the rights of the child and parents, which were originally limited by judicial action. This action may also often involve a change in the legal status of the child. Both actions seem to fall clearly within the judicial function.

SUMMARY

The fundamental idea of the juvenile court is that the state must step in and execute guardianship over a child found under such adverse social or individual conditions that they encourage the development of crime. Furthermore, the juvenile court takes the position that the youngster should not be treated as a criminal or legally charged with a crime, but should be held as a ward of the state, thus, receiving the care, trust, and discipline that are accorded the neglected and dependent child, and which, as the act states, shall approximate as nearly as possible responsible care given by parents. The juvenile court law concept was first formulated in 1899 by the Chicago Bar Association which sponsored the act ultimately legislated by the State of Illinois. The first such juvenile court as we know it today, was initiated in Cook County, Illinois. This county was the only county that had the facilities to carry out the high demands expected of the new juvenile court system.

The principle of *Mens Rea*, which was adapted from Roman law is related to the juvenile court concept. Under this doctrine a child of seven is held to be incapable of having the criminal intent that is a necessary ingredient of a crime between seven and fourteen he is deemed presumptively incapable; and after fourteen years of age he is deemed presumptively capable. An additional legal antecedent of the juvenile court was the doctrine of *Parens Patriae*—the state as the guardian of its ward, the child—by which the state has the right to intervene in the family and alter or terminate parental rights. This doctrine originally developed out of appeals for justice in behalf of neglected and dependent children of the king's chancellor in feudal England.

Although the concept of the juvenile court and probation was "invented" in England with a subsequent transplant to the United States, it can be said that the system was much more highly developed in the United States. The social systems prevailing in the nineteenth century in the United States played an important role in intensifying the movement for reform in the treatment of children. Industrialization, immigration, and poverty were driving people into cities by the thousands, with a resultant overcrowding and destruction of family life.

Therefore, the juvenile court was established essentially as a response to social problems because of society's concern over the callous, indifferent treatment of children accused of criminal activity.

Within twenty-five years, after the authorization by the Illinois Legislature in 1899 of the first juvenile court, every state but two had authorized such courts. The rapid spread of the juvenile court was in effect a response of society to widespread conditions that created special difficulties for children, mass immigration and rapid urbanization that followed industrialization produced slums where families were crowded into unsavory housing. On the streets, children were exposed to vice and crime. The strong paternalism that had marked American and European family life gave way to the destruction and loss of control of children. The juvenile court came to be seen as an effort to produce social justice by offsetting some of these conditions.

There are many significant acts that proved to be important to the development of the Juvenile Court, such as the Social Security Act of 1935 and the Public Health Service Act, which greatly stimulated the growth of grants to states for expanding and improving community health services. The movement to provide separate institutions for child offenders grew out of three interrelated, historical factors. Despite the glowing language written about these new schools, they were little better than prisons; neither in architecture nor in personality did they differ from the conventional prison. While it is true that the first superintendents were educators and men of some vision, they could accomplish little. On the positive side, however, these institutions were a step forward since they exhibited certain crude forms of classification that distinguished the youthful offenders from adult criminals.

Modifications in the juvenile court system, as well as the function of the juvenile court, since its inception are discussed in the latter part of this chapter.

ANNOTATED REFERENCES

Allen, H. and Simonsen, C.E., *Corrections in America: An Introduction*, Glencoe Press, Beverly Hills, Calif. 1975.

> Chapter 17 (press 323–336) focuses in cases relative to chapter 7. Particularly insightful is the discussion on "A Whole New Vocabulary" (pages 327–329) on juvenile delinquency.

Eldefonso, E. and Coffey, A., *Process and Impact of the Juvenile Justice System*, Glencoe Press, Beverly Hills, Calif. 1976.

> This short paperback (215 pages) examines each style of the Juvenile Justice process by juxtoposing explanations of each stage of the process with narrative and dialogue based on a series of juvenile case histories.

Fox, Sanford J., *The Law of Juvenile Courts in a Nutshell*, West Publishing Company, St. Paul, Minnesota, 1971, pp. 1–12.

> In the introduction, Fox discusses the function of the juvenile court. He expounds on the definition of a juvenile court, the relation of juvenile court to judicial structure, and the venue of a juvenile court. This is an excellent resource.

Martin, John M. and Fitzpatrick, Joseph P., *Delinquent Behavior: A Redefinition of the Problem*, Random House, New York, 1965, pp. 35–37.

> To date, this is one of the best presentations of the historical development of the methods of punishment. The methods of punishment have been amply documented by the authors, who focus on the institutional systems of juveniles as well as adults.

Pound, R., "The Juvenile Court and the Law," *National Probation Parole Association Yearbook*, 1944

> This is a classic in the field of information pertaining to juvenile court and the law. Pound provides an excellent summary of various juvenile court systems and the laws that relate to such systems.

Reasons, C.E., "Gault:Procedural Change and Substantive Effort," *Crime and Delinquency*, vol. 16, no. 2, 1970.

Reasons presents an excellent overview of changes in the juvenile courts affected by the Gault decision.

Sloane, H.W., "The Juvenile Court: An Uneasy Partnership of Law and Social Work," *Journal of Family Law*, vol. 5, no. 2, Fall 1965. See also: J. E. Westbrook, "Mens Rea in the Juvenile Court."

Sloane and Westbrook present two views of the relationship between the juvenile court and the philosophy of social work. This is an excellent presentation on the validity of the relationship between probation casework and the juvenile court law.

Task Force Report: Juvenile Delinquency and Crime, The President's Commission on Law Enforcement and Administration of Justice, U.S. Government Printing Office, Washington, D.C., 1967.

This is an excellent resource covering the entire history and development of the juvenile court.

CHAPTER EIGHT legal aspects of the juvenile court

Society has determined that the best way to deal with youthful criminals is to reeducate and rehabilitate them. However, existing methods of treatment and judicial procedures set up for adult criminals do not serve this rehabilitative purpose. Consequently, separate treatment facilities and a separate court have been established for youthful offenders.

Chicago was the birthplace of the juvenile court movement. A group of dedicated citizens laid the cornerstone of a new judicial structure—a juvenile court system. That structure has since grown and expanded, not only within the United States, but throughout much of the world. If a youngster as far away as Formosa gets into difficulty with the law today, he is treated in accordance with a juvenile court law that had its origins in the original Illinois legislation. The impact of those earlier efforts in Illinois has thus been felt throughout the world.

The organization and structure of juvenile courts differ not only throughout the world but also throughout the United States. However the juvenile court system is, in the United States, part of the field of corrections.

THE FIELD OF CORRECTIONS

The field of corrections represents the system by which our society deals with juveniles who are delinquent or show delinquent tendencies and with adults who have been convicted of crimes. Corrections is one of four distinct but interrelated phases in the administration of criminal and juvenile justice. A continuum representing the broad sweep of this process would follow the following sequence:[1]

[1]The Practitioner in Corrections, *California Probation, Parole and Correctional Association* Delores Press, San Francisco, Calif., 1977.p.5

1. *Law Enforcement* is basically collecting evidence about reported offenses as well as detecting and arresting suspected offenders.

2. *Prosecution and Defense* is preparing and presenting cases before the courts.

3. *Judicial Process* is determining and ruling upon legal issues and evidence and the rendering of appropriate decisions. The juvenile court system, in most states, is part of this process. The juvenile court system is an arm of the superior court and, in most states, superior court judges are in control of the juvenile iourt process and are charged with an obligation to see to the rehabilitation of the child. Although the superior court judges are in control of the juvenile court process, the juvenile court procedure, whenever possible, is a nonadversary, informal, and nonpublicized procedure. The publicity that attaches to criminal convictions and punishment renders the criminal court process unsatisfactory for dealing with juvenile offenders. Such publicity renders rehabilitative "machinery" useless. Youth who might otherwise be rehabilitated can be damaged by such publicity, because a serious community stigma is attached to a conviction in the criminal courts. Perhaps even more important, rehabilitation should begin during the court hearing. As a result, juvenile court procedure itself has been altered to achieve a protective rather than an adversary atmosphere. Rules of evidence, court procedure, and sterile formality have been discarded. Thus the juvenile court is informal in nature, and the court, acting in the role of *parens patriae* takes protective jurisdiction over the minor and purports to act on his behalf.

4. *Corrections* is implementing the orders of the court through probation departments or parole agencies and institutions to which the courts make commitments. Treatment methods utilized by the adult courts are incompatable with the correctional-oriented philosophy of the juvenile court. The criminal courts incarcerate lawbreakers, not only for rehabilitative purposes but also for the purpose of protecting society from harm and detering others from criminal acts. In order to realize these purposes, institutionalization may be severe and long in duration, and this type of treatment is likely to make the offender even more antisocial than he was before. On the other hand, rehabilitation requires individualized treatment.

As part of the administration of criminal and juvenile justice, corrections is based upon a philosophy of serving and preserving society through the rehabilitation of the offender. The purpose of any correctional program is to make services available, within a client-restricted status designed to protect society, which will enable the offender to become a useful, productive citizen.

The correctional process includes a professional methodology that has been synthesized from the findings of the behavioral sciences. It operates through certain agencies that administer the system, specifically probation, parole, and various types of institutions.

JUVENILE COURT JURISDICTION

The juvenile court cannot act unless it has jurisdiction over a person. In order to act in any particular case, a court must have power, or jurisdiction, over both the person and the subject matter involved. In other words, the juvenile court must cover both *who* may be brought before the court and *why* he is appearing before the court. The laws which created the juvenile courts that operate in the United States differ considerably in regard to both the persons and the subject matter over which these courts have jurisdiction. Thus, they are far from uniform. In a strict sense, it is incorrect to speak of a juvenile court or juvenile court systems as if juvenile courts throughout the country were uniform in their structure, philosophy, and activities. The reasons for such radical diversity are:

1. The laws setting up juvenile courts are often far from clear.

2. Most of the persons working on such courts, usually including the judges, are socially directed, sometimes to the detriment of the legal rights of persons involved in cases that come before them.

3. A subsubstantial number of juvenile court judges serve only part time and are untrained in law; even full-time judges are often untrained in law.

4. Few courts have a staff competent to administer the law properly either in its legal or its social ramifications.[2]

The jurisdiction of the juvenile court (as pointed out in Chapter seven) is *equity jurisdiction*, which has five characteristics:

1. *It is relatively informal in its procedure*—a characteristic going back to the origins of English equity, when one who sought relief in equity presented to the Chancellor an English bill, that is, an informal petition in English, whereas one who sought relief in a court of law had to buy a Latin writ and follow it up with a formal statement of his case (called a Declaration), likewise in Latin.

2. *As with all equity jurisdiction, it is remedial not punitive.*

[2]W S. Fort, "The Juvenile Court Examines Itself," *National Probation Parole Association.Vol. 5, No. 4, Oct. 1959, p. 404.*

3. *It acts preventively in advance of any specific wrongdoing.*

4. *It employs administrative rather than adversary methods.*

5. *It can adapt its action to the circircumstances of individual cases and so achieve a high degree of individualization, which is demanded by justice if not always by security.*[3]

LEGAL PRINCIPLES

There is nothing magical or revolutionary about the legal principles upon which the juvenile court rests. These concepts did not spring fully mature from the brow of the Illinois legislature in 1899, as some chroniclers would have us believe. Rather, they have an ancient lineage; they had their childhood and adolescence.[4]

The legal principles of the juvenile court system were never more clearly stated than by the Supreme Court of Pennsylvania over 125 years ago. Under an 1826 statute, a fourteen-year-old girl, Mary Ann Krouse, had been committed at the request of her mother to the house of refuge for "vicious conduct." A habeus corpus proceeding was brought on the child's behalf, claiming she was deprived of her liberty without due process of law and without trial by jury, a claim that is still heard today in many juvenile cases. However, in holding that Mary Ann was not being deprived of her liberty and that her constitutional rights were not otherwise infringed, the court said:

> *The House of Refuge is not a prison but a school. Where reformation, and not punishment, is the end, it may indeed be used as a prison for juvenile convicts who else would be comitted to a common jail; and in respect to these, the constitutionality of the Act which incorporated it, stands clear of controversy. . . . The object of the charity is the reformation by training its inmates to industry; by imbuing their minds with principles of morality and religion; by furnishing them with means to earn a living; and, above all, by separating them from the corrupting influence and improper associates, to this end may not the natural parents, when unequal to the task of education, or unworthy of it, be superseded by the* parens patriae, *or common guardian of the community.*
>
> *It is to be remembered that the public has a paramount interest in the virtue and knowledge of its members, and that of strict right, the business of education belongs to it. That parents are ordinarily entrusted with it is because it can seldom be entrusted to better hands; but where they are*

3R. Pound, "The Juvenile Court and the Law," *Crime and Delinquency*, Vol. 10, No. 4, Oct. 1965, *pp. 448–449.* See also: H. E. Allen and C. E. Simonsen, *Corrections in America: An Introduction,* Glencoe Press, Beverly Hills, Calif., 1975, pp.324–327.
4Fort, "Juvenile Court Examines Itself," p. 404.

incompetent or corrupt what is there to prevent the public from withdrawing their faculties, as they obviously are at its sufference? The right of parental control is a natural but not an inalienable one. It is not accepted by the Declaration of Rights out of the subject of ordinary legislation; and it consequently remains subject to the ordinary legislative bar, which, if wantonly or inconveniently used, would soon be constitutionally restricted, but the competency of which as the government is constituted cannot be doubted. As to the abridgment of indefeasible rights by the confinement of the person, it is no more than what is borne to a greater or lesser extent in any school, and we know of no natural right to exemption from restraints which conduce to an infant's welfare. [5]

These legal principles were consistently adhered to during the nineteenth century; by 1899 they were fully accepted as part of American jurisprudence and thus provided a firm legal foundation upon which to build the juvenile court structure. [6]

SOCIAL PRINCIPLES

What was new about the juvenile court was that it was the first true offspring of the union of law and "the public good," because it was the first court designed to deal separately and solely with the lawbreaking behavior of a child and the conditions which caused that behavior, in a particular child, hence its motto, "individualized justice." In other words, the law offender who steals a candy bar is to be given theoretically as much consideration as one who burglarizes a home. The concern is to be focused on the dynamics of the reasons for one's action and methods to prevent recurrence. Thus, the juvenile court system is a product of the marriage of two ancient and honored lines fundamental in the development of man—the law and the public good. The soundness of these lines is eloquently shown by the phenomenal growth and development that attended its childhood. But it is still in infancy; and, as is so often true with children, it is having growing pains, lots of them, and will have many more. [7]

CHARACTERISTICS OF THE JUVENILE COURT

From the doctrine of *parens patriae* the term ward or wardship has been adopted to include youngsters who are found to come within the court's jurisdiction. Black defines a ward as "a person, especially an infant, placed by authority of law under the care of a guardian."

[5]*Ibid.*
[6]*Ibid.*
[7]*Ibid.*

The structure of the juvenile court and its position or status in the state's organizational pattern vary among, and even within, states. Relatively few are separate, independent courts. Most are part of a circuit, district, superior, county, common pleas, probate, or municipal court. In a few jurisdictions, family courts have been established to deal with both children's and domestic relations' cases. Even where the jurisdiction of children's cases is in a court that is organizationally part of a larger system, however, the judge assigned to hear children's cases often operates his court quite independently.

It is worth mentioning again that, although there is variation among and within states, on the jurisdiction of court's hearing of children's cases generally included *delinquency, neglect, and dependency cases.* Delinquency includes cases of children alleged to have committed an offense that if committed by an adult would be a crime. It also includes cases of children alleged to have violated specific ordinances or regulatory laws that apply only to children, such as curfew regulations, school attendance laws, restrictions on the use of alcohol and tobacco, and children variously designated as beyond control, ungovernable, incorrigible, runaway, or in need of supervision. According to U.S. Department of Health, Education, and Welfare (Juvenile Court Status in 1976) the latter two groups account for over 29 percent of the total number of delinquent children appearing before children's courts and between 30 percent and 35 percent of the population of state institutions for delinquent children. In addition to the cases of delinquent, neglected, and dependent children, children's courts may deal with other types of actions involving children: adoption, termination of parental rights, appointment of a guardian of the person of a minor, custody, contributing to the delinquency of a minor, and neglect-dependent cases.[8]

In some states, major offenses such as capital crimes are excluded from a juvenile court's jurisdiction. In other states, the jurisdiction of the juvenile court is concurrent with that of the criminal court in more serious offenses.

REFERRALS AND PROCEDURAL REQUIREMENTS

Most juveniles who appear in juvenile court are sent there by the police. Extensive screening and informal adjustment by the police on the street and at the police station reduce significantly the number of apprehended juveniles referred to the court. Parents, social agencies, and others may also have recourse to the court.

When a complaint is received, juvenile court statutes frequently provide that the court shall make a preliminary inquiry to determine whether the interests of the court or the public require court action. The inquiry may vary from a cursory investigation to a full-fledged social study involving contact with numerous persons and agencies in the community. It may include a hearing at which the child, his parents, and their attorney representing the child are present. In many juvenile

[8]*Task Force Report,* p.4.

A minor appearing before the juvenile court referee. Photo courtesy of Santa Clara County Juvenile Probation Department, San Jose, Calif.

courts, especially in the larger metropolitan areas, the preliminary screening function, known as intake, is performed by a special division of the probation department. Dependent upon his judgment as to basis for the court's jurisdiction, the sufficiency of evidence, and the desirability of court action, the intake officer may dismiss the case, authorize the filing of a petition, or, in many courts, dispose of the case by "informal adjustment." In many juvenile courts, approximately one-half of the cases referred there are informally adjusted at intake by referral to another agency, by continuation on "informal probation", or in some other way.

During their growth, juvenile courts and their personnel were somewhat like federal judges in that they were relatively free from criticism. Criticism would not likely erupt unless certain practices had defeated their own purposes. Juvenile courts were able to exercise a range of discretion not available nor allowed in adult criminal courts, and until recently, the juvenile courts were able to operate quite freely. The change to procedural safeguards was largely attributable to the school of legal realism, which used the judicial process as one in which the judge makes the law. [9]

[9] J. Mack, "The Juvenile Court," *Harvard Law Review*, vol. 23, no. w3, 1909, p. 104. For an up-to-date critique of this topic, refer to *Juvenile Justice Information Systems: A National Assessment*, National Institute for Juvenile Justice and Delinquency Prevention, Reno, Nevada, 1977.

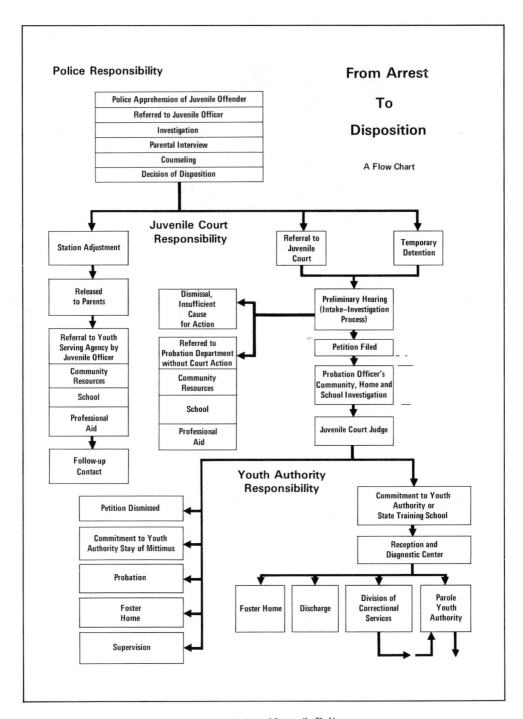

Police Responsibility

From Arrest

To

Disposition

A Flow Chart

Police Apprehension of Juvenile Offender
Referred to Juvenile Officer
Investigation
Parental Interview
Counseling
Decision of Disposition

Juvenile Court Responsibility

Station Adjustment

Referral to Juvenile Court

Temporary Detention

Released to Parents

Dismissal, Insufficient Cause for Action

Preliminary Hearing (Intake–Investigation Process)

Referral to Youth Serving Agency by Juvenile Officer

Referred to Probation Department without Court Action

Petition Filed

Community Resources

Community Resources

Probation Officer's Community, Home and School Investigation

School

School

Professional Aid

Professional Aid

Juvenile Court Judge

Follow-up Contact

Youth Authority Responsibility

Petition Dismissed

Commitment to Youth Authority or State Training School

Commitment to Youth Authority Stay of Mittimus

Reception and Diagnostic Center

Probation

Foster Home

Foster Home

Discharge

Division of Correctional Services

Parole Youth Authority

Supervision

Source. Richard W. Kobetz, *The Police Role and Juvenile Delinquency*, reproduced by permission of the International Association Chiefs of Police, Washington, D.C., 1971, p. 117.

CRITICISMS OF THE JUVENILE COURT SYSTEM

At present, few in public life are satisfied with the capacity of the juvenile justice system to fulfill its original mandate, as a matter of fact, many also disagree about what the mandate should be. Studies conducted by the President's Commission on Law Enforcement and Administration of Justice, legislative inquiries in various states, and reports by informed observers compel the conclusion that the great hopes originally held for the juvenile court have not been fulfilled. Few government and state organizations, as well as academicians in the field of law enforcement and corrections, find the juvenile justice system useful or beneficial to the youths involved in it. According to these professional groups, the juvenile justice system has not succeeded significantly in rehabilitating delinquent youth, in reducing or even stemming the tide of juvenile criminality, or in bringing justice and compassion to the child offender. Unfortunately, the only way to measure success or failure of the juvenile court system is by the number of recidivists (young adults who are reappearing before the juvenile courts) throughout the United States. Statistics presented in chapter 3 indicate that many juveniles are reappearing before juvenile courts throughout the nation. Apparently many juveniles are not profiting from their first contact with the juvenile court and are not being rehabilitated.

There have been many disparaging editorials, critical articles appearing in professional journals, and numerous protests from the press regarding the ability of the juvenile court system to act in the best interests of the juvenile. Former United States Supreme Court Justice Fortas, when announcing the decision in *Kent* vs. *United States*, vividly described the nation's concern with the juvenile court system:

> *While there can be no doubt of the original laudable purpose of the Juvenile Courts, studies and critiques in recent years raise serious questions as to whether actual performance measures well enough against theoretical purpose to make tolerable the community of the process from the reach of constitutional guarantees applicable to adults. There is much evidence that some Juvenile Courts . . . lack the personnel, facilities, and techniques to perform adequately as representatives of the State in a parens patriae capacity, at least with respect to children charged with law violation.*

There are many other reasons for the failure of the juvenile courts to rehabilitate juvenile offenders. Besides the lack of personnel, facilities, technqiues, and the community's continual unwillingness to provide the resources necessary to permit the juvenile courts to realize their potential, there is a great deal of concern about the lack of training and qualifications of those judges who sit on the juvenile court bench. A recent study by the Center for the Behavioral Sciences of juvenile court judges revealed that 50 percent of the judges had not received undergraduate degrees, one-fifth had not had the opportunity to receive college educations, one-fifth were not members of the bar. Furthermore, according to this study, almost three-quarters devote less than one-fourth of their time to juvenile and family matters, and judicial hearings often are little more than attenuated interviews of ten of fifteen minutes' duration. The National Council on Crime and Delinquency, in their study of the Family Court of Cook County (Chicago), states that it averages a little over fifteen minutes' per hearing—about one-half the time the council estimates is needed for proper consideration of the issues. Another study by the state of California, referred to as the California Governor's Special Study Commission on Juvenile Justice (1960), concluded that the average time spent on a juvenile court case is approximately ten to fifteen minutes. The report further states:

> An appropriate question is whether the beneficient values of the Juvenile Court hearing implied by the philosophy expressed in the law can be achieved in the abbreviated time which most Juvenile Courts devote to each case. To what extent, for example, can a Judge make a significant impact on the errant child and his parents in what is almost an assembly line judicial process? A corollary question is whether the Juvenile Court Judge can actually explore in a brief hearing the behavior complexities presented by each case?

Other resources are equally lacking, such as court services and placement possibilities for children. Because of the inadequate court services and placement facilities, juvenile court judges have taken "the easy way out" and committed increasing numbers of children to even more inadequate state "reform schools." Because of lack of discretion in the use of placement possibilities, a revolving-door policy of *parole* has developed. In other words, *children have been released to the community no better prepared for the future than when they were removed from the community.* Supervision after release from correctional institutes has been minimal.

It is no wonder, then, why students of the juvenile court have become extremely critical of its operation. The lack of facilities, underdeveloped and understaffed personnel, lack of training and qualifications of the judges sitting on the juvenile court benches (who have extremely broad powers over children's lives), and the noticeable lack of set procedures by the juvenile courts have resulted in efforts by individuals and organizations interested in civil liberties—notably the American Civil Liberties Union—to press for reforms. The President's Commission on Law Enforcement and Administration of Justice in 1967, pointed out that there is:

> Increasing evidence that the informal procedures, contrary to the original expectation, may themselves constitute a further obstacle to effective treatment of the delinquent to the extent that they engender in the child a

> *sense of injustice provoked by seemingly all-powerful and challengeless exercise of authority by Judges and Probation Officers.* [10]

Efforts by the American Civil Liberties Union have resulted in several landmark decisions by the U.S. Supreme Court. These decisions have attacked the *flexibility* of the juvenile court system. In general, it is the flexibility of the juvenile court system that commends its retention. But this flexibility must operate only on children who actually belong in the system in the first place, for it retains all the coercive powers of the criminal courts. Thus, there can be no justification for denying the child those rights that are required to assure a fundamentally fair determination of guilt or innocence. It is not the juvenile court that is the gateway to treatment; it is the child's acts. [11]

COURT DECISIONS: IMPACT ON JUVENILE COURT PROCEDURES

During the early days of the development of the juvenile court, statutes establishing such courts contained few, if any, specific procedural requirements. Many provided simply that the court hearing should be conducted in an "informal manner," a degree of generality that reflects the desire of the proponents of juvenile courts to eliminate the adversary procedures of adjudication which were justified on the ground that more specific procedures would be destructive for several reasons. First, the *formal process*—charges, jury trials, by counsel, evidentiary restrictions, motions and countermotions, the protection against self-incrimination—was inescapably identified with criminal law; whereas it was the objective of the juvenile court movement to eliminate the atmosphere and presuppositions of criminal law in dealing with child offenders. [12] Second, *adversary procedures* for determining whether a person committed a criminal act with a criminal state of mind were not useful for ascertaining the full picture of the child's behavior, including not only the conduct that brought him to court, but the full pattern of his prior behavior and relationships. [13] Third *criminal procedures* would put the child on one side and the court on the other, creating a tone of combat and contentiousness that would destroy the desired cooperation of each child in the

---

[10] President's Commission on Law Enforcement and Administration of Justice, *The Challenge of Crime in a Free Society,* Washington, D.C., U.S. Government Printing Office, 1967, p. 85. See also: George B. James Jr.: *Gault and The Juvenile Court Restoration,* Ann Arbor, Mich., Institute of Continual Lesson Education, 1976.

[11] J. E. Glen, "The Coming Juvenile Court System," *Youth Authority Quarterly,* vol. 23, no 3, Fall 1970, p.2

[12] Task Force Report, p. 28.

[13] *Ibid.*

common effort to help him.[14] Furthermore, during the development of the juvenile court, upper court rulings were rather rare and provided few guidelines, and, when the juvenile court was challenged, the courts proved receptive to the spirit of the juvenile delinquency laws. Courts have, in the past, indicated that the juvenile court proceedings were *civil* and *not criminal;* therefore, the juvenile courts were an extension of equities to deal compassionately with children, and were addressed to the salvation rather than the punishment of the child. The upper courts, during the development of the juvenile court procedures, did not play a significant role in formalizing guidelines for procedural requirements. An opinion of the Pennsylvania Supreme Court of 1905 provides a good lesson of changing fashions of ideas about dealing with children.[15] The child, said the Appellate Court stated that

> *no one who is charged with a criminal offense shall be deprived of law, liberty, or property without due process of law. To save a child from becoming a criminal or from continuing a career of crime, to end in mature years in public punishment and disgrace, the Legislature surely may provide for the salvation of such a child, if its parents or guardian be unable or unwilling to do so. . . . The natural parent needs no process to temporarily deprive his child of its liberty . . . to save it and to shield it from the consequences of persistence of a career of waywardness, nor is the State when compelled as parens patriae, to take the place of the father for the same purpose, required to adopt any process as a means of placing its hands upon the child to lead it into one of its courts. When the child gets there and the court, with the power to save it, determines on its salvation, it . . . is immaterial how it got there. The Act simply provides how children who ought to be saved may reach the court to be saved. If experience should show that there ought to be other ways for it to get there, the Legislature can, and undoubtedly will, adopt them and they will never be regarded as undue processes for depriving a child of its liberty or property as a penalty for crime committed. . . . [The Act is not for the child of a child charged with a crime, but is mercifully to save it from such an ordeal, with the prison or penitentiary in its wake, if the child's own good and the best interests of the State justifies such salvation.]*[16]

In recent years, however, much of this has been changed. Since the second half of the twentieth century, the upper courts have been playing a significant role in forging the procedural "requirements" of the juvenile courts. Many studies have proven that, although the juvenile court's rehabilitative objectives and protective philosophy are uniformly endorsed, considerable question has been raised as to whether the court as constituted at present is providing sufficient legal safeguards.

[14]*Ibid.*
[15]*Ibid.*, p.29.
[16]*Ibid.* [*Commonwealth* v. *Fisher,* 213 Pa. 48, 53, 54 (1905)].

The impact of the upper courts on the juvenile court process is clearly pointed out by Sanford J. Fox, Professor of Law and noted author:[17]

> *Courts also have played a significant role informing a jurisprudence for juvenile justice, especially the Supreme Court's decision* In re Gault, *378 U.S. 1, 87 S. Ct. 1428 (1967), serving to invoke the concept of Due Process and its derivatives as the basic structure of actions in its Juvenile Court. This mandate has been both enthusiastically embraced and stoutly resisted by many engaged in the Juvenile Court process, a diversity that is often reflected in court opinions. Paradoxically, the increasing number of Juvenile Court decisions being appealed to higher courts also tends to produce a somewhat unsettled state of law by virute of the fact that the Appellate Judges still have relatively little* ratio decidendi *to borrow from each other, and must rely more on individual conceptions of the needs of justice in particular circumstances than they do in areas of law, such as torts or commercial relations which have lengthy traditions of consensus.*

THE ROLE OF ATTORNEYS IN JUVENILE COURT HEARINGS

The state and federal courts have taken an active role on the issue of the right to counsel. Authorities in the field of justice hold the belief that no single action contains more potential for achieving procedural justice for the child in the juvenile court than provision of counsel. The presence of an independent legal representative of the child, or his parent, is the keystone of the whole structure of guarantees that a minimal system of procedural justice requires. The rights to confront one's accusers, to cross-examine witnesses, to present evidence and testimony of one's own, to be affected by prejudcial and unreliable evidence, to participate meaningfully in the dispositional decision, to make an appeal, has substantial meaning for the overwhelming majority of persons brought before the juvenile court only if they are provided with competent lawyers who can invoke those rights effectively. The President's Commission on Law Enforcement and Administration of Justice pointed out that lawyers do not play a major role in representing children in the juvenile courts. A study, preliminary to the recommendations that led to the enactment of the New York Family Court Act in 1961, showed that in the New York City Children's Court in 1959, 92 percent of the respondents were not represented by counsel. Similar results were found by the study that preceded the recommendations for the subsequent major revision of the California Juvenile Court Law. Another study, based on a survey of juenile court judges serving the nation's largest metropolitan areas, revealed that lawyers appear on behalf of children in less than 5 percent of delinquency cases and only somewhat more frequently in

[17]S. J. Fox, *The Law of Juvenile Court in a Nutshell*, West Publishing Co., St. Paul, Minn., 1971 (Preface).

neglect and dependency cases. The study also revealed that the lawyers who appear in juvenile court are almost always retained lawyers rather than assigned or defender system lawyers.

Fears have been expressed that lawyers will inevitably make juvenile court proceedings adversary. No doubt this is partly true, but it is partly desireable. Informality is often abused. The juvenile courts deal with cases in which facts are disputed and in which, therefore, rules of evidence, confrontation of witnesses, and other adversary procedures are called for. They deal with many cases involving conduct that can lead to incarceration or close supervision for long periods, and therefore juveniles often need the same safeguards that are granted to adults. And, in all cases, children need advocates to speak for them and guard their interests, particularly when disposition decisions are made. It is the disposition stage where the opportunity arises to offer individualized treatment plans and in which the danger lies that the court's coercive power will be applied without adequate knowledge of the circumstances.

The matter of representation by counsel was made clear by the U.S. Supreme Court in *Kent* v. *United States.*

> *The right to representation by counsel is not a grudging gesture to a ritualistic requirement. It is of the essence of justice. Appointment of counsel without affording an opportunity for hearing on a "critically important" decision is tantamount to denial of counsel.*[18]

It is essential that counsel be appointed by juvenile court for those who are unable to provide their lawyers. Experience under the prevailing system, in which children are free to seek counsel of their own choice, reveals how empty of meaning the rights is for those typically the subjects of the juvenile court proceedings. Moreover, providing counsel only when the child is sophisticated enough to be aware of his need to ask for one or when he fails to waive his announced right is not enough as experience in numerous jurisdictions reveals.

THE GAULT DECISION

The United States Supreme Court in 1967 returned a landmark decision which is certain to lead to broad reformation of legal proceedings across the land. The various fundamentals of fairness were enunciated by the Supreme Court in the case of *In re Matter of Gault.* The *Gault* decision gave juveniles substantially the same constitutional protection adults receive in criminal trials. The Court dramatically stated that "under the Constitution the condition of being a boy does not justify a kangaroo court." The Supreme Court, in a fifty-six page opinion by former Justice Abe Fortas, stated that the supposed benefits of the juvenile process have

[18]*Kent v. United States* (1966) 383 U.S. 541, 18 L. Ed. 527, 87 S. Ct. 1045.

not always worked and that the features of the juvenile system, which its proponents have asserted are of unique benefit, will not be impaired by constitutional domestication. The Supreme Court, using this Arizona juvenile's case as a springboard, concluded that juveniles, like adults, are entitled to the following Bill of Rights safeguards:

1. Notice of the charges placed against him.

2. The right to have an attorney's assistance.

3. The right to confront and cross-examine complainants and other witnesses.

4. Protection against self-incrimination, including the privilege of remaining silent.

5. The right to transcript of the proceedings.

6. The right to have the case reviewed in higher courts.

In directing the new approach to the handling of juveniles, the majority opinion stated:

> We now hold that, absent a valid confession, a determination of delinquency and an order to commitment to a state institution cannot be sustained in the absence of sworn testimony subject to the opportunity for cross-examination in accordance with our law and Constitutional requirements.

Since *Gault*, most courts and legislatures have gone further in attempting to assure a fair hearing in a juvenile court. The integrity of the fact-finding process has been the hallmark of this trend.

THE MIRANDA DECISION

The *Gault* decision also had a significant impact in the area of admissibility of evidence. Several juvenile courts throughout the United States have taken the position that statements made by the child during police investigation and intake (probation investigation) are inadmissible at the adjudicatory hearing unless the minor was notified of his rights under *Miranda* v. *Arizona*. The *Miranda* decision requires that certain legal requisities be fulfilled when a police officer engages a suspect on the street and questions him. The officer must advise the suspect that (1) *he has the right to remain silent; (2) he has the right to speak to an attorney; (3) if he wishes an attorney, but cannot afford one, the state will provide him with one:* and (4) *anything the suspect says may be held against him. The Miranda* decision, of course, applies to police interrogation, as well as to interrogation by probation officers; and since the *Gault* decision, most states require that *Miranda* warnings be applicable to juveniles.

The courts have focused on the capacity of a child to make an intelligent and knowing waiver of his rights under *Miranda* and have found:

> *The Appellate Courts in New York, where juvenile jurisdiction is limited to children who commit delinquent acts before their 16th birthday, have held that a child's out-of-court statements made while in custody are admissible only if his parent or guardian joined in the waiver against privilege of self-incrimination. The California and Illinois Supreme Courts, on the other hand, have held that a mature youth is capable in appropriate circumstances, of waiving his rights without parental advice. The most recent California decision admitted a statement by a 15-year-old who was questioned by Police and an Assistant District Attorney without informing his parents.* [19]

As pointed out by the Associate Counsel of Crime and Delinquency, Jeffrey E. Glen, the California decision is inconsistent with the United States Supreme Court's insistence that a person subject to possible coercion through law enforcement investigation and interrogation requires the shelter and protection of counsel unless he is able to compete, particularly in psychological terms, with his interrogators. Glen further points out that the one rationale of the Juvenile court is to protect the child from the rigors of the full criminal process because of his immaturity. It is unrealistic, therefore, to treat him, as an adult when he is being questioned or interrogated by police. The California courts, according to Glen, recognize the need to involve the parents in the waiver decision in the juvenile court itself, which requires that the parent as well as the child be notified of the child's *Miranda* rights. Thus, the holdings of the California Courts are inconsistent with both constitutional theory governing interrogation and juvenile court theory requiring special protection for the immature. [20]

THE RIGHT TO JURY TRIAL

Like bail, jury trial in juvenile proceedings is not granted in most states. The Supreme Court ruled, in June 1971, that juveniles charged with crimes for which an adult could be punished do not have a constitutional right to trial by jury.

According to the Supreme Court, although the juvenile system of justice may have fallen far short of perfection, the climate of a jury trial should "put an end to what has been an idealistic prospect of an intimate, informal protective proceeding."

The ruling upholds laws existing in most states. Twenty-nine states and the District of Columbia have laws barring jury trials in youth courts, which provide

[19]Glen, "The Coming Juvenile Court," p. 4.
[20]*Ibid.*, pp. 4-5.

for proceedings before a judge in closed hearing. In five other states court rulings are required, and in the remaining states, trials for youths are allowed under certain circumstances.

The Supreme Court decision was based upon cases from Pennsylvania and North Carolina in which teen-agers adjudged to be delinquent petitioned for jury trials.

The area of jury trials has proven particularly troublesome to the courts. Since the inception of the juvenile courts, jury trial for children in juvenile court has been prevented by statutes in several states as well as in the District of Columbia. California had two cases appealed on this subject. "Juvenile Court proceedings are not primarily criminal in nature; therefore, trial by jury is not a Constitutional requirement."[21]

The second case made reference to *Gault:*

> *To adopt trial by jury in the Juvenile Court would "introduce a strong tone of criminality into the proceedings," destructive of the beneficial purposes of the Juvenile Court Law, not warranted as a due process of law safeguard of individual rights.*[22]

There are certain exceptions, as some states have statutes providing for jury trial; however, the juveniles must demand trial by jury, or the juvenile judge, on his own motion, calls for a jury trial.

> *The record discloses that counsel made no demand for a jury trial at the time of the hearing before the County Court. It appears that the County Court had jurisdiction of the person, jurisdiction of the subject matter, and jurisdiction to render the particular judgment which was rendered, and that the petition for Habeus Corpus should be denied.*[23]

SELF-INCRIMINATION[24]

The protection against self-incrimination applies to juveniles as well as adults. No exceptions were noted. Even when confessions are obtained after advisement of legal rights, the questions of intelligent and voluntary waiver must be resolved prior to their use as admissible evidence in court.

> *The youth of the petitioner, the long detention, the failure to send for his*

[21]*In re R.L.* (1969) 83 Cal., Rptr. 81.

[22]*In re T.R.S.* (1969) 1 Cal. App. 3d 178, 81 Cal. Rptr. 574.

[23]*In Ex parte Norris* (1954 Okla. Crim.) 268 P 2d 302. Other states which allow for jury upon demand in juvenile cases are Texas, Tennessee, Nevada, and Georgia.

[24]Eldefonso, *Youth Problems,* Chapter 4. See also: E. Eldefonso and W. Hartinber. *Control Treatment, and Rehabilitation of Youthful Offenders.* Revisions Calif., 1976, Chapters 2 and 5.

parents, the failure immediately to bring him before the Judge of the Juvenile Court, the failure to see to it that he had advice of a lawyer or a friend—all these combine to make us conclude that the formal confession on which this conviction may have rested was obtained in violation of due process. [25]

Interrogation of the youthful suspect, has been under considerable attack by civil rights organizations and groups. Therefore, the appellate courts have given numerous decisions regarding the interrogation of children suspected of having committed crimes. Confessions by juveniles are often incriminating, and, when obtained by law enforcement agencies, they have been offered in evidence in juvenile court or in criminal court hearings. The factors determining the admissibility of confessions in juvenile or criminal court hearings depend upon compliance with legal obligations outlined in the *Miranda* and other court decisions. Sanford J. Fox discusses the legal obligations (i.e., the legality of an arrest or detention, and notice to parents, as well as compliance with norms directly concerned with interrogations)[26] and comments on arrest practice:

> *Having the admissibility of confessions relate to the adherence to specific duties by law enforcement officers involves two distinct policy considerations. There may be the desire to compel compliance with the duties by making inadmissibility the penalty for non-compliance. This is the basic reason for a Federally guaranteed exclusionary rule for the fruits of an illegal search and seizure. . . .*
>
> *Second, it may be that the rules of inadmissibility are a means to an end more fundamental than controlling certain Police behavior. The prevailing conception of "justice" may dictate, for example, that confessions be made only through the voluntary choice of the child and are "not the product of ignorance of rights or of adolescent fantasy, fright or despair. . . . ."*
>
> *Current Constitutional doctrine is an amalgam of the penalty-for-non-compliance rule and the purity-of-procedures desideratum. The strong reference in* Gallegos *to an abhorrence of secret inquisitions and interrogation circumstances that are inherently coercive has received its most profound and institutionalizing support in Miranda v. Arizona. . . .* [27]

The late Chief Justice Warren, delivering the majority decision in *Miranda v. Arizona,* placed the "purity" factor—that is the free exercise of protection against self-incrimination—into proper perspective:

[25]*Gallegos v. State,* (1962) 370 U.S. 49, 8 L. 2d 325, 82S. Ct. 1209.
[26]Fox, "Juvenile Court in a Nutshell," pp. 21-22.
[27]*Ibid.,* p. 22.

> *The current practice of incommunicado interrogation is at odds with one of our Nation's most cherished principles—that the individual may not be compelled to incriminate himself unless adequate protection devices are employed to dispel the compulsion inherent in custodial surroundings, no statement obtained from the defendant can truly be the product of his free choice.* [28]

The *Miranda* requirements have been adopted by the juvenile court process; furthermore, it is quite possible that an additional requirement in juvenile interrogations, which was not specified in *Miranda*, have been brought forth in the case of *Gault*. More direct and binding, the *Gault* ruling in 1967 discusses self-incrimination:

> *It would be entirely unrealistic to carve out of the Fifth Amendment all statements by juveniles on the ground that these cannot lead to "criminal" involvement. In the first place, juvenile proceedings to determine "delinquency," which may lead to commitment to a state institution, must be regarded as "criminal" for the purpose of the privilege against self-incrimination. We conclude that the Constitutional privilege aginst self-incrimination is applicable in the case of juveniles as it is with respect to adults.* [29]

The United States Supreme Court extended the protection against self-incrimination—the Fifth Amendment—to children, and warned that admissions of children are of doubtful value. Children must be advised of their constitutional rights "so that they fully appreciate that remaining silent is an absolute right which neither fear nor promise can affect." This privilege of silence applies, of course, not merely before the police, but before probation officers, school authorities, courts, and anyone else whom the child believes to have public authority over him. The United States Supreme Court concluded that the constitutional privilege against self-incrimination is applicable in the case of juveniles as it is with respect to adults.

The difficult question as to to who may waive a child's constitutional rights was not clearly passed upon by the Supreme Court. Certain points are, however, obvious. No person can waive a right unless he personally, and in his particular mental and emotional condition, understands the consequences of waiving it. No person can waive a right for a child except (1) a lawyer or, (2) a parent who understands the right and the effect of waiver, or (3) a child sufficiently mature and comprehending to make an intelligent decision. A waiver is meaningless if given under stress, pressure, or fear; or if it is given as the result of promises of better treatment or other award.

---

[28]*Miranda v. Arizona*, 384 U.S., 86 S. Ct. 1602 (1966).
[29]*In re Gault* (1967) 387 U.S. 1 18 L. Ed. 527, 87 S. Ct. 1428.

DOUBLE JEOPARDY

As juvenile proceedings are still considered noncriminal and nonpenal, double jeopardy has yet to become an issue. In 1953, a California juvenile was certified back to the juvenile court after being confined fifteen months at a California institution. He was then certified to an adult court from the juvenile court; subsequently, he was committed to a state prison. Appeal, based on double jeopardy, was denied. The constitutional provisions against double jeopardy were held not to apply to this case, "for the reason that the proceedings in the Juvenile Court was not a criminal prosecution."[30]

In a later case, a juvenile was remanded to an adult court after a preliminary hearing.

> *Consequently, it was not improper for the Juvenile Court to conduct a hearing before determining whether or not to waive its jurisdiction. To hold that jeopardy attached at that point would preclude the full and informal investigation in the interests of the minor and the community which Congress thought necessary to achieve the solitary remedial purposes of a Juvenile Court system.*[31]

However, once a juvenile stands trial for an offense, and a disposition has been made for that specific offense, juvenile courts are reluctant to subject the juvenile to another trial. In *Garza v. State*, judgment was reversed, and the prosecution was ordered to be dismissed.

> *Conviction of the defendent for murder violated principles of fundamental fairness and constituted a deprivation of due process where prior to such conviction, which occurred after defendant reached the age of 17 years, defendent upon petition of the District Attorney, had been adjudged a delinquent child on basis of the same act of murder and had been held in custody as a delinquent child.*[32]

RULES OF EVIDENCE

The usual rules of evidence applicable in adult civil cases are applicable to juvenile cases, thus excluding most hearsay and most opinions. Furthermore, testimony should be under oath and only competent material and relevant evidence under rules applicable to civil cases should be admitted in evidence. The amount of proof required, however, varies from state to state, and some states indicated a *propon-*

[30]*People v. Silverstein* (1953) 121 CA 2d 140, 262 P 2d 656.
[31]*U.S. v. Dickerson* (1959) 106 App. DC 221 F 2d 487.
[32]*Garza v. State* (1963) 369 SW 2d 36.

derance of evidence as being sufficient. However, the issue was recently resolved by the United States Supreme Court:

> We therefore hold, in agreement with Chief Justice Fuld in dissent in the Court of Appeals, "that, where a 12-year-old is charged with an act of stealing which renders him liable to confinement for as long as six years, then as a matter of due process . . . the case against him must be proved beyond a reasonable doubt."[33]

Due process as stated in the Fourteenth Amendment is now becoming applicable to delinquent proceedings in juvenile courts. The law has been stated by the courts, and when due process is ignored or circumvented, the juvenile courts are subject to sharp criticisms:

> There is evidence, in fact, that there may be grounds for concern that the child receives the worst of both worlds; that he gets neither the protection accorded to adults nor the solicitous care and regenerative treatment postulated for children.[34]

It was stated again in *Gault*:

> We do not mean . . . to indicate that the hearing to be held must conform with all the requirements of the criminal trial or even of the usual administrative setting; but we do hold that the hearing must measure up to the essentials of due process and fair treatment.[35]

It seems clear that marked changes have taken place in American juvenile courts. It appears that the juvenile court process, in order to keep pace with our rapidly changing society, is due for significant changes. The decisions by the United States Supreme Court and the state appellate courts have had a tremendous impact upon the juvenile court system throughout the United States. Of all the decisions handed down by the upper courts, the most important and significant, with regard to its impact on the juvenile court process, is the decision *In re: Gault* (See Appendix A). The key points of this decision follow:

1. *Limitation.* While the procedural requirement would almost certainly be expanded to include other cases, a court may only rule upon questions directly before it. The Gault decision is, therefore, limited to "proceedings by which a determination is made as to whether a juvenile is a 'delinquent' as a result of alleged misconduct on his

[33]*In re Winship* (1970) 38 LW 4253.
[34]*Kent v. U.S.* (1966) 383 U.S. 541, 18 L. Ed. 84, 87 S. Ct. 1045.
[35]*In re Gault* (1967) 387 U.S. 1, 18 L. Ed. 527, 87 S. Ct. 1428.

part, with the consequence that he may be committed to a state institution."

2. *General Philosophy.* Neither man nor child can be allowed to stand condemned by methods that flout constitutional requirements of due process of law. "Unbridled discretion, however benevolently motivated, is frequently a poor substitute for principle and procedure. . . . We do not mean . . . to indicate that the hearings to be held must conform with all of the requirements of a criminal trial or even of the usual administrative hearings; but we do hold that the hearing must measure up to the essentials of due process and fair treatment."

3. *Notice.* The Supreme Court makes three requirements as to the notice that must be given prior to a hearing in which the parents might lose custody or the child might lose liberty. The notice, which may be a copy of the Petition, must be (a) in writing; (b) it must give reasonable details of the misconduct; (c) it must be served sufficiently in advance of the hearing to allow time to prepare a defense; (d) it must give the time, date, and place of hearing; (e) at the arraignment as well as at the fact and disposition hearings, the Court cannot consider any charges or claims against the child which were not included in the notice.

4. *Right to a Lawyer.* The Supreme Court requires that both the child and the parents must be notified, and in a manner they can understand, that they have an absolute right to a lawyer, at public expense, if necessary.

5. *Self-Incrimination.* The Supreme Court extends the protection against self-incrimination—the so-called Fifth Amendment—to children as completely as it has heretofore done to adults, and warns that admissions of children are of doubtful value. The warning to children must also be done so that they fully appreciate that remaining silent is an absolute right that neither fear nor promise can affect. The privilege of silence applies, of course, not merely to the police, but to probation officers, school authorities, courts, and anyone else whom the child believes to have public authority over him. "We conclude that the constitutional privilege against slef-incrimination is applicable in the case of juveniles as it is with respect to adults."

6. *Confrontation.* Unless there is a constitutionally valid admission of the essential facts charged against a child, he has a right to confront the witnesses against him, to hear their testimony, to have them under oath, and to cross-examine them.

7. *Rules of Evidence.* The usual rules of evidence applicable in adult, civil cases are applicable, thus excluding most hearsay and most opinions. "Testimony should be under oath and only competent material and relevant evidence under rules applicable to civil cases should be admitted in evidence."

8. *Waiver.* The difficult question of who may waive a child's constitutional rights was not clearly passed upon. Certain points are, however, obvious. No person can waive a right unless he, personally and in his particular mental and emotional condition, understands the consequences of waiving it. No person can waive a right for a child except (a) a lawyer, (b) a parent who understands the right and the effect of waiver, or (c) a child sufficiently mature and comprehending to make an intelligent decision. A waiver is meaningless if given under threats, pressure, or fear; or if given as the result of promises of better treatment or other reward.

9. *Police Interrogation.* Before interviewing a child at the accusatory stage, the police must first be sure that the child and his parents understand that they have (a) a right to a lawyer, (b) a right to remain silent, and (c) a right not to be fingerprinted. A waiver of such rights must be by a person comprehending the meaning of the right and the effect of the waiver.

10. *Trial Transcript.* The Supreme Court set no requirements as to the right to a court reporter or tape recorder or transcript. It suggested, however, that some form or record of the evidence would be desirable. "The consequences of failure to provide an appeal, to record the proceedings, or to make findings or state the grounds for the juvenile court's conclusion may be to throw a burden upon the machinery for habeas corpus, to saddle the reviewing process with the burden of attempting to reconstruct a record, and to impose upon the juvenile judge the unseemly duty of testifying under cross-examination as to the events that transpired in the hearings before him."

11. *Not Mentioned.* It should be noted that the Supreme Court did not require (a) jury trials, (b) public trials, (c) public access to records, or (d) appeal as of right, nor did it so much as suggest a contradiction of the juvenile court philosophy or method other than to confer on children the basic constitutional rights enjoyed by adults."[36]

Although there are many criticisms of the juvenile court process, no fair-

[36]Santa Clara Juvenile Probation Department, Training Bulletin No. 21, "United States Supreme Court Decision—*In re: Gault.*"

minded citizen would argue with the fact that there are practical reasons for maintaining a juvenile court system with jurisdiction over criminal law violations committed by children. There are many rehabilitative facets to the juvenile justice system that would not be available if the criminal courts assumed jurisdiction of juvenile court cases. The criminal courts have a continual *backlog* of cases. The juvenile court goal of *maximum diversion* of cases from the juvenile justice system is applied in criminal courts only in such borderline criminal cases as alcohol and drug offenses. The public trials of criminal courts would attach a *stigma* to juvenile court hearings. Civil and political rights would be *forfeited*. The impossibility *of the sealing* of records in adult criminal courts and many other factors, once again, make the juvenile courts indespensible regardless of their many shortcomings.

SUMMARY

The initial section of this chapter discusses juvenile delinquency in relation to law enforcement, prosecution and defense, the judicial process (including the juvenile court system), and corrections (including probation, parole, and correctional institutions).

In order to act in any particular case, a court must have power, or jurisdiction, over both the person and the subject matter involved. In other words, the juvenile court must cover both *who* may be brought before the Court and *why* he is appearing before the court. The laws that create juvenile courts in the United States differ considerably with regard to both the persons and the subject matter over which these courts are given jurisdiction. The jurisdiction of the juvenile court is *equity jurisdiction*. The five characteristics of equity jurisdiction are: (1) it is relatively informal in its procedures; (2) it is remedial not punitive; (3) it acts preventively in advance of any specific wrongdoing; (4) it employs administrative rather than adversary methods; (5) it can adapt its actions to the circumstances of individual cases.

The *legal principles* upon which the juvenile court system rests were stated by the Supreme Court of Pennsylvania over 12 years ago in the case of a fourteen-year-old girl Mary Ann Krouse.

With regard to social principles, the concern is focused on the dynamics of the reasons for one's possible actions and how to prevent their recurrence; in other words, the concept of "individualized justice" is advocated.

The characteristics or traits of the juvenile courts differ throughout the United States. Although there are some wide variations with regard to philosophy, procedure, and functions of the juvenile court there are certain traits that are similar. For example, the proceedings are divided into three stages: *the pre-judicial stage,* commonly referred to as "detention hearing," the *jurisdictional hearing* where the facts are established by presentation of evidence or testimony, and the *dispositional hearing* in which the court must decide what would most likely prevent the juvenile from becoming involved in further difficulties. From the time a youth is placed in custody, these three stages must comply with a definite time schedule.

There are many criticisms of the juvenile court system: the lack of personnel, facilities, techniques, and the community's continual unwillingness to provide the resources necessary to permit the juvenile court to realize its potential. There is also a great deal of concern about the lack of training and qualification of those judges that sit on the juvenile court bench. Studies vividly portray the lack of educational qualifications of judges throughout the United States. Furthermore, such studies conclude that the average time spent on a juvenile court case is approximately ten to fifteen minutes. There is a question as to whether a juvenile court judge can actually explore the behavior complexities presented in each case in such a brief hearing.

Court decisions, particularly the decision pertaining to *Gault v. Arizona*, have had a significant impact on juvenile court proceedings. The *Gault* decision, *Kent v. United States*, *Miranda v. Arizona*, are other significant decisions by the upper courts. Since the *Gault* decision has had the greatest affect on the procedures of the juvenile court, the final section of this chapter reemphasizes and outlines briefly the key points of this decision.

ANNOTATED REFERENCES

Advisory Council of Judges of the National Crime and Delinquency, *Procedure and Evidence in the Juvenile Court*, National Council on Crime and Delinquency, 1977.

> This council deals with the entire juvenile court process. Petitioning processes as well as problems in obtaining evidence in juvenile court hearings, are thoroughly analyzed in nontechnical language.

Eldefonso, E. and Hartinger, W., *Control, Treatment and Rehabilitation of Youthful Offenders*, Glencoe Press, Beverly Hills, Calif. 1976

> Chapters 2 and 5 examines the complexity of problems confronting the juvenile court system in terms of the quality of representation (legal counsel) of minors in juvenile courts throughout the United States.

Fox, Sanford J., *The Law of Juvenile Courts in a Nutshell*, West Publishing Company, St. Paul Minnesota, 1971, pp. 13-73.

> Fox explores the entire question of jurisdiction of the juvenile court. Topics such as age limitations, double jeopardy and related problems, children's criminal conduct, noncriminal conduct, neglect and dependency are reviewed and analyzed. This is an important resource for students who want a vivid and seemingly accurate description of the topic of jurisdiction in a criminal court.

Ketcham, Orman W. and Pulsen, Monrad G., *Juvenile Courts: Cases and Materials*, The Foundation Press, Inc., Mineola, New York, 1967, chap. 11.

This chapter covers the power of the juvenile court in relationship to noncriminal and criminal conduct of minors. Cases are presented that which portray the problem of attempting to differentiate betweeen the offenses considered criminal and noncriminal which are processed through the juvenile courts. See also: Orman W. Ketcham, "Legal Renaissance in the Juvenile Court," *Northwestern University Law Review,* vol. 60, November/December 1965, pp. 585-97. Ketcham's article provides some useful recent analysis of the juvenile court system as well as useful comments on the problems of justice for juveniles.

Kenney, J.P. and Pursuit, Dan G., *Police Work With Juveniles and the Administration of Juvenile Justice,* 4th ed., 1974, Charles C Thomas, Springfield, Illinois.

This is a relevant resource covering the police role in adhering to the juvenile court law when investigating and disposing of cases.

Vinter, Robert D., "The Juvenile Court as an Institution," *Task Force Report, Juvenile Delinquency and Youth Crime,* The President's Commission on Law Enforcement and Administration of Justice, U.S. Government Printing Office, Washington, D.C., 1967, appendix C.

This report explores some of the major difficulties in the system of juvenile justice and suggests lines of remedial action. See also Noah Weinstein's *Supreme Court Decisions and Juvenile Justice,* National Council of Juvenile Court Justice, Reno, Nevada, 1973.

CHAPTER NINE probation—parole: trends in juvenile justice

In the nineteenth century, probation was frequently defined as a suspension of sentence, with the understanding that further delinquency would result in punishment. Today probation is more likely to be defined as "a consciously planned treatment process," "a helping process that changes a law violator into a law abider," "a new and therapeutic experience with authority," or "psychotherapy aimed at changing distorted or unrealistic attitudes."[1]

The experts in the field who use these definitions also review probation as having a different meaning to the delinquent and to the general public. The probationer himself may see the probation officer as a person in authority who checks on him and who has the authority to send him away. It is not uncommon for the delinquent to picture the probation officer as hostile or at least unfriendly; the probation officer, however, sees himself as a helping person, one who is treating the delinquent. The general public considers probation as a second chance; if the delinquent can change his behavior, he need not lose his liberty.

The Children's Bureau in Washington defines probation as a "legal status in which a child, following adjudication in a delinquent case, is permitted to remain in the community, subject to supervision by the court through the court's proba-

---

[1]For further information on legal and social components of probation, see a workshop report compiled by the Department of Health, Education, and Welfare in 1972 "Training for Juvenile Probation Officers."

tion department or an agency designated by the court, and subject to being returned to the court at any time during probation."[2]

In each of these definitions there is a recognition that the court sees the need for the delinquent to change. Having violated the code of the community, he is given the opportunity to change; if he does not, then other measures are taken by the court. According to this view, the delinquent who does not need to change because his behavior was atypical for him, should not be placed on probation, and admonishment and warning from the court regarding his own responsibility for his action should be sufficient.

But when the court, through its study of the adolescent and his family, finds that change is necessary, several dispositions are possible. Generally they are limited to (1) probation and/or placement in a relative's home or a foster family home, or (2) commitment to a suitable institution or agency for treatment. Whatever the disposition, all the parties concerned should recognize that the court believes that the delinquent needs a change and as a result of its study has selected this way as the most likely path. The disposition is designed both to aid the adolescent and to protect the community, as the court has the joint responsibility of serving both.

The court's disposition which perceives the need for change and provides the method to be used to accomplish it, is frequently regarded as punishment by the probationer. Having done wrong, the individual must make up for it. On some occasions, the delinquent may regard the disposition of probation as "getting away" with lawbreaking, and may react to probation rules with contempt. Such responses have lent credence to the cry of "mollycoddling" by those who have no faith in probation as a method of changing the individual's attitudes and behavior. From another viewpoint, the court's disposition is regarded as an expression of the community's recognition that the delinquent needs to be helped with his social problems. For example, a boy was referred to court for participating in a car theft. He was not the instigator, but had followed the lead of the other boys, lest he be considered "chicken." Investigation revealed that this was an isolated incident and that generally he could be relied upon to use good judgment. The judge, knowing this, could effectively point out the responsibility of each boy for his behavior and the fallacy of trying to prove one's manhood through delinquent behavior.

THE GOALS OF PROBATION

Because of the differing needs of individual delinquents, the goals of probation vary from immediate to long-range, from limited to broad, from mere stopping of the delinquent behavior to rehabilitation of the individual. The minimum goal of stopping delinquent behavior is generally accepted. Should goals be higher?

[2]*Standards for Specialized Courts Dealing with Children*, Children's Bureau, Department of Health, Education, and Welfare, Washington, D.C., 1974, p. 18.

Should the goals be to help the delinquent achieve his highest potential? Should probation continue until the delinquent has made an adequate social adjustment in the community, perhaps through planning regarding his life situation? Phrasing this another way, should probation terminate when the youth is considered law-abiding, or should it continue in order to resolve other social or emotional problems?

If the answer is that the probation officer should assist with only those problems that are related to delinquent behavior, the question arises concerning how this separation of problems can be determined. Can we delineate areas of a client's life that are the concern of a probation officer and those that are not? Should a probation officer work with a delinquent youth's dating problems, for example? Or is this beyond the limits of duty?

It is felt that the following factors affect the goals of probation:

1. The situation and capacity of the client.

2. The culture and environment of the youth and his family.

3. The concept of probation held by the judge and the probation staff.

4. The quality and quantity of staff as they affect the service available to the youth and his family.

5. The court's situation in the community and the availability of community resources.

THE PROBATION PLAN

To meet the goals of probation, the probation plan needs to be tailored to the individual and to have within it the elements of change required by the court. Stereotyped rules and conditions should be eliminated. The philosophy of the juvenile court movement is based upon the individual child. Falling back on standard probation conditions for all delinquents denies the uniqueness of the individual approach necessary for successful probation.

How the probation plan is arrived at will be discussed in the next section. However, the probation officer is responsible for formulating the plan; the judge may approve it, modify it, or disapprove it. It is the probation officer who has the responsibility for carrying out the details of the plan along with the delinquent.

Some courts set down rules of probation, but it seems better to leave the details of limitations of activities to the supervisory authority vested in the probation officer. For example, matters such as keeping probation appointments, attending school, and the limiting of travel should be left to the authority of the probation officer.[3]

[3]*Ibid.*, pp. 18–19.

Although the general treatment plan may be agreed upon at the time of the hearing, it would be unwise to make this a part of the court order since the plan may need to be modified as treatment progresses. The probation officer should be permitted to take such action within the scope of his authority.

The probation plan is subject to different interpretations by the delinquent and court personnel. It can be considered by the delinquent as the punishment allotted for wrongdoing, or as the framework within which social treatment can be accomplished as envisioned by the court. It can also be interpreted as neither punishment nor rehabilitation, but a social plan focused on the welfare of the adolescent and the community. This plan requires that the youth control his behavior in specific ways, and is designed to help him effect an adequate adjustment with the help of the probation officer.

THE ROLE OF THE PROBATION OFFICER

The juvenile probation officer has two roles, and there must be no conflict between these roles. He must be considered, first, as a court officer or "arm of the court" and, second, as a correctional social worker.

AS A COURT OFFICER

As an officer of the juvenile court the probation officer has several responsibilities:

1. He is a creature of the statute and must work only within those limitations. He is only an agent of the court and has no authority to change orders of the court or to disregard those orders.

2. He makes investigations and determines whether a child should appear before the court by filing a petition.

3. He makes factual objective reports to the court so that the court may arrive at an intelligent decision.

4. He makes suggestions and recommendations to the court.

5. He keeps the court informed on the progress made by the court's wards.

6. He is a legal representative of the juvenile court.

AS A CORRECTIONAL SOCIAL WORKER

The probation officer performs the following functions in his capacity as a correctional social worker:

1. He conducts a social investigation, makes a subjective analysis, and works out a realistic plan for each case he presents to the court.

2. He makes certain that no child is placed on probation until a specific plan has been formulated.

3. He supervises, consults, and guides both the ward and his family. There is little point in granting probation unless a plan is prepared and adequate follow-up is continued until the child no longer needs it.

4. He represents the child's best interests to the court.

AS A SOCIAL DIAGNOSTICIAN

From the time the adolescent and his parents come to the attention of the court, the probation officer is assessing them as individuals and as members of a family and members of the community. The social study made by the probation officer is designed to (1) identify and evaluate the factors causing the delinquent behavior, and (2) develop and recommend a necessary program that will eliminate or alleviate these factors.

During the interval that the probation officer is making the social study for the court's use, he is also preparing the delinquent and his parents for the hearing. He tries to learn the meaning of his total experience to the youth and at the same time to convey to him the purpose of the court and the functions of the staff members who will deal with him. In some cases, the social study will reveal that the delinquent does not need the services of the court—that there are other community agencies available to meet his needs.[4] In these situations, the roll of the probation officer is to enable the delinquent to accept the referral—and to give the agency, to which he is referred, adequate information regarding him so that the referral will be accomplished.

In still other cases, the study will point out that the delinquent does not need any social services. His behavior was atypical; yet social control can be maintained without relying on probation or other measures. In these situations, the judge can use the social study prepared by the probation officer as a way of making the hearing a positive experience for this child. Here again, the point is that the court's purpose is to serve the child; it can do this best if the remarks made by the judge to the child are based on an understanding of that child.

The material obtained by the social study comes from many sources, including the delinquent himself, his parents or relatives, the school, the police, social agencies, professional personnel such as doctors and ministers, and other interested and informed people concerned with the delinquent. Selection of what material goes into the report in order to give a clear picture of this youth is at the core of the

[4]*Ibid.*, p. 97.

probation officer's job. Information from these sources needs to be blended and evaluated. When reports have been received from other professional people, these should be incorporated into the study in order to formulate the probation plan. This method offers the judge a unified, comprehensive report rather than a set of reports that may need consolidating.

As the person responsible for the social study, the probation officer needs to be able to work with ease and confidence with the people providing information. He needs to know when to refer the delinquent for psychological testing or for psychiatric study and how to use the information obtained from these sources. His evaluation of the material in the social study is the basis of the probation plan that defines the means of helping the delinquent to achieve responsible behavior.

It is commonly agreed that, although the probation officer should not be exclusively a psychotherapist, the degree to which he is involved depends on the nature of the case. It is generally agreed that the probation officer is a correctional social worker whose function is to provide treatment consistent with the philosophy of social work as practiced today. It is concluded that the probation officer should not engage in psychotherapy, but should only ask questions, make statements, and require conduct on the part of the delinquent as defined by the legal description of the probation officer's duties. However, the probation officer in his use of social case work should be able to build on the strength of his relationship with the delinquent in order to work out a sound probation plan. There are other descriptions of the probation officer's function, however, and all point out that he should use all his skills and knowledge in the appropriate social work method (casework, group work, community organization) to assist the delinquent.

AS A CONTROLLING PERSON IN THE DELINQUENT'S LIFE

When the need for the delinquent to change has been recognized and approval has been given to the probation plan, both the delinquent and probation officer are responsible for implementing the plan.

The limitations set by the court for the delinquent youth are restraints that are appropriate and often essential facets of the plan to assist the youth and protect the community. The probation officer is present to help the delinquent to understand and comply with the probation plan; he is also available to help the client with problems, as they relate to delinquent behavior. The goal of both is to restore the delinquent from his restricted supervised status to legal freedom. Until it is safe to do this, the probation officer is expected to provide the necessary special controls and relationship resources.

The question often arises as to whether the probation officer can be both a controlling and helping person. Some people believe that control exerted over the probationer is antitherapeutic because it is resented by the probationer. Others hold that there is necessarily authority in the helping relationship. It can be a

An important function of probation services is the use of
authority. Authority, if used judiciously, can be an extremely important tool. If, however, authority is misused or
abrogated, probation services will be of little assistance to
persons they are meant to serve. The probation officer must
understand the authority the court has invested in him or
her as an officer of the court. Photo courtesy of Santa Clara
County Juvenile Probation Department, San Jose, Calif.

positive force; for, if the probation officer abrogates his authority, the delinquent
loses an opportunity to deal with the problem of authority in personal and social
relationships.

But how far does the control or the help function go? Does the probation
officer have the right to tell the probationer to shave off his mustache or cut his
hair? Can he require him to wear nonpointed shoes?

The answers to these questions lie in the goal that is set when the probation
plan is made. In general, this goal will be to help the client develop socially acceptable standards and adequate personal and social controls. In the process of developing these, they cannot be at any point too alien to him. The probation officer
and the delinquent need to find a comfortable way of working together—one
within the cultural system of the delinquent.[5] If the attempt is made by the probation officer to get the client to adopt a different set of cultural values, then the
probation officer's plan becomes a form of coercion against which the delinquent
will rebel. The plan should be designated to assist, not to trap, the probationer.

The most common problems of probation are those involving social relationships. Should the probation officer control the delinquent's selection of friends, or
his association with other probationers? Should certain hangouts be permitted?
Are there times when the probation officer takes over the authority of the parent?
Here again, the answers lie in understanding what is the individual goal of proba-

[5]Ibid., p. 66.

As a Controlling Person in the Delinquent's Life   197

tion. The effort is to assist the delinquent in establishing a more satisfactory and acceptable pattern of behavior. How far can he himself go in establishing healthy social relationships? Does he need control for a period of time, or is guidance enough so that he develops the control needed?

There are certain legal boundaries to which the delinquent is held by the probation officer. One of these is school attendance. If the delinquent is of school age and in good health, he must attend school. The efforts of the probation officer are again twofold: to help the youth accept school and gain interest in it; and to assist the school in understanding and planning to meet the needs of the youth. In some cases, the court may help the community evaluate school attendance requirements as they affect the youth of the community.

The control plan for the delinquent is set up to help him achieve good citizenship. He must live within the law. The probation officer identifies with the mores of the community and with the law. He represents the law-abiding citizen. For example, if the probationer admits that he has been shoplifting, the probation officer handles this in an appropriate manner—by re-referring the youth to the court for another disposition, by forcing the delinquent to return the merchandise, or to purchase the articles taken. The manner in which this is done can be therapeutic or can convince a youth that (1) he can outsmart adults when caught, or (2) no one will understand him. In no case can the probation officer ignore the delinquent. The delinquent needs to know that there are adults that he can't seduce into delinquency as silent partners.

In some courts, a new petition is filed for each delinquent act. In others, the supervising probation officer is consulted before a new petition is filed. It is generally believed that when a new petition is being considered, the supervising probation officer should be consulted. Based on his understanding of the delinquent, the supervising probation officer often can contribute important knowledge in making this decision.

AS AN AGENT OF CHANGE

Concern with change, the most characteristic common element of the methods of social work, is also at the core of the probation officer's job. Change must be planned, and the plan must be followed thoughtfully. Both the delinquent and the probation officer need to understand and agree on the goals toward which they are striving. The process of positive change may come about through:

1. *Interaction* between the delinquent and the probation officer, through the help given directly to the delinquent and/or members of his family.

2. *Referral* of the delinquent to other resources and the help he receives

through these services. The knowledge of other resources and the ability to help the delinquent use them makes the probation officer more effective.

3. *Creation of new resources* to enable the individual to solve his problems.[6]

The probation officer also serves as an agent of change in relation to both the court and the total community. Where he observes that policies or procedures of the court need revision, it is his obligation to work for constructive change. Within the community, he should point out what additional services are needed for the youth. Generally he should work through the channels provided by the court, rather than independently.

The concept of the probation officer as an agent of change raises many questions:

1. If the family is the basic problem, does the probation officer work with them, or refer them to a social agency?

2. Is probation child-centered to the exclusion of parents?

3. If the delinquency involved is group-participation, should the probation officer take the responsibility for intervention with the group when not all members of the group are under court jurisdiction?

4. To what extent should the probation officer function as an agent of community change? Should he organize and lead a youth group?

In dealing with the question of family, the Children's Bureau in its publication, *Standards for Specialized Courts Dealing with Children*, states:

> *In certain situations, much of the work of the probation officer may have to be done with parents. Although the parents of a child on probation are not themselves on probation or under supervision, they should be aware of the fact that their behavior and ability to help and control the child may have a bearing on the success of the service. If, for example, the parents are interfering with the probation officer or are failing to abide by a restraining order of the court, the probation officer may have to bring the case back to court.[7]*

The question of group participation has often triggered discussions pertaining to the responsibility for probation of individuals not officially under court jurisdiction. Naturally, there are many sharp differences as to the use of official versus

[6]W. W. Boehm, "Objectives of the Social Work Curriculum of the Future," *Social Work Curriculum Study*, vol. 1, Council on Social Education, New York, 1959, p. 131.
[7]"Training for Juvenile Probation Officers," *op. cit.*, p. 5.

unofficial probation. Throughout many workshops in the country, it is agreed by participants that regardless of the kind of intervention the probation officer attempts, he must have the knowledge to identify the kinds of problems and the appropriate ways to deal with them—for example, intervention with the family, with the peer group, or with the community.

The question of the probation officer as a community organizer drew the attention of workshop participants at Haven's Hill Lodge, Michigan, in 1960. Some of the participants meeting under the auspices of the Children's Bureau, viewed the probation officer's role as being limited to the casework function of overcoming the distortions in the attitudes of clients. Others viewed his role as that of a social worker who deals with many aspects of the community as a way of meeting the treatment needs of the delinquent. This latter group believed the probation officer must ally himself with groups seeking the solution to those community problems that are causative factors in the delinquent's behavior leading to referral in court. One person reasoned that if the probation officer understands, as the result of a careful study, the various factors that lead to the poor adjustment of the delinquent within the community, then he has the responsibility of dealing with those pressures as they impinge on the behavior of the youngster and as they impinge on the activities of other youngsters, who at this point may or may not have come to the attention of the court.

Does this indicate that the probation officer should take responsibility for any and all problems the delinquent might have? The consensus of the Michigan workshop was that it is the function of the probation officer to provide community leadership that is aimed at encouraging and helping the community to develop resources to deal with such problems. For example, the probation officer might attend meetings of community organizations and encourage their interest in various problems faced by the youth in the community, such as the need for organized social activities for teen-agers, or the problem of employment during summer vacations.

"The court is in a particularly good position to see the gaps in services which exist in the community, to bring these gaps to the attention of planning groups in the community, and to work with them to secure more adequate services."[8]

The size of the probation staff, the resources of the community, and the policies of a given court determine how much of a community organizer the probation officer will be. Juvenile courts, along with other community agencies, have the responsibility for bringing about wholesome changes in the community. Each individual probation officer should be assigned his part of that responsibility in a way that will not dissipate his effectiveness in meeting the demands of his case load.

The question of how circumscribed or how broad the community organization role should be in the probation task needs to be given more thought because of the wide divergence of opinion in the field.

[8]*Standard Family Court Act*, National Probation and Parole Association, New York, 1976, pp. 28–29. *Standard Juvenile Court Act*, 8th ed., National Council on Crime and Delinquency, New York, 1970, pp. 31–32. *Standards for Specialized Courts*, pp. 43–44.

ADMINISTRATIVE–MANAGEMENT ASPECTS

An indispensable precondition to effective probation services is an effective working relationship with the judge and the probation officer; each must have a clear understanding of his role in the process. This means that all channels of communication should be open between the judge and the probation officer in order to provide a free exchange of ideas.

It is often pointed out that probation officers occasionally do not respect the rights of judges to be final decision-makers regarding plans set up by courts for delinquent youths. This refers to those instances where the decision of a judge disagrees with the recommendations of a probation officer. In such situations, both judge and probation officer need to look for ways to collaborate effectively. In some instances, a judge may need help in accepting knowledgeable recommendations based on a thorough study of the delinquent before him; in others, a probation officer may need to understand that a judge has taken other factors into consideration in making his decision. It should be remembered that in deciding a case a judge must take into consideration the protection of the community. Also some judges, in certain types of cases, may be motivated by community reaction. As judge and probation officer work together, the judge tends to become more "case-conscious" and the probation officer becomes more "community-conscious." Thus, the occasions of differences between the recommendation of the probation officer and the plan accepted by the judge diminish and boil down to those cases where legal principle dictates something other than the recommendation made to the judge by the probation officer.

Most authorities in the field agree that the family should be informed of the recommendation, but they should also be told that the judge has the authority to follow, modify, or reject it. It is recognized that both judge and probation officer must be accountable. The judge is ultimately responsible for the probation plan, but this does not make the probation officer any less responsible than the judge for the kind of plan that is developed.

Regarding the administrative aspects of his work, *the probation officer must understand the framework in which he works and recognize how procedures affect practical goals.* Administration is a process in itself that requires thoughtful scrutiny to make it most effective. One of the key administrative personnel who contributes to the quality of service is the supervisor.[9]

How the job can be defined and divided is the research task. There are certain areas of knowledge, skills, and attitudes necessary for effective performance. The knowledge, skills, and attitudes enumerated below are those considered by the experts in the field to be the most important; an effort has been made to list them in the order of their importance.

[9]Advisory Committee on Social Welfare Education, *Social Workers for California,* Regents of the University of California, Los Angeles, 1971, p. 34.

FUNCTION OF THE JUVENILE COURT

The function of the juvenile court is to determine when society has the right to enter into a child's life and, when this is the case, how to deal with him on an individualized basis.

LAW

Knowledge of the law is a prerequisite for the adequate functioning of the probation officer. He needs to have an understanding of the philosophy and the role of law in society. The principles, strengths, and weaknesses of the law and the legal system need to be understood in order to apply knowledge of social work in the court. With respect for the law should come an improvement in the relationships between the lawyers and probation officers. In the language of the social worker, the court is the legal system. The probation officer must see himself in relation to law. While much of the knowledge of law must come through service training, the basic respect for law should be taught by the universities to all students of social work.

HUMAN GROWTH AND CHANGE

Knowledge of the dynamics of human behavior and of personality development enables the probation officer to understand the reasons behind a youth's actions. Knowledge of psychopathology aids in the recognition of disturbed youths and parents. There are many delinquents in the probation officer's case load who lack the social and personal resources needed to adjust without help. Many become delinquent because of situational factors and then react defiantly to the process of being taken into custody and appearing in the juvenile court. The behavior of some others is due to neurotic conflicts or psychosis. A still greater number suffer from behavioral disorders characterized by poor impulse control, sometimes termed "acting-out" behavior.

Understanding the behavior and attitudes of this variety of persons requires both sociological and psychological knowledge. In some cases it is important to have sufficient recognition of pathology so that the probation officer does not attempt to deal with an emotionally ill person, but instead refers him to other professional resources.

SOCIOLOGY AND DELINQUENCY

Knowledge of social phenomena, class values, cultural patterns, and economic influences is needed as background to understand the behavior patterns of many youths. Knowledge of earlier efforts to deal with delinquency; of the role of the police; of the background, philosophy, and structure of the juvenile court; of the uses made of detention and of training schools; of the efforts to prevent delinquency; of the treatment agencies such as child guidance clinics; and of the extent of the current problem—all such knowledge is needed by the probation officer.

THE COMMUNITY

Knowledge of the power structure of the community, of its social resources, how it reacts to various types of delinquent behavior, and what methods of social action can be gained in securing new resources for youth—these fields should also be familiar to the probation officer seeking to serve delinquency. Knowledge of the power structure and of the economic and bureaucratic organization of the community offers an understanding of how these determine what can be accomplished.

SELF

In probation work, the officer himself helps the adolescent modify his behavior. It is the relationship with the delinquent that is the major treatment tool. The better the probation officer understands his own attitudes and beliefs, the better he can manage to discipline himself and to use the developing relationship in a professional way. Knowledge of self mitigates against the probation officer working out his personal conflicts through his clients.

ROLES OF OTHER PERSONNEL

To avoid a conflict of approach to the delinquent and his family, the roles of other persons serving him need to be clearly defined and understood. Knowledge of the proper role of the police and of juvenile bureaus and of information regarding detention facilities and the appropriate use of the detention, and the contribution to be expected from detention personnel are all needed by the probation officer. In order to integrate the functions of the court with the functions of the other agencies in the community, knowledge of the various roles of these agencies is essential.

AUTHORITY

Knowledge of authority—its use and misuse—must be emphasized as one of the keys to effective probation. Although the professional literature offers many definitions of authority, referring both to its sociological and psychological aspects, perhaps the dictionary version offers and adequate frame of reference.

Authority is: (1) the right to command and to enforce obedience; the right to act by virtue of office, and (2) the power derived from intellectual or moral superiority, from reputation, or from whatever else commands influence, respect, or esteem; as the authority of wisdom.

Persons coming before the court generally know its power to restrain the delinquent or remove him from his home, and commit him to an institution or appropriate facility. Knowledge of the proper application of social controls determines whether the delinquent can benefit from the court experience or not.

RECORDS AND THEIR USE

How and why records are kept is essential knowledge. The probation officer should be both student and critic of his own practice, and recording what he does gives him this opportunity. Each court will determine the social record that suits its needs. Often the probation officers are impatient with the amount of time needed for recording, but few would eliminate it. The case record serves as a protection to the client, as a possible resource, and as a way to develop skill and to gain new knowledge. The chief function of the record itself is to describe the situation, what the delinquent is doing about it, and the suggested plan for assisting him.

There are many other factors that should be considered when discussing the role of the probation officer. Attitudes and personality factors, such as sensitivity to client needs, objectivity, nonjudgmental attitude, personal integrity, motivation to learn, development into a well-rounded person, and a commitment to serve the delinquent, are all important, but they are beyond the scope of this chapter.

FUTURE TRENDS IN THE JUVENILE JUSTICE SYSTEM

The infusion of the adversary process into the juvenile justice system as a result of the *Gault* decision had a revolutionary impact on the procedural aspects of the juvenile court and its components. For the first time, the juvenile had a strong voice in the system's decisions through his attorney. Defense council's appearance on the scene resulted in a significant increase in the pressure upon practitioners of juvenile justice to defend their actions. Initially, the "advocate" maximized his impact on the system. Attorneys could easily exploit witnesses gathered through hurried, or less than diligent, police work; by social workers categorizations of juveniles which were frequently made on hastily compiled, inaccurate information; and untrained judges called upon by the system to uphold "the minor's best interests."

To some extent, practitioners in the field of juvenile corrections have "turned the corner" and increased their proficiency in dealing with youthful offenders; thus, making it more difficult for any advocate of special interests to manipulate the system and its processes.

No sooner had the field of juvenile corrections stabilized somewhat when Congress commenced putting immense pressure on juvenile courts throughout the nation to demonstrate the clear benefits of their federally funded programs. The message from the federal government was clear: Show us that what you are doing has resulted in the correction of effective approaches to the nation's problems of juvenile crime; show us that your activities have generated information useful in devising these approaches, or, we will reconsider the budget levels appropriate for such activities.

Funding agencies were no longer giving state and county governments a "free ride" in funding programs dealing with the juvenile offender.

Again, practitioners in the field reacted.

In Massachusetts, for example, nearly all juvenile institutions have been closed and replaced by community alternatives; Vermont, too, has followed along the same lines. California, through its probation subsidy programs, has moved in the same direction. Future prospects offer even greater use of these kings of community arrangements when handling our juvenile offenders. Finally, the juvenile justice system—a system permeated with a "don't rock the boat" attitude—has responded to the challenge. It was recognized that court intervention "may well do more harm than good." And it was also recognized that probation, in some instances, was a farce. And, carrying the "awakening" one step further, it was acknowledged that conditions in training schools can only be described as "distressing."

REACTING TO PROBLEMS

Any one who has followed the juvenile justice field knows that since 1899, when the first juvenile court law was enacted in Cook County, Illinois, the problems that have erupted have, fortunately, not been without some workable solutions. Unfortunately, practitioners in this field are continually "reacting" to such problems instead of moving to the forefront and seeking remedies to problems "bubbling beneath the surface."

Recent trends in the development of the juvenile justice system as a whole will have a substantial impact on the role of all components of the system. These trends and their consequences should be of primary concern to practitioners, especially to administrators in the field of juvenile justice. These trends and their consequences must be considered together in predicting the roles of practitioners within the system.

TRENDS AND THEIR FUTURE CONSEQUENCES

The basic nature of the juvenile justice system will change significantly. More so than ever, the court will take a "legalistic" view of the case before them. More and more, full disclosure of the factual case on each side—that is the side of the juvenile and that of the practitioner—will be the rule; and not the exception. Within the past several years, legislators have taken a tougher approach to juvenile crime. There is no doubt that cries of "community-based corrections and diversion programs in the field of juvenile (and adult correction) have flopped," have influenced such legislators. There has been one study in particular by the *National Observer* (January 5, 1975), entitled "Reform Is A Flop," which suggests that efforts to rehabilitate the juvenile and adult offender have shown little or no positive results. Given these dismal evaluations, and national frustrations with what appears to be an evergrowing juvenile crime rate, the current reaction advocating a hard realism that calls for an increased use of state institutions may not be surprising. Indeed, reflecting such views, several states have modified their juvenile court laws to reflect a "tougher approach."

Witness the recent headline article of a local California newspaper (*Mercury-News*, San Jose, California, Sunday, October 10, 1976):

'Get Tough' Law for Juveniles

Juveniles who commit violent crimes will be dealt with more harshly under a new California 'get tough' law. . . .

The law, which takes effect January 1, 1977, prescribes that juveniles aged 16 and 17 suspected of such crimes as burglary, armed robbery, and kidnap can be tried as adults. There can be exceptions, but the effect won't be known until the law has been in operation. . . .

A provision in the law calls for the District Attorney's office to take cases involving youths who have broken adult statute laws to juvenile court. Apparently, a juvenile probation officer files a petition outlining the offenses and presents it to the court.

The District Attorney's office will advise in these cases whether the crime is a misdemeanor or a felony. The final decision, however, will rest with the judge hearing the case. . . .

[There is] a provision in the law that would commit 16 and 17-year-olds to state prison for a variety of violent crimes. . . . [There is a section in the law] that allows judges to commit [a youngster] to the California Youth Authority two years longer than at present, or until they are 23.

Because of the "get tough" laws in California, and in other states, the role of the practitioner (probation officers, social workers, police, etc.) in the juvenile justice system will change drastically. The environment will become even more legalistic. The practitioner must build a strong case. The juvenile offender (defender) will find greater need for "discovery motions," and the judge must be prepared to supervise the adversary proceedings to insure its effectiveness and to prevent delays. Greater preparation based upon a more thorough knowledge of the facts will require a high degree of interpersonal skills. Witnesses will need to be thoroughly interrogated in advance of the "trial"; because, in essence, it will, indeed, be a trial. The technology of crime will need to be mastered. More time will be needed and therefore, for the same number of cases, more judges, district attorneys, and public defenders.

A major change in the juvenile court hearing will be the use of plea bargaining. This is not to say it is not being utilized at this time; the increase will, however, be staggering. Negotiations, rather than "the best interests of the child," (and in some cases unfortunately, the community) will be the tools. In these cases, the judge will play the mediator rather than the decider.

Perhaps the most significant change in the juvenile justice system—and this is not to say the change is not a positive one—will be the selection of judges. Selection will be strictly through abilities instead of seniority or "it's-your-turn-lists."

The growth of management capacity will be one of the major changes of the next decade. Although presently nonexistent, the art of justice management is being discovered. Once a cadre of managers are trained and active in the field, even the smaller officers will seek out the people who can help their organizations to function effectively—eliminating the present fragmentation. This trend is now reaching components of both the criminal and juvenile justice system. Both an increase in interpersonal skills and an awareness of management information will come as a result of intelligent people trying to make the system work. Effectiveness measures will be established after many decades of floundering and goal identification. When these measures are discovered, masses of operations and priorities will be changed.

Work loads will change as more of the *status offenders* are diverted into other channels. Narcotic offenses will also fall under "the juvenile diversionary plans"; but the diversion will, in most cases, be court supervised.

In a speech to a chapter meeting of the California Probation Parole Correction Association at Davis, California, on April 15, 1976, the keynote speaker, R. Parness, a noted lecturer, author, and academician, made some provocative predictions:

1. Within the next year, a *voluntary* treatment program for those in prisons [and juvenile institutions] will be eliminated;

2. Within the next five years, *involuntary* treatment programs for those on parole will be eliminated—in fact, the concept of parole will die away.

3. Within the next ten years, involuntary treatment programs for those not institutionalized but under court jurisdictions will be eliminated—i.e., the elimination of probation as we know it;

4. The rapidly growing trend in professional publications—one now

spread to mass publications, periodicals, and newspapers—argues that the optimism of the behavioral sciences at the turn of the century is no longer warranted by our experience. Instead, the new view holds that

a. Most crime is not the result of any sicknesses;

b. Even when some sickness is the cause of a serious crime, we have no way of knowing which offender is truly sick, what the sickness is, how to treat it, or when the patient is cured. Hence, let us dispense with involuntary treatment of convicted criminals. (Although most of this reasoning is still directed at institutions, its obvious bearing on probation and parole is apparent.)

5. Increasingly, people must recognize their personal and individual responsibility for their acts, which—when wrong—are subject to society's condemnation and retribution in the form of punishment rather than society's tacit approval as formerly under the "treatment concept." This new perspective reflects not only what the public wants but also fosters the kind of rehabilitation we are really striving for, i.e., the nonrepetition of criminal behavior, pure and simple.

These predictions by Parness carry additional weight when one considers the study by Robert Martinson of the City University of New York. After examining the results of 231 rehabilitation programs conducted around the country from 1945 to 1967, Martinson concluded: "With few and isolated exceptions, the rehabilitative efforts that have been supported so far have had no appreciable effect on recidivism."

Martinson was not referring only to adult programs.

James Q. Wilson of Harvard University carried Martinson's statement one step further in his well-publicized book, *Thinking About Crime.* Wilson argued that the primary purpose of prisons—and in most cases juvenile institutions qualify—is to isolate and punish. He writes that the certainty of punishment will deter more people from committing criminal acts. Several studies support this thesis. According to Gordon Tullock of Virginia Polytechnic Institute: "There is no question any longer . . . that punishment does cut down on crime."

There is no doubt that support for the rehabilitative ideal has been eroded at both ends of the ideological spectrum.

> *With the apparent fall of the rehabilitative ideal, we are quite possibly at the threshold of a major new penal reform movement. The Age of Enlightment brought to a largely retributive tradition a humanitarian philosophy: the unitarian view of man, the importance of deterrence in punishment, and the humanistic development of the penitentiary system. The science of society and behavior had, by the late Nineteenth Century, generated some understanding of the causes of crime and, therefore,*

corresponding sanctions for treatment. Referred to as the positive school of corrections, this movement has since become identified with rehabilitation, . . . individualization of sanctions, and indeterminate sentencing, which in turn have come to be identified with gross disparity and often inhumanity in the name of treatment. It should not take too many reports before the positivist movement is likely to be pronounced dead. . . .[10]

COURT DECISIONS: ANOTHER INFLUENCE

Yet another influence likely to impinge on the juvenile court of the future is Supreme Court decisions. In essence, the frequently cited Supreme Court decisions in the matter of *Kent, Gault,* and *Winship* are probably the first of many tending to isolate rights, as opposed to needs.

Constitutional protection of juvenile rights is likely to emphasize an increasing requirement that bifurcated hearings replace the traditional juvenile court hearings which are both jurisdictional and dispositional simultaneously.

Bifurcated hearings, in effect, procedurally distinguish between rights and needs. In sharp contrast to the *parens patriae* of feudal England and of early American juvenile courts, the concept of "due process" is likely to gain increasing emphasis in the jurisdictional part of juvenile court hearings. Put simply, the part of the juvenile court hearing in which the jurisdiction of the court over the juvenile is determined is likely to appear increasingly similar to the adult criminal courts. Rules of evidence and adversary attorneys arguing for the prosecution and for the offense are often likely to appear in *all* juvenile court hearings—but certainly in all "contested hearings"—in the future. The forerunner of this change seems to be the present emphasis placed on advising juveniles of their constitutional rights.

Rules of evidence for *adult* criminal hearings are likely also to become the standard of proof in future *juvenile* court matters. It is not inconceivable that the legal concept of *mens rea* will completely replace the common law concept of *parens patriae*. In other words, the juvenile justice system is likely to find not only that it must prove that the *actus reus* (illegal act) was committed by the juvenile, but also that the *mens rea* (illegal intent) was also present when the act was committed. Inundated by what may appear to be harsh technicalities, the juvenile court may conceivably find that these preliminary procedures help rather than hinder its ultimate success. This is likely to occur in the process of first isolating the juvenile's rights and then, once his rights have been protected, taking care of his needs.

On a broader social spectrum, the needs of the community must also be included. Protection of community members from assaultive juveniles will come of necessity and must be weighted against the needs of a juvenile following diag-

[10]Kellogg, Frederick K., Contained in a review of Andrew Van Hirch's book, *Doing Justice: The Choice of Punishments;* Report of the Committee for the Study of Incarceration, Hill and Wang, New York, 1976. Kellog's review was in December 1976's *Federal Probation*, p. 79.

nosis. In other words, protection of the juvenile's rights, followed by sophisticated diagnosis of his needs, should not overshadow the needs of the community to be protected—particularly if the juvenile is diagnosed as violently assaultive.

Amid growing concern for the protection of the community, juvenile justice is likely to witness a steady increase in concern for the needs for the juvenile as well. And it is likely that the conflict of needs will increase and only be resolved in favor of the community. But insofar as the juvenile will always have the need to adjust to the community, resolving community needs will remain in the best interest of the individual juvenile.

SUMMARY

There are numerous definitions of probation, but perhaps the most acceptable is the definition proposed by the Children's Bureau: probation is "a legal status in which a child, following adjudication in a delinquent case, is permitted to remain within the community, subject to supervision by the court through the court's Probation Department or an agency designated by the court, and subject to being returned to the court at any time during probation."

The goals of probation vary, obviously, because of the distinct needs of individual delinquents. However, all such variations should lead to the minimum goal of stopping delinquent behavior.

The following factors affect the goals of probation: (1) the situation and capacity of the client; (2) the culture and environment of the youth and his family; (3) the concept of probation held by the judge and the probation staff; (4) the quality and quantity of the staff, as they effect the services available to the youth and his family; and (5) the court's situation in the community and the availability of community resources.

The juvenile probation officer has two roles that must not conflict. He must be considered first, as a court officer or "arm of the court" and, second, as a correctional social worker.

As a *social diagnostician,* the probation officer must (1) identify and evaluate factors causing the delinquent behavior and (2) develop and recommend a necessary program that will eliminate or alleviate these factors.

As an *agent of change,* the most characteristic elements of positive change may come about through (1) the interaction between the delinquent and the probation officer; (2) the referral of the delinquent to other resources and the help he receives from these services; and (3) the creation of new resources.

An indispensable precondition to the affected probation services is an effective working relationship between the judge and the probation officer. Each must have a clear understanding of his role in the process. This means that all channels of communication should be open between the judge and the probation officer in order to provide a free exchange of ideas.

In order to be effective, the probation officer must have knowledge of (1) the function of the juvenile court, (2) criminal law, (3) human growth and change, (4) sociology and delinquency, (5) the community, (6) self, (7) roles of the other personnel, (8) authority, and, finally, (9) records and their use.

Chapter 9 closes with a succinct discussion of the future role of components in the juvenile justice system.

ANNOTATED REFERENCES

Amos, William E. and Manella, Raymond L., *Readings in the Administrations of Institutions Toward Delinquent Youths,* Charles C Thomas, Springfield, Illinois, 1974.

This is an excellent discussion of the types of institution available for delinquent youngsters throughout the United States as well as the types of probation and correctional service.

Crime and Delinquency Literature, Information Center, National Council on Crime and Delinquency, vol. 2, no. 2., April 1970.

This publication gives a great deal of information on publications in the area of crime and delinquency, including probation services.

Davis, S. M., *Rights of Juveniles: The Juvenile Justice System,* Clark Boardman Co., 1974.

Davis discusses the functions of the probation officer in nontechnical language. This is an excellent source for those who are interested in the multitudinal tasks probation officers are expected to perform.

Imlay, C. H. and Reid, E. L., "The Probation Office, Sentencing and the Winds of Change," *Federal Probation,* vol. 34, Dec 1975, no. 4, pp. 9–19.

This article gives an in-depth contemporary study of probation services.

Joint Commission on Correctional Manpower and Training, Inc., *A Time to Act: Final Report,* Joint Commission on Correctional Manpower and Training, Washington, D.C., 1969.

The commission discusses the demands on manpowern as well as educational resources for correctional purposes. This is an in-depth study of the training necessary in order to be a correctional worker and the opportunities available in this field.

Turner, David R., *Probation and Parole Officer,* Arco Publishing Co., New York, 1969.

If the student is in training for positions in probation services, this particular volume is a must. It is a civil service primer that discusses the functions of probation and parole officers, as well as the knowledge that must be obtained in order to secure a position in the field. Numerous test questions are applicable to the field of probation and parole and serve as an excellent guide for test-taking.

Vedder, Clyde B., and Kay, Barbara A., *Probation and Parole*, Charles C Thomas, Inc., Springfield, Illinois, 1974.

The authors discuss the numerous functions and assignments that must be carried by probation officers and the great degree of knowledge necessary in order to carry out such functions. Casework services, court work, and understanding of the offender is discussed. This is an excellent source for the beginning student who has limited knowledge of correctional work.

CHAPTER TEN police services for juveniles

The primary responsibility of law enforcement is the control and prevention of crime and delinquency through the enforcement of laws that are necessary for the good order of society. Since many criminal acts are committed by minors under the age of eighteen years, a large proportion of police work involves the detection, investigation, apprehension, and referral of these juveniles. In addition, law enforcement agencies are concerned with minors who come to their attention for noncriminal reasons. The initial handling of neglected children, for example, is often a police matter; and police officers also have the responsibility of dealing with runaway, incorrigible, and wayward youngsters.

Because most juveniles charged with delinquency are apprehended by police, the first contact obviously is an important one and undoubtedly leaves a lasting impression on the child. If he is intimidated and frightened, he is not apt to respond favorably to efforts to help him. On the contrary, he will very likely tend to withdraw and resist any efforts on his behalf.

Consequently, there is a real necessity for knowledge and training in juvenile problems. The police officer who apprehends a child must know how to work with that child. He must know how to dispel the child's fear and put him at ease so that he will be cooperative and responsive.

THE AWARENESS OF THE POLICE

Law enforcement officials have always been concerned with the control of juvenile crime; however, within the last three decades, police organizations began placing particular emphasis on their work with juveniles, and a definite trend in the development of police services for juveniles has been established. While the growth of the delinquency programs throughout the nation contributed to the increased emphasis on juvenile police work, other factors were probably equally responsible. The policeman who walked a beat several years ago had a greater opportunity to know more intimately the inhabitants and social institutions in the area he patroled and could easily resolve minor law enforcement problems, but the replacement of

The arresting officer, ultimately, has to make the important decision to place a youngster in custody. If the decision is to deliver the minor to the custody of the probation officer (juvenile hall), all pertinent data must accompany the minor. Photo courtesy of Michael Johnson, Santa Clara County Probation Department and the Campbell Police Department, Campbell, Calif.

the foot officer by motorized patrol units reduced personal contact between the police officer and the inhabitants of his area. Although the public have demanded a return to the "foot patrol" officer, administration of police agencies find it impossible to comply due to insufficient manpower. The fact remains that patrol vehicles covers more territory is difficult to dismiss.

At the same time, within the last several decades, there has been an apparent decrease in the effectiveness of family controls. As a result, police and other public agencies have been compelled to assume greater responsibility in containing juvenile antisocial behavior. Public demand for more activity in the field of juvenile control, and growing realization that apprehension and punishment alone are not sufficient to stem the tide of delinquency, also contributed to the increasing emphasis on juvenile police work.

Law enforcement officers, although generally aware of the primary factors that produce criminal behavior, are not basically concerned with the "why" of human behavior. They are employed, trained, and directed to find answers of "what, how, when, who, and where." The police officer must use fruitfully the *anaysis of motive and of causation* as an investigative aid in searching for the perpetrator of a crime; however, the immediate primary goal is to *detect, identify,* and *apprehend* the individual.[1] It is incumbent upon the police administrator to expend his efforts and his resources as effectively as possible to minimize opportunities for crime. The "problem" of delinquency for the police administrator is not one of probing the philosophical and political roots of our social and economic systems. Nor is it the police administrator's obligation to engage in the longitudinal or cross-bisectional psychological evaluations of the delinquents. The American citizen generally has not indicated that the police should do more than protect their persons and their property. The concept of the thief catcher remains. It has been solely through the works of the police officers themselves that duties beyond the traditional ones have been adopted—despite the public.

The problem of congestion in urban communities and increased migration to the suburban areas have caused law enforcement problems. Law enforcement in a changing community has caused a great deal of concern for practitioners in the field; the International Association of Chiefs of Police have attempted to channel information down to local law enforcement agencies. George W. O'Connor and Nelson A. Watson have commented that there are law enforcement problems in

> *a nation on the move from the farm to the city—such as the United States. The technological and industrial facets of our economy have met to bring people into the crowd of centralized living. We have moved from a farm-based economy to a city-centered economy. The compression of persons into our urban centers has added to the complexity of our concern . . . the density of population in our cities serves only to bring persons into conflict with increased frequency . . . the phenomenom of juvenile delinquency and youthful criminology represent the end products of diverse, complex, and presently insoluble social and personal problems.[2]*

It is clear that the law enforcement arm of our various governmental executives has been developed to protect the community by reducing the opportunity for criminal behavior. The job has been made more difficult because of the vast social changes during the past half century. Changes such as population density, social mobility, social deprivation, saturation of communication media with status-orienated advertising, and other social innovations have increased both the desires and the opportunities for crime.

IMPORTANCE OF THE POLICE ROLE

Most juveniles involved in delinquent behavior are taken into custody by the police. A few of these youngsters are referred to the family court (juvenile court) by

[1]G. W. O'Connor and N. A. Watson, *Juvenile Delinquency and Youth Crime: The Police Role,* International Association Chiefs of Police, Washington, D.C. 1964, p. 17.
[2]*Ibid.,* p. 16.

parents, guardians, or relatives who are unable to cope with their incorrigible behavior. Other sources of referrals to the juvenile court are schools, churches, or social agencies. However, most juveniles usually have their initial contact with legal authorities through the police officer. How to conduct himself with a child is only one phase of the police officer's role.

An important task is how the police officer performs the function of referral disposition to other agencies; he must make some crucial decisions in dealing with youngsters taken into custody. The arresting officer must answer some extremely important questions: What should a police officer do with a child taken into custody for commiting a delinquent act? What action should an officer take when a child is suffering from neglect or abuse? What exactly is the role to be played by the police officer in a community's program to control juvenile delinquency and to protect and further the welfare of young people?

The importance of these questions is readily understood. The police-juvenile relationship is a matter that requires careful consideration and planning in every community.

Primary among the factors affecting police services for juveniles in any community is the authority the police force has over juveniles, and also the functions assumed by the police department with regard to juveniles.

The extent of local police authority and responsibility, and the manner in which local forces exercise them, depend on both the particular powers given a local police force by law, as affected by judicial interpretation, and on the limitations provided by law. The attitude and policy of the department head may also have some effect. As a result of these variables the number and types of functions carried out by police departments in one community may exceed, or differ from, those undertaken in another.

Four functions, however, are the main concern of all police departments. Stemming directly from the customary legislative mandate that the police shall be responsible for the protection of life and property and for the maintenance of law and order, these functions apply to juveniles and adults alike.

1. *Control of crime and violations of the law.* This includes apprehension and referral for prosecution, or for other appropriate action, of persons who have committed crimes or other offenses.

2. *Enforcement of regulations.* This means enforcement of a vast number of restrictions imposed by law on people's day-to-day activities for the purposes of protecting the safety and rights of the general public. Traffic regulations are examples of such restrictions.

3. *Rendering of general assistance.* A function readily excepted by the police in most places, is the rendering of general assistance in a variety of cases having little relation to crime control or regulation. Some examples of these forms of assistance are: helping to locate lost or runaway children, searching for lost property and maintaining service for restoring to the owner lost property that has been

found, and aiding persons locked out of their homes. These duties police have accepted largely as a matter of custom.

4. *Prevention of delinquency in crime.* So far as juveniles are concerned, the developments mentioned in practice apply principally to known or suspected delinquents, or to children who are neglected. Police interests in juveniles has not been limited, however, to those already in need. A function, now engaged in many police departments to varying degrees is the prevention of delinquency in crime. Thus, in many communities the police act to prevent delinquency by enforcing laws, ordinances, or regulations. Quite frequently, too, it is the policy of the police to act protectively toward children who are found wandering the streets late at night, or under circumstances that might be harmful to them. In these cases the police return the child to his home and possibly counsel the parents or guardian on the need to give more supervisory care.

In addition to pursuing these more or less customary preventive activities, some police departments have now extended their work to include recreation character-building programs, safety-education programs, and counseling service. The counseling service is directed toward children and young people who have come to the attention of the police because of behavior that suggests they are particularly vulnerable to delinquency.

A considerable number of communities have made definite progress toward giving sharper definition to police service for juveniles and how it should be carried out. To summarize some of these local developments, many police departments now give greater attention to training their officers in those modern concepts of law enforcement to emphasize protection, treatment, and rehabilitation of the child. In many places, officers have been appointed to work with children. In a considerable number of communities, units or divisions have been established to carry on the work with juveniles. Special procedures have likewise been devised for rehabilitating and, at the same time, steering the juvenile away from the public exposure and shame so often visited upon the adult. *The Task Force Report: Juvenile Delinquency and Youth Crime*, delineates some of these special procedures. It recommends the following:

1. The police should promptly determine which cases are suitable for pre-judicial disposition. Where there are juvenile specialists, they should be present at the station house for as many hours of the day as possible and available on call when absent, to facilitate speedy pre-judicial decisions. The police should have written standards for release, for referral to nonjudicial sources, and for referral to the juvenile court. They should not be precluded from making nonjudicial referrals in juvenile cases involving minor criminal acts, non-criminal delinquent behavior, and violations of probation and

parole. While referral policies for probation and parole violators require close coordination between the police and other authorities, an automatic bar to adjustment seems unnecessary. Rather, there should be an area of discussion and a clear understanding that adjustments must immediately be reported by the police to the court or correctional agents concerned.

2. The standards for release and adjustment should be sent to all agencies of delinquency control and should be reviewed and appraised jointly at periodic intervals. There should be made a basis for in-service training that would consider, besides the decision-making duties of the police, materials pertinent to increasing an understanding of juvenile behavior and making more effective use of nonjudicial community resources.

3. In cases where information on the child is needed, it should be sought through home visits as well as through official records, and the police should be aided or replaced, by paid case aides drawn from the nieghborhood within the police district and selected for their knowledge of the community and their ability to communicate easily with juveniles and their families.

4. In addition to outright release and referrals to nonjudicial agencies with or without warning, the police should have the option to refer directly to the juvenile court specific classes of cases, including those of more serious offenders, repeated offenders for whom other and persistent, redirecting efforts have failed, and certain parole and probation violators.

5. The police should not undertake to redirect juveniles by such means as conducting quasi-judicial hearings or imposing special duties or personal obligations.[3]

   Finally, in those communities that have given particular attention to the problem of young people, the relation of the police to other community agencies should be strengthened and clarified so that the police have a better understanding of what can, and what should, be done for children through use of other resources in the community. In order to insure complete understanding and clarification, coordination with other delinquency control agencies, particularly the court, efficient deployment of juvenile specialists, and

[3]The President's Commission on Law Enforcement and Administration of Justice, *Task Force Report: Juvenile Delinquency and Youth Crime,* U.S. Government Printing Office, Washington, D.C., 1967, p. 19. See also J. P. Gibbs, *Crime Punishment and Deterrence,* Scientific Publishing Co., Inc., New York, 1975.

better training for both specialists and regular patrolmen is, obviously, quite necessary.

Naturally, some of these activities of the police in regard to children, and particularly the "prevention" activities, have not gone unquestioned. For example, the issue has been raised by many citizens and by some police officers themselves as to whether programs involving such matters as recreation and unofficial probation are not beyond the proper scope of police work and more the obligation of other agencies. Also, in regard to procedures affecting known delinquents, the opinion has been expressed in some quarters that the police should simply turn all children directly over to the juvenile court authorities, without undertaking further service for them. Once again, the original premise of this chapter is underscored: in every community, police services for juveniles depend on the functions assigned to, or assumed by, the police department, and on how these functions are carried out. *Therefore, police services to a particular community depend upon what the community expects or demands.* One of the chief aims of this chapter is to outline various types of practices in regard to these functions insofar as they affect children, to offer opinion as to how certain of the functions might be best carried out, and to help determine whether, in certain instances, a particular function is a proper concern of the police.

JUVENILES AND POLICE PHILOSOPHY

Modern Western society has developed the institution of the police as a specialized social agency to preserve the peace, to protect life and property from attacks by criminals and from injury by the careless and inadvertent offender, and to enforce laws. In recent years the traditional police role has been broadened to include many aspects of social service formerly the exclusive concern of specialized social institutions such as churches, schools, and public welfare agencies. The police today cannot be excused from applying their utmost efforts toward prevention, identification, and early reversal of aberrant antisocial processes: the vicious cycle of school dropouts, unemployment, crime, and welfare dependents that vitally concerns all organized agencies of society, including the police.[4]

In handling offenders, concepts of punishment and retribution, now outdated, must be abandoned in favor of therapy and rehabilitation. Society cannot

---

[4]N. A. Watson and R. N. Walker, *Training Police for Work with Juveniles*, International Association of Chiefs of Police, Washington, D.C., 1965, p. 1. See also T. F. Adams, *Introduction to the Administration of Justice: An Overview of the Justice System and Its Components*, Prentice-Hall, Inc., Englewood Cliffs, New Jersey, 1975 Chapters 5, 6.

afford mounting recidivism and unchecked escalation of delinquent behavior from petty to capital crimes.[5]

Basic police responsibility for both juveniles and adults is placed on policemen on the beat, whether on foot or in a motor vehicle. They are primarily responsible for maintaining law and order, with occasional help from specialized personnel, e.g., the juvenile unit, available in larger departments. Patrolmen themselves, however are in no sense relieved of basic responsibility and authority for police-juvenile relations since they remain the key persons for deterring and controlling antisocial acts affecting all citizens, including minors. The police job consists primarily of investigation, apprehension, and preventive patrol.[6]

Clearly, every police officer must be well-trained in the principles and practices that are peculiar to police relations with juveniles as specified by laws and police regulations. The juvenile unit is available as a referral and supportive element to assist the patrolman, as requested, with cases involving juveniles, but the large share of such work remains with the patrolman in routine day-to-day duties on his beat.[7]

Every police officer must studiously avoid any action that will solidify or reinforce undesirable behaviors. As in relations between a physician and his patient, the offender is not to be harmed by police actions, however well-intentioned these may be. In this connection, psychological abuse, in the form of threats, accusations, and recriminations are likely, in the long run, to be much more harmful to juveniles than physical abuse.

Nowhere in police philosophy is there anything about punishment by the police; nowhere is there anything about rehabilitating or reforming the offender. These are not police functions. Moreover, nowhere is there anything specific about juveniles in this philosophy. *Juveniles are not exempt from the enforcement of the law.* They must be held to answer for their wrongs against society. Tender years, immaturity, irresponsibility are not *excuses* for theft, vandalism, or violence. The fact that a person is an adult does not always permit police to use force in arresting him; nor does the fact that one is a juvenile, per se, require that no force be used. What is unnecessary or excessive force is determined by the extent of the circumstances, of which age is but one factor. This is not to say that there are no differences in handling juveniles and adults. However, insofar as the realization of basic objectives is concerned—the vigorous and successful completion of the job given the police by society—there are no fundamental philosophical or policy differences. There are *adaptations* of these philosophical concepts which, while they do not in any way modify the basic objectives, result in procedural differences in the handling of juveniles as compared to adults.[8]

This is not to say that law enforcement agencies throughout the nation are not

[5]*Ibid.*
[6]*Ibid.*
[7]*Ibid.*
[8]O'Connor and Watson, *Police Role,* p. 33.

Although police services for juveniles should be based on rehabilitation, realistic appraisal of arrest situations dictates that caution should always be exercised when taking someone into custody. Arresting a juvenile can be an extremely dangerous task. Photo courtesy of Berkeley Police Department, Berkeley, Calif.

concerned about rehabilitation. The police department, of course, subscribes to the public policy, generally held throughout the nation, which dictates that the primary objective or programs for dealing with juvenile delinquents and youthful criminals is rehabilitation; law enforcement programs, practices, and procedures are devised to implement that policy.

In summary, the philosophy of police-juvenile relations should be based on:

1. *Respect* for individual personality whether a suspect or victim is involved.

2. *Accepted* criteria of human relations.

3. *Therapy* rather than punishment as a final goal.

4. *Crime prevention* and deterrence rather than apprehensions, detection, and court procedures.

5. *Police initiative* and active cooperation with all local youth-serving agencies and institutions in efforts to decrease delinquency.[9]

In police-juvenile relations, one often hears the admonition that an officer

[9]Watson and Walker, *Training Police*, p. 2.

must be a policeman first and a juvenile specialist second; every officer by his oath of office is aware of this. But there is nothing in the basic role of the police officer that prevents effective performance by the officer as a juvenile specialist.[10]

There is no justifiable philosophical basis for a different approach to juveniles by juvenile specialists as contrasted with other officers. From the point of view of the community, the juveniles, parents, the courts, and anyone else involved, a policeman is a policeman. The major problem relative to police handling of juveniles is *adequate training* of all officers and *policies* and *procedures acceptable to the people* of the community, the courts, and the police for discharging these responsibilities.[11] The important principles and approved practices must be a part of the operational armament of all patrolmen.

The objective sought by the police in handling juvenile offenders, then, even those guilty of serious crimes, is protection and rehabilitation. To this end, the police are willing and anxious to cooperate with other community agencies, both public and private. Stark realism based upon firsthand experience impels police agencies to assert that there are some young people who prove to be incorrigible and irrevocably committed to criminal ways. It must be admitted, however, that it is impossible to tell in advance which ones they are. Therefore, the arresting officer must condition himself in all cases to promote and encourage reform, but not at the expense of not practicing sound arrest procedures. Utilizing a cautious approach to all arrest situations is a must.[12]

SPECIALIZATION[13]

There have been many opinions expressed about the role of the police in programs designed to control and prevent juvenile delinquency. Modern police thinking accepts the theory of rehabilitation as being a realistic approach in most cases, and police departments have adopted techniques and methods designed to further that purpose.

Special training units within the police department, participation in the community efforts, and official stress on prevention rather than arrest and prosecution are some of the measures being devised implemented throughout the country. It is

[10]*Ibid.*

[11]*Ibid.*

[12]O'Connor and Watson, *Police Role,* p. 33.

[13]For additional reading in the area of specialization refer to: E. Eldefonso, *Youth Problems and Law Enforcement,* Prentice-Hall, Englewood Cliffs, New Jersey, Essentials of Law Enforcement Series, Chapter 5, 1971.; E. Eldefonso and W. Hartinger, *Control, Treatment and Rehabilitation of Youthful Offenders,* Glencoe Press, Beverly Hills, Cal., 1976; E. Eldefonso, and A. Coffey, *Process and Impact of the Juvenile Justice System,* Glencoe Press, Beverly Hills, Cal., 1976.

generally agreed that these activities constitute a major police role in the prevention and control of juvenile delinquency.[14]

Law enforcement agencies, recognizing the growing challenge of juvenile delinquency, have extended activities to meet the challenge and its effect upon the welfare of the community and its citizens. Police departments have organized special units within the structure of the department, staffed with personnel having qualifications in this particular field. Special training of personnel has been inaugurated to stress the importance of rehabilitation of youthful offenders rather than punitive action in all cases.

The purpose of such a unit is concentration on the understanding, control, and suppression of juvenile delinquency; the elimination of detrimental influences; and the protection of delinquent, dependent, neglected, and mistreated minors. Generally speaking these special units have the same objectives as the entire department. However, in view of the fact that the juvenile court laws are essentially protective and rehabilitative, it is frequently necessary to modify the procedures established for the handling of adults by law enforcement when dealing with juveniles.

Specialized juvenile units in police departments are known by various names in the United States. They are called, for example, *crime prevention bureaus, youth aid bureaus, juvenile bureaus, juvenile divisions,* and *juvenile control bureaus.*

The following duties are considered appropriate for juvenile control units:

1. Processing into disposition juvenile cases investigated by other units, with a possible exception of traffic cases.

2. Special patrolling of known juvenile hangouts where conditions are harmful to the welfare of children unknown or suspected.

3. Maintenance of records on juvenile cases.

4. Planning and coordinating a delinquency prevention program.

The question of a juvenile officer's responsibility for the investigation of offenses is a significant one in those departments big enough to allow for a great deal of specialization. Some such departments hold investigation by juvenile officers to a minimum, assigning cases to be cleared to an appropriate squad without reference to the age of the person thought to have committed the offense. In others, the juvenile control routinely investigates certain offenses connected with juveniles. In this latter instance, a juvenile control unit might be given responsibility for investigating and processing to disposition such specific cases as:

1. Offenses concerning children and the family, such as neglect, abuse, or abandonment.

[14]A. Coffey, E. Eldefonso and W. Hartenger, *Human Relations: Law Enforcement in a Changing Community,* 2nd ed., Prentice Hall, Inc., Englewood, N.J., 1976, Chapters 4, 7, 8, and 10.

2. Adults contributing to the delinquency of minors; employing minors in injurious, immoral or improper vocations or practices; and admitting minors to improper places.

3. Processing, possession, or sale of obscene literature when children are involved.

4. Bicycle thefts.

5. Offenses committed on school property.

6. Offenses involving juveniles, except forcible rape.

7. Gang warfare among juveniles, and other such cases.

It is particularly important for the juvenile control unit to have separate quarters in a police station. If possible, the outside entrance to these quarters should be located so that children and their parents can come and go without passing through other quarters in the building. But access to the other sections should be easy and convenient for the juvenile offenders.

Whether or not to assign officers to specialized duty in connection with juvenile cases, the extent and degree of specialization, and the duties and responsibilities of the specialists are important questions for police administrators. The decision to specialize is based on a theory that a specialist, because of superior knowledge and more intimate acquaintance with the problems, can do a better job. In large, more complex communities, the need for specialization in large police departments is probably both essential and inevitable. Therefore, the question is not whether to specialize, but just what added duties should the specialists assume and what should they take away from other personnel.

Problems in Specialization

Movement toward specialization to work with juveniles has, of course, produced its problems. Police executives have had to experiment and evolve policies largely by trial and error. There are some dangers in specialization:

1. Danger exists in that there may be a tendency for nonspecialized personnel to *ignore matters that the specialist really should handle.*

2. *Overemphasis on specialization* may produce inhibition to effective communication and may also generate morale problems. Remarks by a patrolman such as "Forget it—that's a job for the Daiper Dicks" are not entirely fictitious.

3. Another potentially dangerous situation is the *overdependence of the executive policy maker on the naturally biased viewpoint of the specialist to whom he turns for guidance.* Such policy decisions are likely to per-

petuate difficulties by subordinating general objectives to those of the speciality.

4. Certain *administrative problems* are concomitant with the decision to specialize. The first of these is how and on what basis to select a specialist. Other problems concern training, duties, and pay of such people. These questions, like the others, have no simple and universally applicable answers. What is good and proper in one community could be quite out of line in another.

5. The source of personnel for special assignments and promotions is ultimately the *patrol division*. The very nature of police organization makes this inevitable. We have here what is at once a paradox and a dilemma. The patrol division is generally conceded to be the backbone of the police organization. As such, it should be strong and dynamic. Police officials should seek ways to make the patrol more efficient and effective. Cutting off the cream of the personnel to handle specialists', duties defeats this aim to a degree. The dilemma results from the fact that the best people possible for specialized assignments (including assignments to the juvenile control unit) are usually selected, but in so doing police agencies run the risk of leaving the patrol force with the least-qualified men. This process can have an unfortunate psychological effect in that the patrol division comes to be regarded as the part of the organization to begin in and to get out of as quickly as possible. It is looked upon only as a stepping-stone to better things—the least desirable of police assignments since the so-called best men do not stay there.

Despite the potential "dangerous problems," some specialization is necessary. One reason is that the formula for handling juvenile cases arising from provisions of the law and juvenile court procedures would, in many instances, take officers away from their regular duties too frequently and too long, whereas this follow-up work can be performed economically by specialists. Even if every officer could be trained to do the job well, it would be administratively unsound to have every man try to handle to completion all details on every child. Then, too, without some specialization there would be some desirable programs that would never get off the ground. Only someone with a special interest and the necessary background can take the initiative to "spark" such programs.

In summary, then, the decision to establish a separate functional unit that is responsible for matters related to juveniles must be based on demonstrated need for more effective utilization of departmental manpower. Need may be evaluated in a number of ways, such as:

1. The inability of regular investigators to clear cases involving juveniles.

2. The extent to which juvenile case processing removes patrolmen from their beats for an extended period of time.

3. Community insistence on police involvement in nonpolice youth programs.

4. Desirability of assigning a juvenile court officer to present cases.

5. The extent to which the department is required to provide social background data to the juvenile court.

As previously indicated, juvenile officers must be selected from the group of experienced line officers. This selection should be open and competitive to assure that the best-suited men are chosen from all of those available. Juvenile officers should be assigned rather than appointed. Preservice training should be required to assure adequacy of knowledge and skills required in the new position.

Finally, except in the very largest departments, the juvenile unit should be a subsidiary of the criminal investigation unit, and juvenile unit responsibilities should center about providing follow-up investigation and staff assistance functions.

AREAS OF CONTROVERSY

The use of records, fingerprints, and photographs in police work with juveniles often gives rise to controversy.[15] There is, of course, room for differences of opinion about certain aspects of these subjects. But very often they are approached in a one-sided manner, either with unrealistic sentimentality, or with a complete lack of understanding or sympathy for the goal of rehabilitation for delinquent youths. It is not within the scope of this chapter to go into the differences of opinion about certain aspects of these subjects. It is sufficient to say that records, fingerprints, and photographs are important police tools and should be maintained.

RECORDS

Adequate records relating to children alleged or known to be delinquents should certainly be maintained by the police. There are several reasons for such records:

1. To provide information, for the police themselves, the court, and other interested agencies, on all police contacts, past and present, with a given juvenile.

2. To define delinquency areas.

[15]Portions of this section have been adapted from: *Police Services for Juveniles*, U.S. Department of Health, Education and Welfare, U.S. Government Printing Office, Washington, D.C., 1974, pp. 27–31.

3. To throw light on community conditions that may contribute to delinquency.

4. For use in evaluating delinquency-prevention programs.

Such records as are maintained should be as brief as practicable and to the point. For example, the patrol officer's report form for taking a child into custody should cover all the facts needed, but should be simple and brief enough to insure the officer's cooperative participation in the report system.

There is little question records should be maintained in all cases wherein a bona fide complaint is received, as when an investigation is made, or a child is taken into custody, in other words, in any case involving a child that requires action and disposition by police.

The records on an offense committed by a child should include a record of the complaint and of its clearance; if the child is taken into custody, there should also be a booking entry.

There should also be a record of the investigation in a juvenile case, including any social background information. It has been suggested that this record should be made available only to the juvenile court and the probation department and to social agencies having a legitimate interest in a case. There should be complete understanding and formal agreement among the various agencies affected as to the use that may be made of the information of police records.

The question of which method should be used for maintaining juvenile records often gives police departments difficulty. Generally, all police records should be integrated in a single centralized system. However, in providing for segmentation of juvenile records within the centralized system (if the department has a juvenile division), there are great advantages in permitting that unit to maintain specialized records. For example, a case of a missing child reported in one precinct station and found in another could probably be cleared more promptly through separate juvenile unit files then it could through central record systems.

A cleared entry on the complaint or offense records for a case involving a juvenile should refer to the juvenile's file by code, including only such additional information, exclusive of his name, as may be needed for adequate cross-reference.

FINGERPRINTS AND PHOTOGRAPHS

Another perplexing issue in the handling of juveniles by police is that of determining operational standards for applying the identification processes to arrested youths. This question is not limited to cases involving juveniles. However, the need for clarity in policy is far more apparent at the youth level.

Perhaps in no other areas are there strong feelings such as those in relation to fingerprinting and photographing. Many arguments have been advanced by both proponents and opponents. Some of these arguments are based on emotion, while others appear to center about factual case histories that are cited to prove or disprove the value of prints and photographs.

Some state laws forbid both fingerprinting and photographing of children except by order of the juvenile court. Elsewhere, the practice is determined by the policy of the police department; some departments fingerprint all children taken into custody and suspected of serious offenses. Photographing is less widespread than fingerprinting, but practice follows a similar pattern. There are those who oppose fingerprinting juveniles on the grounds that such practice stigmatizes the youngster and associates him in the public mind with criminal procedures. On the opposite side of the argument, there are those who advocate the use of such a method in that it is the most accurate method of identification. In other words, it gives a complete record. It is the consensus of law enforcement personnel that the use of fingerprint records cannot be considered apart from the use of other types of records. Therefore, professionals in the field suggest that the same safeguards that apply to other records of juveniles apply with special force to fingerprints, which are basically a form of record. Generally, it is agreed, that:

1. No juvenile fingerprints should be recorded in a criminal section of any essential fingerprint registry.

2. Because of the criminal connotations associated with fingerprinting in the minds of many people, their use should be held to occasions where identification hinges upon evidence available only through their use and where sanctioned by law or juvenile court policies.

3. In many jurisdictions, the consent of the juvenile court must be obtained before such procedures are utilized.

4. Such fingerprints should be destroyed after its purpose has been served.

The rules pertaining to use of fingerprint records should also be applied to photographs, and such use should be authorized only when: (1) the juvenile has been taken into custody as a suspect in the commission of a *serious* offense such as robbery, rape, homicide, manslaughter, or burglary; (2) the juvenile has a *long history* of delinquency, involving numerous violations of the law, and there is reasonable grounds to assume that this pattern of behavior may continue; (3) the juvenile is a runaway and *refuses to reveal his identity*.

An important factor to be considered in the use of fingerprints and photographs is the need for *positive identifications*, and this should be the major consideration in the development and implication of the policy for fingerprinting. Thus, a person whose identity is verified by parents immediately after an arrest may not be fingerprinted unless there is evidentiary material for which comparison prints are needed. On the other hand, a youngster who has been caught in a burglary should be fingerprinted so that the prints from future or past burglary scenes may be compared against a single or complete file of known offenders. The use of fingerprints in this fashion is considered by law enforcement agencies as a vital, investigative aid, and the age of the burglar cannot reasonably be offered as the basis for using or excluding such a technique. The psychological and emotional trauma of the burglary itself is what really counts rather than any trauma supposedly associated with the arrest and ensuing identification procedures.

RIGHTS OF JUVENILES

The indispensable precondition for the authority of the juvenile court to act in any case brought before it is the *factual* determination that the child or parent was engaged in conduct specified in the law to impower court action. Concern for the child's welfare may lead to attempts to mold the adjudicatory process to avoid unnecessary harm to the child. But it has been a single defect of the administration of juvenile justice that often this concern has been allowed to interfere substantially with the goals of fairness and reliability in the adjudicatory process.[16]

There have been significant changes in juvenile court laws throughout the United States. Such changes have been attributed to the 1967 decision of the U.S. Supreme Court in the *Gault* case (refer to Appendix A). The decision by the Supreme Court in *Gault* v. *Arizona* has influenced some courts to adopt criminal court procedures with prosecutors appearing in behalf of the state. The constitutional rights extended to children appearing in juvenile court are worth reviewing:

1. *Notice* to comply with due process requirements, must be given sufficiently in advance of scheduled court proceedings so that reasonable opportunity to prepare will be afforded, and it must be.

2. The child and his parents must be *notified* of the child's right to be represented by counsel retained by them, or if they are unable to afford counsel, that counsel will be appointed to represent the child.

3. The child has the *right* to confront and cross-examine witnesses who testify, and he has the right to remain silent—that is to exercise "the Constitutional privilege, against self-incrimination'—at the hearing. "After a valid confession, a determination of delinquency and an order of commitment to a state institution cannot be sustained in the absence of sworn testimony subjected to the opportunity for cross-examination."

The Supreme Court also spoke about other matters such as *taking a child into custody, detention, interrogation,* and statements made by the child in custody. The law of the case, however, consists of the three holdings on *(1) notice, (2) counsel,* and *(3) self-incrimination* described above.

[16]*Ibid.*

EVIDENCE

Perhaps the height of the juvenile court's procedural informality is its failure to differentiate clearly between the *adjudication hearing*, whose purpose is to determine the truth of the allegations and the petition, and the *disposition proceeding*, at which the juvenile's background is considered in connection with deciding what to do with him. In many juvenile courts, the two questions are dealt with in the same proceeding or are separated only in the minority of cases in which the petition's allegations are at issue. Even where adjudication and disposition are dealt with separately, the social reports, containing material about the background and character that might make objective examination of the facts of the case difficult, are often given to the judge before adjudication.

To lessen the danger that information relevant only to *disposition* will color factual questions of involvement and jurisdictional basis of action, the Children's Bureau has for some time recommended bifurcating juvenile court hearings (separate hearings into jurisdictional and dispositional). Similarly, in the trial of criminal cases there is a sharp judicial distinction between the trial on the issue of guilt and the sentencing determination. By adopting such a procedure, it makes possible a controlled and relatively narrowly focused inquiry into the facts of the alleged conduct of adjudication, and more general and searching inquiry into facts bearing upon the need for supervision and disposition. Thus, this procedure reduces the danger that the limitations of the adjudicatory hearing will unduly narrow the dispositional determination and that the demands of information appropriate to the dispositional hearing will unduly enlarge the scope of the adjudicatory hearing. As a result, it seems that many courts are gradually restoring the various procedures and safeguards of the traditional criminal court hearing.

Sensitivity to rules of evidence, issues, and facts of the case are becoming more predominant in juvenile court hearings and the nonadversary atmosphere that once prevailed is quickly disappearing.

Due process for children has now been held to entitle them to such criminal procedural rights as the right to jury trial (*Piland* v. *Clark County Juvenile Court*, 457 P. 2d. 523-Nev. 1969), the right to suppress evidence seized in violation of the Fourth amendment (*Ciulla* v. *State*, 434 S.W. 2d 948-Tex. Civ. App. 1968), and the right not to be placed twice in jeopardy in the juvenile court (*Matter of Fonseca*, 229 N.Y.S. 2d 493-Sup. Ct. Kings Co. 1969).

The procedures that a police agency follows in gathering evidence of an offense involving a juvenile should be identical with those used in investigation of cases involving adult suspects. The degree of proof required is no less for juveniles than adults, and every care must be exercised to assure the rights of the child as those rights served to protect him from unwarranted treatment or correction.[17]

[17]O'Connor and Watson, *Police Role*, p. 54.

THE ADMONISHING OF JUVENILE OFFENDERS

Other aspects of procedural due process have also received the recent attention of the courts. In 1963 the Supreme Court ruled on the appeal case of *Gideon* v. *Wainwright*. The effect of this ruling was that new trials could be demanded by anyone convicted of a crime without legal counsel. Moving closer to the functions of police, in 1964 a decision was handed down in the case of *Escobedo* v. *Illinois*. This decision, based on a five to four majority, provided the constitutional right of an indigent to be provided with legal counsel at the time of police interrogation. In June 1966, again by five to four majority, the court ruled on the case of *Miranda* v. *Arizona*. The *Miranda* decision had the effect of providing legal counsel for persons suspected of crimes during police questioning. Since this and the previous rulings were made on the basis of constitutional rights, law enforcement found itself compelled to regard many traditional investigative methods as "unconstitutional."

These rules have been applied to the juvenile court process and does apply (*Dorado*, *Escobedo*, and *Miranda* decisions) to the following situations:

1. When a police officer takes a youth into custody, does the officer have to advise the youth of his rights to remain silent and get legal counsel?

2. When a law enforcement officer is engaged in conversation with a youth on probation or parole, does the officer have to advise the youth of his rights?

3. Does a probation officer interviewing a youth already in custody at juvenile hall have to advise the youth of his rights?

4. Does a probation officer in the same situation have to advise a youth of his rights if that youth is under supervision as a ward of the court?

5. Can a minor contract to waive his rights?

As a result of the *Dorado* and *Escobedo* decisions, the courts handed down a ruling requiring *police officers to admonish suspects* at the time of arrest. The United States Supreme Court subsequently ruled that California's method of admonishing was best, and suggested that all states adopt similar procedures.

The *Miranda* decision requires that certain legal requisites be fulfilled when an officer engages a suspect on the street and questions him. The officer must advise the suspect that he has a right to *remain silent*; that he has a right to *speak to an attorney*; that if he wishes an *attorney*, but cannot afford one, the *state* will provide him with one; and, that anything the suspect says may be held *against* him.

The question then arises as to the admonishing of ten to twelve-year-olds. Would a youth of that age be able to understand what he was waiving? (It is commonly accepted that, although the youth may not understand the consequences of his waiver, nevertheless he should be admonished. The courts are of the opinion that it is within the jurisdiction of the court to determine whether the youth is fit to waive his rights or whether he has knowledge of what was involved.

On the problem of admonishing during the conversation between a law enforcement officer and a suspect who is a minor, it is common practice to admonish the minor if the officer is trying to *discover* what part the youth played in an offense. If, however, an officer is talking *casually* with a youth who spontaneously reveals his participation in an offense for which he is subsequently taken before the court, the officer need not have interrupted the conversation to admonish the youth. Any evidence revealed by a minor in that manner was felt to be acceptable in a court hearing for determination of jurisdiction and wardship.

A copy of the police report, which includes a record of the admonition, does not accompany the probation officer's report to the court. Is it necessary then for the probation officer also to admonish the youth, since he is presenting his own report to the court? Technically, there is no need for the probation officer again to advise a youth of his rights. However, if a probation officer has any doubts that the youth has been admonished, or if he was questioning the youth with an eye toward obtaining a *confession*, the probation officer should definitely admonish the youth again. It is suggested, however, that the probation officer admonish the youth in any case to ensure the admission of all evidence and testimony in the determination of wardship and the acceptance of the recommended disposition. In most cases, it is a matter of policy that the juvenile probation officers are presently admonishing youths in all cases.

The admonition of youths on probation does not differ significantly. Usually, if a youth is on probation and commits a law violation, he should be admonished. However, if a youth on probation commits an offense that would fall in the category of predelinquent (i.e., truancy, incorrigibility, lewd and immoral conduct), he need not be admonished. The admonition is always necessary when *establishing* wardship. Furthermore, all "felony-type" offense cases involving minors, whether court wards or not, would require an admonition.

In regard to the question of proper admonition through more than one day of questioning, or after a change in the officer conducting the questioning of a suspect, or prior to written statement, it is most desirable to admonish *immediately at the time of arrest*, at the scene of the arrest if possible; to have a *written record* of the admonition in the police report; to admonish *prior* to any written statement made by the suspect; and to admonish the suspect *again* at the start of each new day of questioning. If a differrnt officer should assume the questioning of a suspect, that officer should also admonish the suspect.

In summary then:

1. You should admonish *all* youthful suspects, regardless of their age.

2. You *need not* interrupt, to admonish, any spontaneous conversation in which a youth reveals his participation in an offense.

3. If a youth is a *on probation* and commits an offense that would fall under the classification of *law violation* (Section 602 of the Welfare and Institutions Code of the State of California), he should be admonished. If he is involved in an offense that can be considered a *"non-Penal Code"* violation (Section 601 of the Welfare and Institutions Code of the State of California), he need not be admonished.

4. Each officer questioning the suspect should admonish him.

ARREST VERSUS DETENTION

The matter of detention poses critical problems for police officers, both as to *whether* the child should be detained and as to *where* he should be detained.

Detention should be utilized only when it is needed to protect the welfare of the juvenile, protect the community, or guarantee the appearance of a child and family in court. No child should be detained as punishment or simply for the convenience of authorities. Nor should a child be detained because he comes from a "bad home." Even though the home is "bad," it may be worse to subject the child to detention care.

There is considerable reason to believe that at present many children are being held in secured custody unnecessarily. Numerous surveys conducted by the National Probation and Parole Association attest to this fact. Many children are placed in secured custody and subsequently released without ever being referred to the juvenile court. Of the children referred to the court, experience has shown that the majority of them can be safely allowed to remain in their homes pending juvenile court hearing. Many children are being held in secured custody without real need.

The general lack of adequate facilities for the detention of delinquent children has long been an aggravating problem for the police. Where the community has no separate facility for the care and custody of delinquent children, it has been necessary to place the arrested youths in jail. Obviously, juveniles should not be held in jail; there is nothing in jail to contribute to their rehabilitation. A number of states have specifically forbidden or placed stringent restrictions on the use of jails for the detention of children. Yet there remains the fact that few communities provide separate detention facilities, and that in many communities that lack such facilities, there are occasionally children who need to be held in secured custody. What is the police officer to do in such a case? In the absence of any other solution than confinement in the jail, the police officer should see to it that the detention period is as brief as possible, that special care is given the child, and that the juvenile is quartered apart from adults in jail.

In those communities that possess a detention home and in which the police department has assigned special officers for work with children, the youngster who is to be detained should be conducted to the facility by a juvenile officer in an unmarked car if possible. The officer should also be aware of the fact that detention is a frightening experience to most children and he should therefore reassure the child and his family by describing the detention facility and the procedures that will be followed there.

Law enforcement personnel play a significant role in alleviating the crowded conditions in juvenile halls throughout the United States. Policemen inherit a great deal of discretionary authority as to the manner in which a juvenile offender is processed. Not every adult wrongdoer is brought to trial for his misconduct, nor is every juvenile offender put through the mill of official processing. It is impossible to determine how many potential subjects of formal legal action are eliminated from the system at an early point, but bits and pieces of information when put together portray a law enforcement and judicial system that uses, and appears to value, substantial discretion, particularly in the initial stages of handling.

For various reasons, and to different extents, every community is committed to informal handling. Statistics reveal that many juvenile offenders come into official contact with the police; they do not reveal the number of unofficial contacts on the street or in the station house. In cases of more than brief or casual contact, a trip to the station house for questioning by the arresting officer or juvenile specialist is usually required. The dispositions available to the police range from outright release, usually to the parents, to referral to the juvenile court. Court referral may mean citation, filing of a complaint, or physical removal of the child to detention awaiting formal action. Between these extremes are referral to community resources selected by the officer and station adjustment, by which is meant the juvenile's release on one or more conditions. Across the country, it is clear, discretionary action by the police in screening juvenile offenders accounts for the removal of significant numbers from juvenile hall and the formal juvenile justice system.

The conditions under which a child may be taken into custody will generally be found in a state's juvenile court law.

Many state juvenile court laws contain the provision that "any child found violating any law or ordinance, or whose surroundings are such as to endanger his welfare, may be taken into custody without a warrant."

This particular provision pertaining to apprehension without warrant as quoted from the Standard Juvenile Act is certainly broad enough to meet all practical contingencies.

Only a relatively small proportion of the total number of delinquent children with whom the police have contact need to be taken into custody. The majority of this group give the police no particular trouble other than concern for their welfare. But, there is a small group of adolescent delinquents—generally to be found in the upper age limits of the juvenile court jurisdiction—whose behavior can give the police a great deal of trouble, and make the process of taking them into custody a serious matter. Utmost care should be taken when placing this type of youngster into custody. Such a youngster can be considered quite dangerous due to his inability to control his impulses and due to inconsistencies in his reactions to stress.

If a child is taken into custody, it should be the *duty of the police officer* to locate the parents, or guardian or custodian of the child as soon as possible. For this purpose, and for this purpose alone, the child may be held by the police temporarily.

The officer then, whenever possible, should return the child to his parents, with a notice (citation) to the parents that the child's and their presence may be required by the juvenile probation department. However, if the parents cannot be found within a reasonable period of time, or, if, generally after consulting with the parents, the officer is of the opinion that the interests of the child or the safety of the community warrant the child's detention, the officer should take the child to the place of detention or shelter designated by the court in accordance with agreed written procedures.

INVESTIGATION OF JUVENILE OFFENSES

The juvenile delinquency problem confronting every law enforcement agency consists primarily of the need to develop and apply procedures for dealing with youths which reflect an awareness of, and an appreciation for, the unique legal system that is invoked. Realistically, police officers gather information from persons and from things in every criminal case they handle. According to O'Connor and Watson ("Juvenile Delinquency and Youth Crime") the techniques for such processes are not amendable to variations according to age of the suspect; therefore, *in the area of routine crime investigation, few if any differences are noted between cases involving adult suspects and those involving youths.*

Although the investigative techniques pertaining to juveniles and adults are quite similar, there are psychological and legal theoretical concepts that dictate the need for diversity of action in the areas of case preparation, disposition, and prevention.

The diversity of action, however, occurs only after the identity of the suspect is known. Once the age of the suspect is determined, the application of different techniques is appropriate. The changes in procedure are dictated primarily by statute and the local juvenile court. The rules against photographing, fingerprinting, and record-keeping do not originate from within the police establishment. Such departmental orders as exist simply translate legal requirements into terms appropriate to departmental procedures. Although the factors affecting the juvenile—those said to cause his delinquent behavior—are not unlike those affecting the adult, society has said quite loudly and clearly that children are not to be held criminally responsible for their acts. Society is of the opinion, and rightfully so, that the chances of redirecting a wayward youth are greater—because of his flexible nature and changing personality structure—than are the chances of changing an adult who has become more set in his ways.

Another concept directing law enforcement agencies in dealing with youth is the one that holds juveniles not to understand and not to have internalized the social, moral, and legal codes of our culture. Obviously, the use of chronological age as the basis of defining criminal responsibility is unreal, although easily administered. However, the statutes in all states utilize chronological age and law enforcement agencies have no alternative but to adhere to the juvenile court law. The fallacies of such a procedure are clearly recognized by individual officers, and this recognition produces a reaction against the system of juvenile justice which spreads and tends to create dissatisfaction.

All juvenile offenses should be fairly and completely investigated as possible. Some police officers are said to show a tendency to neglect certain facts in the investigation of juvenile offenses on the *assumption* that the juvenile court does not need or require detailed facts and evidence. This assumption, as this book attempts to communicate, is incorrect. Full information concerning the case is always needed to sustain petitions.

The techniques utilized in the investigation of offenses will be those developed by police science, as that is taught in the best police academies and treated in standard texts on police investigation. Although a definitive treatment of such techniques is not possible in this chapter, the highlights of investigating juvenile offenses will be discussed.

The specialized work of criminal investigation has two primary purposes:

> *(1)   the gathering of facts and other information for examination to determine whether a criminal violation has been perpetrated and, if there is a violation, the identity of the violator; and*
>
> *(2)   the collection, preservation, and preparation of evidence that will be admissible and effective before a court or jury to convict a defendant standing trial for his actions.*
>
> *In fulfilling these two purposes, the investigator must adhere to and be guided by Constitutional law. His evidence in a criminal case must be admissible in a court of law and must follow the basic rule for all investigators that evidence secured against a defendant in the violation of his Constitutional rights will not be admitted into evidence.*
>
> *The criminal investigator must be searching constantly for new and more refined methods of investigation, just as the crime community is never idle in devising new patterns of crime.*

It must be recognized that it is *not* the function of the police officers to do casework and that they do not make comprehensive case studies. The social information they do secure, during the investigation of a juvenile crime, must be limited to that needed for a general understanding of a youngster's situation so that he may be referred to the proper source for help.

There are many factors, then, that the police officer must undertake in the full investigation of a case. The following are factors that should be included in such an investigation:

1. Factors of the offense, including all details necessary to sustain a petition in court.

2. Record of any previous police action.

3. Record of any previous court or social agency action.

4. Attitudes of the child, his parents, and the complainant in the offense toward the act.

5. Adjustment of the child at home, school, and the community.

Any variety of methods is utilized by the police agencies in reporting the offense to and communicating with the probation department. Generally, in delivering a minor to the probation department, it is incumbent upon the police officer to submit a cursory report, providing essential details, and to follow up a day or two later with a full written report. Some agencies send juvenile officers to complete the investigation and then report orally with a supplementary report to the investigating probation officer. Such information might include:

1. Facts of the offense, which gave the juvenile court jurisdiction over the case and personal data about the juvenile.

2. Information about any codelinquent or the complainant, including a statement regarding injuries or damages.

3. Any reasons for requesting juvenile court action other than, or in addition to, the specific offense.

4. A brief summary of any significant factors revealed in the investigation.

Every police officer has an obligation to familiarize himself thoroughly with the juvenile court philosophy and procedures so that he may interpret them to the child's parents. However, the officer should avoid giving any suggestions as to what the probation department's study will lead to or what the court disposition may be, since these are matters outside his jurisdiction. There is no reason, however, why the arresting officer should not insure the child and his family that the study made by the probation department will help the judge to make a disposition that will not be punitive but will be in the best interests of the child, his family, and the community.

GUIDELINES FOR POLICE DISPOSITION[18]

After a police officer has made a thorough investigation of a delinquency case, he is ready to make a choice of disposition. The following are some of the ways in which an officer may dispose of a delinquency case.

[18]*Police Services for Juveniles,* op. cit., pp. 29–31.

Referral to the Juvenile Court

The criteria for referral to the juvenile court are as follows:

1. The particular offense committed by the child is of a *serious nature*.

2. The child is *known* or has in the past been known to the *juvenile court*.

3. The child has a *record of repeated delinquency* extending over a period of time.

4. The child and his parents have shown themselves *unable or unwilling* to cooperate with agencies of nonauthoritative character.

5. Casework with the child by *nonauthoritative agency has failed* in the past.

6. Treatment services needed by the child can be *obtained only* through the court and the probation department.

7. The child *denies* the offense, and the officer believes judicial determination is called for; and there *is sufficient evidence* to warrant referral, or the officer believes the child is in need of aid.

Release to Parents or Guardians Without Referral

Generally speaking, a delinquent's own home is the best place for him, whether he is referred to an agency in the community for treatment or not. Before releasing a child to his own home without other referral, however, a police officer should look for evidence of the parents' interest in the welfare of their child and of the family's ability to meet his problems. Certain criteria that might lead a police officer to select this disposition for a delinquent case are as follows:

1. The offense is *minor* in nature, and there is no apparent need for treatment.

2. The child shows *no habitual* delinquency pattern.

3. The family situation is *stable*.

4. The *relationship* between the child and his parents is *good*. The parents seem aware of the child's problems and are able to cope with them.

5. Adequate help is *being given* by public or voluntary agencies in the community.

In actual practice, *release to parents or guardians* without referral is probably the disposition most frequently made by the police officers in regard to delinquency cases. There is some question, however, whether this disposition should be used as often as it is. The release to parents or guardians might be more successful if the child and parents were referred to another agency in the community for help.

There are indications that police officers do not use nonauthoritative treatment resources to the maximum advantage. It is true that in many communities such resources are either limited or nonexistent, but it seems likely that in many places these resources are not utilized more than they are because of the failure on the part of the police or of the agencies, or of both, to work out a more cooperative and mutually helpful relationship.

The delinquent who would be an appropriate referral to a social agency is a child who is not referred to the juvenile court, but whose delinquency is sufficiently serious to demand professional attention that he cannot receive from his parents. This is a child whose misconduct is just beginning rather than one whose pattern of antisocial behavior is serious and well established. In many cases the family of such a juvenile might also be referred to an agency.

In order to make a referral to the appropriate agency, a police officer must know about the needs of the child and his family and also about their willingness to ask help of such treatment resources.

In preparing a child and his family for referral, the officer should do a constructive job of explaining the functions of the agency. He should describe the special skills of the workers employed in the agency and how they are able to help the children and parents with specific problems. The officer should make it clear that problems can be solved only through the joint efforts of the agency and the child or his parents, and that the agency cannot undertake to help them without their active interest and participation.

The officer should also provide specific information as to contact. Agency referrals can be made in many of a number of ways:

1. By the *police* themselves, either by an individual officer, or by a special referral unit.

2. Through the intake division of the *probation department* of the juvenile court.

3. By an information and *referral* division of the community welfare council or council of social agencies.

INTERVIEWS AND INTERROGATIONS

The interview, broadly defined, is used in every stage of the criminal process and is probably the most common device used by man to influence others by command, direction, guidance, suggestion, entreaty, or merely by expressing opinions. The interview is probably the most important means that the police officer has for carrying out his investigation.

While conducting their investigation, investigators will make extensive use of the interview and interrogation. The reputation of the department, as well as the effectiveness of the police officer's work may depend on how well he carries out this particular task. Although interviewing and interrogation appear to be similar, there are some basic differences in the methods utilized.

An *interview* is a serious conference or conversation between two or more persons with the definite purpose of either *obtaining certain information* from the person interviewed about himself or about another, or of *effecting a change* in his behavior or attitudes. It differs from ordinary conversation in that it has the purpose of influencing another person in a planned direction, whether it be that of making him willing to give information or to change his conduct. Ideas are exchanged not only through words, however. The skilled interviewer also relies upon his observation or gestures, tone of voice, inflections of speech, facial expression, and all the other means of expression used by human beings, consciously or subconsciously.

> *It may be concluded readily that the process of interviewing as defined covers a large area and could include that of speaking with suspicious persons on the streets, talking with witnesses to gain information and clear understanding regarding a particular offense or investigation, or obtaining information with reference to the background of police applicants, criminal suspects, informants, or any number of persons. Through the process known as* interviewing, *the police officer and investigator will learn a great deal of information and facts which are of extreme importance to him if he is to fulfill his assignments in a forthright manner.*[19]

The following are basic to police interviewing:

1. *Listening* is better than talking. The police officer will not learn much if he does all the talking.

2. *Play a "waiting game."* Sometimes a person will "give," sometimes he will not. Information—that is significant information—cannot be forced out of the interviewee. While it is true that the police officer is usually pressed for time, the interview situation must be cultivated in such a way as to allow the subject to express himself. Permit him to talk at his own speed. Questions should be for the purpose of directing the subject's conversation into productive channels.

3. *The location of the interview is important.* Privacy is a necessity. If there are telephones or other distractions, the subject will not feel at ease and will resist.

4. *Asking questions and writing down the answers verbatim is not interviewing.* If this were so, a tape recorder would do a better job. The

[19]E. Eldefonso, A. Coffey, and R. C. Grace, *Principles of Law Enforcement*, 2nd ed., John Wiley and Sons, Inc., New York, 1974, pp. 246–247.

interviewer should apply himself completely to the interview, then write down these notes immediately afterward.

5. *Two is company; more, a crowd in an interview.* Generally, only one person should be in an interview at a time. Exceptions occur (where a family conference is conducted, for example), but usually the purpose of an interview will be defeated if more than the interviewer and the subject are present. If the youngster is to be interviewed, the parents can be cordially excused and what has been discussed can be presented to them later.

6. *"Who does what?" should be made clear.* The interviewer should explain who and what he is, what his purpose are, and where he stands in relation to the subject. Doubts, surmise, and suspicion negate an interview.

7. To understand the subject, it is necessary, when possible, to see things from his point of view. The police officer must avoid "talking down" to him. *And, the interviewer should use language the interviewee can understand.* Much valuable information can be gathered by correspondence and telephone; however, personal interviews are basic in securing the kind of information and insight that are necessary for preparing an adequate report.

The aim of the police officer in the interview is to learn as much as possible about the facts of the offense, and, when appropriate, about the child who is believed to have committed the offense, all knowledge that will help him to dispose of the case in the best interests of the community and the child.

In contrast, *interrogation* may be defined as:

Interviewing and counseling techniques are important tools for practitioners in the field of probation and parole.

The questioning of a person who is suspected of, has confessed to, or in fact has committed a crime or public offense. Interrogation is an art, *and competent interrogators are rare in the police profession. Much skill, experience, and training are necessary before a person is considered a master at interrogation. The one factor that distinguishes the interrogation from the interview is the atmosphere in which each is conducted. The atmosphere of the interview is usually more relaxed and the person is more likely to "open up" and supply the desired information. . . . On the other hand, an interrogation usually is conducted with a person who is reluctant, for any number of reasons, to converse with a law enforcement officer. The atmosphere and tenor of the conversation is not as relaxed as in the interview, and the success or failure of the interrogation depends in large part, as stated before, on the skill and ability of the interrogator to develop the hidden knowledge or information possessed by the person being interrogated.*[20]

Recently, the United States Supreme Court has placed several restrictions on the police in this vitally important area (interviewing and interrogating). These restrictions have already been discussed in a previous chapter and briefly reviewed at the beginning of this chapter, and, therefore, will not be repeated. But, whether these restrictions are a safeguard against the "overzealous" police as charged by some or are a well-meaning but unrealistic erosion of necessary police authority is still a moot question. The practical result is the serious curtailment of the effectiveness of interrogation and interviewing as a police technique in many cases, especially with suspects who are, in fact, guilty and who have learned to rely on these restrictions for protection from punishment. In more cases than not, the police cannot prove guilt through physical evidence, such as fingerprints or through witnesses simply because there are none. Under these circumstances, it is necessary to question the suspect and to check out his statements. His alibi or any discrepancies in his answers may be the only source of proof of guilt short of his confession. If he cannot be interviewed or interrogated adequately, even this source or proof is cut off. Moreover, if he is innocent, he is denied an opportunity to prove it without being formally charged.

The police officer must be aware of the present emphasis of the courts on statements and confessions. Formerly, the pertinent question was: "Is the confession true?," but today the emphasis seems to be whether or not the statement, admission, or confession is free, voluntary, without coercion of any kind, and is made in the full and complete awareness and understanding of all the defendant's Constitutional rights. This emphasis by the courts in interpreting the Fourth, Fifth, *and* Fourteenth Amendments to the *U.S. Constitution places very severe restrictions on the investigator. Many previously tried and proven techniques of investigators are*

[20]Eldefonso, Coffey and Grace, *Principles of Law Enforcement,* pp. 251–252.

no longer of any value or use. Today's police investigator must develop and use new techniques which for the present are acceptable to the courts.[21]

There are certain attitudes and types of behavior that every police officer should avoid in interviewing and interrogating, since they destroy respect for law enforcement and accomplish no good whatsoever. These can be listed as follows:

1. Using profanity or obscenity.

2. Branding children with epithets such as "thief," "liar," or "tramp."

3. Losing temper.

4. Telling falsehoods.

5. Using physical force.

6. Making promises that cannot be kept.[22]

One final note regarding interviewing and interrogation is that whenever possible, and especially in the cases of children under the age of thirteen, the interview or interrogation should take place in the presence of the parents, or guardians of the minor in order to protect the rights and best interests of the child. In most cases this is possible, except when the presence of the parents or guardians would tend to interfere with the officer's duty to obtain the facts surrounding the alleged offense, or where the parents or guardians have themselves participated in or contributed to the conduct of the minor being investigated (dependency, neglect, or abused children cases). There may well be instances in which the presence of the parents will tend to "block" or impede investigation; in such a case, the officer may refuse such parents the right to be present at the interview. The officer, however, must always remember that he may be charged with having obtained a statement from the minor by means of duress or by the infringement of the minor's guaranteed rights.

SUMMARY

Chapter 11 moves into an area of direct police services for juveniles. The primary responsibility of police is the control and prevention of crime and delinquency through the enforcement of laws that are necessary for the good order of society. Understanding and expertise in the handling of juvenile matters is necessary because most juveniles charged with delinquency are apprehended by the police and, therefore, the first contact is an important one that undoubtedly leaves a lasting impression upon the child. The police officer, therefore, who apprehends a child must know how to work with that type of child.

The police role is extremely important and special procedures set up to work

[21]*Ibid.*, pp. 251–252.
[22]*Ibid.*, p. 252.

with juveniles must be developed. There are several recommendations in this chapter taken from the *Task Force Report* as to written standards for *release, referral, nonjudicial sources, and for referral to the juvenile court.* Regarding the placement philosophy directed toward juveniles, it is important to note that nowhere in *police philosophy is it indicated that juveniles are not exempt from the enforcement of the law.* The fact that a person is an adult does not always permit police to use force in arresting him; nor does the fact that one is a juvenile, per se, require that no force be utilized. What is unnecessary or excessive force is determined by the extent of the circumstances, of which age is but one factor. This is not to say that there are no differences in handing juveniles and adults. However, insofar as the realization of basic objectives is concerned—the vigorous and successful completion of the job given the police by society—there are no fundamental, philosophical, or policy differences. There are adaptations of these philosophical concepts which, while they do not in any way modify the basic objectives, result in procedural differences in handling of juveniles as compared to adults.

Specialization in law enforcement has brought forth a great deal of controversial discussion. Specialization by juvenile control units may be considered appropriate in the following areas: (1) processing and disposition of juvenile cases investigated by the units; (2) special patrolling of known juvenile hangouts where conditions are harmful to the welfare of children; (3) maintenance of records on juvenile cases; (4) planning and coordinating a delinquency prevention program. The reason for specialization is that the formula for handling juvenile cases arising from provisions of the law and juvenile court procedures would, in many instances, take officers away from their regular duties too frequently and too long, whereas this follow-up work can be done economically by specialists.

Areas of controversy such as *records, fingerprinting, and photographing,* are explored. The use of records, fingerprints, and photographs in police work with juveniles is a necessary police tool and cannot be eliminated; however, there are procedures that can be utilized to improve such services.

The *rights of juveniles* as well as the gathering of *evidence* and the arriving at a *disposition* are discussed. The admonishing of juvenile offenders utilizes the knowledge gained in the *Dorado* and *Escondido* decisions, the *Gault* decision, the *Miranda* decision, and other important high court decisions pertaining to rules of evidence and investigation.

ANNOTATED REFERENCES

Carter, R. M. and Klein, M. W., *Back on The Street: The Discussion of Juvenile Offenders.* Prentice-Hall, Englewood Cliffs, N.J. 1976.

> This is a relevant reference in the area of procedures pertaining to the handling of juvenile offenses. Carter and Klein stress the importance of the first contact between the juvenile and formal legal authorities. The behavior of the police is a decisive element in the process of delinquents and is discussed in nontechnical language by the authors.

Eldefonso, Edward, and Coffey, Alan, *Process and Impact of the Juvenile Justice System*, Glencoe Press, Beverly Hills, Calif., 1976.

> Chapter 2 of this paperback gives additional reading in the area of investigation.

Gibbons, Don C., *Changing the Law-Breaker*, 2nd ed. Prentice-Hall, Inc., Englewood Cliffs, N.J., 1976.

> This is an excellent general discussion of juvenile delinquency—causes, topology, and the role of law enforcement.

Hamann, Albert D., "Factors to Consider When Handling Young Offenders," *Police Work*, Police Science Technology Department, Milwaukee Technical College, Milwaukee, Wisconsin, December 1968.

> Hamann, who is with the University of Wisconsin, University Extension, Institute of Governmental Affairs, is responsible for law enforcement education and training. Therefore, Hamann's article in *Police Work* is the result of a great deal of experience and kndowledge in the area of police work with juveniles. This article points out the importance of "how police officers view their roles." Hamann is of the opinion that how the police officers view these roles plays an important part in how he reacts to demands of that role. Hamann also discusses specialization, interviewing the juvenile, arresting the juvenile, searching the juvenile, and selecting the proper disposition. See, also, in this same issue of *Police Work*, Judge George A. Bowman, Jr.'s dissertation on "The Police and Juveniles" in which he discusses the necessity of being *objective* when investigating juvenile offenses. Personal likes and dislikes, according to Judge Bowman, are not a part of proper police work.

Peirson, N., *Police Operations*, Nelson-Hall, Publishers, Chicago. 1976.

> This author discusses the basic responsibility of law enforcement officers when dealing with law violator—including the youthful offender. Above the basic responsibility, the authors discuss the methods and materials that affect the police response to crime.

U.S. Department of Health, Education, and Welfare, *Police Services for Juveniles*, U.S. Government Printing Office, Washington, D.C., 1974.

> This paperback presents an overview of the subject title. In nontechnical language, the report discusses the importance of the police role, police services for alleged delinquents, police services for neglected children, offenses by adults against juveniles, organization and training of police for work with juveniles, and prevention activities and related police programs for juveniles. This report brings together some current opinion and information about police services for juveniles; it is an extremely important resource for students.

CHAPTER ELEVEN police services for neglected and abused children

Neglected and abused children are complicated social and legal problems. When a child's home environment is seriously detrimental to his or her normal development, the intervention of the social and legal agencies may be essential for the protection of the child.

Childhood is a successful period for most persons in the sense that they have enough care and protection from their parents, relatives, and family to enable then to grow up to be reasonably competent adults. However, for some people, childhood is severely marred by parental failure or inadequacy. Family failure may be bizarre and obvious, as it is for a child who is completely deserted or who is physically hurt by angry or violent parents, or it may be untraumatic and corroding, as it is for a child who feels so unwanted at home and confused in his family relationships that he loses his motivation and drive. Experience has shown that children who have been shortchanged through parental neglect or abuse can be helped in many ways, particularly if their troubles are recognized at an early date and if sensitive, appropriate help is made available to the family and the child in any way that is adapted to the needs of the individual situation.

The conditions that indicate separately or collectively the need for action include:

1. Lack of physical care and protection.

2. Lack of supervision, guidance, and discipline.

3. Exploitation of children.

Police Services for Neglected and Abused Children **247**

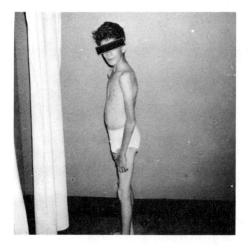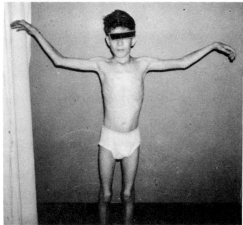

These illustrations vividly depict lack of physical care and protection—an extreme case of deprivation and neglect. Cases of malnutrition due to improper diet are not an uncommon sight in juvenile courts of America. Photo courtesy of Santa Clara County Juvenile Probation Department, San Jose, Calif.

4. Lack of protection from degrading conditions.

5. Abuse and fear of physical cruelty.

These neglected children become visible to the community in a variety of ways:

1. Two small children quarreled fretfully in a filthy room, while their baby brother lies wet and listless on a bare, stained mattress. Their older sister comes carrying a bag of potato chips and for a few moments, there is the noise of children arguing over food. Their mother will not be home until the early hours of the morning, and when she comes, she is likely to be drunk. Their father is a stranger to them. They live a cold, lonely, uncertain existence.

2. In another neighborhood, a six-year-old boy quietly enters his front door after school. His mother greets him with a blow on the chin which knocks him across the room. He makes no sound; experience has taught him better. His mother, standing in the middle of a precisely ordered living room, glares at him: "You're 10 minutes late! Were you looking for trouble, something to steal maybe? I'll teach you to disobey me!" The boy has no defense, he is silent,

trying to shut out the real world by escaping into a world of fantasy.[1]

The Report of the Assembly Interim Committee on Social Welfare reveals that neglected and abused children also become visible to the community in a dramatic fashion. The most dramatic, and most rare, according to this committee, is when a child actually suffers trauma about the body (i.e., burned, beaten, or starved to death) and police arrest the parents. The assembly committee cites the more common examples:

1. Seven-year-old Michael is a source of great concern to his grandmother who has observed his mother administer excessive, erratic beatings, and shower him with gifts. He is having difficulty in school and has twice run away to his grandmother's house, begging her to let him stay.

2. Six-month-old Susie is brought to the hospital with body bruises and a broken arm which, her mother explains, resulted from a fall from her high chair. X-rays reveal other partially healed breaks that the mother does not mention, causing the examining doctor to suspect that the injuries were not accidental.

3. Johnny is frequently absent from school. When he does come, both his body and his clothing are filthy. The school representative who visits the home is confronted with an appalling odor, filth, and disorder. Two preschoolers are seen eating cold leftover food out of its original tin.

4. Mrs. B. committed suicide two months ago, leaving her husband and four children. Mr. B. is determined to keep the children and has had several inadequate housekeepers, none of whom actually mistreated the youngsters. Mr. B. quit his job and decided to stay home with the children himself. He now has applied for financial assistance.

5. Three small children are stranded with their parents in a broken-down car in a service station. The manager calls Travelers' Aid be-

---

[1]*Protective Services for Children,* Report of the Assembly Interim Committee on Social Welfare, Assembly of the State of California, January 1967, p. 6. See also: L. Young, *Wednesday's Children,* McGraw-Hill, New York, 1964. V. De Francis, *Protecting The Child Victim of Sex Crimes,* The American Humane Association, Children's Division, Denver, Colorado, 1969; V. De Francis, *Child Protective Services: A National Survey,* The American Human Association, Children's Division, Denver Colorado, 1967; Ray E. Helfer, *The Battered Child,* The University of Chicago Press, Chicago, 1968.

cause the children looked so poorly cared for and because he has overheard the father offering to give the youngest to a station employee.

These vivid illustrations of how neglected and abused children in any community may become visible, dramatically or otherwise, to different persons in different ways. The problems of these children arise from various kinds of parental failures and parental inadequacies. Some of the children have parents who are desperately trying to live up to the demands of being a parent, and who can and will make use of help from any agency to improve their work as parents. Others have parents who are so preoccupied with their own problems and their own needs that they cannot carry the responsibility for children and, in these cases, alternative plans must be made for the children's own good.[2]

The inability of parents to provide a physical setting that is reasonably clean, safe, and comfortable is common in *neglect situations*. The inability of the mother or father to regularly provide food that is nourishing and well prepared is another facet of breakdown in child nurture. The inability to provide comfortable and reasonably becoming clothes, suitable for school and play, summer and winter, and to keep them clean and mended so that the child's appearance does not embarrass him or set him apart from his group is frequently another part of the parents' failure.

The lack of established, orderly daily routine is usually a symptom of family breakdown. These are disorganized households. Meals are irregular. The house is in a disarray. It is dirty, sometimes filthy. Broken windows or stairs and rough or splintered floors are a constant source of physical danger to children. Beds are broken, springs sag, mattresses and bedclothes, if indeed there are any, are not clean. The plumbing leaks; frequently it is out of order. Body cleanliness for children, as well as for adults, is often neglected and may lead to skin or scalp infections that isolate and embarrass children.

In the great majority of households that lack physical care and good protection for children, two factors are present: *poverty* and *inadequate housing*. Such situations are particularly pertinent to large family groups.

DEFINING NEGLECT AND ABUSE[3]

The standards and criteria of neglect and abuse, as well as those statutes that supposedly defined such cases as falling in these categories are dangerously vague.

The line between neglect and abuse is sometimes difficult to draw, but the two can generally be distinguished in the following way: the *neglectful parent* usually does not *consciously* intend to harm his child, but through failure to meet the child's

[2]Helfer. *The Battered Child, op. cit.,* p. 175–199.
[3]*Protective Services for Children,* pp. 7–8. See also E. Eldefonso and A. Coffey, *Process and Impact of the Juvenile Justice System,* Glencoe Press, Beverly Hills, Calif., 1976, Chap. 1.

health, nutritional, comfort, and emotional needs, he exposes the child to severe risks.

> The neglect statutes are concerned with parental behavior not as behavior per se, but only and solely as it adversely affects the child in those areas of the child's life about which the statutes have expressed concern. Each child embodies his own unique combination of physical, psychological, and social components; no child has quite the same strengths or weaknesses as another or exactly the same relationship with his family. The parental failure which markedly damages one child might leave another quite untouched. This interaction between the child and his family is the essence of a neglect situation, the imponderable which defies statutory constraint. . . . Each case involving neglected children must involve first the finding of the facts governing the given situation, as they are developed through testimony, and then the application of the legal principles controlling these facts. Obviously, this is peculiarly and exclusively a judicial function and through its repetition many times over, the courts slowly pick out, decision by decision, the law of neglect.[4]

The Assembly Interim Committee on Social Welfare that reported to the California legislature in 1967 gave some examples of *neglect*, such as the father who left his four small children alone in a car with a book of matches. Although nothing happened to them, he was charged with neglect. One month later, he left two of the children alone in the car. One, a little girl, lit some matches and subsequently died of burns. Many parents may leave children alone at a time of emergency or under unusual circumstances, but it is those parents who habitually leave their children alone who expose them to the greatest risks.

Living requires some exposure to risks. The more serious the risk, the longer and more repeatedly the child is exposed to it, the greater is the neglect. In some cases of neglect, such as feeding, an occasional missed meal is no great concern, but continual failure to feed children results in malnutrition or starvation.

Besides failure to feed, neglect includes leaving children alone, maintaining them in an unsanitary condition, keeping them out of school, failing to keep them clean and adequately dressed, and ignoring their medical needs. *Neglect, then, is the failure to exercise the care that the circumstances justly demand.* It embraces willful as well as unintentional disregard of duty. It is not a term of fixed and measured meaning. It takes its context always from specific circumstances and its meaning varies as the context of surrounding circumstances changes.

As in the case of feeding, concrete circumstances and conditions determine the existence and extent of neglect. A parent who leaves his children in a parked car for a few moments while he runs in to buy a package of cigarettes would not be

---

[4]T. D. Gill, "The Legal Nature of Neglect," *National Probation and Parole Association*, vol. 6, no. 1, Jan. 1960, pp. 5–6.

considered neglectful according to prevailing community standards. But a parent who leaves his children in the car all day, particularly if they are very young and the sun is hot or there is a great deal of traffic, is probably neglectful, since the likelihood of harm over the long run is very substantial. A parent who sends his six-year-old child out to play during the day is not neglectful, but if he locks his three-year-old out at night, especially in the winter time, he is being neglectful.

> *In the landmark case of* People v. Pierson, *68 N.E. 243 (1903), which, although it involved criminal prosecution for a medical neglect, nevertheless dealt squarely with the same issue that confronts a juvenile court, the New York court stated that "a reasonable amount of discretion is vested in parents charged with the duty of maintaining and bringing up children; and . . . the standard is at what time would an* ordinarily prudent person, *solicitous for the welfare of his child, and anxious to promote his recovery, deem it necessary to call in the services of a physician.* [5]

Most neglectful families show neglect in a variety of ways. A young Sacramento mother, whose husband was imprisoned on a narcotics violation, was overwhelmed with the care of five little boys, the oldest of whom was five. She sat watching television all day long, while the boys defecated, vomited, and urinated in the house, tracked mud in with their bare feet, and fed themselves uncooked maggoty oats from a bag in the kitchen cupboard. When a complaint brought a probation officer to the scene, she found the boys filthy, emaciated, and covered with sores, the house overrun with insects and varmints, and an unbearable stench permeating the atmosphere. On the basis of the combination of circumstances, the situation was classified as one of general neglect. It was the extreme conditions in the home, the evidence of the duration of these conditions for a considerable period of time, and the very youthful age of the children that defined these circumstances as neglect.

Research, examination of neglect cases, and statutes pertaining to neglect reveal that the nature of neglect normally falls into one of the following categories: moral neglect, custody conflict, medical neglect, emotional neglect, and educational neglect.[6] These categories are expounded upon and defined by Thomas D. Gill in his article entitled, "The Legal Nature of Neglect."

> **Moral Neglect:** *The sole purpose of the court's inquiry into the behavior of the parent, whether it be willful or unconscious defection from duty, whether it be an act of commission such as getting intoxicated or a deed of omission such as failing to buy food, is the determination of what harm, if any, this behavior has caused, is causing, or if uncorrected can be reasonably anticipated to cause in the future to the child. The neglect statutes are*

[5]*Ibid.*, p. 7.
[6]*Ibid.*, pp. 8–13.

not penal and were not designed to vent community indignation over the allegedly offending parent. If, therefore, a causal relationship between the questioned parental conduct and the well-being of the child is not established, there can be no finding of neglect. It follows that a parent can conceivably be a convicted community offender without impugning his status as a parent if the offense in question falls short of infringing upon the protective interest of the child.

It is particularly in cases of moral neglect that confusion about the essential connection between what the parent has done and what the child has suffered is likely to ensue. Situations primarily identified with moral sensibilities form themselves into two general groups: those billed around a specific moral defection, often highlighted by an arrest, and those presenting a parent whose life history has been consistently unsuccessful, immoral, and anti-social.

A typical illustration of the former category is the married woman who, separated from her husband and living with her children on a dependency allotment, becomes illicitly involved with another man. She becomes pregnant; her neighbors register complaints; she is arrested; the agency providing assistance files a petition of alleged neglect. The hearing discloses acceptable behavior on the mother's part prior to the marital separation and acceptable care at other levels of her two children, aged two and four. There is no moral neglect because these youngsters are not old enough to be aware of the implications of their mother's behavior, and her past pattern does not suggest that her present difficulties must inevitably continue into the future; moral sense may not be outraged for it exists. Were the children of this situation 11 and 13 years old, these same set of facts could conceivably produce a totally different finding, dependent, of course, on the degree of impact on these older children, who have achieved an age of moral sensitivity.

In the second group, composed of parents who have lived but intermittently within the accepted moral and social boundaries of the community, the neglect petition is triggered not by a single breakdown but rather by an accumulation of events, a pattern shot through with anti-social behavior which, it is usually contended, advertises the moral bankruptcy of the mother or father and results in an ethically structureless family environment most prejudicial to moral development.

Representative of this group is the mother whose continuous clashes with the law and the conventions over a period of years have led to a previous commitment and placement of the children. Now a social derelict, she has by chance partner another child, upon whose behalf a neglect petition is immediately filed for it.

Custody Conflict: *Prudence must be exercised by family casework agencies to avoid bringing to the juvenile court under the guise of neglect, a* custody situation which could be determined in a suit between the parents in a court of proper domestic jurisdiction. Generally, such cases are selfishly motivated: the petitioning parent is far more interested in embarrassing or punishing his spouse than safeguarding the child. Even when promoted by genuine concern for the child, such an action rarely produces evidence justifying a finding of neglect since it normally hinges on family disharmony and the idiosyncrasies of the couple. To conclude that one of two parents might better serve the best interest of the child is a far cry from determining that the other has been guilty of neglect; lacking evidence of neglect, a juvenile court cannot award custody to one parent. There is, of course, the occasional case where parental competition has completely undermined the security and routine of the home to the great detriment and neglect of the child.

Medical Neglect: *In the field of medical neglect, specifically cited as an area of concern by the statutes of approximately half of the states as well as by the 1959 revision of the Standard Juvenile Court Act, it appears to be well established that the state can intervene and order medical treatment in those cases where the life of the child is dependent upon his receiving it, and this without regard to any religious objection. As was said by the U.S. Supreme Court in* Prince v. Mass.*, "Parents may be free to become martyrs themselves, but they are not free to make martyrs of their children." Once, however, the saving of the child's life is not the issue, the courts are not in accord. Operations to correct crippling, disfigurements, and handicaps, even of the most devious sort, which the parents have refused to authorize, have not consistently been approved by the court, particularly if the recommended operation involves a substantial element of risk of the child's life. In such cases the courts have not been willing to say that the judgment of the parents in refusing was unreasonable.*

Emotional Neglect: *However preoccupied the state may be with the medical and the physical care of the child, any desire it may have to protect the same child's emotional well-being is but slightly supported by recorded evidence. Except for the recently enacted legislation in Minnesota, no state laws specifically holds emotional life of the child worthy of protection. The 1949 edition of the Standard Juvenile Court Act held the parent responsible for providing medical, psychological, or psychiatric care for their child. In the 1959 edition the words "psychological or psychiatric" do not appear; they were eliminated largely in response to the Children's Bureau's reservation concerning the legal recognition of emotional neglect. . . . To deny the existence of emotional neglect is to affirm that a child can live happily and successfully without love—which no one believes. The law is inconsistent: in trustee cases involving children it emphasizes often and eloquently the irreplaceable gift of maternal or parental love: then, when the gift has* *been withheld, it professes that the child has suffered no hurt which necessitates protective help.*

Educational Neglect: *Educational neglect is one of the few fields where the community's standard of performance has been specifically spelled out for the court by the state or local law. The requirement of school attendance, procedures for fulfilling them, and permissible exceptions are all uniformly proscribed in the governing educational code. For all of this alleged definitiveness, the decisions involving educational neglect rarely resolve themselves with any greater ease than do any of the others.*

It is first genuinely necessary to determine whether the action seeking the court's help has been brought in the proper form. "Nonattendance" which finds the child at home during his absences from school with the knowledge of his parents because of claimed illness or for other reasons, can conceivably be the result of neglectful parental handling. Truancy, on the other hand, which finds the child out of school without the knowledge and presumably against the wishes of his parents, furnishes a basis for neglect unless the routines of the home and the supervision of the parents can be found to have contributed substantially to the child's actions by denying him the reasonable guidance to which he is entitled. It could, for example, be true that the alleged truancy of a child left by his working parents to get himself up and to school stems more from the laxity of such a parental arrangement than as an attitude of the child's parents, since, in these cases, the delicate needle of court action can quiver mercilessly between delinquency and neglect, it is generally helpful to trace back the attendance pattern of the children in the family for several years, for in the total pattern is ordinarily found the answer to whether we are dealing with a child hostile to school or with parents indifferent to educational responsibilities.[7]

In contrast to the neglectful parent, the abusive parent intends to harm his child and does so by *overt action.* Sexual assault, mutilation, tying up in a dark closet—these are examples of abuse.

The literature on abuse shows that children may be beaten with irons and ironing cords, sticks, wires or lead pipes. They may be tortured with lighted cigarettes, scalding water, or hot stoves. Beloved pets may be tormented and killed before their eyes and the children threatened with the same fate. Parents have twisted their offsprings' arms and legs until they broke, slammed them against a wall until their skulls are fractured, and even bitten them.

The forms of abuse inflicted on children are a negative testimony to the ingenuity of man. Pool cues, baseball bats, TV aerials, rubber hoses, and oars have been used as battering instruments. Children have been gassed, given electric

[7]*Ibid.,* pp. 10–13.

shocks, burned alive, drowned in bath tubs, and suffocated with plastic bags or pillows[8] (see illustrations).

In the total picture of neglect, the percentage of abused children is small. Parents who are physically cruel to children are usually suffering from pathological conditions.

Physical punishment is a common form of punishment; the practice differs among cultural groups. What may appear severe to some is not considered so by others. Brutal treatment is, at times, associated with fanaticism and rigid, unreasonable behavior standards. Beatings are administered with self-righteous ferver. Both physical and psychological damage to the ihild can be severe and may have far-reaching consequences.

Ninety percent of abusive parents show no remorse. They blame their children for being "monsters," "idiots," or "crazy." *Characteristically, abuse of children is not related to a child's misbehavior.* And the parents give seemingly irrelevant reasons for attacking their children.

Medical and social work literature, in the last few years, has reported on the phenomenon of physical abuse inflicted on infants and young children by their parents. This is commonly referred to as the "Battered-Child Syndrome" in which children have sustained serious injuries to bone and soft tissues that resulted, on some occaisons, in permanent crippling or in death.

Apparently, only superficial facts are available about parents who inflict such injuries. Actual experience indicates that (1) adults who inflict injuries on children are *likely to repeat the attack;* (2) the adult is *not reacting to a specific behavior* but to his own feelings; and (3) police warning, court action, and probationary status have been *ineffective as deterrents.* In these circumstances, young children are dependent on the social, medical, and legal agencies for protection.

LEGAL PROVISIONS

The laws relating to neglect of children vary widely from state to state; some outline a specific definition of neglect, and others define the term very broadly or leave the definition to administrative discretion. The laws of New York State are somewhat typical of those that define neglect in specific terms. They are applied to children under sixteen whose parents, or guardians fail to provide them with the physical accessories of life, needed medical attention, and occupational opportunities. They apply also to abandoned children, to those under unlawful or improper supervision in an illegal place, or to a child in such need of care or control "as to injure or endanger the morals or health of himself or others." Mental incapacity of a parent, together with cruelty, immorality, depravity, are specific reasons for court considering parents unfit to care for their children. In addition, children who are left in someone's care by their parents without being visited by

[8]Helfer, *The Battered Child, op. cit.,* pp. 43–56.

them or without payment for their support for a year may be considered abandoned children and therefore in need of the state's protection.

Research reveals that California, Illinois, Maryland, Massachusetts, Minnesota, Missouri, and Rhode Island have laws defining neglect in terms similar to those of the laws of New York State. Minnesota has one unusual provision. A child may be considered neglected "who is without proper parental care because of the emotional, mental, or physical disability or state of immaturity of his parent, guardian or other custodian." Emotional factors in neglect are not elsewhere specifically mentioned in law, although many laws refer to mental incapacity of parent, and courts have recognized this as including emotional neglect.

A few states define neglect in rather broad terms. Colorado statutes, for example, charge county welfare departments with responsibility for "care and treatment of dependent and handicapped children." Dependent and neglected children are considered together, in that the statutes describe seven grounds for dependency and neglect and make no differentiation between dependency and neglect. The agency, therefore, has defined neglect in more specific terms as a guide to working with children in need of help. Laws of the District of Columbia leave definition of neglect to administrative determination. Similarly, the Ohio General Code states that "child welfare has power and duty to make investigations concerning any child reported to be in need of care, protection or service."

With all variations in legal provisions relating to neglect, agencies are in general agreement that *the most effective laws place emphasis on the responsibility of the community to act in behalf of the children rather than against parents.* These laws direct attention to the needs of children and the right and responsibility of the community to intervene in their behalf rather than stressing punitive measures against parents. With such emphasis, a protective service can then be a family-centered service offered in the best interests of a child, with the goal of strengthening or rehabilitating the child's family where necessary and possible.

Community definitions of neglect, reflecting as they must community expectations of parents, differ even more widely than statutory definitions. More and more, however, cities and states are regarding child neglect as a social problem requiring treatment by community action to remedy inadequacies or dangers in the social scene, and by casework services to improve and strengthen parental functioning and enable children to remain with their own familes.

SOURCES OF REFERRALS

The most frequent referral agencies are law enforcement agencies; this is followed by interested individuals in the community, including relatives, then the schools, public assistance agencies, other social agencies in the community, and health agencies and workers, including physicians, public health nurses, and hospitals.

Most agencies accept referrals of families receiving public assistance in the community on the same basis as any family not receiving such assistance. There are some agencies, however, that upon receiving a report of neglect about a family that is found to be receiving public assistance, first screens the case, then with the local department of welfare to determine whether that agency is able to give the needed services through its regular staff.

Several of the public agencies have responsibility for the administration of "child welfare and public assistance services," usually through separate divisions or departments. These agencies have found it necessary to work out clear procedures between the two divisions for serving families in which there are questions of neglect. In most of the agencies throughout the United States, the public assistance worker retains responsibility for administering the assistance payment and for decisions regarding eligibility, while the child-welfare worker assumes primary responsibility for casework service and planning.

EXTENT OF THE PROBLEM

No exact figures are available on the numbers of neglected children in the United States. In California, police report more than 100,000 cases are referred for some type of official action each year. In most of these cases, nothing is done beyond on-the-spot warning or counseling by the police officer. It is impossible to estimate how many of these dismissed children would fall into the category of children needing protection, but it is reasonable to assume that it would be a substantial number. It is not always easy, as previously indicated, to draw the line between neglected and delinquent children. A significant number of youngsters picked up by police for "delinquency tendencies," which includes truancy from school, running away, incorrigibility, and possession of alcohol, could just as appropriately have been given the neglect label, since the delinquent act reflected parental inadequacy or lack of concern.

Whatever the actual incidence, the numbers of neglected children seem to be growing, both absolutely and in proportion to the population. Statistics released from the various social agencies seem to substantiate this fact. The statistical picture of the increase in dependent and neglected cases is vividly portrayed when one reviews the annual statistical report compiled by the Santa Clara County Juvenile Probation Department, considered by many professionals as one of the most progressive departments in the United States. Santa Clara County is rather heavily populated and has fairly adequate living standards. The 1975–76 Annual Report of the Santa Clara Country Juvenile Probation Department cited these figures: "New referrals involving dependency and neglect increased during 1975–76 over our experience in 1974–75. There were 2869 new referrals received during the year compared to 2078 in 1974–75. The difference represented a significant gain in new referrals involving dependency and neglect." It must be remembered that these were probably thoroughly severe cases of neglect, sufficient to warrant probation department attention.

All estimates of child neglect in California may vary according to the scope of the definition used; estimates of abuse vary also, but in smaller range. With various incomplete reporting services, the officially known number of beaten and battered children is about 150,000 annually in the nation as a whole.

Most studies of cases of *child abuse* reveal that the children involved are proportionately young. This is understandable, since young children are relatively incapable of self-defense, more vulnerable to injury, less likely to be in contact with outsiders, and more likely to be a parental burden and irritant than older children.

The Children's Division of the American Humane Association did a study of 662 cases of child abuse reported in newspapers in 1962. Ninety percent of the children were ten years of age or younger. The majority, 50 percent were under four. Nearly one child of every four died as a result of the parentally inflicted injuries and of those who died, over 80 percent were children under four.[9]

In a Kansas study, out of 85 known cases of child abuse, most were children under three and one-third were under six months. Fourteen deaths occurred—all of children under four years.[10]

In the first nine months of Illinois' reporting law, 363 suspected victims of abuse were found. The majority, 247, were under five, 99 were under one year, and 59 were under six months.

The above figures relating to neglected and abused children reflect the more obvious results of family breakdown, neglect, and mistreatment of children. Less is known about chronic neglect situations where crisis does not demand immediate action. Children's court, again, reports that evidence of neglect of long duration is often found in situations of children who have been charged with delinquent acts; cases coming into the family court on matters of nonsupport also frequently give evidence of serious and long-standing neglect.

CONTRIBUTING FACTORS[11]

There are factors other than the personal characteristics of parents[12] which predispose toward the mistreatment of children.

One question that inevitably rises is the effect of *social and economic status* on the incidence of child neglect and abuse. Are most of the cases found among low-income families, and, if so, is the inability to meet children's emotional and physical needs a general characteristic of low-income parents? Many thoughtful people

---

[9]Childrens Division: The American Humane Association, *Protecting the Battered Child*, Denver, 1962. For a contemporary point of view, see E. W. Brown, *Child Neglect and Delinquency: A Digest of Case Law*, Juvenile Justice Textbook Series, National Council of Juvenile Court Judges, Reno, Nevada, 1975.

[10]M. Rosenhein, ed., *Pursuing Justice for the Child*, University of Chicago Press, Chicago, 1976, pp. 303–310.

[11]*Protective Services for Children*, p. 75.

[12]*Ibid.*, pp. 12–14.

have assumed that the problem is confined to low-income families, who are viewed as unstable, disorganized, and lacking in goals of planning ability.

One researcher in the field makes a distinction between "problem" and "stable" low-income families.[13] The latter, which comprised the majority of low-income families, take good care of their children and expect others to do the same. Cool or indifferent families are deviants from the general social norms that prevail among poor persons. Child-rearing patterns may be different among classes, but accepted behavior at any social level does not include harming one's children.

Another study, this time of families receiving welfare assistance in Chicago, resulted in similar findings. The profile of family disorganization was not typical of the lowest economic group, the welfare recipient. The report observed, "The Public has gained a false image of a mother who is shiftless and lazy, unwilling to work, promiscuous and neglectful of her children." This study found very few mothers, not more than 3 percent, who fit this image in one or more ways.[14]

Yet, the experts agreed that while the majority of low-income persons are good parents, the *proportion* of abused and neglected children is greater among this group. Low-income persons are more accustomed to seeing maltreated children. They are less likely than middle-income individuals to report such cases to the authorities, with whom they often do not identify. The low-income group exerts less pressure, either formal or informal, against neglectful parents, and they tend to be more tolerant of corporal punishment than is the middle class.

The low-income group may do little to discourage child neglect and abuse among its ranks. At the same time, a lower-class family whose behavior is deviant in the area of child care is often very visible to the outside community. A family's request for financial assistance, for example, exposes it to an initial investigation and continuing contact that under other circumstances would be summarily rejected as an invasion of privacy. Children from prosperous homes may be shielded from official view or sent away to school if the parents cannot handle them. In general, low-income families, with low prestige and frequent ignorance of official methods, have less means of concealing deviant behavior, and less motivation for doing so than the middle-class parent who fears the censure of his peers and loss of status. The lower-income parent has less to lose by the discovery of his behavior, and takes less pains to hide it.

Finally, there is no doubt that low-income parents may have to face more obstacles to family living than those with higher incomes. Lack of work skills may force parents to move from place to place in search of a job, regardless of what this does to a child's associations and schooling. Lack of money makes it difficult to find adequate housing, provide nourishing meals, or pay for baby-sitters when the parent wants a night out, regardless of how well-meaning they may be.

The majority of low-income families are stable, but the disorganized and

[13]A. Roberts, *Childhood Deprivation,* Charles C Thomas, Springfield, Illinois, 1975, Chap. 2.
[14]Welfare Council of Metropolitan Chicago, *Facts, Fallacies and Future—Summary of a Study of the ADC Program in Cook County,* Chicago, 1962.

broken families from any class are likely to end up at the low-income level. Disorganized families, some of whom are used to a higher standard and all of whom have difficulty in ordering their lives, are ill equipped to cope with the burdens of managing on a minimal budget. Low income only increases their inadequacy as parents. It is also possible that low income per se can produce, as well as aggravate, inadequacy.

Among *minority ethnic groups*, the greater proportion of neglected children may be found on the basis of low income alone. In particular, American Indians who have moved away from the reservation often find difficulty in meeting parental responsibilities. After moving from the firm authority and tradition of the tribe, they do not know what parental behavior is expected in the outside community.

But it would be a mistake to believe that child neglect and abuse are primarily minority problems or confined to any particular group. Expert witnesses before the California Legislature Assembly Committee on Social Welfare stressed that the cases with which they were familiar cut across all ethnic, racial, religious, and economic lines. One witness, Mrs. Wanda Schernerhorn of the Los Angeles County Schools, made this comment when asked whether most neglected children come primarily from minority communities:

> *I would say that it certainly is a problem in minority areas for many years. That neglect of children in the sense we are discussing occurs as much in Caucasian families as it does in minority families. I have encountered indescribable neglect in Caucasian families. And I would say that my experience with minority families basically has been one of affection for children, of concern for children, perhaps accompanied by ignorance of how to care for them. But the kind of complete oblivion to the needs of children, I would find much more likely in the Caucasian family than in a minority group. And this again is probably not a fair generalization.*

The *continued growth of urban centers* is perhaps one of the most important factors fostering child neglect and abuse. Once, in a small town, a two-year-old was tied outside on a broiling August day. Within an hour, several people had reported his plight to the sheriff. In an urban area, passersby might be disturbed by the suffering of a little girl in the hot sun, but they would not know the family and would probably not know whom to call. Community concern for neglected children is less likely to be expressed on the neighborhood level in our growing urban areas. This in itself makes mistreatment a more likely occurrence.

PUBLIC ACTION THROUGH PROTECTIVE SERVICES[15]

Given the extent and magnitude of the cruelty and disregard parents can show

[15]*Protective Services for Children*, pp. 18–24. See also: W. C. Gordon, *The Family Court: Advantages and Problems, Juvenile Justice*, National Council of Juvenile Court Judges. Vol. 25, no. 3, Nov. 1974.

toward their children, what is being done to help these children, what more can be done, and who should do it?

First of all, it must be recognized that *abusive and neglectful parents are not going to change by themselves.* "Unless pathological familes receive continuing and persistent, personalized help they have neither the volition nor the means to conform to society's norms. People do not spontaneously decide one fine Monday morning that they are going to change their way of living, proceed to do so at the price of enormous effort, and then maintain the change, especially when they have neither the strength nor incentive and no conviction that it would benefit them anyway. For people as passive as those in our study the idea that an occasional lecture or threat will accomplish such change is patently absurd."[16]

Secondly, the harm they do to their children is, by and large, *something the children cannot survive without physical and emotional scars.* The child who has been consistently harmed by his parents is not going to outgrow his problems as an adult. The less that is done for him, the less will be his resiliency and ability to cope with life's problems as time goes on. His personal and emotional handicaps will be compounded with time,[17] until, as an adult, he is unable to be a good parent. And so the cycle continues.

Not only do neglected and abused children become poor parents, but *they may develop into delinquents, criminals, psychotics, and adult social problem cases.* The effect spreads beyond themselves and their children. The reasons for this are obvious. "Children who are abused present a problem to the community, aside from society's moral and legal obligation to help them. They develop patterns of living without parental supervision and discipline, and often hate and resent all persons in authority. They have untreated illnesses and suffer from lack of needed medical care. They may develop destructive behavior patterns in an unconscious effort to secure acceptance and gratification of their needs. They often fail in school and are unable to adjust to persons outside the home."[18]

THE ROLE OF THE JUVENILE COURT: RIGHTS OF PARENTS AND CHILDREN UNDER THE LAW[19]

If the cycle of parental inadequacy and cruelty is to be broken, and its broader social effects prevented, intervention is necessary. The founders of the Children's Division of the American Humane Association recognized this event in the last

[16]Young, *Wednesday's Children*, pp. 145–146. See also N. Weinstein: *Legal Rights of Children*, Juvenile Justice Textbook Series, National Council of Juvenile Court Judges, Reno, Nevada, 1975.
[17]R. G. Stennett, "Emotional Handicap in the Elementary Years: Phase of Disease," *American Journal of Orthopsychiatry*, April 1966, p. 449.
[18]Tennessee Department of Public Welfare, "A Project in Protective Services," *Tennessee Public Welfare Record*, August 1966, p. 78.
[19]*Protective Services for Children*, pp. 22–21.

century. The original child protective services, however, were rescue operations, with punishment of the parent and removal of the child from the home as the goals. Now punishment of the parent is recognized as a blind alley. If the goal of helping a child is to take precedence, initial efforts must be made to maintain the child with the family. Where this cannot be done and where a child's life and well-being are endangered, then placement outside the home should be sought.

The legal concept of taking a child for protection is based on the concept of the state as *parents patriae* (discussed in chapter 8), which means the state's concern as the guardian of social interests and the concept that the state has both the right and the duty to see that the physical, mental, and moral welfare of its children is safeguarded. In this country, the rights of the control and custody of children are ordinarily fixed in the home and by the natural parent. In the absence of abnormal circumstances, the state has only a limited concern with the child's upbringing, however, it is also clear that the state has the authority to protect a child whose parents fail to do so. The concept of the state's authority as superior to that of neglectful parents has developed in the last century and represents the community's concern for its children.

The rights and responsibilities of parents are specifically set forth in the welfare institutions and the civil, probate, and penal codes. These rights and duties can only be overruled by a court. Parents have the right to bring up their children and the duty to do so properly. The right of a parent extends to the placement of his child in a home for temporary or permanent care, but such a placement does not alter his responsibility for the child's well-being, support, and education. The parent may also place his child for adoption or relinquish him to an adoption agency.

> *The authority of a parent over a child is not limited, so long as it is exercised so as not to endanger the child's safety or morals, or to interfere unjustly with the child's welfare. While the parent has the right to inflict reasonable and moderate punishment on the child for the punishment of disobedience and the enforcement of parental authority.*[20]

The rights of a child have been summarized as follows:

1. *The child is a person in his own right. A considerable body of statutory laws spell out his rights to care, teaching, training, and treatment. These add up to birth rights to live, grow, and develop to the fullest potentialities of his individual capacity.*

2. *However, the law presumes that the child is too mature and inexperienced to be left to fend and defend for himself, to make his own choices and decisions, and to realize his rights wisely and responsibly.*

[20]M. R. Ward, *California Juvenile Laws,* Legal Book Store, Los Angeles, California, 1976, p. 25 (from 46 C.J. 1221).

3. *Consequently, the law requires that the exercise of the child's right shall be entrusted to other persons capable of, and interested in, acting for the child during his childhood.*

4. *..The law makes it a duty of parents to take up this responsibility for their own children.*

5. *..It makes it a duty of the State to supplement and substitute for parental efforts whenever needed to further the best interests and welfare of the child.*[21]

With the growth of laws to protect the rights of children, juvenile and adult courts have established an essential role in the protective field; however, the court's role is limited and it cannot deal with many of the situations that threaten children.

Adults who attack children are likely to repeat the incident, but this cannot be proven in an individual case. Because it takes place in the privacy of the home, abuse and neglect, especially of preschool children, is rarely witnessed; in addition, infants and toddlers, who bear the greatest brunt of mistreatment, cannot speak out on their own behalf. Usually a child under seven is not considered a competent witness; furthermore, his story may be confused out of fear of parental retaliation or out of a sense of family love. As a result, it is very difficult to demonstrate clear and present danger unless a child has already been severely harmed. Even then, the court has no real method of resolving the situation except incarceration of the parent or removal of the child from the home.

Criminal charges against a parent are usually very difficult to prove and punishing the parent does not seem to alleviate nor necessarily deter him from further acts of abuse. Since guilt must be proved beyond a reasonable doubt, lack of evidence may make it impossible to obtain a conviction. Witnesses are protected against self-incrimination and a parent may not be forced to testify against his own interests. When such prosecution fails, the parent may feel even more punitive toward his child, more immune from outside interference, and more justified in his actions. In addition, the publicity that surrounds a child often makes it more difficult to work with the parent afterwards. Even when legal action against the parent might be possible, the child's interests are usually better served by not pressing charges.

Because juvenile court actions on behalf of a child are not criminal prosecutions against any person, proof of guilt beyond a reasonable doubt is not required. However, recently, the United States Supreme Court ruled that proceedings on the juvenile court level must adhere to the same rule as applied in adult courts, which clearly states "that proof beyond a reasonable doubt is required." This decision does not affect the cases presented to the court on the petitions filed alleging

---

[21]I. Weissman, "Legal Guardianship of Children," *The Social Welfare Forum*, National Conference of Social Work, 155 D, Sept. 1973, p. 74.

delinquent or predelinquent behavior. The cases pertaining to neglected and abused children, however, differ significantly. These cases must be fully documented according to the rules of evidence as presented in the cases prosecuted under the general law by the district attorney. It is not unusual, therefore, to find many instances of how the police and court system fall short in protecting the rights and well-being of children. In some cases, a home situation gives every sign that it will develop into danger for the child, but it has not done so as yet. In other situations, mistreatment of the child has apparently already occurred, but it cannot be proven, or, when it is proven, the parent is put on probation or given a light sentence and the family resumes life as before without further assistance. Testimony before the California Legislature Assembly Committee on Social Welfare reveals that there are many cases where court intervention comes too late, after the parent has seriously injured the youngster. The Los Angeles County Probation Department testified to the following:

> We feel that society must accept the fact that some parents are inadequate in some ways and would remain inadequate. These situations call for long-term, realistic planning which would not include taking these children in and out of their homes, in and out of court, and in and out of foster homes, but rather provide a kind of service, for example, parental aid, and leaving the children at home. An agency small enough, and with its entire focus on the protection of children, could provide this sort of service.
>
> The police will only pick a child up when the situation is provable, e.g., so they have to go on provables. So a lot of times when they get out and can't prove anything, police resort to what they call "counsel and release," very simply counsel and tell the parents not to do it any more. . . . We seldom, only in extreme situations, get the first contact with the police. Usually when we get it, the police have been out several times.
>
> In other words, this is what we are saying, it has to be within the framework of the law. And anything physically and psychologically could be happening to the child while the slow wheels of the law grind out. This is not really protecting the youngster.

Numerous examples[22] were brought to the attention of the Assembly Interim Committee on Social Welfare vividly portraying tragic incidences where the wheels of justice were simply too slow.

[22]*Standards for Specialized Courts Dealing with Children*, Children's Bureau Publication, no. 346, Washington, D.C., 1964, p. 24; *Child Welfare Services*, Children's Bureau Publication, no. 359, Washington, D.C., 1957, p. 11; J. P. Kenny and D. G. Pursuit, *Police Work with Juveniles*, 4th ed., Charles C Thomas, Springfield, Ill. 1976; *Municipal Police Administration*, 6th ed., International City Managers Association, Chicago, 1966.

THE POLICE ROLE IN CASES OF NEGLECTED AND ABUSED CHILDREN

Reports of abusive treatment from any source, or the observation by police officers of bruises and injuries suffered by the child, are sufficient reasons to make a thorough investigation of the family situation, to seek medical opinion, and, where available and indicated, psychiatric advice. Parents are likely to be evasive in discussing their relationship to a child, and likely to be suspicious of agency action. Occasionally, parents are relieved to express their true feelings about the child and to participate in planning for his care outside the home.

Generally, the role of the police in cases of neglected and abused children can be broken down into the following categories: *receiving and investigating, verifying, evaluating and disposing of complaints.*

RECEIVING AND INVESTIGATING COMPLAINTS

Situations involving neglect of children usually are brought to the attention of the police by someone other than the parents. Sometimes instances of neglect are observed by police while responding to other complaints, such as domestic disturbances. Many of these complaints concern children caught in the middle of family crises, such as destitution, loss of the home, violent fights of the parents, and parental threats of suicide. These crises often lead to children being left alone, locked in closets, undernourished, or severely beaten. The following examples are typical of the many complaints received each year by the police throughout the country:

1. Responded to a complaint concerning three children, ages two to six, left alone in a parked car for several hours. Observation indicated that the children were dirty and unkempt, cold and hungry, poorly clothed, and in need of medical care.

2. Responded to a domestic disturbance, where drinking parents had been fighting. Children were frightened and appeared to have been abused by the parent. The home was in disorder.

3. Responded to a complaint about several children, ages three to seven, left alone in a small apartment for several hours. Complaint indicated that this situation was not new, but was being reported to an official agency for the first time.

A variety of sources point out the authority and the responsibility of the police for receiving and responding to complaints of the type illustrated. These authorities[23] see the police department as an appropriate agency for investigating

[23]For a detailed discussion of agencies investigating complaints of neglect and delinquent cases refer to: A. F. Brandstetter and J. J. Brennan, "Prevention Through the Police," *Delinquency Prevention,* Prentice-Hall, Inc., Englewood Cliffs, N.J. 1967, Chap. 10.

complaints of this type, petitioning for a court hearing, and referring cases to community welfare agencies. They contend that recognized police procedures in some cases of neglected and abused children are, in many respects, similar to those used in cases of delinquency and that investigation of offenses is primarily a police function. Another authority states that the police are permanently in the field of child protection since no other community service is organized to perform all of the functions related to neglected and abused children.[24]

In some communities, one or more social agencies may have, by statute or charter, a responsibility for providing protective services on behalf of children who are neglected or abused. Therefore, it is incumbent upon each agency involved to plan in a cooperative manner and to coordinate their efforts in responding to complaints about neglected and abused children.

This is not to say that overlapping will not exist regarding law enforcement agencies and community agencies receiving and responding to complaints about neglect and abuse. Such overlapping is essential when we consider the fact that the police department, or any other community agency, cannot by itself handle all complaints of neglected and abused children that arise in a community. Although the police department is in the best position to accord immediate response to emergency complaints regarding neglectful and abused situations, the brunt of receiving and investigating complaints should not fall solely on the law enforcement agency. If, however, a private or public agency resonds to a complaint regarding a case of neglect or abuse, the responding agency should be cognizant of the fact that if the children are in *immediate danger*, the police department should be called into the situation during the initial phase of the investigation.

A police officer who is called in on the case of a neglected or abused child should first make a thorough investigation of the facts and circumstances of the case. He can decide whether the case requires further action, and, if so, whether this should be court action or adjustment through a nonauthoritative agency. If court action is warranted, the investigating officer must decide whether it should be on behalf of the child in the juvenile court or directed at the adult involved in the case, necessitating a complaint being filed and the matter being heard on the adult court level.

It is often difficult for the investigating officer to make a thorough investigation of the neglected or abused case. The reasons for such difficulty are: (1) the child concerned may be either too young to give an accurate account of what has occurred or too afraid to tell the officer the true story; (2) the very neighbor who called the case to the attention of the police may later be reluctant to testify against the parents of the child. Under such circumstances, the police officer is often hard-pressed to make an adequate investigation of the situation surrounding the offense.

Because the complaining parties may be reluctant to testify, the officer, in his contacts with reporting or complaining neighbors, will have to persuade them that

[24]*Ibid.*

they should cooperate with the authorities in order to protect the child concerned. Whenever possible, he should promise them that their names will not be involved in further action on the case unless they are needed to prove the case legally.

In dealing with the parents of an allegedly neglected or abused child, the officer investigating the case must keep in mind the many pressures that may have caused the parents to be guilty of such mistreatment. It may be helpful if the officer lets the parents know that he understands about such pressures and encourages them to talk about their problems as they see them. In this way, the officer may be able to see possible strengths in the family that could be drawn upon (in the report to the agency to which the case may be referred) to bring about an intelligent adjustment.

The officer should also ascertain whether the present instance of neglect or abuse is an *isolated incident* or whether it is part of a *long-time pattern* of neglect and abuse. If the situation is one of long-time neglect or abuse, court action should be initiated.

In the area of investigating complaints—particularly where court action appears to be the possible disposition—the investigating officer should take the following evidentiary steps in order to strengthen his case in juvenile court: (1) he should obtain visual proof (colored photographs) in order to prove that undesirable conditions exist; (2) he should call upon appropriate persons (i.e., neighbors, deputy probation officers, school personnel, etc.) to witness such conditions; (3) and in a case where cruelty on the part of a parent toward a child is indicated, he should ask a licensed physician to make a physical examination of the child so that the physican can testity in court about the child's condition.

VERIFYING COMPLAINTS

The initial question that should concern the police in responding to reported complaints of abuse or neglect of a child is "Does neglect or abuse exist?" This fact should be established by a proficient police investigation, based on knowledge of law and of the offenses governed by law, rules of evidence, and previous police experience in handling such complaints. Methods of gathering evidence, besides the process indicated above, include statements of witnesses and complainants, interviews with parents and children, and general observations.

EVALUATING COMPLAINTS

After observing and investigating home conditions and discussing the case with the family and witnesses, an evaluation of the situation is made by the police officer. This evaluation should include those aspects of the case regarded as *legally* and *socially* significant: the seriousness of the situation, the need for immediate protection of the child, observations concerning the physical conditions of the child, attitudes of parents, statement of witnesses, and general conditions of the home. This evaluation is not a social history, since it differs in purpose, scope, and degree, but is simply a process for arriving at a police disposition.

CASE DISPOSITION

A number of cases can be closed by a *warning* or a *reprimand*. In dealing with neglect and abuse situations it is important for the police officer to be aware of the many pressures that may cause parents to neglect or abuse their children. Rather than being willful, the neglected or abused child may be the symptom of the fact that these pressures have mounted and we find that the offending parent or parents are unable to cope with the problem. In such cases, the police officer may find it more suitable to refer the parents to a social agency for help. Through such means as interviewing techniques, the police officer should try to differentiate between those who want to be and can be helped by social agencies and those who have shown, by willful neglect of the children, that they need the authoritative service of the court.

A police officer should be informed about the community agencies that can be of service in working with neglected and abused cases. Definite policies for referrals should be arranged between the police and such agencies. Smoothly working relations with the agencies will enable the police department to explain their services to parents in need of referral.

Minor instances of neglect or misconduct by parents toward their children may most appropriately be dealt with by a reprimand regarding the matter and a warning of the possible consequences if the act is repeated. For example, a police officer may be dispatched in response to a neighbor's reports that a child is being beaten. Upon investigating, the officer may find no conclusive evidence that the beating is beyond the normal discipline within parental perogatives. However, *if the facts warrant it*, the officer may want to make it clear to the parents that under certain circumstances such an incident could lead to further action by the police in behalf of the child.

On the other hand, there are instances where the officer, before disposing of certain cases, should check the records of the police department and of the community agencies to determine whether the family has been known previously. In any event, adequate records should be maintained regarding the complaint, normal facts of the action, and the police disposition.

A referral to the juvenile probation department (or the agency legally assigned to handle such a referral), involving the neglected or abused child, is called for when: (1) the alleged neglect constitutes an *immediate danger* to the health and welfare of the child and the facts on hand are sufficient to support a petition; or (2) the alleged neglect does not constitute immediate danger to the health or welfare of the child, but there is reason to believe that court action or service is needed to *protect or aid the child* and the facts on hand are sufficient to support a petition.

The Police Role in Cases of Neglected and Abused Children   **269**

If these conditions do not strictly apply, the police may first try other dispositions, if the department policy and agreement with the local courts permit such steps. Policies relative to court action against adults should be worked out jointly by the police department, the juvenile court, and the prosecuting attorney's office.

TAKING THE NEGLECTED AND ABUSED CHILD INTO PROTECTIVE CUSTODY

Taking children into custody is primarily a police function. By law, the police have the responsibility and authority to take into custody a child in danger of violence or serious injury. This authority may also be vested in other administrative agencies, such as a society for the prevention of cruelty to children. Usually, such an agency is guided in its authority by law.

When questions arise as to the need to take a child into custody, the police, if possible, should consult with special agencies about the desirability of such action. Distinction should be made between the desirability of taking children into custody and statutory grounds for such action. The police cannot take children into custody merely upon the request of an individual or social agency. They must determine whether sufficient grounds exist for such action. Since the police have the responsibility and the authority, the final action to take children into custody must rest with them. Where another community agency has such powers under the law, that agency may, of course, also take such action.

Not all children taken into custody by the police must come under the jurisdiction of the court. Exceptions are lost children and children left alone because of an emergency family situation, such as hospitalization of one or both parents. Such children may be held temporarily pending arrangements by the parents for permanent care or return home.

The lack of adequate shelter care facilities for neglected and abused children presents just about as great a problem for the police as the lack of detention facilities for children needing secure custody. Often, as is the case in many states, the only shelter care offered is the facility used for delinquents. In many of the more progressive states such as California and Colorado, the law specifically provides for separate facilities for delinquents and neglected or abused children. What type of services does the children's shelter provide? What it is, what it does, who it serves, is answered by one of the most progressive departments in the nation, Santa Clara County Juvenile Probation Department (California), which attempts to answer the question by providing a brochure to the clientele and agencies with whom they deal. The substance of the brochure is partially summarized here:

> *The Children's Shelter is operated by the Santa Clara County Juvenile Probation Department for boys and girls taken into protective custody under the Juvenile Court Law.*

Protective custody involves situations of neglect, abuse, absence of parents, extreme poverty, or genuinely unfit home. Lost or wandering children also are received at the Shelter.

Boys and girls from infancy through age 17 are accommodated and the Shelter receives children at any hour when they are brought by the proper authorities.

Even before the State Legislature decreed in 1961 that separate facilities must be maintained for dependent as compared to delinquent children, Santa Clara County was established in this area.

METHOD OF OPERATION

Children are admitted to the Shelter only on the basis of facts submitted by a law enforcement agency or probation officer. A neighbor or relative knowing of neglect or abuse cannot take it upon himself to bring a child to the Shelter; he must notify the proper authorities.

The Shelter is a temporary holding facility only, where children are kept until it can be determined what disposition will be made of their case.

This disposition will involve either (1) sending the child home if conditions have improved, (2) sending the child to a responsible relative or foster home, or (3) sending the child to a privately operated instition.

Such disposition can be made only by the Juvenile Court after the child legally has been declared a Dependent Child of the Court.

Approximately two weeks elapse between the time a child is admitted to the Shelter and a disposition. Children staying for a longer period at the Shelter in almost every case are awaiting an opening in an agency or institution chosen for them.

Once the Juvenile Court has taken jurisdiction of the Dependent Child it reviews the case annually until it is dismissed. Meanwhile, case-work services are maintained through Juvenile Probation Department, which is the administrative arm of the Court.

PROGRAM OF THE SHELTER

In view of the great range in ages and the daily population change, it is necessary to follow a precise schedule if order is to be maintained among boys and girls whose lives bear the stamp of disorganization and neglect.

For many of them the Shelter experience may be their first acquaintance with the valuable disciplines of proper rising and bed-time, personal grooming and the proper care of quarters and belongings.

Even so, the Director and counselors strive to maintain a homelike atmosphere, keeping externally imposed controls and regimentation to a minimum and exercising reasonable permissiveness of activity and expression.

There are no locked doors and the building layout and decor are so planned as to reflect as little of the institutional look as possible.

On the more formal side, a program is arranged so that children staying for more than just a few days attend public schools in the immediate area. Children may attend religious services on Sunday.

Older children are assigned to various jobs around the Shelter, such as assisting with the care of the toddler group, helping in the kitchen and dining hall, and performing certain housekeeping chores.

Good behavior is encouraged by means of a point system and selection of a "boy and girl of the week" who receive small prizes for their achievement.

Each child is given a physical examination by a physician who makes regular calls at the Shelter. A doctor is always available and a Registered Nurse is on the premises 24 hours a day. The services of the Santa Clara Valley Medical Center are used for emergencies as well as private medical centers.

There are many opportunities for wholesome recreation. There is a well equipped playground, an athletic field, and an ample supply of toys and games for indoor and outdoor enjoyment. Civic groups and social clubs have donated almost all of this type of equipment.

TV is available on a supervised schedule. On Friday nights a feature-length movie is shown, and local theatre managers have been very cooperative in admitting custody children free to worthwhile programs.

PARENTAL AUTHORITY

As is the case with all other placements in County Institutions made by the Juvenile Court, parents are liable for the cost of keeping their children at the Shelter. Collection is based upon ability to pay.

Parents are allowed to visit their children once within the first 24 hours after admission to the Shelter and thereafter on Sunday from 1:30 to 2:30 P.M.

The Santa Clara County Juvenile Probation Department's facility for neglected and abused children, unfortunately, is not practiced nationally or, for that matter, within the state itself. The lack of adequate shelter care facilities for neglected and abused children presents just about as great a problem for the police as the lack of detention facilities for children needing secure custody. Often the only shelter care offered is the facility used for delinquents. On many occasions these facilities are totally inadequate. The plight of their institutional care was brought to the attention of the public recently via television. On January 4, 1977, NBC presented a documentary on child abuse. In this author's opinion, this documentary gives a vivid picture of the neglected and physically abused child syndrome. The report was factual and revealed the completely inadequate care and supervision accorded children in trouble in *some* states.

In those communities where specific facilities for shelter care exist, arrangements should also be made whereby police officers can have access to the shelter at any time of the day or night. In communities where no adequate or separate facilities exist, it is the obvious responsibility of the police to work vigorously with other groups in an effort to bring about the establishment of such facilities.

The police should put a neglected or abused child in shelter only when *absolutely necessary*—that is, when the health and welfare of the child is in immediate danger. Otherwise, the child should be allowed to remain with the parents, pending further consideration of the case by the authorities, or study and recommendation by the social agency called in.

The police should be certain to let the juvenile court and the parents know when a child is being placed in shelter. If school is in session, the school authorities should also be notified, either by the parents, the court, or the police.

Statutes of some states provide certain safeguards governing the process by which children are placed in shelter care. For example, a number of state juvenile court statutes, similar to the Standard Family Juvenile Court Acts, provide that no child shall be held in detention or shelter care longer than forty-eight hours, excluding Sundays and holidays, unless a petition has been filed.

SUMMARY

Neglected and abused children are complicated social and legal problems. This chapter attempts to resolve some of the social and legal complications that police officers are confronted with when working with these types of youngsters. The conditions that indicate the need for action on the part of social or law enforcement agencies include: (1) lack of physical care and protection; (2) lack of supervision, guidance, and discipline; (3) exploitation of children; (4) lack of protection from degrading conditions; (5) abuse and fear of physical cruelty. These neglected and abused youngsters become visible to the community in a variety of ways; examples of actual cases quite vividly portray the tragic situation.

The line between *neglect* and *abuse* is sometimes difficult to draw, but the two can generally be distinguished. The *neglectful parent* usually does not *consciously* intend to harm his child, but through failure to meet the child's health, nutritional, comfort, and emotional needs, exposes the child to severe risks. Neglect, then, is the failure to exercise the care that the circumstances justly demand. It embraces willful as well as unintentional disregard of duty. There are several types of neglect: *moral neglect, custody conflict, medical neglect, emotional neglect, and educational neglect.*

In contrast to the neglectful parent, the *abusive parent intends* to harm his child and does so by *overt* action. Sexual assault, mutilation, tying up a child in a dark closet—these are some examples of abuse. In the total picture of neglect, the percentage of abused children is small. Parents who are cruel to children are usually suffering from pathological conditions. Furthermore, 90 percent of abusive parents show no remorse. They blame the children for being "monsters," "idiots," or "crazy." Characteristically, abuse of children is not related to a child's misbehavior. Actual experience also indicates that: (1) adults who inflict injuries on children are likely to repeat the attack; (2) the adult is not reacting to a specific behavior but to his own feelings; and (3) police warnings, court action, and probationary status have been ineffective as deterrents.

The laws relating to neglect of children vary widely from state to state. Some states are quite specific in defining neglect and others define the term very broadly, leaving the definition to administrative discretion. Along these lines, the laws of New York, California, Illinois, Maryland, Massachusetts, Minnesota, Missouri, and Rhode Island are analyzed.

There are many factors, other than the personal characteristics of parents, that predispose parents to mistreatment of children. Factors such as social and economic status; minority ethnic groups (the greater proportion of neglected children may be found on the basis of low income alone); and the continued growth of urban centers, which is perhaps one of the most important factors fostering child neglect and abuse. The type of action available through community services are discussed as well as the role of the juvenile court and rights of parents and children under the law.

The police have a difficult role in cases of neglected and abused children. What do the law enforcement agencies do when receiving and investigating complaints? How does the arresting officer verify such complaints? In evaluating complaints received, evaluation should include certain aspects—what are these aspects? And finally, in arriving at a disposition what are the guidelines that must be followed? These questions are answered in this chapter. Taking the neglected and abused child into protective custody presents an extremely difficult problem. By law the police have the responsibility and authority to take into custody a child in danger of violence or serious injury. This authority may also be invested in other administrative agencies such as a society for the prevention of cruelty to children. Usually, such an agency is guided in its authority by law.

ANNOTATED REFERENCES

Browne, E. W., *Child Neglect: A Digest of Case Laws*. Juvenile Justice Textbook Series, National Council of Juvenile Court Judges, Reno, Nevada, 1975.

This book is a special edition on "neglect" and, thus, its entire focus is devoted to evaluating and resolving problems that confront social as well as law enforcement agencies in the area of neglected and abused children. Browne's discussion should prove extremely interesting to students of law enforcement.

Flammong, C. J., "Reflections on the Police Juvenile Enterprise." *Juvenile Justice,* National Council of Juvenile Court Judges, Reno, Nevada, Vol. 24, No. 1, 1973, pp. 23–27.

Part 4 entitled "Legal Aspects" includes two chapters that are directly related to police work: chapter 10, "The Law and Abused Children," and chapter 11, "The Role of the Law Enforcement Agency." Both areas are discussed by knowledgeable practitioners and academicians.

Kahn, Alfred J., *Planning Community Services for Children in Trouble,* Columbia University Press, New York, 1968.

Chapter 9 of this volume covers an area in which law enforcement officers should have some knowledge: protective services and the community's response to alleged neglected and abused children. The manner in which such children are identified and the expertise utilized by law enforcement agencies in responding to such neglected and abused situations are discussed.

Heifer, Ray E. and Kempe, C. Henry, eds., *The Battered Child,* 2nd ed., University of Chicago Press, Chicago, 1974.

This work discusses the investigative and follow-up activities that may be expected of police. It asserts that many cases will need referral by the police authority to public child welfare agencies for protective services.

Young, Leotine, *Wednesday's Children,* McGraw-Hill, New York, 1964.

Some of the examples in this chapter pertaining to neglected and abused children were taken from Young's book. For an extensive, vivid discussion, and interesting case studies, the student should refer to this source.

CHAPTER TWELVE police relationships with other agencies

In almost every aspect of their work with juveniles, the police must have contact with at least one other agency in the community. It must be recognized that the police services are only a part of the total community effort to promote the welfare of children and young people. For police services to be made more effective, then, they must be planned in relationship to the overall community program as well as to the services offered by individual agencies.

COMMUNITY PLANNING

Experience has shown the public and private agencies in communities that they can do a much more effective and economical job in meeting the social needs of people if they plan and coordinate their efforts. Therefore, in many communities the agencies have gotten together to form community planning bodies, known by such names as "Health and Welfare Council," "Council of Social Agencies," "Community Council," and the like.

As a major public service in the community, the police department should take part in the community planning and be a member of any coordinating council that may exist. *The Special Juvenile Delinquency Project—International Association of Chiefs of Police* query on police services revealed that 48 percent of the police departments responding were not represented on community planning bodies. Of course, it is possible that in many communities there were no such planning bodies to which the police could belong. Where this is the case the police should join with other interested agencies and persons to establish a council. Consultative services for this purpose are available from Community Chest and Council of America, Inc., The National Council on Crime and Delinquency, and from various state departments.

277

Insofar as services to children are concerned, the police department might bring to the attention of the planning bodies such matters as:

1. The delinquency rate

2. Focal points of delinquency and crime in the community.

3. Various services that are lacking and are needed for families and children.

4. Inadequacy of detention or shelter care facilities.

5. Need for new laws or revision or repeal of existing laws.

6. Need for greater interpretation to the public of existing laws.

7. Need for additional personnel to serve juveniles.

8. Need for assistance in conducting community programs.[1]

The community planning meetings are also the place to work out problems as to which agency can best conduct programs to meet the various community needs.

Association with the community planning body thus gives the police an opportunity to understand better their own position in the composite picture of services to the community; to bring the services and their needs to the attention of other agencies and the public; and to learn what resources can be called upon for assistance when needed.

WORKING RELATIONSHIPS WITH INDIVIDUAL AGENCIES

Although police officers, and particularly special juvenile officers, should be familiar with the contribution and operation of all agencies in the community (an up-to-date directory of agencies can be of great value), it is clear that the major part of their work with children will involve contact with only a limited number of agencies. This contact should normally be close and continuous and, therefore, the relationship should be based on a clear understanding and amicable acceptance of the role of each of the participants.

The agencies with which the police have most frequent contact are the juvenile court and its probation department, public welfare department, recreation and other such group-work agencies, private family and childrens' agencies, and the public schools. There will be specific matters about which the police will have to reach agreement with each of these agencies. In every case, however, a few fundamental arrangements will apply, among which are the following:

1. One or more representatives of the police department should meet

[1]*Police Services for Juveniles*, Children's Bureau, Department of Health, Education and Welfare, Washington, D.C., 1974, pp. 44-45.

with the executive and other key administrative personnel of the other agency to plan jointly how the two agencies can work together to serve juveniles and their families.

2. Agreements resulting from such joint planning should be put in writing whenever possible so that they will be available to members of the police department and of the other agency who did not attend the meeting.

3. The police department and the other agency should arrange for a guest speaker from each agency to appear before staff members of the other to explain his own agency's functions and what it can contribute to the work of the other.

4. The police should invite speakers from the social casework field and from recreation work to appear before conferences of law enforcement agencies.[2]

As stated earlier, special problems will have to be worked out with the individual agencies concerned, as in the following instances.

WITH THE JUVENILE COURT

A number of matters call for meeting and agreement by the police and juvenile court (including the probation department). Some examples are:

1. Each should interpret to the other the framework of administrative policy and procedure within which it operates. Organization charts are useful for this. Legal provisions controlling functions and programs should be thoroughly explained.

2. The specific functions of the police and of the court should be carefully defined, with particular attention given to the extent of the police investigation and the type of report to be submitted to the probation department.

3. Definite policies governing detention and shelter care should be worked out, covering both delinquent and neglected children.

4. An arrangement should be made so that the police officers do not need to attend juvenile court hearings to testify, *except when the facts in the case are disputed.*

5. A method should be worked out for the juvenile court to inform the police about the final disposition of cases initiated by the police.

[2]*Ibid.,* pp. 45–46.

WITH CASEWORK AGENCIES

Some of the important areas that should be clarified in the police-social work agencies are.[3]

1. Definite agreement should be reached as to the types of cases that the police are to refer to the treatment agency.

2. Methods of referral should be agreed upon.

3. Police officers should become well acquainted with the agency's intake workers, with whom they will work on most cases. Understanding between the worker and the police officer will make it easier for the police to get questions and problems settled.

WITH THE SCHOOLS

The schools and the police department frequently have occasion to work together in the cases of juveniles who are in need of special types of help from community agencies. Policies must be jointly formulated to:[4]

1. Define the role of the police in relation to truants, clarifying the relationship between attendance officers and police officers.

2. Specify the violations of law within the school building that school officials will report to the police for investigation.

3. Specify procedures that an officer will follow in taking a child into custody at school or interviewing a youngster at school.

4. Establish police responsibility for the protection of children from adults loitering around school grounds with unlawful intent.

5. Specify the extent to which school records will be made available to police officers and police records to school personnel.

6. Set forth police responsibility for regulating juvenile pedestrian traffic to and from school and for aiding in traffic safety education.

7. Provide for police services in handling large crowds at athletic meets and social functions.

WITH RECREATION AND OTHER GROUP-WORK AGENCIES

In meeting with executives and appropriate employees of individual leisure-time agencies, the police should try to reach an agreement on a number of matters.[5]

[3]*Ibid.*, p. 47.
[4]*Ibid.*, pp. 47–48.
[5]*Ibid.*, p. 48.

1. The type of cases to be referred to the leisure-time agency.

2. The use of leisure-time agencies' facilities for police interview purposes.

3. Arrangements for the police officer to visit the leisure-time agency as a friend interested in observing its constructive activities.

4. The procedures that an officer will follow in taking a child into custody at a recreational agency or in interviewing a child at a recreational facility.

5. Law violations that take place on agency property that will be reported to the police for investigation.

WITH HEALTH AGENCIES

There are many occasions when a police officer can make use of a community's health facilities for serving the needs of children or their parents. City hospitals, private hospitals, specialized health clinics, county and city health departments, and emergency clinics are among the types of health facilities with which the police should be well acquainted. To insure proper use of health facilities:[6]

1. A police officer should be thoroughly familiar with the intake policies of both public and private hospitals and outpatient clinics, so that he can make appropriate referrals to these facilities.

2. Agreement should be worked out regarding the use of hospital and health agency records by the police. The availability of such records or any interpretation of them can be very helpful in police investigations.

WITH STATE AGENCIES

Police departments need to develop a working relationship with appropriate state agencies, particularly those concerned with:[7]

1. Licensing business establishments

2. Licensing foster homes and institutions for children.

3. Institutional care of emotionally disturbed and mentally retarded children.

[6]*Ibid.*, p. 48.
[7]*Ibid.*, pp. 49–50.

4. The correctional program for delinquents in training schools and on placement or parole.

5. Highway traffic.

6. Child labor laws.

7. Protection of constitutional rights and interpretations of statutes.

LACK OF UNDERSTANDING BETWEEN AGENCIES

Many of the problems engendered by children eventually bring both the children and their parents into contact with the police. It is obvious, however, that the police cannot undertake to correct situations like these except insofar as the conduct amounts to a violation of the law. Other aspects are social, ethical or moral, economic, and psychological, and are properly the responsibility of other community agencies. This leads us to an external source of difficulty: *the lack of understanding and coordination of effort among community agencies including the police and the courts.*

There is often a lack of communication between the police and other youth-serving agencies in the community resulting in mutual criticism and feelings of hostility. Police sometimes say such agencies fail to advise them of action taken concerning juveniles brought to their attention. Agency personnel, on the other hand, often attribute the hostility and bad behavior of the juveniles turned over to them by the police to the unsympathetic "treatment" given them by the police. Social agency personnel, including probation officers and even some judges, see the police as unnecessarily harsh and hard and oriented toward punishment as the only effective treatment. On the other side, some police see such agency personnel as unrealistically soft and permissive even to the extent of being "played for suckers" by cunning, worldly wise "young punks." Feelings such as these on both sides are certainly not conducive to effective communication to say nothing of real cooperation.

Police relationships with the *Juvenile Court* are not always harmonious. It frequently happens that there is better understanding between police juvenile officers and the Juvenile Court than there is between other police officers and the Court. This is not solely due to the fact that juvenile officers work more closely with Court personnel. In this respect, some police officers are guilty of overgeneralizing just as most humans are. Here again the fault is not all one-sided. There are, no doubt, some Juvenile Courts that are not as good as others and their deficiencies are sometimes the result of limited facilities and resources available to the Court. The same is true of police departments. It is well, however, for police to bear in mind

---

[8]Quoted from N. A. Watson, "Community Failure," *Police Chief,* Charles C. Thomas, Springfield, Illinois, 1964, by permission of the publisher.

that the Juvenile Court is here to stay, and police should do their best to make the working relationship as productive as possible.

The most frequent criticism of the Juvenile Court by police is that the Court fails to take positive and strong action. Some police feel that Probation is not effective as a corrective measure and that referral to various welfare and other social agencies is practically useless. On the other hand, one of the criticisms levels at the police sometimes is that they are too eager to have erring juveniles put in detention or committed to institutions. There is a feeling on the part of some police, unquestionably justified in some cases, that action taken by the Court in regard to certain juveniles is not strong enough. Police have noted at times a feeling that "You can't do anything to us; we're juveniles." They attribute this attitude of irresponsibility to the fact that juveniles caught in various offenses have been let off with leniency by the Court. It may also grow out of the philosophy of the Juvenile Court system, well known to some children, that juvenile offenders may not be fingerprinted, photographed, or jailed, and that their identities will not be made public. These procedures are in accord with the modern concept of a juvenile corrections procedure that does not consider their offenses criminal (short of capital and certain other heinous offenses) and whose objective is rehabilitation, not punishment. Police are often disturbed because a boy who has repeatedly been in trouble with the law is released on probation or otherwise rather than sent to some institution. They sometimes point to delays and a backlog of cases in Juvenile Court as evidence of the ineffectiveness of the system.

Procedural requirements specified in the law or laid down by the Juvenile Court receive police criticism also. Some of the procedures are considered by police to be unrealistic, ponderous, or downright obstructionistic. These restrictions affect such basic police techniques as interrogation and detention. In some places, upon arresting a juvenile for a criminal offence police are required to turn the youth over immediately to a Probation Officer, making it impossible for them to conduct an adequate interview in many instances. Police are then prevented or at least inhibited in discharging their responsibility for clearing up other offenses in which the juvenile has been involved. It is also likely that the Court will be deprived of that information, which certainly ought to be considered in deciding what to do with the offender. Knowledge of whether the current offense is the first or the fifteenth burglary clearly should be of some practical value aside from the police objective of clearing offenses. Other facets the police should explore concern the possible criminal involvement of adults and/or other juveniles. Unless the police are given ample opportunity to investigate the case fully—including holding the offender long enough to conduct a complete interrogation—the other juveniles involved might not be afforded the ministrations of the Court. In another jurisdiction, there is a flat prohibition against taking an apprehended juvenile to a police station for interview or any other purpose. In terms of practical police operations, this puts the police officer on the beat in an awkward position when he has to try to make sense out of a mass of contradictory statements and evasions through methodical interview.

Probation as a function of the Court is regarded in some places as ineffective. Police often point to the fact that Probation Officers are so overloaded with cases that they cannot adequately supervise anyone. Other complaints center around the police viewpoint of the Probation Officer as being primarily oriented toward the best interests of the offender rather than the best interests of the community. They feel that he is, therefore, inclined to take chances on behalf of his charges that sometimes work out to the detriment of some innocent party. In police conversations, one hears it said that the welfare of the community must take precedence over the welfare of the individual. This is one of the reasons police feel that certain juvenile offenders do not deserve Probation—there is good reason to believe they will continue their antisocial and criminal ways and letting them out on Probation means that someone will be victimized.

Police also often feel that Probation Officers fail to get the full story from juveniles. They claim the Probation Officers overstress their striving for empathy and understanding and do not bring out all the sordid details of the crime because to do so would cause the juvenile pain. They feel that Probation Officers do not understand the harsh realities of the police job and are not as concerned as they should be with the plight of the victims of the crime. These feelings are by no means universal in police circles, but are a fairly representative summary of the kinds of problems evolving from Probation as seen by the police.

Criticism of the Court sometimes deplores the lack of uniformity in the procedures required of police and the lack of clear guides for police to follow in implementing the Court's dicta. Police in border jurisdictions are frequently troubled by differences in age limits, regulations relative to liquor sales, and other details. In regard to purchasing beer, for example, juveniles in certain locations can circumvent the law in their area by simply driving to a neighboring jurisdiction where the law is more "liberal." Many police officers feel very strongly that while the philosophy on which Juvenile Court procedures are based is commendable in its intent, it is weak and ineffective in its application, especially concerning recidivists. One well-known and highly respected police executive, widely acknowledged as a leader in the police profession, expressed the view that most of the police problems in the juvenile field can be laid directly at the door of the Juvenile Court in its attempt to treat with kindness and decency antisocial youths who deliberately seek to take advantage of it.

SUMMARY

Investigation, arrest, and report writing are the basics of police work with both juvenile and adult offenders. There is, however, another aspect of police work with *juveniles* that transcends the basic exigencies mentioned. As pointed out at the very beginning of Chapter 12, "in almost every aspect of their work with juveniles, the police must have contact with at least one other agency in the community." Thus, in order to be an effective contributor in promoting the welfare of young people in their community, it is incumbent upon police agencies to cultivate positive liaisons with public and private community agencies.

The potential for hostile relations with community agencies is always crouching in the background and the latter part of Chapter 12 discusses the ramifications of this ill will.

The agencies with which the police have most frequent contact are the juvenile court and its probation department, the public welfare department, the recreation and other such group-work agencies, private family and children's agencies, and the public schools. In dealing with agencies, the police should endeavor to make a few fundamental arrangements and arrive at procedural agreements.

ANNOTATED REFERENCES

Coffey, Alan, Eldefonso, Edward, and Hartinger, Walter, *Human Relations: Law Enforcement in a Changing Community*, 2nd ed., Prentice-Hall, Inc., N.J., 1976.

> Chapter 12 of this volume relates to the type of programs that law enforcement agencies within a community should become involved in if they wish to enhance their image and lines of communications. This portion of the volume deals with community relations programs, public support, success of such programs, and the actual construciton of programs pertaining to the enhancement of police-community relations.

Jenkins, Herbert T., "Utilizing Community Resources," *Police and the Changing Community, Selected Readings*, ed. N. A. Watson, International Association of Chiefs of Police, Washington, D.C., 1965.

> This article is devoted entirely to the use of law enforcement agencies and community resources. Law enforcement agencies should have some understanding of the resources available in the community, and this article gives a fairly acceptable account of such resources. See also in the same reader: E. Wilson Purdy, "Meeting Current Problems," and Curtis Brostron, "Use of Community Civic Groups in Strategic Planning."

O'Brien, K. and Marcus, M., *Juvenile Diversion—A Selected Bibliography*, National Institute of Law Enforcement and Criminal Justice, Washington, D.C., 1976.

> Use of community resources is detailed here.

Phelps, Thomas R., *Juvenile Delinquency—A Contemporary View*, Goodyear Publishing Co., Pacific Palisades, Calif., 1976.

A significant section of this text is devoted to community action for delinquency control.

Treger, H., *The Police–Social Work Team. A New Model for Interprofessional Cooperation: A University Demonstration Project in Manpower Training and Development*, Charles C. Thomas, Publishers, Springfield, Illinois, 1975.

A model of interprofessional cooperation.

CHAPTER THIRTEEN rights and liabilities of minors

Although the laws pertaining to *rights and liabilities of minors*[1] are basic throughout the country, there is a great deal of variation throughout the states in the area of age—minority and majority. Therefore, the age limitations presented here may or may not be applicable to the state in which the reader resides. Such age variations should be taken into consideration when reading and/or interpreting the laws.

The laws of the United States and each state are divided into major divisions: criminal laws and civil laws. *Civil law* is that body of law contained both in statutes and in the decisions of courts of law which apply to society as a whole and define the rights, duties, obligations, and liabilities of citizens. *Criminal law* is that code of law that defines offenses against the state and provides punishment for individual convicted of violations of criminal laws. Violation of civil law could be an offense against one or several persons and not necessarily an offense against the state. To enforce civil law, an individual normally initiates a lawsuit in the civil courts.

The district attorney can initiate a criminal action. In order to dispose of criminal and civil actions, there are municipal courts that handle minor crimes and civil law suits that are under specific sums set up by each state. A superior court handles major crimes (called felonies) and civil law suits in excess of the amount designated by the municipal court of each state as well as family law cases.[2]

TORTS

A tort is a harm done to one's person, property, or reputation by another. A person suffering this harm must show that the party inflicting it had a duty to do or refrain from doing it. Furthermore, he must show that this duty was violated in a neglect-

[1]For further detailed information see: "Rights and Liabilities of Minors," *Department of the California Youth Authority,* 1976 by W. E. Thornton, Chief Probation Officer Sacramento County, California.
[2]"Youth and the Law," *Palo Alto Unified School District,* Community Council of Northern Santa Clara County, California, 1972, p. 1.

ful or deliberate manner, and that such act was the approximate cause of the injury suffered.

The layman always presumes that when harm occurs, someone must be responsible and therefore liable for damages. This is false assumption, because many accidents do occur in which neither party is negligent. In these unavoidable accidents, no recovery can be obtained. Many states have the rule of *contributory negligence,* which provides that if both parties are negligent, neither party can recover. These two rules may be summed up briefly by saying that, if neither party is negligent, there can be no recovery in damages for either; if both parties are negligent there is no recovery for either.

Most of these situations in regard to torts, which are dealt with by the probation, parole, or police officer, involve a deliberate act. The minor deliberately breaks a window, deliberately steals an automobile, deliberately strikes a person. They are intentional torts, against a person or property of another. The victim of the minor's intentional act has suffered a harm and may be legally entitled to payment for damages.

In order to understand what constitutes damages, it is necessary to analyze the different types briefly:

> Compensating damages. *Damages are normally awarded for the express purpose of giving the victim compensation for the actual damage suffered. The theory is to return the victim, as nearly as possible, to his former position. If the window was broken, pay to get it replaced; if the victim was injured, pay for all medical and hospital bills, and so on. Special damages may be awarded for pain and suffering resulting from injury, loss of limbs, hospitalization, and inability to work.*

> Punitive or exemplary damages. *Most states allow the victim not only money for actual damages suffered, but where the act is deliberate the victim, in addition, may recover damages for the sake of example and by way of punishing the wrongdoer.*

In every crime there is also a tort action when the victim, suffers some harm. If the victim is injured deliberately, the wrongdoer is liable for criminal action; if property is stolen and not recovered, civil action will apply; or if an automobile is stolen and subsequently recovered, civil action will apply. Damages in terms of money will usually be awarded for the actual loss suffered, plus punitive damages to teach the wrongdoer a lesson.

There are, then, really two separate actions involved in a crime. The first is represented by the *People of the State versus the Defendant* (or in a juvenile court proceeding a petition is filed on behalf of the minor alleging commission of a particular act specified as a low violation). These proceedings are brought into either criminal court or the juvenile court.

The second is a civil action, which may be brought by the victim in a civil court against the defendant for tort. Recovery is in payment of money for loss suffered and in punitive damages, if such are allowable.

The two actions are separate and distinct, brought into different courts by different parties, with different causes of action and with different types of judgment. The criminal court is the people against the defendant, while the civil aciton is a remedy by the victim for loss suffered. A criminal conviction, or a juvenile court proceeding, does not cancel out the civil action for money damages.

> Example. *A person steals an automobile. The wrongdoer may be prosecuted in a criminal court for auto theft; the victim may sue the wrongdoer in a civil court for damages in a tort action.*

> Example. *A person strikes another; the injured party may sign a complaint and have the wrongdoer prosecuted for battery in a criminal court; he may also sue in civil court for money damages in a tort action.*

A recovery in a civil action for tort does not bar criminal action for the same fact any more than a conviction in a criminal case bars a civil action.

LIABILITY OF MINOR FOR HIS TORTS

There is much confusion in the general public's mind regarding the liability of the minor for his own deliberate torts. The rule in many states is that a minor is liable for his own torts in the same manner as if he were an adult. This simply means that a minor must face civil liability for his willful misconduct or negligence. There are obvious cases where the child is so young that he does not know the consequences of his wrongful act and to penalize him for his lack of understanding would be unjust. While all children are civilly liable for actual damages caused, they are not liable for punitive or exemplary damages unless the child is capable of knowing the act was wrong.

When the minor's civil liability is examined carefully, it is found that the victim has a right to be compensated; however, it is usually ascertained that the minor has no assets to satisfy a judgment. There is a remedy, but once this remedy is reduced to a judgment, there is little the victim can do to recover. Because of this, claimants generally make little effort to seek a judgment, but seek aid in the juvenile court. The juvenile court, of course, as a term of probation, may order the minor to make restitution to the victim. However, the litigation involving civil matters rightfully belong in the proper civil court and cannot be litigated in the juvenile court. There is a conflict among juvenile court judges as to whether or not restitution should be a part of juvenile court procedure, and whether the parties should best be left to civil remedies in the proper court.

The procedure to sue a minor in a civil matter will be discussed later, but it is well to examine the process of holding the minor to a judgment once obtained:

1. Sue the minor in tort through guardian ad litem.

2. Obtain judgment award.

3. Execute this judgment on any real or personal property the minor has.

4. Return judgment unsatisfied if minor has no assets, or a deficiency if minor does not have sufficient assets to completely satisfy the total judgment.

5. A judgment may be executed any time within ten years and, after that, may be renewed for a like period if execution is not possible.

6. Keep judgment alive and executed when minor does acquire property, even if he has reached a majority.

It is important to realize that mere minority is not a bar to recovery in a civil action. A foolish act on the part of a fifteen- or sixteen-year-old child may result in a large money judgment against him. Ten or twenty years later, when the child has grown, married, or has acquired property and assets, he may be subject to an execution of this judgment. The law has provided a remedy for the victim of a minor's deliberate or negligent act, and enforcement of it by execution of judgment may occur many years later.

PARENTS' LIABILITY FOR TORTS OF THEIR CHILDREN

Parental liability for the torts of children is an area that has received wide discussion. For example, the law in California, prior to a statutory enactment in 1955, had been that parents were usually not liable. It is only by direct statutory provision that the rule is relaxed or modified.

The rule was that minors themselves were liable for their torts, but the mere relationship of the parent and child did not impute liability.

Most states subscribe to the California law pertaining to parents' liability for torts of their children. Victims of minors' intentional torts were surprised to learn that they were unable to hold the parents responsible. The exceptions to the rule of no liability by parents were as follows:

1. If the minor acted as an agent of the parents, the parents were liable. The parents actually had to authorize the child to perform the act, and it is doubtful if many parents order a child to steal a car or commit a burglary. One would have to show the child did the wrongful act at the parents' order, or at least implied constructive authorization.

2. If the parents did provide the child with a dangerous instrument,

and should have known that damage could be caused, they were liable. Examples could be: a BB gun in the city, a knife, possibly fire crackers.

3. Where the *parents know* that the child is following a course of careless or intentional acts that may cause harm to others, they must take *reasonable steps* to control his conduct. However, the question of "notice" and what is considered "reasonable" are two areas that generally would bar recovery from parents for willful misconduct of the child.

> Example. *Parents of a four-year-old child, who had violent propensities, were liable for damages caused when the child attacked the baby-sitter. Parents had knowledge of this conduct and failed to warn the baby-sitter.*

It is always difficult to show that parents could reasonably know their minor child would commit a law violation and cause damage to another, and even more difficult to show what "reasonable steps" should have been taken to prevent it.

It is generally presumed that parents do not authorize, order, or allow their children to steal cars, break and enter, or commit vandalism, and usually cannot be held on notice that their children will do these acts. What the parents can do to prevent these acts is also open to speculation. Thus, in most cases, the parents are not liable for the torts of their children.

STATUTORY PROVISIONS IMPUTING LIABILITY TO PARENTS FOR CHILD'S WILLFUL ACTS

In several states, including California, there are two specific statutes that make parents civilly liable for the intentional torts of their minor children. Both of these actions, however, refer to willful and intentional acts which cause damage to another's property and not negligent acts.

> Section 16074 of the California Educational Code imputes liability to the parents for any willful act that causes damages to school-property. *The implication, however, is that the child must be a pupil and that if he willfully breaks windows, cuts chairs or books, or commits any vandalism, the school board may sue the parents. This section also covers parental liability for books and supplies loaned to the child and not returned.*

> Section 1714.1, a 1955 provision of the Civil Code of California, makes the parent or parents having custody or control over a minor child severally and jointly liable for any damages that a child

willfully causes to the property of another. *The limitation is $500 that may be recovered for each individual willful act by the child.*

The above section does not mean that the minor himself is not liable for the full amount of the damage he caused, but his parents are liable for up to $750. If the damage caused was willful and the actual cost for repair was $1,000, the parent is liable for only $750. Obviously, the total amount that can be collected, however would be actual damages of $1,000. The victim would be wise to join both the parents and the minor in the action and to seek a recovery in the form of a judgment against both.

However, Section 1714.1 probably does not apply where the minor is *not* subject to the control of the parents, i.e., he is emancipated and living alone. Examples of this are married minors, minors in the armed forces, minors who, by implication, are declared emancipated and are living alone. This section would also probably not include a parent who, by court decree or other means, has been deprived of custody. Examples of this may be where parents are divorced and the minor is living with the parent who was awarded custody. The other parent would not have custody and control, and thus it would appear he would escape imputed liability. The same would apply to children who have been removed from their parents' custody and placed in foster homes or institutions by the courts.

Many other questions also arise which are at present unanswered. What if the parent having custody or control specifically orders the minor *not* to do a certain act and he nevertheless willfully does this act and causes harm to another's property? Is the victim to hold the parents liable? This section covers damage to "property" and apparently does not cover damages to "person." Suppose a seventeen-year-old causes physical harm to another. How about the twenty-year-old living at home who robs a gas station and spends the money? Does the state hold the parents liable?

What of the sixteen-year-old who willfully steals a car, but negligently has an accident that damages the stolen car as well as the auto of the third person? The damage caused was not willful, but was accidentally caused by the negligent operation of the stolen car. Are the parents liable for the damages to the stolen car? Damages to the car of the third person? The medical expenses of an injured third party? These questions, and many more, will arise in future litigation and be answered then.

It must be remembered that this action against the parent is a civil remedy for the plaintiff. The litigation arises in a lower civil court. The proper place for filing the complaint for damages is either in the justice or municipal court, and it is not an action to be litigated in the juvenile court. This is purely a civil matter and should not be confused with juvenile court proceedings.

The juvenile court proceeding is one in which a petition is filed on behalf of the child, and jurisdiction is over the child, not the parents. The juvenile court may make reasonable orders over the parents regarding restitution, but it has no jurisdiction to litigate a civil issue that concerns the parental liability for the tort of the minor.

CRIMINAL RESPONSIBILITY OF PARENTS FOR THE ACTS OF THEIR CHILDREN

Throughout the country there is a growing demand to make the parents responsible in criminal proceedings for willful violations of the law by their children. One of the basic doctrines of criminal law is that the offender must have willfully violated a specific criminal statute; knowing that such act is a violation is not necessary, but he must have intentionally committed the act. There are exceptions to this general rule which involve criminal negligence, but for our purposes the general rule is basic.

The basic question is, does the law punish parents with criminal proceedings for wrongful acts of their children based on the parent-child *relationship?* Is the state going to prosecute parents for being incapable of controlling their children?

At the present time, to this author's knowledge, no state has a statute that attempts to make parents *criminally responsible* for law violations committed by their children. The only statute that in many states has implications of criminal liability, relates to the sections pertaining to *contributing to the delinquency of a minor.* Such a section often provides that "a person who commits any act or omits the performance of any duty, which act or omission causes or tends to cause or encourage any person under [age to be determined by the respective state to come within the jurisdiction of the juvenile court [such jurisdiction refers to provisions for which a minor may be declared a ward of the court is guilty of a misdemeanor."

If a minor commits a law violation, what must his parents have done or not done in order to be charged with contributing to his delinquency? Can parents be convicted under such a section if they are incapable of controlling their children, or if they are doing all a reasonable parent could do, even though their children commit law violations? The answer seems to be that there is nothing in the mere parent-child relationship that makes a parent criminally liable for his child's violations of the law. In order to convict, it would seem that the parent must have aided, counselled, or authorized the child to commit a crime, and not merely have been passive in exercising control.

The only statutes that seem to impute criminal liability are local curfew ordinances. These generally provide that if the minor is on the streets after a certain hour, he is guilty of a misdemeanor. It also provides that any parent, guardian, or other adult having custody of the minor is also guilty of a misdemeanor if they allow or permit the minor to be on the streets after a designated hour.

If the parent gave consent for the minor to be out after the designated hour, or actually ordered the child to be on the street, it is quite possible that a case for conspiracy or aiding and abetting the child to violate the ordinance could be shown. Under these circumstances the parent would probably be liable. The problem, of course, comes when the parent has no knowledge that the minor is out after the curfew hour, or has told the minor to be home before that time. If this is the case, can the parent be charged with willfully and unlawfully violating that ordinance? It does not appear that conviction can be sustained unless there was an intentional violation by the parent, and, if the parent did not approve the minor being sent out after the designated hour, or specifically ordered him to be home, the parent is guilty of nothing.

Again, the prosecution of the criminal aspects of these ordinances against the parent is one for the district attorney or city attorney. This is a criminal proceeding against the parents based on their willful and unlawful violation of the specific ordinance. The action is in the lower court (justice or municipal), and parents are entitled to a jury trial. There have been few violations under these sections. These curfew ordinances have been an attempt to keep the minors off the streets and away from public places after a designated hour, unless they are accompanied by an adult or are on their way home from recreational pursuit.

Therefore, take the above factors into consideration, it can be concluded that the relationship of parent and child does not, in itself, create criminal liability of the parent for law violations by the child. Incompetent or incapable parents must commit some overt act, or fail to perform some specific legal duty that violates a statute, before they may be prosecuted for their child's misconduct.

CONTRACTS

What is a contract? A contract is an agreement between two or more parties under which each of them agrees to do or to refrain from doing some act. In order to be binding, there must be an offer and an acceptance of the offer. A contract may be made by custom where acceptance is implied. There must also be an exchange of consideration, which means an exchange of cash, property, or some other benefit.[3]

In simple terms, a contract is an agreement between competent parties to do or refrain from doing some act that is supported by a consideration. All of us each day make contracts. Some are made by mere custom where consent is implied, some are oral, some are written, some executed, and some remain to be executed. A minor's contract, like that of an adult, when all legal prerequisites are met, is valid and binding—with certain exceptions.

However, the law seeks to protect a minor from some of his own imprudent acts. Because of his age, he lacks sound judgment. So that advantage will not be taken of him, the law provides him with a "way out." Even though the contract is otherwise binding, the law gives the minor a voidable option. That is to say, most contracts entered into by a minor (in most states, a youth under eighteen years of age) with an adult are voidable. It is voidable at the minor's option; nevertheless, the adult is bound and does not have the same privilege of voidability. Note that most of the contracts of a minor are not *void*, but voidable at the minor's option. It may be generally said that adults contracting with minors *do so at their own risk,* and the law discourages such dealings.

[3]*Ibid.,* p. 1.

There are few situations in which a minor's contract is not voidable, but actually void. A youngster (who is considered a minor; any state legislature can set any specific age as majority) cannot give a delegation of power or make any contract regarding real property or make any contract relative to personal property not in his immediate possession or control. Any such contract is void, not voidable, and no act on the minor's part to disaffirm is necessary.

The general rule, then, is that any contract entered into by a minor is voidable at the minor's option. The minor may refuse to perform his obligations and not be liable in damages for the breach. The adult who contracted with the minor, however, must perform. The minor may, of course, refuse to perform and use his age as a defense.

The minor may intentionally and willfully misrepresent his age, i.e., falsely state that he is over the statutory age as set by a state, and yet this in itself will not prevent him from disaffirming the contract. The law gives him the voidable option, and he is not liable in a tort action for false misrepresentation of age, nor will this misrepresentation bind him to a contract. These rules apply whether the minor is buyer or seller. There are dangers inherent in entering contractual relationships with the minor.

In California, for example, minors under eighteen years are treated below as follows:

> Minor under eighteen. *The minor under eighteen may disaffirm his contract. He is not liable for damage done to the article, and if he has lost the article purchased, he is not liable to reimburse the seller. The same rule seems to apply if the minor under eighteen is the seller rather than the buyer. He may recover the article sold, and need not return the money received from the sale, if he no longer has it.*
>
> *He can always recover his property from the adult-buyer, unless the article has passed into the hands of an innocent purchaser from the adult-buyer. The innocent third party is not a party to the minor-seller and the adult-buyer transaction, and to penalize him would be unjust. The law protects this third person who was in no way involved in the voidable contract transaction.*
>
> Exceptions. *There are some* exceptions *to the voidable aspect of the minor's contract. The voidable ones are as follows:*
>
> When a minor is living alone he may contract for necessities of life. *It may well be seen that many minors are "on their own" and if their contracts were voidable, it would be almost impossible for them to rent rooms, buy groceries, purchase clothes, and so forth. Adults would be reluctant to deal with them, as their contracts would normally be voidable. The law seeks to give the minor living alone the status of an adult. In contract law, it comes to the things necessary for existence. What these things are is the difficult question. They probably would not include jewelry, watches, automobiles, etc.*

A minor who is eighteen years old has the same legal rights of contract as an adult. *Note that this applies to both male and female, and once this status has been reached, the minor has forever lost the power to disaffirm any contract on the basis of minority. Of course, the contract must have been entered into subsequent to reaching this status in order to be binding.*

Note also that a parent is not liable for contracts entered into by his minor child. If the parent enters into a contractual relationship in behalf of the minor child, he, of course, becomes bound in his individual capacity. A parent can be a cosigner on a note or contract with his minor child and could not deny his own liability when the minor sought to rescind the contract because of his age. This might result in an unusual situation where the minor could not be bound, but the cosigning parent may be legally liable in event of the minor's breach of contract. Adults contracting with minors would be wise to bind the parents in the transaction, so that the parents accept liability in case the minor seeks rescision or refuses to perform.

There may be some questions, however, where a minor enters a contract for necessities and fails to pay. It may well be that the parent has an obligation of support under state law and may be liable on the minor's contract for these necessities of life, or at least liable to pay for a fair amount of these necessities.

While the general rules of contracts relating to minors have been discussed, there are specific sections granting consent to minors to enter into binding contracts. These are generally enacted to allow such contracts that are deemed necessary to the minor and thus allow adults to contract with no fear of rescision by the minor. For example:

1. Minors may contract bank deposits allowing minors to open savings accounts and make withdrawals. Similar provisions are made in regard to savings and loan associations and building and loan associations.

2. A female minor may sign relinquishment for the adoption of a child, and also make contract with a hospital for medical or surgical care in regard to pregnancy if she is married.

3. Married minors may contract with a hospital for medical or surgical care. In the event of annulment the right of consent continues.

4. A minor in the armed forces is able to contract for any medical care when necessary for himself.

5. A minor who is married may enter into a property settlement agreement in reference to the marriage.

6. If over sixteen, a minor make make a contract of insurance for himself, with a member of the family as beneficiary.

CRIMINAL SUITS BY AND AGAINST MINORS.

MINOR AS A PLAINTIFF

A minor, like an adult, always has a civil remedy when his rights are invaded. He has protection both in the law of torts and contracts against adults or other minors. The minor may enforce his rights by civil action, or other legal proceedings, in the same manner as a person of full age, except that a guardian must initiate the proceeding. The theory behind this is that the minor lacks sound discretion and good judgment, so the law seeks to protect from his own imprudent acts. The requirement that he proceed through a guardian is intended to more fully protect his rights. The parents of a minor unmarried child are his natural general guardians and are such by their parent-child relationship.

The minor, if he is the plaintiff in an action, must appear by and with his guardian. The complaint should clearly indicate this so that the defendant is put on notice as to the plaintiff's status. If the minor fails to proceed through his guardian, and does obtain a judgment, it will not be void because of failure to have a guardian appointed. The best procedure is to have a guardian appointed by the court for the proceedings, even though the guardian is the natural parent and by law the general guardian.

> In California, if the minor is over fourteen years of age, he must nominate and approve his own guardian. This permits the fourteen-year-old minor to choose whomever he pleases to assist in representing his interests, and the courts will appoint this nominee, unless he is not a fit and proper person. These appointments are generally done on affidavit of the minor and the guardian ad litem before issuance of a complaint and summons upon the defendant. A guardian ad litem is an adult appointed by the court for the express purpose of the litigation, and the jurisdiction of the guardian is limited to the litigation. The guardian ad litem appointed by the court for a fourteen-year-old or older minor must be so appointed on the nomination of the minor, or at least his appointment must be ratified by the minor. If either of these are not done, the judgment may be disaffirmed by the minor. This, again, is to permit a child over fourteen to choose his own guardian and to protect his right given him by the statute.

The point to remember is that, although the ages differ in different states, the basic premise as indicated above is similar.

The plaintiff minor under fourteen years does not have the right to select his guardian *ad litem*. A friend or relative may apply to the court for appointment, and after being duly appointed may proceed with the complaint and summons on the minor's behalf. Even though the minor has a general guardian, the court in which an action or proceeding is prosecuted may appoint a guardian ad litem if the court

The apparent liability statute imputes liability from child to parent for $500 in each tort. The minor is liable for full damages of his tort, but the parent is restricted to $500 for each tort. The plaintiff may now proceed against the minor child and the parents. The plaintiff may join both parents and child in the action and seek a judgment against both. The factual issues against both parent and child are the same, so that they may be severally and jointly liable. The parents, however, have a $500 limitation while the minor has an unlimited amount for his own torts. If the total situation is under $500, the plaintiff could join the parent and child in the same action.

PARENT AND CHILD

This section on the parent and child relationship will cover only the more perplexing problems. It is not an attempt to outline the voluminous material on the subject.

DOMICILE AND RESIDENCE

Domicile and residence become important in deciding the proper court for action, eligibility for various county services, and juvenile court jurisdiction. *Domicile* means physical presence and intention to make a place a home. Residence may be merely a temporary place of abode. The terms, however, are many times used synonymously and, for the purposes here, they will be so used. The child's residence is controlled by his parents. Neither parent of a legitimate child has any greater right than the other over the custody of the child. The husband selects the location of the home. It is a general rule of law that the residence of the wife and children is that of the husband-father. The residence of the father determines that of the child during the father's lifetime. However, if he has abandoned the child, or if a court has awarded custody to the mother, the child's residence becomes that of the mother. If the parents are separated and living apart, the residence of the child becomes that of the parent actually having physical custody of the child. This may not be true if the custody order of the court vests custody in one parent, while the other parent or third person in fact has physical custody and is caring for the child.

A child who has been abandoned is a *foundling*. He gains residence in the state and country where he is found. Subsequent finding of either parent may change the child's residence but not in such a manner so that the child will suffer from this change of residence.

An unmarried minor who has a parent living may not obtain a residence by acts of his own. This is subject to the rules of emancipation that will be discussed later.

The adopted child, of course, acquires the residence of his adopting parents and loses that of his natural parents. Once adopted, the same rule applies as if his adoptive parents were his natural parents. The child on adoption relinquishes all rights to his natural parents and may inherit from and through his adoptive parents. The natural parents are no longer liable for the child's support and are relieved from all parental duties.

PARENTAL AUTHORITY

A parent may use reasonable physical force to discipline his children, but this may not be done to excess. The parent has a duty to care for his children, to support them, and be responsible for any of their acts that are imputed to him by the law. The courts will seldom intervene, either through the criminal or juvenile court, to interfere with the way parents rear their children unless the conditions are severely unacceptable. Social agencies and probation officers may, on occasion, seek to have children removed from their natural parents, through "neglect" or "dependency" petitions in juvenile court and placed in foster homes. The line between neglect and the rights of parents to rear their children must be balanced against the state's interests in the rights the children have in being provided with substantial opportunity and a chance for a successful future life.

The juvenile court law does not contemplate the taking of children from their parents and breaking up of family ties merely because, in the estimation of probation officers and courts, the children can be better provided for or more wisely trained as wards of the state. Probably from mere consideration of helpful and hygenic living and systematic education and training, this would be true in the case of thousands of families of wealth and respectability. It is only in instances where there is demonstrated incapacity, akin to criminal neglect, that the state is justified in interfering with the natural relationship of parent and child.

The evidence to support the allegation that the child is being neglected by his parents must be clear and convincing before the juvenile court can intervene. Each case must, of course, be examined on its own merits, and while it may be clearly in the best interests of the child to be removed from his parents, the vested interests of the parents' authority over their children must be heavily considered. The supremacy of the parents in their own home in regard to the control of their children is generally recognized.

feels that it is expedient even if the minor appears with his general guardian. The court, representing the minor's best interest, may require a guardian ad litem even though the parent objects.

A minor in the United States may have a right to prosecute a civil action through a guardian ad litem, but situations arise where his suits may be settled without court action. The law again attempts to protect the minor against himself and requires that this compromise be handled by those who are competent. A disputed claim of the minor must be approved by the superior court. This also brings the whole matter before the court and does not permit the parents to give a release of the action which might be unjust to the minor. The parents may have the approval of the superior court to compromise, and the funds may be held by them in trust for the minor. The funds, however, are the child's not the parents', and they may be required to post bond and account to the court. The court may require that a guardian be appointed to administer the funds. This guardian would in most instances be the parents, although the normal rule is that minors over fourteen years may choose their own guardians. The parents have a right to be appointed guardian if the minor is under fourteen, and unless there is some very compelling reason not to, the court will appoint the parent guardian of the minor under fourteen years. The parents are, by the very nature of the parent-child relationship, the natural guardians of their child, and their interest is almost the same as an invested property right. Therefore, parents, when available, have almost a right to be appointed their child's guardian in any matter that requires such appointments.

MINOR AS A DEFENDANT

The minor who is being sued, i.e., the defendant in an action, must also be protected. State laws recognize that a minor defendant does not have the knowledge or experience to protect himself against suits, and he may well have a legal defense to the action. It would be unjust to allow the plaintiff to take advantage of a minor's inexperience and possibly to obtain a default judgment against him.

The plaintiff, when suing a minor, must serve the defendant personally if he is over fourteen years of age—the age varies from state to state—and if the minor is under fourteen years, in addition to serving the summons on him personally, he must serve the father, mother, or guardian. If there is no father, mother, or guardian in the state, service must be made either on the person having the care, custody, and control of the minor or on the person with whom he resides or in whose service he is employed.

Should the plaintiff fail to make this service as required, the court in which the action is filed lacks jurisdiction and a judgment is voidable. The plaintiff should name the parents, if there are parents, as the general guardians when bringing the suit against the minor defendant, and serve all the parties named.

The defendant minor over fourteen must apply for appointment of a guardian ad litem within ten days after receiving a service of summons. If the defendant is under fourteen (if over fourteen and he fails to apply for appointment of guardian ad litem, a relative, friend, or any other party to the action may apply for the court to appoint a guardian ad litem to assist in defending the action), the court on its own motion may also appoint a guardian ad litem to protect the interests of the child.

The plaintiff suing a defendant minor often makes application to the court for the appointment of the guardian ad litem so that the action may proceed. A judgment obtained against a minor defendant by default, unless a guardian ad litem was appointed, may be set aside. Thus, plaintiffs have the burden of proper service, as well as making certain that a guardian ad litem is appointed. The court acquires jurisdiction over a defendant minor, to authorize the appointment of a guardian ad litem, only when service of summons on the defendant minor has been made.

Note that when the minor is the plaintiff and fails to have a guardian ad litem appointed but obtains a judgment, a judgment is not voidable by the defendant because of a failure to appoint a guardian. However, if the minor is the defendant and a judgment is obtained without a guardian ad litem being appointed, the situation is not the same. The judgment may be set aside. The minor in both cases may have the judgment set aside, but in neither case can the adverse adult part to the action do the same.

The child may expect support and education from his parents. The father is primarily responsible for this, but the mother must assist to the extent of her ability. This is, of course, subject to the "station in life rule," and the ability of the respective parents. The father is under no legal obligation to send his children to college, no matter what his financial condition may be. The father, unless his parental authority has been taken away by the courts, is the one to decide the extent of the education of his children beyond what is provided by the school system of the state. His duty to support is reciprocal between parent and child. The adult child has a duty to support his parents if they are unable to support themselves. If a parent abandoned his child while the child was under sixteen years, and this abandonment continued for over two years, the adult child may be relieved of any responsibility to support his parent.

Should the father fail to provide the necessities for his minor children, and if a third party assumes this responsibility, the third party may hold the father liable for the funds expended upon this minor child for the necessities of life. This applies when this third party is the county, a relative, or some charitable agency. The father is not liable for compensation to the other parent or relative without an agreement for compensation when the child has abandoned the father without just cause.

PARENTS' RIGHTS IN PROPERTY OF THEIR CHILDREN

A minor child, like an adult, may own and dispose of his own property. The mere fact of being a parent gives no right over property owned by the child. Parents may not exercise control over property of their children by sale, lease, or destruction. This, of course, is subject to the commonsensical rule that the parent may restrict the child in the use of his property when such restriction is for the best interest of the child. The relationship of parent gives a certain control over the custody and conduct of the minor child, but nothing inherent in this relationship makes the property of the child that of the parents. The minor having a right to own and dispose of his own property is usually handicapped because of the voidable nature of his contracts, and adult buyers are very cautious concerning their dealings with them. Generally, the minor is prohibited from making a contract dealing with his real property when he is under eighteen years (remember, minor age varies in states) and cannot give a valid power of attorney. A minor may dispose of his property by will only if he is over eighteeen, and if under eighteen, his property will be distributed by the law of intestate succession at his death.

The father and mother are equally entitled to the custody and services of their minor children. They are entitled to have their children work for them without compensation. However, if the minor chooses to work for someone else for wages, the parents are entitled to the child's wages. This simply means that all earnings of the minor legally belong to the parents, and the child has no right to keep any part of these earnings. If either parent is dead, the other is entitled to these earnings; and if the parents are separated, the parent having legal or physical custody is entitled to the earnings. The mother of an illegitimate child is entitled to that child's earnings.

The employer of a minor must have some protection for compensating the minor directly for services performed, so the law permits an employer to pay wages directly to the minor *until notified to pay only to parents.* The parents of an employed minor may notify the employer to pay them for the child's employment, and if the employer refuses and pays the child instead, the parents still may collect from the employer.

These earnings are not similar to property the minor receives such as a gift, inheritance, or will, as this type of property belongs only to the minor child. Earnings of a minor child are part of the services the parent is entitled to receive from the parent-child relationship, and earnings belong only to the parents. However, parents may relinquish their rights to the earnings of a child and permit the child to keep them. If this occurs, in fact or by implication, the earnings then belong to the child, and the parent has no further control over the money.

EMANCIPATION

Upon reaching the age of majority, or entering into a lawful marriage, a child is emancipated (set on his own), by operation of the law, from the right of the parent to control him and to receive his earnings.

A parent may emancipate his child by voluntarily relinquishing the right to control him and to receive his earnings. This emancipation may be accomplished by express agreement, by involuntary agreement of parent and child as to the child's freedom from control, or it may be implied from such acts as reasonably indicate consent on the part of the parent and child. After complete emancipation, the child is in every respect his own person and may claim his earnings as against the parents and may bring court action for personal injuries resulting from the parents' ordinary negligence; however, the child must obviously be old enough to work and care for himself.[4]

This *voluntary emancipation* on the part of the parents is not so extensive a doctrine as most presume. Such a voluntary emancipation of minors *under the majority age* does not enlarge a minor's right to contract for necessities, nor does it permit suit without a guardian, or enlarge his political rights, or release him from the jurisdiction of any court orders.

It is doubtful that the parents may escape liability for the child's support by releasing the child from their control. The primary liability to support a minor child lies with the father, and it would be counter to sound logic to permit the father to evade this responsibility by an agreement with a minor child. Certainly the county or some third person who assumes the support of the child could have looked to the father for reimbursement. However, a third party cannot expect reimbursement from the father of an emancipated child when the father has been abandoned by the child. It appears logical, however, that a criminal action of failure to provide could be instigated against the father if he refused to support his minor child. This would not apply if the father is willing to have the child returned home to live and the child refuses.

Emancipation or release from parental authority may result even without the consent of the parents. A minor when enlisting in the armed forces is no longer under the control of his parents. A lawful court order, either in a civil court or in the juvenile court, may release the child from one or both parents. These orders may or may not release the parents from the liability of support. A guardianship procedure may completely divest the parents from any control over the child, or a juvenile court action may also deprive the parents of all control. A stepparent adoption relieves the natural father or mother of all control and interests in the child and places control with the stepparent.

The marriage of a minor child emancipates the child from control of his parents. This appears true even in the case of a voidable marriage, and until the parent proceeds with annulment action, the child is not under the control of his parents. There is no case law as a guide, but it would appear that if the annulment is granted, the minor once again would be under the control of his parents. Emancipation would only be temporary, and the parental control would resume when the marriage is declared not to have existed. However, if the marriage is dissolved by divorce, it may be that the dissolution does not return the minor to parents' control.

The above question remains unanswered by statute or case law. It would appear the parents no longer are liable to support a married minor child. This obligation is assumed by the spouse of the married minor child. Mutuality of support between husband and wife is the controlling factor in such a case, and the parental obligation of support would cease. This may not apply to annulment of an

[4]*Ibid.*, p. 18.

underage marriage, and it may well be that the parents of the minor child assume this liability of support and that the spouse of the minor child is relieved of this support obligation.

SUMMARY

There are two types of laws in the United States: *criminal law* and *civil law.* Civil law is that body of law, contained in both statutes and in decisions of courts of law, which applies to society as a whole and defines the rights, duties, obligations, and liabilities of citizens. Criminal law is that code of law which defines offenses against the state and provides punishment for individuals convicted of violations of criminal law.

What is a contract? A contract is an agreement between two or more parties under which each of them agree to do or to refrain from doing some act. In order to be binding, there must be an offer and acceptance of the offer.

Is a minor's contract valid? A minor's contract, when all legal presumptions are met, is valid and binding with certain exceptions. The reason for having certain exceptions is that the law seeks to protect a minor from his own lack of sound judgment and to prevent adults from taking advantage of him.

Another division of civil law deals with torts. What is a tort? A tort is a harm done to the person, property, or reputation of another person by a person who had a legal duty to refrain from doing that act. The harm may be caused by a deliberate act or negligence or lack of care of the actor.

The minor is liable for all of his torts in the same manner as if he were an adult. On occasion there may be cases where the minor is too young to realize the consequences of his wrong act, but children as young as five years of age have been held liable for their torts.

Upon reaching majority, the adult child has a duty to support his parents if they are unable to support themselves. The child, however, is not liable for such support if the parents abandoned the child.

The parents have a legal right to all earnings of their child. Such earnings may be paid directly to the parents or indirectly to the child and channeled to the parents. However, if the parents inform the minor's employer that all wages should be paid to them and the employer does not respond to their request, he is liable for a duplication of wages—one to the minor and one to the parents if it is so requested. Except for the earnings and services of the child, the minor's property is his own and is not the property of his parents. The parents cannot take possession of the child's property, unless they are appointed guardians for that purpose.

A minor child is liable for his or her own wrongful acts (torts) that result in injury to another person or damage to property, or both, unless the child is so young that he is incapable of knowing the consequence of his acts. These acts may involve both a civil wrong and a criminal act. Parents are normally not liable for the wrongful actions of their children except in certain circumstances. If the minor child is acting as an agent of the parents, or if the parents have authorized the act, the parents become liable. If the parent provides the child with a dangerous instrument such as BB gun (in the city), a knife, firecrackers, and so on, where it can reasonably be expected that some injury or damage could result to a third person, the parent may be held liable. If the parents know that a child is engaged in a course of careless or intentional acts that may cause harm to others, they may be held liable if they do not take reasonable steps to control the child.

ANNOTATED REFERENCES

Holtzoff, Alexander, ''The Power of Probation and Parole Officers to Search and Seize,'' *Federal Probation,* vol. 28, no. 1, December 1967

> This article is a close scrutiny of the possibilities of violating the constitutional rights of probationeers or parolees.

Devlin, Patrick Arthur, ''The Police in a Changing Society,'' *The Journal of Criminal Law, Criminology and Police Science,* vol. 57, no. 2, June 1966.

> Devlin discusses the role of the police officer in his attempts to enforce laws in a rapidly changing society. This article gives an overall view of the problems confronted by the police in the area of police powers in relation to arrest, search, and detention.

Eldefonso, Edward and Hartinger, W., *Control, Treatment, and Rehabilitation of Juvenile Offenders,* Glencoe Press, Beverly Hills, Calif., 1976.

> Chapters 1 and 2 of this text cover material discussed in Chapter 13 of *Youthful Offender.*

Sheridan, William H., ed., *Standards for Juvenile and Family Courts,* U.S. Department of Health, Education, and Welfare, Children's Bureau, U.S. Government Printing Office, Washington, D.C., 1975.

> In chapter 2 Sheridan discusses terms and definitions. Legal custody, guardianship of the person, parental rights and responsibilities, and other important areas are also discussed. There is a chart on page 24 which gives a vivid picture of the totality of parental rights and responsibilities.

CHAPTER FOURTEEN special problems

There are some problems—special problems—that police officers handle and that require a great deal of flexibility and thought. Problems posed by juvenile gangs and their abuse of narcotics and alcoholic beverages, to say nothing of the perplexing problems of sex offenses, cannot be considered routine. All these problems take specific expertise; hence, the prospective police officer should have some understanding of their salient features.

DELINQUENT SUBCULTURE: JUVENILE GANGS

The special problem of juvenile gangs takes into account the "delinquent subculture" as it is found among adolescent males in lower social-economic areas of large urban surroundings. Youth gangs in America today are a lethal, everincreasing problem. Gangs are now employing deadlier weapons and, as police are learning, are proving more difficult to handle than the juvenile gangs of the 1950s and 1960s. The main problem, according to the United States Justice Department's Law Enforcement Assistant Administration (LEAA),[1] is that gangs have discovered a deadly contrivance—the gun. Also, gangs have shifted a major part of their operations from the street to the school. The author of the report, Walter B. Miller of Harvard's Center for Criminal Justice, concludes:

1. Today, gang violence is a much more serious problem during any previous period; and, it appears, the reason is the "extraordinary increase in the availability and use" of handguns by gang members.

2. From 1972 through 1974, five of the six cities recorded 525 gang-related murders—about 24 percent of all juvenile homicides for those cities.

3. Junior and senior high schools are being terrorized by gangs.

[1] W. B. Miller, *Violence by Youth Clubs and Youth Groups as a Crime Problem in Major American Cities. Interim Report,* Office of Juvenile Justice and Delinquency Prevention, Washington, D.C., 1976, pp. 1–2.

4. New York, Chicago, Los Angeles, Philadelphia, Detroit, and San Francisco (the cities from which the studies originate) report that from 760 gangs with 28,500 members to 2700 gangs with 81,500 members.

5. The study further indicates that, although female crime continues to increase, "urban youth gangs continue to be a predominantly male enterprise." Female participation in gangs continues to be the "carrying of weapons for boys, serving in female auxillaries and frequently offering their impugned honor as a reason for rumble between rival gangs."[2]

Miller, an anthropologist, whose interest in gangs dates back to 1954, spent more than a year studying present-day gangs in New York, Chicago, Los Angeles, Philadelphia, Detroit and San Francisco, which, according to the author of the report, have thriving gang problems. Along these lines, Captain Francis J. Daly, commander of the Youth Aid Division of the New York Police Department stated: "Ten years ago we had nothing in New York City. [However] about 1971, it started up again in the Bronx." Daly added that the problem has leveled off, "somewhat," but the "activities are certainly much more violent than . . . in the 1950s. Weapons are much more available." Daly further stated: "Another difference between now and the old days is that innocent people are more often the victims of gang criminality. In the old days, they spent much more time on rumbles against each other. Now, there are more robberies, burglaries, and shakedowns against non-gang members."[3]

Miller's report indicates that the weapons are much more sophisticated—no longer are homemade zip guns in style. Instead, the easy-to-obtain Smith and Wesson .38, utilized by many police departments, is the gang's weapon. "[The 38s] are not that difficult to get," stated Los Angeles Police Captain William J. Riddle, commanding officer of the Juvenile Division, "everytime a million more guns are sold to the public, more of them reach gangs and other criminals through such means as burglaries."[4]

Perhaps the most serious problems with gangs, ascertained Miller, is the fact that they have centered their activities around the educational facilities of urban areas. The public schools, according to Miller, are being turned into "battlegrounds." And the targets are not only members of rival gangs, but also students who are nonmembers. The report indicates that "the shooting and killing of teachers by gang members" is much in evidence in Chicago and Philadelphia. According to Miller, "the violence has led to 'territorialization' of schools —meaning that gangs actually claim 'ownership' of such areas as a cafeteria or gym. And 'as owners of school facilities,' gang members have assumed the right to

[2]Ibid., pp. 2–3.
[3]Ibid., pp. 3–5.
[4]Ibid.

collect 'fees' from other students for a variety of 'privileges' which can be defined as passing through the hallways, using the gym, not being assaulted and of simply going to school."[5]

In the cities studied, gangs have, basically, intimidated the educational system.

Like the gangs of the 1950s and 1960s, today's gangs are for the most part, Miller reports, "confined to the slum areas of big cities." The gang members, who are usually associated by ethnic background, range in age from twelve to twenty-one. Although the Black, Mexican, and Puerto Rican ethnic groups are highly representative, the increase of Anglo-Americans is a new phenomenon. Miller elaborates:[6]

> *Accepted doctrine for many years has been that oriental youths posed negligible problems in juvenile delinquency or gang activity. This accepted tenet has been seriously undermined by the events of the 1970s—not only by the violent activities of the new immigrated 'Hong Kong Chinese,' but by the development in several cities of gangs of Philippinos, Japanese, and other Asian groups. The estimated number of Asian gangs is now almost equal to that of white gangs and may exceed in their number in the near future.*

San Francisco, according to the report, has, probably, the most significant problem in the area of Chinese gangs.

No relief is in sight; instead, the report indicates, "the likelihood that gang problems will continue to beset major cities during the next few years appears high."

GANGS NOT A NEW PHENOMENON

The word "gang" has a long history in the United States, and some of that history sheds light on contemporary use of the term and on present social attitudes toward designated groups of adolescents throughout the country. In early English usage, gang was often employed as a synonym for "a going," "a walking," or "a journey." In this sense, it traces its origin to the Scandinavian languages. As early as 1340, there was an Anglo-Saxon derivation that had a common meaning of "a number of things used together or forming a complete set." These meanings were eventually combined so that gang came to stand for a crew of a ship or companies of mariners.

Although the word gang is usually associated with antisocial behavior or rebellion against authority, the gang in itself is not inherently vicious. Group activity is a necessary part of a growing child's life. The gang becomes dangerous if the

[5]*Ibid.*, p. 6.
[6]*Ibid.*, p. 7.

street life from which it springs offers opportunities for delinquency and if the leader of a gang is a bad influence. To the youngster who is in danger of becoming a delinquent, gang life often becomes particularly attractive. With others of his own age who may be as neglected as he is, he may get recognition and acceptance by adopting the ways of the gang. In such a manner, the goal he seeks—the satisfaction of a well-defined and well-approved ego—is obtained.

The influence of the gang, whether negative or positive, is particularly effective because it often completely answers a boy's needs. His desire for companionship and adventure is satisfied. He gets the feeling of belonging and being loyal to a group. If the gang is delinquency-oriented, the tougher the boy is the more recognition he gets. Furthermore, he may also find the discipline he needs. Gangs develop their own codes and rules of behavior, and demand that their members rigidly abide by them. Because a gang's control over a boy's conduct often becomes stronger than the control of his family, or of larger social units, attitudes and behavior patterns may result in delinquent activities.[7]

The etymology of the word gang provides a starting point from which to examine contemporary social views about juvenile gangs.[8] The social views are constructed from an amalgam of fact, myth, and stereotype and, like all other such views, they tend to elicit and to preserve the process they seek to describe. It is one of the noteworthy insights of social science that isolating and labeling forms of behavior tends to solidify, and sometimes increase, such behavior. Labeling provides a definitional framework for recognition of a phenomenon, and this adds a further dimension to its previous characteristics.[9]

Cloward and Ohlin indicated in their book *Delinquency and Opportunity* that a "delinquent act is defined by two essential elements: It is behavior that violates basic norms of the society, and when officially known, it evokes a judgment by agents of criminal justice that such norms have been violated."[10] In other words, a delinquent act is an antisocial act that transgresses upon the right of others, and when it comes to the attention of law enforcement agents, a judgment is imposed.

When one speaks of a subculture, it refers to knowledge, beliefs, values, codes, tastes, and prejudices that are traditional among certain groups in our society.

The group we are concerned about here is one in which certain forms of delinquent activity are essential requirements for the performance of the dominant role supported by the subculture.[11]

These delinquent activities are a direct defiance of the dominant culture of our middle-class society.

---

[7]Winters, *Crime and Kids*, Charles C Thomas, Springfield, Illinois, 1969, p. 96. See also: G. Geis, *Juvenile Gangs*, President's Committee on Juvenile Delinquency and Youth Crime, Government Printing Office, Washington, D.C., June 1965, p. 2.
[8]Winters, *op. cit.*, p. 97.
[9]*Ibid.*

THEORIES OF DELINQUENT SUBCULTURE

Albert K. Cohen in describing the development of the delinquent subculture in *Delinquent Boys*, calls attention to a crucial condition for the emergence of a new cultural form, namely the existence of a number of individuals who have similar problems of adjustment and who at the same time are in effective interaction with one another. These interacting individuals burdened with comparable problems may be the entire membership of a group or only certain members circumscribed within it. The adjustment problems of the working-class boy, according to Cohen, are that he is unable to live in accordance with the middle-class standard of the dominant culture because of his disadvantageous social position.[12]

The working-class boy's problem is one of "status-frustration," the origins of which begin in his early exposure to lower-class socialization. Yet all about him he sees prized the middle-class values of achieving an occupational position of economic advantage and social prestige.

The workingboy's aspirations are not necessarily considered a step toward economic mobility. "Advancement" and "promotion" are not so important in the working class; "planning" and "foresight" are outside the range of values. The "pinch of the present" is far more demanding than the promise of the future. A "run of good luck" is to furnish the wherewithal for buying what is wanted, not for starting a savings account. "Pay off" is considered an immediate need, not eventual upgrading. The "ethic of responsibility" for the down-and-out in this family is imperative to the extent that one branch of the family will spend all it has for another in need; and the "law of reciprocity" holds, namely, in times of stress the same is expected in return.

One is honest with particular persons, not honest in general. Persons in this socio-economic group feel more at home in their own families and in their immediate neighborhood and are ill at ease in secondary social contacts. Emotions appear to be released more spontaneously, and there is free expression of aggression with no hesitancy to assert what is right. Little attempt is made to cultivate polish, sophistication, "fluency," "appearance," and "personality," all considered so necessary in the middle-class world.[13]

In contrast, the middle-class culture values ambition as a virtue; lack of it is a serious defect. Responsibility is individual; and reliance and resourcefulness are considered essentials. Skills have to be developed in order that there may be tangible achievements through outstanding performances, either in the scholastic, the athletic, or the artistic areas. Forethought, conscious planning, and budgeting of time are valued highly. Manners, courtesy, charm, and other skills in relation-

---

[10]Richard A. Cloward and Lloyd E. Ohlin, *Delinquency and Opportunity*, Free Press, Glencoe, Illinois, 1960, p. 3.

[11]Albert K. Cohen, *Delinquent Boys*, Free Press, Glencoe, Illinois, 1955, p. 7.

[12]*Ibid.*, p. 59.

[13]*Ibid.*, p. 135.

ships are the basis for "selling" of self to others. Aggression is controlled; and violence and physical combat are frowned upon. Recreation has to be such that it is considered, "wholesome," "constructive," and not a "waste of time." Property must be respected. To achieve status and success, Cohen states, these are the ground rules of the prevailing culture in the United States.[14]

This socialization to lower-class values handicaps the working-class boy from achievement in the middle-class status system. Nevertheless, he must compete where achievement is judged by middle-class standards of behavior and performance.

The lower-class boy finds the delinquent subculture a solution to his problems. It gives him a chance to belong, to amount to something, to develop his masculinity, to fight middle-class society.

This solution for the "status-frustration" problem may not appear to be acceptable behavior, but it may appeal more than the already institutionalized solutions. When youngsters find it impossible to achieve status, according to middle-class standards, then they turn to the development of "characteristics they do possess and the kinds of conduct of which they are capable."[15]

Mob or gang action sets up its own "positive morality" a value structure to justify its conduct with a rapid transition into behavior according to the new "group standards" with emergence of a distinctive subculture."[16] These new values that emerge, according to Cohen, are opposed to the larger cultural structure. The mechanism of "reaction formation" takes place in which the delinquent seeks to obtain unequivocal status by repudiating, once and for all, the norms of the middle-class culture.[17]

There is strong hostility and contempt for those who are not a member of the delinquent subculture. Antisocial behavior is indulged in simply because it is held to be disreputable by the dominant class. In order to gain status in the delinquent gang, a member must constantly exhibit his defiance of middle-class norms.

Among boys of the working class, the most common response is not that of becoming a member of the delinquent gang but that of hanging out on the street corner. The stable corner boy accepts this way of life, and tries to make the best of his predicament. He withdraws, "as far as possible into a sheltering community of like-minded working-class children pretty much avoiding delinquency."[18]

This is the juvenile who continues to remain in the lower-class community employed as a "blue-collar" worker or an "unskilled" laborer and aimlessly hangs around the street corner during his idle leisure hours. In part, this is an explanation of why one finds that not every boy living in a lower-class urban community is a juvenile delinquent.

[14]*Ibid.*, pp. 94–97.
[15]*Ibid.*, pp. 89–91.
[16]*Ibid.*, p. 66.
[17]*Ibid.*, p. 65.
[18]*Ibid.*, p. 135

The corner-boy way of life "temperizes with middle-class morality, the full-fledged delinquent subculture does not." The boy who "breaks clean with middle-class morality" has no inhibitions against aggressive and hostile behavior toward the sources of his frustration. The corner boy who has not embraced delinquent subculture still temperizes with middle-class norms by inhibiting his hostility and aggression against the middle class. "On the other hand, delinquent subculture legitimizes aggression."[19]

Cohen contends that the delinquent subculture is nonutilitarian, malicious and negativistic. By nonutilitarian, he means that the boys really do not want the things they steal. They steal for the glory, for the "hell of it," for the status. By malice he means, "an enjoyment in the discomfort of others, a delight in the defiance of taboos itself." By negativisitic he means that the delinquent subculture negates the values of the middle-class culture. Other characteristics are short-term hedonism, by which he means that the gang has very little interest in long-range goals, planned activity, or practice to develop skills. The group is intolerant of restraints that limited its autonomy apart from those arising from informal pressures within the group itself. Relations with other groups tend to be indifferent, hostile or rebellious.[20]

According to Cohen, the delinquent subculture is a solution to the problems of status and success for the male rather than the female.[21] Female delinquency is usually establishing a satisfactory relationship with the opposite sex.

The final question, then, is—would one find a delinquent subculture in the middle-class culture? Cohen failed to give a concise answer but indicated that it is conceivable that much of the delinquency found in "over-privileged" neighborhoods may be the same, in terms of both content and etiology. However, that the subcultural delinquency would differ in quality as well as in frequency from that found in the working class.[22]

Paul W. Tappan in his book, *Crime, Justice, and Corrections,* questioned the hypothesis that the working class craves success as defined by Cohen in the *American Dream* or that they may turn to crime in order to succeed. He further doubts that delinquent norms derive from a reaction formation. Few working-class children experience such ambivalence toward the middle-class as to produce this emotional mechanism.[23]

In fact, Tappan feels that whether or not antisocial norms will prevail in particiular families depend very largely upon the "under the roof" patterns of the

[19]Walter C. Reckless, *The Crime Problem,* Appleton-Century-Crofts, Inc., New York, 3rd ed., 1965. pp. 314–316.
[20]Cohen, p. 23.
[21]*Ibid.,* pp. 25–28.
[22]*Ibid.,* p. 143.
[23]*Ibid.,* pp. 159–160.

particular home, upon its reference groups, and upon the controls that are exerted through the family line.[24]

Another critique of Cohen's book was written by John I. Kitsuse and David Dietrick in the *Sociological Review* in which they indicated the weak points in this explanation of the delinquent subculture. According to these sociologists, Cohen does not present adequate support for his formulation of the problem of the working-class boy. The working-class boy faces a problem of adjustment "to the degree to which he values the good opinion of the middle-class standards himself." Thus, it would appear that the working-class boy's problem is a minor one if it depends on the degree to which he values middle-class persons.[25] Cohen's explanation of the problem of adjustment implies that the lower working-class youths are dissatisfied with their position, which may be true of some, but not all.

Another discrepancy in Cohen's book is that the methodology used is untestable. Data concerning the psychological dynamics of a population is difficult to obtain, if not impossible. The theory should also include an explanation of the persistence of the subculture if it is to meet an adequate test. In conclusion, Kitsuse and Dietrick indicated that Cohen's description of the middle-class system implies that it is not that the working-class boy's status aspirations that are frustrated, but rather that he does not want to strive for status in the system.[26]

Richard Cloward and Lloyd Ohlin in their book, *Delinquency and Opportunity* attempted to explain two questions: Why do delinquent norms or rules of conduct develop? What are the conditions that account for the distinctive content of various systems of delinquent norms, violence, theft, or drug use.[27]

According to Cloward and Ohlin, the delinquent subculture of lower-class adolescents living in an urban setting springs from problems in trying to adjust aspirations and opportunities.

When a person ascribes his failure to injustice in a social system, he may criticize that system; he may become alienated from its established set of social norms. On the other hand, a person may attribute failure to his own faults and reveal an attitude supporting the legitimacy of the existing norms, namely, a "corner-boy response."[28]

The lower-class adolescent who places the blame for lack of opportunity on the established social order negates the values of the dominant order. He seeks support from others for denying legitimacy to official norms and may champion illegitimate means as the preferred way of achieving success.[29] Usually he commits

[24]Paul W. Tappan, *Crime, Justice and Correction*, McGraw-Hill Book Co., New York, 1960, pp. 81–83.
[25]*Ibid.*, p. 183.
[26]John I. Kitsuse and David Dietrick, "Delinquent Boys—A Critique," *American Sociological Review*, April, 1959, Vol. 24, p. 209.
[27]*Ibid.*, p. 210.
[28]Cloward, p. 9.
[29]*Ibid.*, p. 111.

his first act under the fear of disapproval. At this stage, the delinquent needs all the encouragement and reassurance he can obtain to defend his position. He finds that by searching out others with similar experience and who still support one another in common attitudes of alienation from the official system.[30]

Cloward and Ohlin indicate that people who violate the law usually have strong guilt feelings. In order for delinquent adolescents to continue their defiant behavior, they usually have to develop some defense against these feelings. Adolescents in a delinquent gang engage in delinquent acts without experiencing acute guilt feelings because they have come to believe in the legitimacy of these acts, given the social circumstances in which they are placed.[31]

The social milieu, according to Cloward and Ohlin, affects the nature of the defiant response whatever the motivation and social position (age, sex, or socioeconomic level) of the participants in the delinquent subculture. In this setting, each individual occupies a position in both a legitimate and illegitimate opportunity structure. There are differentials in access to legitimate routes to attaining goals successfully. This approach shows the relative availability of illegitimate opportunities and how this availability affects the resolution of adjustment problems leading to defiant behavior. The way in which the problem of adjustment is resolved may depend upon the kind of support given at different points in the social structure to one or another type of illegitimate activity. For example, in order for a criminal subculture to develop among delinquents one expects the social location and illegal means to be available. Manipulation of violence should become a primary avenue to higher status only in areas where the means of violence are socially accepted. Drug addiction and subculture organized around the use of drugs presuppose that persons can secure access to drugs and gain knowledge of how to use them.[32]

On the basis of the theory of "differential opportunity" in which each individual occupies a different opportunity structure, Cloward and Ohlin point out three distinctive delinquent subcultures. The criminal delinquent subculture is one in which the lower-class youth may be associated with and aspire to become a "policy king." The youth has an opportunity to actually perform illegitimate roles because such activity finds support in his immediate neighborhood. He resides in an area in the urban setting in which the "racket" and other illegitimate activities are flourishing and the participants are "successful."

His neighborhood is characterized by close bonds between different age-levels of offenders and between criminal and conventional elements.[33] And, as the apprentice criminal passes from one status to another in the illegitimate opportunity

[30]Ibid., p. 124.
[31]Ibid., p. 126.
[32]Ibid., p. 13.
[33]Ibid., p. 150.

system, he develops ever-widening relationships with the members of the legitimate world.[34]

The conflict subculture of the "boy gangs" develop when a youth resides in an area in which social disorganization has taken place in lower-class urban neighborhoods that lack unity and cohesiveness. In this slum area there are mass housing projects and a high rate of vertical and geographic mobility. Among youths this instability produces powerful pressures for violent behavior.[35] Violence becomes an outlet for release of pressures generated in an unorganized community that is unable to provide access to legitimate success-goals. This youth is also restricted from access to stable criminal opportunity systems; for the slum area contains outcasts of the criminal world. Crimes committed in this area are unorganized, individual, and petty in nature. A youth can thus seize upon an individualized manipulation of violence as a route to status and a way to express anger and frustration.[36]

The retreatist subculture of the Drug User contains youth and young adults whose only interest is in experiences in using drugs. In order for a youth to begin use of illegal drugs, there must be steady sources of supply available. But, because of the restricted availability of drugs, a new user must affiliate with the old users. Hence, the more an individual becomes acculturated to this subculture, the more likely he or she will persist in drug use.[37]

How do adolescents become involved in the use of drugs and the retreatist subculture in the first place? According to Cloward and Ohlin, recruitment is from adolescents who fail in both the legitimate and illegitimate worlds. First, they are unable to aspire realistically to goals approved as legitimate by the broader culture; and second, they are unable to acquire proficiency in the controlled use of violence demanded by the criminal world. Culturally and socially detached from both conventional worlds, they turn inward for their rewards. They are in continuous pursuit of the "kick."

Cloward and Ohlin conclude that the most worthwhile program of prevention is to reorganize the slum communities. Slum neighborhoods are undergoing progressive disintegration. The old structures, which provided social control and avenues of ascent, are breaking down. In order to alter the trend towards violence and retreatism among adolescents, the community must provide legitimate but functional substitutes for these traditional structures.

William Foote Whyte, in his book, *Street Corner Society*, analyzed a "slum" community called Cornerville. The methodology was one of "participant observation" in which Whyte settled in Cornerville and became integrated into the community for a period of three and one-half years. The purpose of Whyte's study was to record the dynamic interrelationship of individuals within a social group.

Cornerville was a slum area composed almost exclusively Italian immigrants

[34]*Ibid.*, pp. 161–165.
[35]*Ibid.*, p. 166.
[36]*Ibid.*, p. 172.
[37]*Ibid.*, p. 176.

and their children. This community was one of the most congested areas (i.e., number of people in square feet) in the United States with a population of approximately 20,000.

Although this study does not indicate a delinquent subculture, it does indicate some of the responses to the middle-class social structure by groups living in a lower socioeconomic setting. In this analysis, Whyte found that there were two main distinctive groups.

The corner boys who centered their social activities at the Norton Street Settlement House had a primary interest in the local community. They would hang out mostly on the street corner during leisure hours after work. An individual in this group was judged according to the way he acted in his personal relations. Whyte found that there was a high rate of social interaciton because of the stable composition of the group and the lack of social assurance outside the group. Mutual obligations arose from actions performed by group members for each other explicitly for the sake of friendship. The leader was the focal point for the organization of the group. When he left, unity gave way to disorganization. In the gang structure each member had his own position, which remained unchanged for a long period of time. The gangs activities proceeded from day to day in a fixed pattern.

The street-corner group described by Whyte is, according to Cohen, the most common response among adolescents living in lower-class urban "slum" areas. The group accepts this way of life and does not aspire toward middle-class standards. Although Whyte found that the group did not get involved in illegitimate activities, they became influenced by the politician and the racketeer who grew up in a similar environment.

The other distinctive group within the slum community was referred to by Whyte as "college boys."

This was a small group that had risen above the corner boys through means of higher education. The primary interest of the group was in social advancement. The activities consisted of membership in the Italian Community Club and the Republican Club. A member was evaluated by his scholastic performance and leadership qualities. He looked upon himself as a superior individual and qualified for a leadership position. He did not tie himself to a group of close friends; instead he was willing to sacrifice friendship with those whose advance was not so fast as his.

The "college boys" would be referred to by Cohen as the group that is willing to compete with middle-class culture in order to aspire to an occupational position of economic advantage and social prestige.

The social structure of Cornerville as a whole conceived of society as a closely knit hierarchial organization in which the positions and obligations of people to one another are defined and recognized. According to Cornerville people, society is made up of "big people"—the college boy, racket boss, and political boss—and of "little people"—corner boys and the Cornerville people.

In conclusion, Whyte indicated that to outsiders, the leading men of the community are the respectable business and professional men—people who have attained middle-class standards. These men, who have been moving up and out of Cornerville, actually have little influence. Not until outsiders are prepared to recognize some of the same men that Cornerville people recognize as leaders will they be able to deal with the actual social structure and bring about a change.[38]

THE SHOOK-UP GENERATION

A popular presentation of delinquent gang as perceived by a layman is that of Harrison Salisbury *The Shook-Up Generation* in which he became a participant observer of juvenile gangs in New York City for a period of three months. Salisbury pointed out that the gangs are "pitiful, tragic, dangerous" and that youth within them find it hard, if not impossible, to break away once a member.[39]

According to Salisbury, gangs are products of social deterioration and are found mainly in the slum areas in a community. Lack of basic security in families, in neighborhoods, and in community life are experienced by the adolescent in this setting. The gang offers a dubious security that exists neither in the present nor in the future.

Salisbury indicates that there are means for working out the problems that have created delinquent gangs. He feels the principle of universal education is unrealistic in that youths learn at different rates, and this creates great difficulty for the slow learner. Different children have different capacities and different chronological age for maturation.

He also feels that social disorganization, which has occurred in many housing projects of "slum" areas, may be improved by making the income requirements more flexible. This would help prevent mobility that is created by having families move when they reach a certain income bracket. In addition, active social work would help to reduce conflict in the housing area and create more stability. Social programs would improve the housekeeping and family life habits of housing tenants and make the projects better places to live.

Schools, Salisbury insists, are in most instances the only place for security and refuge for the lower-class youth who is buffeted by poverty, family inadequacy, lack of formal and informal neighborhood organization.

In conclusion, the theory of a "delinquent subculture" indicates that the lower-class adolescent is unable to aspire to middle-class culture because of early and persistent socialization in the lower-class community. As a result of "status frustration," the adolescent joins the delinquent gang in order to negate the middle-class values of the larger community.

We question, however, the assumption of a doomed struggle by the lower-class adolescent to acquire middle-class standards, a defeat that leads to a "reaction formation" that negates official norms.

[38]*Ibid.*, p. 179.
[39]William F. Whyte, *Street Corner Society,* University of Chicago Press, Chicago, Illinois, 1947, p. 771.

First of all, the lower- and middle-class structures are not so distinctively different. There is an interrelationship of cultural values and socioeconomic mobility that prevents establishment of a caste, or even of a rigid class, system.

In this cultural approach, the sociologists we have cited fail to indicate the most important influence on an adolescent, namely, the family unit. True, many lower-class youths grow up in a highly organized family unit; however, this is not true of all lower-class youths.

Statistics indicate the majority of lower-class adolescents have grown up to become law-abiding citizens.

The delinquent subculture may have some merit in explaining why the delinquent gang defies official norms, however, more empirical knowledge is required about the gang's appeals and functions within its social setting.

POLICE ROLE

Neither punitive methods nor adult-sponsored recreational programs are adequate in coping with street gangs. Revenge or simple punishment will not deter antisocial activities. Such methods only increase tensions and make behavior more hostile and aggressive. The main difficulties facing athletic-recreations and leisure-time programs is that youngsters who need them the most are usually not participants in adult-sponsored activities of this kind. Such activities usually attract youngsters who have not displayed delinquent tendencies. Furthermore, many agencies that are attempting to organize programs with the delinquent youngster are not equipped to integrate into their total programs those autonomous street gangs that have already developed patterns of aggressive behavior. If the punitive approach is unsound, and if the provision of recreation through agencies tends to be ineffective, what other methods can be utilized and where do the police fit in?[40]

Law enforcement agencies throughout the United States recommend that an *area project* approach be adopted. The reason for such a recommendation is quite practical. Under the coordinating council program, each area of the community would have a committee composed of a cross-section of persons living in a particular neighborhood, including representatives of social agencies, schools, labor unions, churches, police, fraternal, and business organizations. One good example of this approach is the area programs being set up by the Economic Opportunity Commission (a federally subsidized agency) throughout the United States. Such intervention groups will try to develop local resources to meet the needs of street gangs in a particular area. By stimulating cohesive community action in various neighborhoods, these programs will neutralize situations inimical to a secure democratic way of life for all neighborhood residents.[41]

The area in which the police can be quite helpful is the identification of poten-

[40]Harrison E. Salisbury, *The Shook-Up Generation*, Publications, Inc., New York, 1958, p. 42.
[41]Winters, p. 58.

tial antisocial gangs and the transmitting of such information to trained workers sent into the streets to work with these gangs. The police should endeavor to obtain information concerning gang members—their backgrounds, prior criminal histories (if any), and extensive data on gang leaders. This approach obviously calls for tact on the part of the investigating officer. These groups generally resent those in authority, and it must be impressed upon each group and its leaders that the objective of the officers is not to take a course of punitive action but to assist the area committee in supplying information concerning the gangs, their members, purposes, and desires.[42]

The area committee, with all information obtainable, can then direct trained workers in efforts to help the clubs along socially constructive lines. If the members of the gang respond positively to accepting and understanding adults, the relationships with such adults will serve as a powerful force for personal and social adjustment.[43]

Unfortunately, the lack of trained workers may make it necessary in many areas for someone else to attempt to perform this task. The police, then, have no alternative but to enter this field. Certainly, under most conditions, the police should not become involved directly in intervention work. If there is no other agency available, however, then someone must take the initiative if effective action is to be instituted against undesirable gang conditions. The approach utilized by the police in such cases is that used by trained intervention workers.

The following suggestions are based on those made by Inspector John E. Winters, commanding officer, Youth Aide Division, Metropolitan Police Department, Washington, D.C., to police officers assigned to gang investigations:

---

1. The investigating officer should not approach a gang with predetermined ideas and suggestions. Because the officer may be in a position to suggest rooms for club meetings, halls for dances, or locations for athletic activities, knowledge of the neighborhood and its resources is a must. Such referrals should only be done, however, if the group expresses a desire for such facilities.

2. The officer must become acquainted with members individually. The individual needs of the youngsters must be determined in order to make intelligent referrals to vocational, casework, or psychiatric services, and to seek assistance of the court if necessary.

3. The most important "tool" of an officer investigating gang activities is his ability to relate to gang members. The officer should have the type of personality that enables him to converse and develop rapport with young people. He should be democratic, and able to accept the difference between his own standards and

[42]*Ibid.*
[43]*Ibid.*

those of the group without trying to impose his thought patterns on them. Club members should neither be protected from the responsibilities for nor the consequences of their antisocial acts.

4. To understand the procedures of various social services available in the community is an important part of the duties of an officer delegated to gang investigations.

5. The police should work in close cooperation with the area committee, if there is one; consult with specialists in casework, group work, and psychiatry.

6. The ultimate objective is a self-governing federation of the various clubs in each area. This is important because through federation, the leadership of individual clubs can be unified and steered toward constructive goals. In short, the police should function to gain the acceptance and confidence of club members and then use all the means at their disposal to work toward their objectives. These objectives, according to Inspector Winters, should be:

 A. The opportunity for the club to enjoy the normal adolescent group life that the street club potentially offers its members.

 B. The gradual development on the part of club members of the feeling that they are needed and important members of the community and that they have a real part to play in the job of making their neighborhood a happier, more comfortable, more secure place in which to live.

 C. The opportunity for club members to develop a close relationship with accepting and understanding police officers, and to create in the minds of these young people the idea that the police want to help, not persecute them.[44]

The recommendations offered by Inspector Winters are made on the premise that when there are other agencies available, the police should not enter the treatment field. Although there is no reason for law enforcement officers not to strike up friendly relationships with these groups, inform interested citizens of the needs of groups, and provide whatever assistance is possible to those who are in the treatment field, treatment itself should be delegated to those who are trained to assume this role.

According to Inspector Winters, it must be borne in mind that:

> though this approach has been successful in some communities, there are those hardbitten, sophisticated, and anti-social groups of young adults and teenagers who would not respond to any reproach. They are believed to

[44]Geis, pp. 3–5.

consist of only a small percentage of the total. The only action that can be taken against these groups is constant surveillance, arrest, and prosecution for unlawful acts. In any determination of police action in a given situation, the welfare of the community must take precedence over the individual. For this reason, all investigations into group situations, whether designed to provide help for the group or to develop sufficiently for prosecution, should be made a matter of record.[45]

Inspector Winters further states:

A file should be maintained in the office of the juvenile unit. This file should identify groups by name and location. Cards on individual members should contain information relating to that individual such as any prior record of criminal activity or reports received on misbehavior, truancy, etc., the results of consultations with parents (a good technique that has produced constructive results), the school attended, etc. It has been established that the mere recording of pertinent information concerning a gang member has a deterring effect on the member with relation to anti-social activity. This file should not be a public record and should not be used as a basis for punitive action except where absolutely necessary. Its main purpose would be to furnish information to the community's coordinating council and, through that council, to the various area committees.[46]

The fact remains that the police department's first approach to a gang situation should be that of a helping agency. That is, the police should assist other agencies and groups to redirect the gang's activities into constructive channels. It is the responsibility of the law enforcement agency, however, to utilize aggressive and consistent action if intervention programs fail and the interests of the community are being threatened.

ADOLESCENT DRUG ABUSE

During the last decade, there has been a continuous increase in the number of adolescents in our society, particularly in the large metropolitan areas, who have become involved in the use of narcotics. This has produced much controversy and discussion in this country; perhaps the most emotionally alarming controversy has been about the nature of its relationship to criminality.

In the past few decades, law enforcement has become an increasingly complex and skilled profession demanding specialized knowledge in many fields. One of

[45]Winters, p. 99.
[46]*Ibid.*

these fields is that of drugs and their abuse. Recent medical advances have brought many new drugs into being and some of them, while invaluable to the practice of medicine, can be abused.

The abuse of drugs is not a new problem for police. The criminal investigation files of our large cities provide ample evidence that thousands of Americans are seeking relief from stress and escape from reality with the aid of opium, morphine, heroin, cocaine, marijuana, codeine, meperidine, and "over-the-counter" and prescription sedatives. These drugs are subject to special laws and regulations. In addition, a number of nonnarcotic drugs are being abused. *Stimulants* (like the amphetamine drugs) and *depressants* (like the barbiturates) head the list. Certain tranquilizers are also increasingly used for nonmedical purposes. And abuse of the hallucinogenic agents—LSD-25, mescaline, and psilocobin—has received considerable publicity.

HISTORICAL PERSPECTIVE

Drug abuse is probably as old as the earliest civilization. Man has used great ingenuity in identifying substances that ease tensions, although for centuries available agents remain relatively static, limited to botanicals and their derivatives. *Amphetamine* and *methamphetamine,* the main stimulant drugs used today, synthesized in the 1920s as part of the search for a substitute for ephedrine. The first clinical use of amphetamine was in 1930, and it became apparent that amphetamines, which stimulated the central nervous system, were effective in retarding fatigue-induced deterioration in psychomotor performance. Used under medical supervision, they had some value for persons required to do routine tasks for prolonged periods over adverse circumstances.

The first barbiturate, Vernol, was introduced in 1903, and a large number of others followed in quick succession. The short-acting barbiturates, especially pentobarbital and amobarbital, have come into widespread use within the last twenty to thirty years.

Amphetamine and barbiturate-type drugs were in widespread use before their dependence-producing properties were recognized. However, the eventual discovery of the ability to cause euphoria, dysphoria, and psychostimulation did not lead to the removal of these drugs from over-the-counter nasal inhalers. Moreover, restricting the legal acquisition of stimulants through prescription medications did not put an end to their misuse or abuse; today, these drugs are part of our major medical and social problems.

As early as 1200 B.C., the hemp plant, *Cannabis Sativa,* was described as a source of long textile fibres, and its "narcotic" properties were documented in Chinese writings by A.D. 200.

> It was first used for such commercial purposes as the production of rope and textiles. It is mentioned in ancient Sanskrit literature, dating from

> *2000–1400 B.C. Later it was utilized for medicinal and anesthetic purposes by Chinese, Hindu, and Arab physicians. Not until the Tenth Century of the Christian Era was it extensively used for intoxicant and euphoric properties in India and Arabic countries. The peoples of Europe were familiarized with the drug through the writings of various romanticists during the Nineteenth Century.[47]*

Its numerous derivatives, which can be smoked, eaten, or drunk, have become know throughout the world by a variety of names, including hashish, bhang, ganja, dagga, and marijuana. Traffic in the use of Cannabis derivatives is now restricted in virtually every civilized country in the world, including those where custom has allowed its introduction into religious rites.

Lysergic acid diethylamide (LSD) was synthesized in 1938, but it was not until five years later, when the drug was accidently ingested in an infinitesimal amount, that its hallucinogenic properties were discovered. Subsequently, LSD was used by several investigators to induce a "model psychosis" thought to resemble schizophrenia. It was soon recognized, however, that the vivid hallucinations, spectacular illusions, and sensory distortions induced were not characteristic of that disorder even though the resulting depersonalization were somewhat similar.

By the early 1960s, an increasing number of persons were using (self-administering) LSD. Its use may have been abetted by the publications of Aldous Huxley and Timothy Leary and his associates, lauding its "consciousness-expanding" qualities. By 1965, the medical literature contained numerous reports of the adverse, and often catastrophic, effects of the drug, particularly among those with preexistent severe psychopathological conditions. Twenty-seven patients with severe complications of self-administration of LSD were admitted to New York's Bellevue Hospital in a four-month period in 1965. Substantial numbers have since been admitted to that and other hospitals for the same abuse.

Today, LSD is recommended for strictly controlled research only, and its legitimate production and distribution are limited to research purposes by the Food and Drug Administration.

The cultivation of the opium poppy for its seed dates back to prehistoric times, probably originating in Mesopotamia. The ancient Egyptians and Persians, and later the Greeks and Romans, used opium extensively for medicinal purposes and sometimes for pleasure-seeking purposes. Among Greek, Roman, and Arabic physicians, opium enjoyed the reputation of a fantasia and was enthusiastically prescribed for all ailments ranging from headache to leprosy. From the Mediterranean area, it was carried to India and China by Arabian traders. The opium poppy is now grown mainly in India, China, Turkey, Iran, and Yugoslavia. *Heroin* is the indirect derivative of the drug opium.

> *More than in the case of other nations, opium has played a crucial and disastrous role in the history of China over the past 200 years. In addition*

[47]*Ibid.*, p. 101.

to retarding economic development, opium cultivation and opium profits have corrupted political life and financed civil disorder and revolution.[48]

In recent years, the smoking of opium has virtually disappeared. The disappearance was probably brought about by the difficulties encountered in smoking without detection. Considerable paraphernalia and advance preparations are required before the smoking may commence. Once the pipe is lit, the opium gives off a distinctive, easily identified odor that will carry for a considerable distance and greatly increase the chances of detection.

YOUTHFUL WORLD OF DRUGS

In a study entitled *Monitoring the Future: A Continuing Study of the Lifestyles and Values of Youth,* 16,000 high school seniors were surveyed in 130 high schools around the country in the spring of 1975. Taken as a whole, they comprise a national cross-section of all seniors enrolled in public and private schools in the continental United States—the high school class of 1975. The findings of the study provided some interesting trends in the levels of drug usage and attitudes relating to drug abuse.

The report indicated that substantial numbers of today's American youth have had experience with the use of illicit substances before leaving high school. In fact, the majority—some 55 percent—have had such experience by age eighteen. About 45 percent of the high school class of '75 had used illicit drugs within the previous year; indeed, over 30 percent had used them within the previous 30-day period.

Comparisons between the class of 1975 and the class of 1969, which was surveyed in an earlier study, indicated that from two to three times as many seniors were using drugs in 1975 as compared with 1969 (see Table 14-1). The number of males who had used marijuana by the senior year increased nearly threefold (from 19 percent to 54 percent); and the number using barbiturates more than threefold (from 5 percent to 18 percent).

Some important distinctions were made in the study between levels of use and between types of drugs utilized. When marijuana was eliminated from the computation, it was ascertained that the number of youths (1975 class) who had used any of the other (more serious) illicit drugs was about one-third of all high school seniors—considerably less than 55 percent using any illicit drug (see Table 14-2).

The majority of the aforementioned youthful population (nonusers for the most part) were still quite conservative about the use of drugs other than marijuana. More than three-fourths of those responding to the survey disapproved of even experimenting with any of the more serious illicit drugs, and most *strongly* disapproved such experimentation. The majority believed that users of all such

[48]David P. Ausubel, *Drug Addiction: Physiological, Psychological and Sociological Aspects,* Random House, New York, 1958, p. 95.

TABLE 14-1.
DRUG USE IN THE HIGH SCHOOL CLASS OF 1975 (MALES AND FEMALES COMBINED, N=16,000)

Span and Frequency

	Lifetime Use				Last 12 months				Last 30 days			
	Any Use	1–2 Times	3–19 Times	20+ Times	Any Use	1–2 Times	3–19 Times	20+ Times	Any Use	1–2 Times	3–19 Times	20+ Times
Marijuana	47.9%	8.7%	14.7%	24.5%	40.4%	8.7%	15.2%	16.6%	27.6%	7.8%	13.6%	6.2%
LSD	11.8	4.8	4.9	2.1	7.6	4.0	3.1	0.5	2.5	1.8	0.6	0.2
Psychedelics other than LSD	14.5	5.3	6.5	2.7	9.7	4.5	4.5	0.8	3.9	2.5	1.2	0.3
Cocaine	9.3	4.4	3.8	1.1	5.9	3.4	2.1	0.5	2.1	1.3	0.6	0.2
Amphetamines	22.6	6.7	9.1	6.9	16.6	5.6	7.7	3.4	8.8	4.2	4.0	0.7
Quaaludes	8.5	3.1	3.6	1.9	5.4	2.4	2.4	0.7	2.3	1.2	0.9	0.2
Barbiturates	17.3	6.2	7.5	3.6	11.0	4.5	5.3	1.2	5.0	2.7	2.0	0.3
Tranquilizers	17.3	7.9	6.9	2.6	10.8	5.3	4.3	1.1	4.4	2.5	1.7	0.2
Heroin	2.3	1.4	0.5	0.4	1.2	0.6	0.3	0.2	0.6	0.2	0.2	0.2
Narcotics other than heroin	9.4	3.8	3.9	1.7	6.0	2.7	2.6	0.6	2.4	1.1	1.1	0.2

	In their lifetime	In the last 12 mo.	In the last mo.
Any illicit drug above	55.0%	44.8%	30.9%
Any illicit drug above other than marijuana	35.3%	26.1%	14.7%
Any illicit drug above (other than marijuana) on 3 or more occasions	23.5%	16.1%	7.1%
Alcohol	90.5 7.5 29.4 53.6	85.0 12.7 39.6 32.7	68.5 22.1 6.0

TABLE 14-2.
COMPARISON OF HIGH SCHOOL SENIORS IN 1969 and 1975 (MALES ONLY)

	Percent of males who have ever used the drug by the end of senior year.			
	Class of 1969[a]		Class of 1975[b]	
Cigarettes:				
Ever used	65.1%		76.8%	
1–2 times only		12.5		28.9
More than 2 times		52.6		47.9
Alcohol:				
Ever used	80.9		91.5	
1–2 times only		12.7		4.6
More than 2 times		68.2		86.9
Marijuana:				
Ever used	19.4		54.2	
1–2 times only		6.6		9.3
More than 2 times		12.8		44.9
Amphetamines:				
Ever used	8.7		19.4	
1– times only		3.4		3.8
More than 2 times		5.3		15.6
Barbiturates:				
Ever used	5.4		18.3	
1–2 times only		2.0		5.8
More than 2 times		3.4		12.5
Psychedelics:				
Ever used	6.0		18.5	
1–2 times only		2.5		7.8
More than 2 times		3.5		10.7
Heroin:				
Ever used	1.2		2.7	
1–2 times only		0.4		2.0
More than 2 times		0.8		0.7

drugs—even experimental users—ran a substantial risk of harming themselves and others. Finally, the majority view of high school seniors on the use of illicit drugs, other than hashish and marijuana, duplicated answers from a national survey of twenty-three-year-old males in 1974; and if the groups of respondents are to be believed, it seems that changes in marijuana laws may have, at most, a moderate effect on use among high school and college youth. It appears that the youth studied seemed to have made a choice about whether to use marijuana—perhaps because nearly all have some exposure to the effects of excess to this drug by the time they leave high school.

Recently, however, there have been indications that "harder" drugs are becoming attractive to high school and college youth. Heroin, which causes powerful addiction, has long been considered the affliction of the criminal, the derelict, and the debauched. It is now increasingly attacking the youth in all segments of metropolitan areas. Dr. Michael M. Baden, the former Deputy Chief Medical Examiner of New York City, stated that heroin use, in the late 1970s, was the leading cause of deaths among teen-agers in New York City, where drug addiction has become a major public health problem apart from its extensive criminal aspects. Amplifying on drug addiction in New York, Dr. Baden reported that hepatitis, tetanus, and endocarditis as well as homicide and suicide are in high incidence among the heroin-user population. The problem is by no means limited to the schools, of course, but as stated previously, a large number of these addicts are of high school age. Some are even younger. They will live short, empty lives with neither hope nor meaning. They no longer have a choice.

Although most of the serious drug problems exist in the heart of the major cities where there are too many people, too little money, and too little to do, the problem can be found everywhere, from the worst slum areas to the wealthiest suburbs.

The common factor underlying drug abuse is the attempt to escape from either physical or emotional problems. Young people are particularly vulnerable. Usually they are introduced to drugs by friends, not by "pushers." It is hard to resist a group when you are the only holdout. It is a well-known fact that gangs, and even otherwise amiable social groups, are often responsible for the introduction of illegal drugs.

The figures mentioned are alarming, but they do not begin to reflect the cost of the abuse of narcotics and certain other drugs. Thousands of drug abusers live for years in the shadow of society—only half alive, only half free.

---

[a] Based on a national study of males, entitled *Youth in Transition* (N=1600). See *Drugs and American Youth* (Ann Arbor: Institute for Social Research, 1973) by Lloyd Johnston.

[b] Based on *Monitoring the Future: A Continuing Study of the Lifestyles and Valse of Youth* (N=16,000, including approximately 8,000 males.)

WHY DRUGS?

To cope intelligently with drug problems, one needs to understand what kinds of appeals drugs offer. While people have used them for a number of reasons, the most basic reason is that the individual involved lacks an adequate personality and fails to identify with adult goals. Because of his inability to formulate some type of identification with mature goals, such a person finds drugs useful in achieving two adjusting objectives: (1) *Creating a pleasure-seeking structure environment for himself in which he can pursue effortless pleasurable activities;* and (2) *eliminating the intrusive demands and responsibilities associated with adult personality status.* A person afflicted with such a crippling personality turns to drugs because they speed him toward hedonistic objectives.

> *After he takes his first few shots, the addict literally exclaims, "Boy, this is what I've been looking for all my life. What could be easier?" By merely injecting a needle under his skin, he satisfies his quest for immediate and effortless pleasure. Apart from the voluptuous thrill of the "kick," he reports increased self-confidence and feelings of self-esteem, decreased anxiety and grandiose illusions (of wealth, power, and omnipotence). Primary needs, such as hunger and sex urges, fade into the background and, although not directly gratified, are rendered so uninsistent as to incapable of generating anxiety or frustration when their satisfaction is threatened or denied. Fear of pain is also satisfied as the threshold for pain perception is raised and as anxiety-producing implications are minimized. In fact, because of the drug's specific inhibition of the self-critical faculty, the environment in general assumes a more benevolent and less stringent aspect.* [49]

In surveying the available literature on drug abuse, it is evident that there are many other explanations and ideas concerning the etiology of drug abuse. Various disciplines (psychology, physiology, sociology, etc.) have contributed to literature on drug abuse. In addition, many kinds of drug users have been delineated, and the causes leading to drug abuse are now thought to be multiple and frequently interrelated. All of the disciplines appear to concentrate on inadequacies of the personalities of the users. David P. Ausubel, apsychiatrist and expert on drug abuse, concludes that:

> *Differential susceptibility to drug addiction is primarily a reflection of the relative adjustment value which narcotics possess for different individuals. At any given moment, a person exposed to narcotics will only become an addict if the drug is able to do something significant for him psychologically, that is, to satisfy certain of his currently important needs.* [50]

[49]*Ibid.*
[50]David P. Ausubel, "Causes and Types of Drug Addiciton," *Key Issues*, Vol. 1, Nov. 1961, p. 12.

Perhaps the most definitive analysis of drug abuse among adolescents is Isador Chein's *The Road to H*. Chein agrees with Ausubel's hypothesis that drug susceptibility is associated with the *adjustive* value of using drugs and concludes that:

> *The evidence indicates that all addicts suffer from deep-rooted major personality disorders. Although psychiatric diagnosis are apt to vary, a particular set of symptoms seems to be common to most juvenile addicts. They are not able to enter into prolonged, close, friendly relations with either peers or adults; they have difficulties in assuming a masculine role; they are frequently overcome by a sense of futility, expectations of failure, and general depression; they are easily frustrated and made anxious, and they find frustration and anxiety intolerable.* [51]

In recent years, drug abuse has moved from city ghettos into the large communities, to middle-class and upper-middle-class neighborhoods and suburbs. Many adults and young people in these more affluent areas, like their less fortunate fellows, have found in drugs an answer to their problems and frustrations—a new excitement and an escape from boredom. Drug abuse initially offers them, as it does to others, a temporary sense of satisfaction and euphoria. Then the drugs proceed to destroy their whole spirit.

The high school student most likely to use drugs, according to a number of high school principals, deans, and suburban psychiatrists, is the bright student who does not participate in school activities, who often has a troubled home life, and feels alienated from society.

Youth is an age of questioning, of learning for oneself what is real and true, a time of keen concern about "Who am I?" For some youths, drugs offer new possibilities in this quest. They also offer an escape from an era of rapid, revolutionary change that leaves adults, as well as youths, bewildered and uneasy as to what tomorrow may bring. The steady dwindling of our environment, the erosion of civil rights, the spread of social injustice, and the decay of leadership in America (revealed dramatically in the final months of the Nixon era and its aftermath) have all provided nefarious examples for youth in America. And offstage is the menace of an obliterating nuclear war or some nameless total catastrophe.

Rapid social changes widen the "generation gap," stated Kenneth Keniston, a psychologist at Yale University, and the here-and-now becomes more important to the youth who "can no longer commit themselves unquestionably to the lifestyles, attitudes, and skills of their parents and other adults. To do so is to condemn one's self to obsolescence in the modern world." Many youths live under tremendous pressure from their parents and others in school, and, to some, school work seems contrived, a form of marking time, and hence irrelevant," stated Dana L. Farnswort, Director of the University Health Services at Harvard University.

---

[51] Isador Chein et al., *The Road To H*, Basic Books, Inc., New York, 1964, p. 14.

PORTRAIT OF AN ADOLESCENT DRUG ABUSER

In general, the addict is a disordered person, undisciplined and insistent on the immediate satisfaction of real or imagined needs. This general description is not very helpful, however, for it might also apply to many nonaddicts. The fact is that recognition of the drug addict, especially when he is obtaining his customary youth dosage, is extremely difficult. The behavior of the drug addict is not well understood, and detection frequently requires the application of sophisticated laboratory techniques.

There are a few overt diagnostic characteristics, such as scars and abscesses that result from intravenous injections, and dilation of the pupils and muscular tremulousness that are caused by the use of cocaine or benzedrine. But it *is* difficult to recognize smokers of marijuana although they sometimes have a characteristic facial flush. And opiate users can only be positively identified by urine analysis, which may detect traces of the drug as much as 10 days after it was last used. Because of this difficulty in recognizing addicts, recognition should be attempted only under hospital conditions, that is, in a drug-free environment that permits prolonged observation and complete physical and laboratory examination.

Although it is extremely difficult to recognize an addict on the basis of immediate physical evidence, as we have noted, there are other indications of addiction that eventually appear in his lifestyle and behavior and that can be observed over a period of time. The tolerant, large-dose, chronic drug abuser may not exhibit obvious physical signs of his drug usage, but he will show signs of social, economic, and emotional deterioration (e.g., downgrading of job or school work, run-down physical condition, and unkempt appearance). Such a person also tends to become unreliable, irritable, and unstable. Various other behavior changes are also quite predominant.

Some characteristics of the adolescent drug user are as follows:

1. He tends to be *materialistic* since, in a sense, he has ceased to believe that his emotional needs can be met in a positive manner.

2. He approaches life with a profound sense of *inadequacy* and *helplessness,* which overwhelms him and causes him to flee from the realities of everyday living. He seeks the comfortable vacuum that the drug offers him. The drug has value for the adolescent not solely because it can provide pleasurable sensations, but because it becomes a buffer between him and the society that he fears.

3. Since he is an escapist, he is *unable to relate* to other people in a meaningful, constructive, realistic fashion. He can only take from others in a dependent and passive manner and is unable to give anything in return in either a physical or an emotional sense.

4. He is usually involved in a *conflictual relationship with parental figures.* He feels that his parents do not understand him and also anticipates

that the parent will act in a manner detrimental to his personal interests. On occasions, it is found that the parents of the drug addict are also inadequate people. They are unable to live up to the criteria expected in a parent-child relationship. This weakness in the parental relationship permeates the entire living situation. Because of relatively instability and immature personality structure, the teen-age drug addict perceives his environmental situation out of perspective. As a result, he experiences great difficulty where only a moderate difficulty should exist.

5. *He perceives the adult world as an unstable place,* and he prefers to seek out new security of an infantile type of relationship. This infantile type of relationship may serve as a protection from dealing with the more complex situations and responsibilities that can be expected of one who aspires to be accepted as an adult.

DOES ADDICTION LEAD TO CRIME?

Some studies suggest that many of the known narcotic addicts had some trouble with the law before they became addicted. Once addicted, they may become even more involved with crime because it costs so much to support the heroin habit. For example, an addict may have to spend from $75 to $100 a day for one day's supply of heroin.

Most authorities agree that the addict's involvement with crime is not a direct effect of the drug itself, but turning to crime is usually the only way of getting that much money. The addict's crimes are nearly always thefts or other crimes against property, and not often crimes of passion or violence.

DRUG ABUSE: LAW ENFORCEMENT PROBLEM

All the drugs commonly abused are either completely outlawed, as are heroin and LSD, or they can be obtained only from the underworld peddler, from thieves, or from diversion of legitimate supplies under the control of physicians, hospitals, or pharmacies. Thus, the drug abuse problem has immediate legal aspects, and law enforcement becomes extremely important.

Problems of enforcement are complicated in the metropolitan areas of cities in which there is a large import/export maritime business. In New York and California the problems of controlling drug abuse are complicated by the smuggling of heroin and marijuana via ships, planes, and motor vehicles coming from abroad. In addition, there are no laws to control the importing of barbiturates and other dangerous drugs.

The problem of narcotics will continue and, without doubt, expand as long as there are ineffective controls at the source of production. Law enforcement is thus continually seeking ways and means of implementing international control. Efforts to increase law enforcement personnel at points of entry in order to insure closer inspection is probably the first step in controlling the illegal drug traffic. Measures to control narcotic traffic depend on the degree of cooperation among nations. At the present there is little effective control over the production of the raw materials for making drugs. This is an area where immediate attention will have to be focused.

International control is only one of the problems confronting law enforcement. As far as adolescents are concerned, as stated earlier, experimentation with the use of drugs is quite prevalent in the schools. Thus, the effective international control of narcotic traffic is of paramount importance to law enforcement agencies. Without "customers" narcotic traffic will dissipate.

Public school teachers can play an important part in the struggle to prevent narcotic use. For they are in position to be able to detect experimentation on the part of youngsters who utilize such drugs for a "thrill."

The search for drugs is one of the most difficult problems faced by an officer. Drugs may be in a solid, powder, or liquid form. in its pure state, the "bulk" of a drug may be very small.

One popular way to carry drugs obtained illegally is to keep them in an old prescription bottle. The officers should be suspicious of any bottle with a worn or dirty label. Illegally obtained drugs are often hidden in the bottom of a cigarette pack. The cigarettes are cut off and the pack appears normal. Drugs may also be found in the belt of pants, cigarette lighters, toothpaste tubes, flashlights, and lipstick tubes which have had their contents removed. Tablets and capsules may be folded into letters, handkerchiefs, personal papers, books and used papers, or secreted in the linings of clothing. Occasionally, drugs may be dissolved into innocent-appearing liquids.

Ways to Determine Illegal Possession, Use, and Source of Drugs

The police may come into contact with drug abusers in many different ways. They may find drugs—or evidence of their use—during a routine check or in the course of an arrest for a totally unconnected offense. They may actually see a person taking drugs, find evidence of unusual behavior or may encounter someone involved in dealing drugs. In each of these cases, the police seek several items of information to build a successful case or to save a life. They must be able to answer the following questions:

1. Does the suspect have drugs in his or her possession?

2. What are the drugs, and where did they come from?

3. Is the possession legal?

4. Has the suspect taken doses of the drugs?

There are literally thousands of drugs on the market. Some require a physician's prescription, but many do not. Prescription drugs can, generally speaking, be purchased only at a pharmacy, but nonprescription items are often bought at supermarkets, variety stores, grocery stores, and newsstands.

A police officer's best approach to questioning relies on the principle that a suspect is innocent until proven guilty. Such an attitude is essential in producing evidence that will be permissible in court, and, incidentally, often results in digging out the greatest amount of helpful evidence. As the questioning proceeds, an officer should remember that many of a subject's answers can be verified later. Questioning often follows this pattern:

Are you sick now? Have you been Ill?
Who is your doctor? Did you receive a prescription?
Is this medicine yours? Does it belong to someone else?
Do you know what it is?
Where was your prescription filled?
When did you last take the medicine?
How long have you been taking the medicine?
What is the medicine being taken for?
Are you under the care of a doctor? Do you take the medicine according to his orders?

By using this pattern of questioning, an officer offers to a suspect a logical alibi and appears, at the same time, ready to believe a story of illness. With this approach, a subject may even volunteer that the medicine is being taken under a doctor's prescription. Whether true or not, an officer is protected legally in case a subject is following the orders of a bona fide physician. At this point an officer should attempt to verify the answers to some questions:

Doctor's name. This should appear on the prescription label and can be verified by telephoning the doctor.
Name of pharmacy. This can be verified by calling the pharmacist.
Prescription date. The pharmacist's records will help there.
How medicine is taken. Check number of tablets or capsules left in the bottle against the number the pharmacist said he dispensed.
Is the medicine the same as that prescribed? Check with the pharmacist. (Pharmacists give all prescriptions an individual number. This appears on the container given to the patient. The pharmacist will need this number to refer back to the original prescription.)

With this procedure, an officer has either confirmed or invalidated a subject's story. Remember that both physicians and pharmacists are generally most helpful and cooperative in these investigations.

TEEN-AGERS, DRINKING, AND THE LAW

Use of alcohol beverages by teen-agers has shown a tremendous increase during the last five years. In 1975, the proportion of male seniors that had been drinking on three or more occasions in their lifetime was almost 90 percent, up nearly 20 percent from 1969. In the state of California alone, the State Department of Health reported that in 1975 alcohol-related arrests increased by 4781—juveniles accounted for 4163 (87 percent) of the aforementioned arrests. Further, in 1975, drunken driving arrests totaled nearly 16 percent of all juvenile alcohol offense arrests, against 10 percent in 1974. A national survey completed in 1974 reported that 63 percent of boys and 54 percent of girls in the seventh grade have had a drink. By the time they reached the twelfth grade, this has increased to 93 percent of the boys and 87 percent of the girls. Drinking among school dropouts, according to the report, is greater than among those remaining in school. Therefore, teen-age drinking is actually higher than reported from information collected from school populations.

All preoccupation with youthful drug abuse have obscured the fact that in every survey, alcohol was the most frequently used and preferred drug. It is by far, the first psyche-altering drug employed.

TRENDS

During the past few years, the established mode has changed significantly. The following trends have been well documented:

1. Drinking during and out of school has extended down to grammar school students and is more frequently encountered than in the past.

2. Girls are involved increasingly in "ever having used" and in regular drinking by the time they graduate from high school. As many girls as boys use alcoholic beverages, but they do not yet use them so often.

3. The combined use of alcohol and other drugs is observed often. Juvenile polydrug use with alcohol as a basic intoxicant is a growing problem.

4. Not only are more youngsters trying alcoholic beverages, but larger numbers are drinking heavily and consistently. Pubescent alcoholism has been diagnosed in a number of pediatric psychiatric clinics.

Generally speaking, it is quite evident from official records that the general public has an attitude of apathy toward enforcement of Alcohol Beverage Control laws throughout the state. Most people, even juries, seem to feel that it is only an ABC violation, and therefore cannot be very serious. Exceptions to this are death or bodily injury, accidents, or crimes of violence. This indifferent attitude by adults is transmitted to minors. Most high school and college students would never stoop to commit petty theft or any similar crime, but they don't give a second thought to an ABC violation, even though it is commonly, in fact, a misdemeanor.

The most important factor in the life of most students is acceptance by their peers. If drinking is favored by a group, it is likely that all its members will drink. It is estimated that 80 percent of high school students throughout the United States consume some alcoholic beverages at some time during their high school career, and, in most cases, they are oblivious to the fact they have committed a crime, or they just "don't care." Occasional drinking, now and then, has been a fairly conventional activity of youth growing up in America.

Adolescents have imbibed both for the effects of the ethanol and for the symbolic meaning of the act of drinking. Partaking of our national intoxicant has often been seen as an important step to adulthood—a treatment for adolescent shyness and anxiety. Drinking thus has the double effect of producing and of justifying disinhibited acting-out behavior. The cultural symbolism of drinking by male adolescents is that it means "being one of the boys" and "being a man."

Youthful imbibing, then, derives directly from our cultural attitudes toward drinking. Although legally forbidden, drinking by those under age tends to be condoned, or at least understood, by most parents and authorities.

THE ADOLESCENT DRINKER

Reports from the National Institute of Alcoholism and Alcohol Abuse confirm the rapid increase in heavy, teen-age drinking. Dr. M. E. Chafetz, Director of NIAAA, said that five percent of young Americans have a drinking problem. The estimated number of problem drinkers between the ages of 12 and 17 is 1.3 million with 750,000 believed to be hardcore alcoholics. A Boston suburb study found that by age 18, seven percent of the boys were problem drinkers. That family, school, or police difficulties. If these estimates are correct, then the teen-ager is drinking just as unwisely as adults, for five to seven percent of adults are also in trouble with their usage of alcohol.

"Drying out" centers report a staggering increase in teen-age crimes. One program in Houston has witnessed an increase in this age group from only six teen-agers to 1200 in two years. Eight- and nine-year-olds have been registered for alcohol detoxification in this and other clinics.

Alcohol Anonymous (AA) has 27 groups for "teen-agers and pre-teen-agers" in Southern California alone. A report form the New York City schools states that 10 percent of the junior and senior high school students are "already, or potential alcoholics."

Many of the well-known signs of tissue damage by alcohol are not seen in pediatric alcoholics. These will come later. Gastronitis and gastrointestinal hemorrhage, though, are present in young and old alike. They are the result of stimulation of hydrochloric acid production and the retardation of acid absorption from the gastroduodenal tract. Inflammatory and ulcerative changes in the mucous membrane result. At Children's Hospital in Los Angeles, patients 12 to 20 years old with alcohol-related ailments like gastritis and internal bleeding are not uncommon.

It is, however, the behavioral toxicity that dominates the picture of problem drinking by teen-agers. Repeated truances, family disruptions, and illegal activities are open signs that alcohol may be the cause. The stealing of beer, wine, or saleable items is well known. The suburban form of this activity is called "garaging." Rowdy group-drinking parties, some of which culminate in the use of dangerous weapons, are regularly reported in the press. Intoxicated youngsters are apt to become involved in malicious mischief at schools, parks, and unoccupied dwellings. The arrest rate for intoxication of those under 18 has tripled during the last decade. Accidental death, a leading cause of lethality in this age group, is particularly frequent among adolescent imbibers. A third to one-half of all accidents are associated with drinking.

Considerable controversy centers around the effects of lowering the legal drinking age in some states and the incidence of car accidents. In Michigan, during the first year that 18-year-olds could legally buy alcoholic beverages, the auto accident rate for those 18 to 20 years of age increased by 119 percent. Arrests in New Jersey rose 60 percent.

On one side of the argument are those who say that these statistics merely reflect normal yearly increases and the differential treatment accorded young drivers by the police. Others view these figures more seriously and believe that young people will die, will be injured on the highway at a rate far exceeding the worst years of the Viet Nam conflict.

Sixty percent of those killed in drunk driving accidents are in their teens. Even in a single year, the jump in alcohol-related accidents is impressive. The California Highway Patrol reported that this in the 12 to 20 age-group rose from 268 in 1973 to 375 in 1974. Traffic injuries rose from 4449 in 1973 to 6252 in 1974.

CAUSES

What causes the teen-ager drinking problem? Why do teen-agers drink? Most experts are of the opinion that drinking is a status symbol. Teen-agers are striving for understanding; they are striving for acceptance by their peers, by their own social group. If a particular group tends to drink or to lean toward this vice, the pressures on each teen-ager to stay in and be one of the group are very strong regardless of the kind or amount of drinking practiced by his or her particular set of friends. Heavy drinking often starts on playgrounds, street corners, and similar areas in which youth gathers. Drinking at special school events and athletic contests has occasionally terminated in riots and forced the cancellation of the event.

Whether a child will drink, and how she or he will behave if drunk, is strongly determined by the culture. It is the culture or subculture that provides cues to family, friends, or mass media and informs youth of what is permitted. In certain subcultures, aggressiveness while drunk is considered normal behavior.

The individual's personality is also a determinate in the development of destructive drinking practices. At times it is difficult to determine whether certain personality features are either the cause or the result of excessive drinking. Diminished personal controls, unpredictable impulses, and antisocial trends are supposed to be predispositions of personality. So they may be, but it should be remembered that alcohol as an intoxicant also induces such behavior.

Young people with personality defects in the area of mood and ego controls do tend to seek out alcohol in order to deal with their feelings of anxiety and instability. If drinking seems to solve their problems, then they are later inclined to turn to it more often and in larger amounts. Not all youthful problem drinkers have a major personality defect. They may be relatively intact psychologically, but may all the same be well advanced in alcoholism because drinking is a cultural or family norm.

POLICE ROLE

On their first encounter with the law and alcoholic beverages, many youngsters receive proper guidance and counseling that result in what seems to be good motivation and direction. Yet the changes are strong that they will not continue this newly won pattern. Many of them have personality weaknesses that need continual bolstering. And frequently, those who have the most obvious personality weaknesses turn out to be the leaders of a particular group, and it takes tremendous courage for a young person to say "No" to his friends. If a boy has a parent who owns a liquor store, then he's a sure winner to be a club president at school. Or, if he happens to work in a grocery or liquor store, the pressures to push a case of beer or two out with the old boxes near the incinerator become tremendous. Even though a youngster repeatedly ignores such urgings, the demands become so great that with an average young man, the desire to succeed with his own group overcomes what that youngster knows to be right. Law enforcement has experienced numerous cases of this type, and it is always disheartening to see the crushed personality when a young man is caught in the act, or subsequent investigation proves to the owner of a market that his employee was not trustworthy.

To prevent overindulgence in such a widespread and cultural-entrenched substance like alcohol seems hardly possible. It is especially difficult since all patterns of usage do not condemn it; some patterns even applaud excessive drinking. Any adolescent who runs counter to cultural pressures, who wishes to abstain from alcohol entirely, should be reinforced in his or her decision. Unfortunately, in a society in which alcohol stands for hospitality, fun, sexuality, and manliness, it is difficult, if not impossible, for most young people to swim against the alcoholic flood.

Exhorting them to renounce drink will rarely work. Instead of proscribing the intake of alcohol, its usage should be wisely prescribed. Children should learn responsible drinking; moderation should be stressed; and drunkenness condemned by parents in words and deeds. An episode of drunkenness that results in the destruction of property, injury, or in passing-out should be met with firm disapproval. Unfortunately, such behavior is often overtly or covertly reinforced.

In the area of possible cures, law enforcement agencies, church and school groups, fraternal and service clubs, as well as parental associations could cooperate in a mass program of communications and make them effective. Persuasively designed and edited handouts and brochures should be considered. As a matter of fact, the system should be incorporated in regular programs dealing with law enforcement, probation, and community self-helps. Another method is a long-range prevention program of educating adults, especially parents, on how to conduct themselves so they will provide good examples of behavior, especially when using alcoholic beverages.

Law enforcement agencies alone cannot eliminate teen-age drinking problems. The burden of work, the increase in population, the slow increase in granting of added personnel (which is true in most agencies) make it impossible to cover all the bases. The most important factor in preventing the use of alcoholic beverage on the part of juveniles is elimination of the causes.

Effective control of the juvenile alcohol problem is not in sight at present. Any program of control requires considerable positive action by the local police and should include the help and support of the vendors of alcoholic beverages. The assistance of interested laypersons and youth-serving agencies should also be enrolled.

SEX OFFENSES

Sex offenders are either a danger to the community or a nuisance that the community need not tolerate. Sex offenses include rape, indecent exposure, exhibitionism, incest, child molesting and homosexuality, as well as a variety of related acts. Legislators have taken the position that sex offenders are different from other types of law violators. Therefore, this has led to legislation that results in placing sex offenders in a state of limbo, somewhere between the criminal and the mentally ill.

Legislation defining sex psychopaths and establishing administrative procedures for their custody, treatment, and release, was passed by some thirteen states between 1937 and 1950 and has been extended to other states since that time. The procedures leading up to legislation were similar in many different jurisdictions. In a review of the development of sex psychopath laws, the late criminologist, Edwin Sutherland, in an article titled "The Diffusion of Sexual Psychopath Laws," noted a sequence characterized by (1) an upspring of fear within the community as a result of a few serious sex crimes, (2) community response in the form of fear and anxiety, leading to (3) the gathering of information from an appointed committee and recommendations that generally were uncritically accepted by state legislatures. Usually, committees proceeded to make recommendations based largely on the absence of facts. Sutherland noted that the laws embodied a set of implicit assumptions that were explicit in much of the popular literature on sex offenses. Such assumptions were largely based on the notion that all sex offenders were potentially dangerous, that they were recidivists, that they can be accurately diagnosed and efficiently treated by psychiatrists. These laws were passed in the name of science, although the scientific method was completely ignored.

Taking various legislative acts into consideration, it can be concluded that the sexual offender is an adult or juvenile who becomes involved in any sexual play (masturbation excluded) that falls outside the socially acceptable scope of normal sexual behavior. Normal sexuality is regarded as heterosexual relations voluntarily and privately practiced in a normal manner by responsible adults, not very closely related. Although such relationships are usually preceded by marriage, there are occasions when marriage does not occur.

Sexual deviation is responsible for the majority of sex crimes. However, although rape and incest are always criminal, such crimes are often committed by sexually deviant people. They are thought of as psychologically abnormal because of their cultural and emotional ties. According to Kinsey,[52] a sex offender is a person who violates a law prohibiting some kind of sexual behavior and is apprehended by the authorities. Furthermore, sex offenders make up a very large segment of the population.

There is an almost universal disregard of the prohibitions of sex offense laws. The ignoring of such laws motivated the following comment from Kinsey:

> *All of these and still other types of sexual behavior are illicit activities, each performance of which is punishable as a crime under the law. The persons involved in these activities, taken as a whole constitute more than 95% of the total male population. Only a relatively small proportion of the males who are sent to penal institutions for sex offenses have been involved in behavior which is materially different from the behavior of most of the males in the population. But it is the total 95% of the male population for which the judge of the board of public safety or church, or civic group demands apprehension, arrest, and conviction, when they call for a clean-up of the sex offenders in a community. It is, in fact, a proposal that 5% of the population should support the other 95% in penal institutions.[53]*

[52]A. C. Kinsey, W. B. Pomeroy, and G. E. Martin, *Sexual Behavior in the Human Male*, W. B. Saunders, Co., Philadelphia and London, 1962, p. 133.
[53]*Ibid.*, p. 134.

Morris Ploscowe, in his book *Sex and Law*, has pointed out that the conclusion that 95 percent of the male population could be jailed because of violations of sex offense laws is an exaggeration. Such a statement, according to Ploscowe, presupposes that such legislation is uniform throughout the country, that all sexual activity except solitary masturbation and normal marital intercourse is universally prohibited, and that these laws invariably prescribe jail and prison sentences for their violation. This, however, is not so. One of the most remarkable features of American sex offense laws, continues Ploscowe, is their wide disparity in the types of sexual behavior prohibited and their extraordinary variation in the penalties imposed for similar offenses.

LAW AND ADOLESCENT SEXUAL OFFENSES

Failure to accord the child in the United States a distinct status position that is closely integrated with the larger structure of American society and the resulting minimum institutionalization of norms for governing adolescent behavior has numerous important implications for defining and sanctioning the sexual conduct of youngsters in American society. Because of the lack of transitional status between childhood and adulthood in the United States, numerous problems have developed in the area of the law and sex offenses. Such a problem has resulted in the following conclusions of Albert J. Reiss, in his article entitled, "Sex Offenses: The Marginal Status of the Adolescent."

1. The perception of adolescent sex offenders as neither child nor adult tends to (a) encourage considerable variation in definition of their sexual offenses; (b) lead to differential treatment and differential adjudication of their cases of sexual behavior on the basis of age, sex, socioeconomic status, and jurisdictional consideration; and (c) obscure the degree to which they are denied the due process of law.

2. The age-based status reference point for evaluating adolescent sexual offenses is a factor in the sanctions applied to their deviation. When adolescent sex offenders are viewed as "not adult," they are generally overprotected and absolved from moral responsibility for their behavior, thereby weakening the moral integration of the total society. When they are viewed as "not children" there often is a tendency to deal more punitively with them than with adults who commit similar sex offenses.

3. The sexual behavior of adolescents is primarily peer-organized and peer-controlled. As such, it reflects the attempt by adolescents to achieve a compromise between being encouraged to behave like adults and being denied the rights and privileges of that status. An examination of the peer-organized basis for adolescent sexual con-

duct provides a normative basis for evaluating their behavior in relation to the larger social structure in which they are held accountable for their behavior.[54]

Taking these conclusions into consideration, one wonders what acts committed by youngsters would be defined as violations of sexual conduct norms. Furthermore, to what degree does a youngster's status as "not child" and "not adult" encourage misinterpretation in the definition of an adolescent's sexual conduct as a sex offense?

Despite some variation in the legal codes from state to state in American society, the statutes define the acts for which violaters are classified as adult sex offenders. Such classification on the part of adults is not complex. However, the problem of defining the juvenile as a sex offender is extremely confusing. Most juvenile court statutes not only define the violation of all criminal statutory codes as sufficient ground for finding of delinquency but also hold that if the child is growing up in a situation undesirable to his welfare, he or she may be adjudicated a delinquent. For all practical purposes, then, the definition of a juvenile sex offender rests with the standards adhered to in a respective juvenile jurisdiction. The statutes, in fact, prescribe that the finding be that the child is a delinquent, and not a specific type of offender.

Juvenile court law statutes are phrased in such general and inclusive terms that *any sexual act* or conduct can be viewed as a delinquent offense. The general provision pertaining to "lewd, immoral, and lascivious behavior" can be construed to cover all deviations from sexual conduct norms. There is considerable ambiguity as to what sexual conduct is to be defined as a violation and what is permitted sexual behavior for adolescents. Juveniles who are held to be guilty of a sex offense often are not charged with a specific sex conduct violation. Categories such as "incorrigibility," "loitering," lewd and immoral conduct," "runaway," and similar charges frequently are the preferred allegations, particularly if the juvenile court has a policy to avoid stigmatizing an individual with a sex offense record. In many jurisdictions, minors are charged with "disturbing the peace" and petitions state the offense as such. The terms "sex offense" and "sexual offender" are not clearly defined, then, for adolescents in legal codes or in adjudication of cases involving the violation of sexual conduct norms.[55]

However, according to Reiss:

> *Adolescents themselves set standards for what is a violation of their sexual codes. The standards in these adolescent codes vary considerably according to the social status position of the adolescent and his family in the larger society. Among young lower-status adolescent boys, perhaps the most*

[54]A. J. Reiss, "Sex Offenses: The Marginal Status of the Adolescent," *Law and Contemporary Problems*, School of Law, Duke University, vol. 25, no. 2, Spring 1960, p. 310.
[55]*Ibid.*, p. 312.

common mode of heterosexual intercourse is the "gang-shag" or "gang bang." A gang of boys usually knows one or more girls who are easy "pick-ups" for the group who will consent to serial intercourse with the members of the gang. To understand this behavior several peer normative factors need to be taken into account. First of all, the girl in the "gang bang" is almost always one who gives her consent. She is not being sexually exploited in any sense of forcible rape. In fact, when she consents to being picked up, she understands that she is to be a partner in the heterosexual coition. Lower-status boys clearly distinguish between "putting it to a girl" (she consents) and "making a girl" (she does not consent). Fewer lower-status boys, particularly delinquent boys, will "make a girl" although almost all frequently engage in heterosexual intercourse and most have at least participated in a gang bang. Most lower-status adolescent boys express the view: "Why should I make a girl when I can get all I want without it." The opportunities for heterosexual coition with consent are ever-present to lower-status boys, so that they negatively sanction forcible rape. This is not to say that some adolescent girls are not forcibly raped by an adolescent boy or even a gang, but the proportion who are is, without doubt, very small.[56]

Regarding the inordinate amount of contacts that girls have with the authorities, Reiss continues:

It is not so much the sexual act of coition that brings the girls to the attention of the legal authorities as it is either of these consequences of the act—pre-marital pregnancy or venereal infection. The couple is seldom caught in the act of coition. Since girls are more likely than boys to be defined as the carriers of the venereal disease, a girl who is picked up by police or juvenile authorities is almost always given a physical examination to determine whether she has had sexual intercourse, now has venereal infection or is pregnant. This is particularly true for runaway girls. Boys seldom are given a complete physical examination for venereal infection as are girls. Even less often are they questioned as to their sex experiences. There is a great variation among jurisdictions in this respect, however, personnel in some are more likely than in others to learn about the sexual deviation of girls. The life chances of a girl before police and juvenile authorities, therefore, are more favorable to definition as a sex delinquent than are the life chances of a boy.

Adolescent boys come to the attention of the court as heterosexual sex offenders usually only when the morality of the girl's family is offended. The most common form of complaint is for the family to define coition as "rape" of their daughter. Research evidence shows that in most cases the

[56]*Ibid.,* pp. 312–13.

boy is not a rapist in any technical sense that force or coercion was used. The act occurred through common consent. The complaint arises because the girl, under family pressure, charges that she did not consent. Although many complaints arise in this way, it does not follow, of course, that some delinquent boys' gangs do not forcibly rape a young girl or that boys individually do not engage in such acts; it is rather to emphasize that available evidence strongly indicates that most heterosexual coition between adolescents occurs through mutual consent. The girl has a reputation. She is sought out or picked up. She knows what is expected of her, consents, and services one or more boys. No money is exchanged. [57]

CLASSIFICATION OF SEXUAL OFFENSES

Incest

Sexual intercourse between two persons, married or not, who are too closely related by blood affinity to be married is considered incest. The element of age is not considered and want of chastity is no defense. Blood relation, in some states, is not necessary. Furthermore, relations between stepmother and stepson are incest until the death of the natural parent.

Sadomasochism

Sadism is a paraphiliac neurosis in which the will to power is sexually accentuated, and masochism is one in which the will to submission is sexually accentuated.

Authorities in the field view masochism as the seeking of what would normally be painful for sexual reasons. Such pain is tied in with domination, humiliation, and degradation.

The attainment of sexual pleasure from acts of cruelty and the infliction of pain is sadism. It is interesting to note that the individual inflicted with this psychological illness is often undersexed rather than oversexed. Sadistic crimes include murder, attempted murder, assault with intent to do bodily harm, battery, bodily injuries, sexual assaults, damage to property, maiming, and other offenses involving bodily harm.

Rape

Rape is defined as an act of sexual intercourse performed with the female, not the wife of the perpetrator, without her consent. Statutory rape is an act of sexual intercourse performed upon the person of a female who is under the age of consent

[57]*Ibid.*, p. 313.

and not the wife of the perpetrator. Regardless how slight the penetration may be, rape is committed if there is penetration.

Necrophilia

Necrophilia (sexual intercourse with a female cadaver) is very uncommon. A necrophiliac either kills a woman and has sexual intercourse with the body or otherwise violates it, or procures corpses which he rapes, mutilates, or uses to commit necrophagy (eating the corpse).

Homosexuality

In homosexuality, sexual desires are directed toward an individual of the same sex. Furthermore, the homosexual is often an individual endowed with characteristics and emotional traits of the opposite sex.

Sodomy and Pederasty

Sodomy, according to penal law, refers to any actual sexual relations between men. The penal law includes sodomy under crimes against nature; oral and anal penetration of a homosexual or heterosexual nature are included, as well as sex acts with animals and birds.

Anal coitus, with a boy as the passive and adult as the active partner, is referred to as pederasty.

Transvestism

A transvestite utilizes the garments of the opposite sex for sexual gratification.

Pedophilia

Pedophilia is an abnormal craving for a child, whether it be female or male, on the part of an adult. However, such behavior is illegal only when it attains overt proportions.

Obscenity and Pornography

The expression, representation, or display to others in certain contexts or situations of something culturally regarded as shocking or repugnant is considered as obscenity. Such obscenity could take the form of displaying the genitals in public.

Pornography is the utilization of obscene and immodest writing and pictures for purposes of leading to certain sexual feats that take place in actual intercourse.

Indecent Exposure

Indecent exposure and acts of exhibitionism are synonymous with the exposure of genitals to women, girls, or young children. Exhibitionism is the exposure of one's self to obtain sexual gratification. Indecent exposure must be indecent, public, and witnessed by more than one person.

Voyeurism and Scoptophilia

Unusual and excessive interest in the viewing of genitalia, sex acts, etc., as a means of obtaining sexual stimulus is called scoptophilia. Voyeurism is a pathological indulgence in viewing some form of nudity as a source of gratification in place of the normal sex act. It should be pointed out that voyeurism is a crime only when the person observed has not given consent.

POLICE ROLE IN PREVENTION AND CONTROL

There are many practical programs that could be constructed to prevent and control the inordinate amount of sexual offenses involving adolescents in the United States. The following are suggestions that could be utilized by law enforcement agencies and communities concerned about the problem:

1. Law enforcement should endeavor to become involved in the *selection* from institutions of potential parolees who have been involved in sexual offenses.

2. Law enforcement officers experienced in the area of deviant sexual behavior should be organized into a squad capable of coping with sex degenerates. Along these lines, a card-index file should be maintained, cataloging all sexual offenders residing within the community. Fingerprints, photographs, and a *modus operandi* should be included with the cards.

3. Areas where sexual offenses appear to have increased should be kept under *special surveillance.* Areas such as parks, theaters, zoos, and public lavatories should be kept under careful observation. Overcrowding tends to produce immorality of all kinds. The number of park keepers should be increased; student teachers in training should receive instructions as to how to deal with problems of undesirable conversation and conduct that may arise in school; prospective teachers should be advised how best to give individual help on matters of sex to all the children.

4. The sex offender should be brought under psychiatric observation

promptly with *minimum* contact with police. When possible, he should be committed for psychiatric examination. He should be held in a hospital, not jail. Police authorities and judges should be given instructions in the nature of the sex offender and his psychopathology. There should be a prepleading probationary investigation, psychiatric observation, and examination. More serious offenders should not be allowed to plead guilty to lesser offenses. The publicity should be carefully controlled for the sake of the rehabilitation of the individual.

5. More *consideration* should be accorded to the handling of victims of sex crimes, particularly children. The *inept handling* of victims is often at the root of the reluctance of parents to complain. Separate facilities should be provided for juveniles, according to the degree of seriousness of the behavior problem.

6. *Copies* of parole and supervisory reports concerning sex degenerates should be filed with the local law enforcement agency.

Prevention is the area that should be expanded, and a preventive program should include the following:

1. Organization of a special squad familiar with methods of coping with sex degenerates.

2. A file should be maintained with complete information on all known sex deviates in the community.

3. A close working relationship with private and state mental institution personnel is necessary in order to obtain fingerprints, photographs, and other pertinent data pertaining to sex degenerates who are capable of committing sex crimes. If the person in question changes residence, this information should be forwarded to the law enforcement agency in the community where the person in question plans to reside.

4. Fingerprinting and photography should be mandatory for all individuals, minor or adult, who are arrested for sexual offenses.

5. Close surveillance of "known areas" where sex degenerates congregate should be maintained by the local police.

In addition to the points for prevention already mentioned, one of the most important weapons to consider is the use of education in combating sex crimes. A specific and detailed educational program should be initiated, directed particularly at: (1) the legislature and other public officials; (2) the public; and (3) the police.[58] To elaborate:

[58]P. Kenney and D. G. Pursuit, *Police Work with Juveniles*, p. 186.

1. Cooperation of the legislature and other public officials should be secured.

2. The general public should be enlightened concerning such matters and be accorded specific instructions as to how to help.

3. Special training should be provided to law enforcement officers with respect to techniques and methods of investigation.[59]

SUMMARY

The influence of a gang, whether negative or positive, is particularly effective because it often completely answers a boy's needs. His desire for adventure and companionship is satisfied. He gets the feeling of belonging and of loyalty to a group. If his gang is delinquently oriented, the tougher he is, the more recognition he gets. Furthermore, he may also find the discipline he needs. Gangs develop their own codes and rules of behavior and demand that their members abide by them rigidly. There are many studies of gangs. Some of the most popular are cited.

Experimentation regarding different approaches to the understanding and control of gang behavior has been carried on in various cities. Law enforcement agencies throughout the United States recommend that an area approach be adopted.

What is the nature of the adolescent who becomes involved in the use of drugs? Although the drug addict is not an individual who has remained aloof from crime, he is rarely many of the sensational things portrayed in the public mind. Those who have worked with the adolescent drug addict recognize him as an emotionally sick individual whose difficulties relate back to a life history of social and emotional maladjustment.

The search for drugs is one of the most difficult problems faced by an officer. Drugs may be in solid, powder, or liquid form. In its pure state, the "bulk" of the drug may be very small. One popular way to carry illegally obtained drugs is to keep them in an old prescription bottle. The officer should be suspicious of any bottle with a worn or dirty label.

Juvenile drinking is often a defiance of adult standards and authority, an attempt to prove manliness, to obtain status in the group; or it may be mere experimentation and curiosity.

Most experts are of the opinion that drinking is a status symbol. Teen-agers are striving for understanding; they are striving for acceptance with their peers, and with their own social group. If that particular group tends to drink or tends toward this vice, to stay in and be one of the group, the teen-ager may participate in whatever form of drinking is practiced by his particular set of friends.

Sex offenses include rape, indecent exposure, exhibitionism, incest, child

[59]*Ibid.*, p. 186.

molesting, and homosexuality, as well as a variety of related acts. Legislators have taken the position that sex offenders are different from other types of law violators. Therefore, this has led to legislation that results in classifying sex offenders indefinitely somewhere between the criminal and the mentally ill.

In view of the development of sex psychopath laws, the late criminologist, Edwin Sutherland, noted a sequence characterized by (1) an upspring of fear within the community as a result of a few serious sex crimes, (2) community response in the form of anxiety, leading to (3) the gathering of information from an appointed committee and recommendations that generally were uncritically accepted by state legislatures.

Failure to accord the child in the United States a distinct status that is closely integrated with the larger structure of American society and the resulting minimum institutionalization of norms for governing adolescent behavior has numerous important implications for defining and sanctioning the sexual conduct of youngsters in American society. Because of the lack of emotional status between childhood and adulthood in the United States, numerous problems have evolved in the area of law and sexual offenses.

ANNOTATED REFERENCES

Carmichael, Benjamin G., "Youth Crime in Urban Communities—Street Hustlers and Their Crimes," *Crime and Delinquency*, April 1975, Vol. 21, No. 2, pp. 139-149.

A detailed analysis of an illicit life style in a large West Coast City.

Caprio, F. S. and Brenner, D. R., *Sexual Behavior: Psycho-Legal Aspects*, Citadel Press, New York, 1961.

Contents covers subject title.

Clark, Robert E., *Reference Group Theory and Delinquency*, Behavioral Publications, New York, 1972.

A scholarly piece of work on the impact of reference groups on youths—particularly the imposing of norms (negative or positive).

De Francis, Vincent, *Protecting the Child Victim of Sex Crimes Committed by Adults*, American Humane Association, Colo., 1969.

The author concentrates on the protection (legal) that can be afforded to a victimized (sexually) child.

Drug Abuse: A White Paper, U. S. Government Printing Office, Washington, D. C., September 1975.

This short 116-page document is a report to the President from the Domestic Council Drug Abuse Task Force. The report includes an assessment of the drug abuse situation in America and strategies aimed at combating the problem.

Levine, S. M., *Narcotics and Drug Abuse,* Anderson Publishing Company, Cincinnati, Ohio, 1973.

The author reviews comprehensively specific drugs and discusses some of the highly controversial subjects inherent in the problem.

Miller, W. B., *Violence by Youth Clubs and Youth Groups as a Crime Problem in Major American Cities—Interim Report.* Office of Juvenile Justice and Delinquency Prevention, Washington, D.C., 1976.

Concise survey that presents a preliminary set of conclusions on the existence, scope, seriousness, and character of violence and other forms of crime by youth gangs and youth groups in American cities.

Vorrath, Harry H., and Brendtro, Larry K., *Positive Peer Culture,* Aldine Publishing Company, Chicago, 1974.

The authors discuss a specific treatment method called "positive peer culture." The aforementioned method capitalizes on the power of peers.

Name Index

Abrahamson, D., 131
Adams, T. C., 219
Alexander, F., 56
Allen, H., 162, 168
Amos, W. E., 211
Ausubel, D. P., 325, 330

Barnes, H. E., 52–53, 56, 59, 139–140
Bayh, B., 135–136
Beeleman, W. C., 85–86, 92
Boehm, W. W., 199
Brandsetter, A. F., 266
Brennan, J. J., 266
Brenner, D. R., 350
Brohel, S., 57
Brown, E., 90
Brown, E. W., 259, 274
Brown, L., 118

California Probation, Parole and Correctional
   Association, 165
Caprio, F. S., 350
Carmichael, B. G., 350
Carter, R. M., 244
Cavan, R., 6, 13, 126, 128, 144
Cheim, I., 331
Children's Bureau, 192, 265, 279
Clark, R. E., 61, 63, 350
Cloward, R., 131, 310–311, 314–316
Coffey, A., 27, 63, 73, 76, 84, 123, 162, 222–223, 240–242,
   245, 250, 285
Cohen, A. K., 61, 129, 131, 311–314, 317
Cohen, L. E., 83
Cromwell, P. F., 54

Davis, S. M., 83, 211
DeFrancis, V., 240, 350
Delinquency Prevention Report, 96
Derbyshire, R. L., 123
Devlin, P. A., 305
Dietrick, D., 314
Dineen, J., 84

Dodson, J., 44
Dugdale, W., 51

Eldefonso, E., 6, 27, 39, 73, 76, 123, 162, 181, 189, 222–223,
   240–242, 245, 250, 285, 305
Ellison, B., 87–88
Empey, L. M., 125
England, R. W., 37
Esselstyn, T. C., 6

Ferdinand, T., 126
Fitzpatrick, J. P., 45, 128, 162
Florence, H. G., 11
Fort, W. S., 167–168
Fortas, A., 173, 178
Fox, S. J., 162, 177, 182
Fredericksen, H., 27
Freud, S., 57

Gans, H. J., 37
Gates, D., 11
Geilli, M. A., 144
Geis, G., 310
Giallombardo, R., 13
Gibbons, D. C., 6, 13, 27, 37, 63, 245
Gibbs, J. P., 218
Gill, T. D., 251
Glen, J. E., 175
Glouch, A., 144
Glueck, S. and E., 55–56, 128, 140, 143
Goddard, H., 51
Gordon, W. C., 261
Grace, R. C., 240–242
Green, N., 6

Hahn, P. H., 127, 129
Hamann, A. D., 245
Hartinger, W., 6, 27, 39, 123, 152, 181, 189, 222–223, 285,
   305
Healy, W., 22
Helfer, R. E., 249–250, 256, 275
Hodges, H. M., Jr., 32

Holtzoff, A., 305
Hooton, E., 54
Hyman, H. R., 130

Imlay, C. H., 211

Jaffe, E., 130
James, G. B., Jr., 175
Jenkins, H. T., 285
Jenkins, R., 25
Johnson, E. H., 127

Kahn, A. J., 275
Kellogg, F. K., 209
Kempe, C. H., 275
Kenney, P., 190, 265, 348
Ketcham, O. W., 189
Killinger, J. C., 54
Kinsey, A. C., 341
Kitsuse, J. I., 314
Klein, M. W., 244
Klineberg, O., 141
Kobetz, R. W., 172
Kolbrin, S., 37
Konopka, G., 7, 27, 127, 144
Korn, R. R., 17–19, 25
Kvaraceus, W., 139

Leonard, R. F., 11
Lerman, P., 157
Levine, S. M., 351
Lombroso, C., 53–54

McCord, 131–133
Mack, J., 171
McKay, H. D., 58, 132
Manella, R. L., 211
Marcus, M., 285
Martin, G. E., 341
Martin, J. M., 45, 109–110, 128, 162
Martin, L., Sgt., 10–11
Martin, L. H., 6
Martinson, R., 208
Matza, D., 128
Mead, M., 34
Merton, R., 128, 131–132
Miller, W., 37, 129, 131, 307–309
Milton, Rector, 10
Monachesi, E., 41
Monahaan, T. P., 44, 131
Mulligan, R. A., 27
Murray, C., 144

Niemeyer, J., 141
Novick, M. B., 98, 101

O'Brien, K. E., 126, 285
O'Connor, G. W., 220–222, 230, 215, 235
Ohlin, L. E., 126, 131, 310–311, 314–316
Olson, 66, 69, 72

Phelps, T. R., 27, 285
Phillipson, M., 133
Pierson, N., 245
Ploscowe, M., 342
Pomeroy, W. B., 341
Porterfield, A. L., 18
Portune, R., 120
Pound, R., 145, 147, 162, 168
Prassel, F. R., 157
Protective Services for Children, 249
Pulsen, M. G., 189
Pursuit, D. G., 190, 265, 348

Reason, C. E., 149, 163
Reckless, W. C., 61, 313
Reece, C. D., 37
Reid, E. L., 211
Reiss, A., 133, 343–344
Rice, A. H., 140
Roberts, A., 260
Rock, R., 57
Rosenheim, M., 259
Roucek, J. S., 42–43
Rubin, S., 13

Salisbury, H. E., 318–319
Sarri, R. C., 73, 75
Schifee, S., 53
Shaw, C. R., 58, 103, 132
Sheldon, W. H., 54
Sheppard, G. H., 66, 69, 72, 118–119, 126
Sheridan, W. H., 305
Shielman, H. M., 144
Simonsen, C. E., 162, 168
Sloane, H. W., 147, 163
Snyder, P. R., 6
Steinburn, T. W., 85–86
Stennett, R., 262
Stullken, E. H., 40, 140
Sussman, F., 13
Sutherland, E. H., 50–60, 129–130, 341

Taft, D. R., 63
Tappan, P., 15, 18, 303–304

Task Force Report, 138, 150, 163, 170, 175, 217–218
Teeters, N. K., 52–53, 59, 139
Thomas, M. P., Jr., 8
Thomas, W. I., 56
Thrasher, F., 58
Toby, J., 131
Treger, H., 286
Tullock, G., 208
Turner, D. R., 211

Ulrich, R., 133
U. S. Dept. of Health, Education and Welfare, 226, 245

Vos, E., 37
Vedder, C. B., 22, 212
Vinter, R. D., 190
Vold, E., 18, 56

Vollmer, A., 52, 63
Vorrath, H. H., 351

Waalkes, W., 68
Walker, R. N., 219–221
Ward, M. R., 263
Warren, R. L., 42–43
Watson, N. A., 120, 215, 219–222, 230, 235, 282
Weinstein, N., 262
Weissman, J., 264
Whyte, W. F., 316–318
Wilson, J. Q., 208
Winters, J. E., 112, 310, 320–322
Wright, G., 9–10

Yoblonski, L., 64
Young, L., 249, 262, 275

Subject Index